John Dillinger

John Dillinger

THE LIFE AND DEATH OF
AMERICA'S FIRST
CELEBRITY CRIMINAL

Dary Matera

CARROLL & GRAF PUBLISHERS
NEW YORK

To Joe Pinkston and Tom Smusyn, whose meticulous research
made this all possible

JOHN DILLINGER
The Life and Death of America's First Celebrity Criminal

Carroll & Graf Publishers
An Imprint of Avalon Publishing Group Inc.
245 West 17th Street
11th Floor
New York, NY 10011

First Carroll & Graf edition 2004

Library of Congress Cataloging-in-Publication Data is available.

ISBN: 0-7867-1354-2

Designed by Paul Paddock
Printed in the United States of America
Distributed by Publishers Group West

Contents

Cast of Characters   vii

Introduction   3

PART I: 1851–1933
A Tommy-Gun Star is Born

    Chapter 1   9

    Chapter 2   21

    Chapter 3   31

PART II: May 1933–January 1934
The Bloody Reign of the Terror Gang

    Chapter 4   47

    Chapter 5   58

    Chapter 6   76

    Chapter 7   94

    Chapter 8   109

    Chapter 9   128

    Chapter 10   147

PART III: January 1934–July 1934
Wanted: Dead or Dead—The End of a Wild Era

    Chapter 11   167

    Chapter 12   186

    Chapter 13   204

Chapter 14   223

Chapter 15   242

Chapter 16   258

Chapter 17   276

Chapter 18   294

Chapter 19   307

Chapter 20   319

Chapter 21   334

Chapter 22   346

EPILOGUE   363

NOTES   372

ACKNOWLEDGMENTS   406

INDEX   407

ABOUT THE AUTHOR   414

Cast of Characters

Historical note: Aside from using numerous aliases, the criminals of the 1930s spelled their names in a multitude of ways in an attempt to thwart law enforcement. The attempt in the narrative is to use the original, the most popular, or the one being used at the time of the incident described.

THE DILLINGER GANGS

1920S PRE-PRISON STINT

John Dillinger

William Edgar "Eddie" Singleton

THE INDIANA STATE PRISON, MICHIGAN CITY SHIRT SHOP BOYS—EARLY 1930S

John Dillinger

Handsome Harry Pierpont

Charles Makley

Russell "Booby" Clark

Homer VanMeter

Earl "The Kid" Northern

Everett Bridgewater

Thaddeus Skeer

Ralston "Blackie" Linton

Frank Bagley

Charles E. Hovious
Ray Lawrence
John "Three Fingered Jack" Hamilton
Whitey Mohler
Sam Goldstine (aka Goldstein, Goldstien)

THE WHITE CAP GANG—1933

John Dillinger
William "The Kid" Shaw
Noble Claycomb
Paul "Lefty" Parker
Hilton "Pizzy Wizzy" Crouch
Harry Copeland

TRANSITION GANG AFTER THE WHITE CAPPERS—1933

John Dillinger
Harry Copeland
Sam Goldstine
John Vinson

THE KENTUCKY/ILLINOIS BUNCH—BRIEFLY EXISTED IN 1933

John Dillinger
Frank Whitehouse
Whitey Mohler
Sam Goldstine
Fred Brenman
Maurice Lanham
James Kirkland

THE TERRIBLE TEN PRISON ESCAPEES—1933

Walter Dietrich
Charles Makley
John Hamilton
Russell Clark
James Jenkins

Edward Shouse
Joseph Fox
Joseph Burns
James Clark
Harry Pierpont

THE TERROR GANG—1933–34

John Dillinger
Harry Pierpont
Charles Makley
John Hamilton
Russell Clark
Edward Shouse
Harry Copeland
  Minor players:
Walter Dietrich
Joseph Burns

TWIN CITY GANG—1934

John Dillinger
Baby Face Nelson (Lester Gillis)
Tommy Carroll
Homer VanMeter
Eugene "Eddie" Green
John Hamilton
John Paul Chase
Pat Reilly
Louis Piquett (Dillinger's crooked attorney was essentially a gang
  member)
Arthur O'Leary (Ditto for Piquett's office manager)
Minor players
Joseph Raymond "Fatso" Negri
Jack Perkins
Arthur "Fish" Johnson

MAJOR PLAYERS IN THE GANGS

Tommy Carroll—Athletic ex-boxer and St. Paul–area enforcer for robber Eddie Green. Expert with a Thompson machine-gun.

John Paul Chase—Loyal friend and associate of Baby Face Nelson. Stayed with Nelson until the bitter end.

James Clark—Terrible Ten escapee had to give up within a few days after eating raw tomatoes that inflamed his ulcer.

Russell "Booby" Clark—Shirt Shop Boy and Terrible Ten escapee partly responsible for the Tucson capture.

Harry Copeland—Graduated from The White Cap Gang to The Terror Gang, then was booted from the fraternity due to his heavy drinking.

Sam Goldstine—Ex Shirt Shop boy popped in and out of various gangs, always arriving with a new spelling to his surname, thus confusing both police and historians.

John "Three Fingered Jack" Hamilton, aka John "Red" Hamilton—Accident prone, bullet magnet lost two fingers in a childhood sleighing accident. Hamilton was a quadruple threat—a Shirt Shop Boy, a Terrible Ten escapee, and the only holdover member of Dillinger's last two gangs. He escaped capture in Tucson because he was recovering from being shot in East Chicago.

James Jenkins—Young Terrible Ten escapee fell out of a getaway car and had a wild adventure on the run until he was shotgunned to death by an Indiana farmer.

Charles Makley—Shirt Shop boy and Terrible Ten member transitioned through numerous Dillinger gangs. Unlike the others who traveled with their favorite molls, Makley preferred to hook up with a local gal wherever he went.

Whitey Mohler—Ex Shirt Shop boy resurfaced during Dillinger's brief Kentucky/Illinois gang, the activities of which are mostly unknown.

Baby Face Nelson—Crazed, quick-triggered bantam killed three of the first six DI/FBI agents slain in the line of duty. Nelson still holds the record for most FBI agents killed by a single person. Often exploded in fits of jealous rage because Dillinger was getting more attention in the press.

Arthur O'Leary—Attorney Louis Piquett's officer manager became a critical Dillinger errand boy, setting up his facial surgery among other things.

Louis Piquett—Dillinger attorney helped him escape from Crown Point prison and performed more illegal functions than legal.

Handsome Harry Pierpont, aka "Pete" Pierpont—Tall hothead with movie-star looks. He was Dillinger's mentor, close friend, and the brains of the gangs he was in.

Pat Reilly—Young trainee arrived at Little Bohemia at the height of the action and still managed to escape with one of the gang's injured molls.

Edward Shouse—Terrible Ten and Terror Gang member had to flee the group when Dillinger's hot-blooded moll, Billie Frechette, began making advances toward him.

William "The Kid" Shaw—Leading man in Dillinger's first post-prison gang had a short criminal career. Shaw left a legacy of interviews afterward pertaining to his days with the yet-to-be-famous Jackrabbit.

William Edgar "Eddie" Singleton—Web-fingered Dillinger cousin and baseball umpire was John Jr.'s first major criminal partner. Abandoned young John during their first stickup.

Homer VanMeter—Shirt Shop boy didn't hook up with Dillinger until his final gang in 1934. VanMeter had his face surgically altered by the same doctor a week after Dillinger had done so.

DILLINGER FAMILY

John Wilson Dillinger—First son of Mathias and Mary Brown Dillinger was John Jr.'s father, a soft-spoken, hard-working grocer and farmer.

Mathias Dillinger—John Jr.'s grandfather immigrated from Metz, France, in 1851.

Elizabeth "Lizzie" Fields—John Wilson's second wife, a Quaker, joined the family in 1912 when John Jr. was nine. The boy and his stepmother got along fine enough. Like John's mother, Lizzie died young (1933), leaving John Sr. a double widow for most of his life. John Sr. and Lizzie had three children: Hubert, Doris, and Frances.

Mary Ellen "Mollie" Lancaster Dillinger—The bandit's mother died of a stroke when he was three.

Audrey Dillinger Hancock—John Jr.'s loyal older sister raised him after their mother died. She had seven children of her own: Fred, Alberta, Norman, Mary, Johnnie, Thelma, and Earl. John Dillinger Jr. was closest to his niece Mary.

Emmett Hancock—Audrey's husband. They married when she was still a teenager.

Beryl Ethel Hovious—John Dillinger Jr.'s only known legal wife, who divorced him during his first prison stint. They had no children. There were rumors, never verified, that Dillinger had a wife and two children prior to his 1924 marriage to seventeen-year-old Beryl.

"Leaping" Lena Pierpoint—Feisty, devoted mother of Harry Pierpont was considered family by John Jr.

THE GUN MOLLS

Patricia Long Cherrington—Friend of Dillinger's true love Billie Frechette. She became the lover of both Harry Copeland and John "Three Fingered Jack" Hamilton. She was the only moll to escape arrest at Little Bohemia.

Bernice Clark, aka Opal Long—Wife of Russell Clark and sister of Patricia Cherrington. She refused to take off her shoes at the hospital following an auto accident because she'd stuffed $4,000 in stolen money inside them.

Marie Marion Conforti—Homer VanMeter's girl. Baby Face Nelson accused her of being a rat and nearly goaded VanMeter into killing her.

Jean Delaney—Moll of Tommy Carroll, miscarried her child after watching him shot down in the streets by the cops.

Pearl Elliott—Widely traveling madam and gangster moll who was once Dillinger's trusted confidant. She later turned on him in an attempt to get the reward money and spring a friend from prison.

Bessie Green—Sour, common-law wife of Eddie Green. Despised her husband's criminal associates.

Polly Hamilton—The Billie Frechette look-alike was Dillinger's last girlfriend. She was a dupe in the East Chicago police plot to assassinate him.

Gladys Hill—Bordello owner and Sam Goldstine's moll.

Mary Kinder—Sprite girlfriend of Handsome Harry Pierpont. Hid the Terrible Ten after the Indiana State prison escape.

Mary Longnacker—Dillinger's girlfriend in mid-1933. She was unfaithful, and inadvertently lured him into a trap that led to his arrest in Ohio.

Helen Wawrzniak Nelson—Teenage bride of Baby Face Nelson. Mother of Nelson's two children.

Anna Sage, aka Anna Chiolak—The infamous Lady in Red; set Dillinger up to be assassinated for the reward money, and as trade-off to fight being deported back to Rumania for running houses of ill repute. She was never Dillinger's girlfriend. She was the lover of ruthless East Chicago police Sgt. Martin Zarkovich.

Ufah Shaw—Wife of William "The Kid" Shaw; played a minor role but was Dillinger's first female gang member.

LAW ENFORCEMENT

Deputy Warden H. D. Claudy—Hated by the cons under his whip, the Indiana State Penitentiary corrections administrator came under fire after the escape of the Terrible Ten.

Assistant Director Hugh Clegg—J. Edgar Hoover sent his high-ranking Division of Investigation underling from Washington, D.C., to St. Paul, Minnesota, to coordinate the efforts to hunt John Dillinger.

Inspector Sam Cowley—Sent from Washington, D.C., to Chicago by J. Edgar Hoover to shepherd the Chicago field office's attempt to capture or kill Dillinger.

Detective Claude Dozier—Hunted Dillinger for the Indiana State Police. Dozier often had to smooth things over with rival police departments to cover for his temperamental boss, Captain Matt Leach.

Prosecutor Robert Estill—Career was ruined after the media took chummy photos of Estill with a smug Dillinger at the Crown Point jail.

Officer James Herron—Unlikely Tucson policeman arrested John Dillinger at the height of the bandit's fame. Assisted by officers Kenneth Mullaney and Milo Walker.

High Sheriff Lillian Holley—Nationally shamed when Dillinger escaped the Crown Point prison in her own squad car.

J. Edgar Hoover—Legendary law enforcement icon can credit John Dillinger with a major assist in helping him create his massive federal police force. In the critical early days, when such a "jackboot" organization faced severe political opposition, Hoover held Dillinger up as the prime example of why his army of Special Agents were needed.

Lt. John Howe—Head of the Chicago Police's "Secret Squad" assigned to find and kill John Dillinger.

Forrest C. Huntington—Former Pinkerton Detective stayed on Dillinger's tail on behalf of the Indiana Banker's Association.

Special Agent Clarence Hurt—Military trained, DI/FBI assassin sent to Chicago to kill John Dillinger. Hurt fired one of the shots that struck the notorious bandit.

Assistant Attorney General Joseph Keenan—The Ohio prosecutor was selected for the federal job because of his knowledge of the Mid-West area where Dillinger was wreaking havoc.

Louis E. Kunkel—Figurehead warden of the Indiana State Penitentiary in Michigan City. Kunkel felt the heat when Dillinger orchestrated the biggest prison escape in Indiana history.

Matthew "Matt" Leach—High-strung head of the Indiana State Police hunted Dillinger feverishly. Leach developed a pronounced stutter during the stress of the ordeal.

Assistant Director Harold "Pop" Nathan—Dispatched from Washington, D.C., by J. Edgar Hoover to hunt John Dillinger.

Sheriff Charles Neel—Harrison County, Indiana, sheriff was taken hostage by the Terrible Ten. Neel ended up befriending and caring for ill escapee James Clark.

Detective Sgt. William Patrick O'Malley—The East Chicago, Indiana, sergeant was John Dillinger's only verified kill. The Jackrabbit took out the beloved Catholic deacon after being shot four times by O'Malley from point-blank range during the robbery of an East Chicago bank. Dillinger was saved by his steel vest. He often lamented having to kill O'Malley and leaving the sergeant's daughters without a father.

Capt. Tim O'Neill—Head of the "East Chicago Five," the Indiana cops who wanted Dillinger permanently silenced to avoid exposure of their own misdeeds.

Chicago DI/FBI Supervisor Melvin Purvis—Most famous of Dillinger's pursuers, the diminutive Purvis was in on the final hit. He was also part of the team that took out Charles "Pretty Boy" Floyd. Purvis became known as "America's Number 1 Special Agent."

Sgt. Frank Reynolds—Chicago Police goon squad's chief assassin had already planted fifteen men before being assigned to go after John Dillinger. Reynolds may have been the only cop Dillinger ever feared.

Inspector W. A. Rorer—Chief of the Minneapolis/St. Paul DI/FBI Field Office was assigned to hunt Dillinger across middle America.

Sheriff Jess Sarber—Lima, Ohio, lawman was unnecessarily beaten to death by a vicious Harry Pierpont and Charles Makley during the breakout of Dillinger from his jail. The savage act would prove to be Pierpont and Makley's undoing.

Sgt. William J. Shanley—Hero cop tried to single-handedly arrest John Hamilton. "Three Fingered" Hamilton killed the popular Shanley instead, a callous act that enraged the public and brought intensified heat upon Dillinger.

Det. Chet Sherman—Tucson cop orchestrated the end of the Terror Gang.

Capt. John Stege—Sgt. Reynold's boss was the head of the Chicago Police's deadly, shoot-first-ask-questions-later goon squad. Assigned to track and kill Dillinger.

Sgt. Martin Zarkovich—Deadly East Chicago, Indiana, cop orchestrated the setup and assassination of John Dillinger for various self-interested reasons, not the least of which was to fight the deportation of his longtime lover Anna Sage, the infamous Lady in Red.

Special Agent Charles Winstead—Military-trained assassin brought in by Hoover to kill John Dillinger. Winstead is credited with firing the shot that terminated the famous outlaw. Left the FBI ten years later.

MISCELLANEOUS

Dr. Harold Bernard Cassidy—Young doctor assisted in the Dillinger facial reconstruction surgery.

Dr. Wilhelm Loeser—German-born surgeon with a shady past operated on the faces of John Dillinger and Homer VanMeter in a mostly failed attempt to disguise their appearances.

Indiana Governor Paul V. McNutt—Hailing from Dillinger's home county, he signed Dillinger's parole papers. The routine act subsequently destroyed his presidential aspirations and motivated him to leave the country.

James Probasco—Speakeasy owner was the middleman who procured Dillinger's plastic surgeon and allowed the operation to take place in his house. It was rumored that angry G-Men dropped him to his death from a building during a brutal interrogation session.

Emil Wanatka—Owner of the Little Bohemia lodge, he wanted to let the well-paying crooks in his midst slide, but caved in to the relentless nagging of his wife and agreed to rat them out. Wanatka created a lucrative museum at Little Bohemia afterward.

Nan Wanatka—Nagged her husband to drop the dime on the Twin Cities gang at Little Bohemia, an act that led to the disaster that occurred there. The Wanatkas' marriage broke up not long afterward.

John Dillinger

Introduction

When all of the known facts about Dillinger are dragged into publicity, it will be found that no desperado in America can approach this bad man's record . . . There are enough angles on [his] tribe and its history to write a great big book.
—Captain Matt Leach, Indiana State Police, 1933

That's precisely what Joe Pinkston and Tom Smusyn did—and it took them nearly a half century. When Pinkston died by his own hand in 1996, he left behind an extraordinary, eighteen-hundred-page gold mine of edited research that covered every aspect of John Dillinger's life.

Pinkston was a former Pinkerton detective, joining the agency when many men who had pursued John Dillinger were still on the force. He later became the co-owner and curator of the John Dillinger Historical Wax Museum in Nashville, Indiana. Smusyn is a Chicago historian who specializes in 1920s and 1930s Americana. Together, they teamed to cut through the myths and legends that have surrounded the famous outlaw, sifting fact from sensationalized fiction.

Newspapers and magazines of Dillinger's era were harvested and cross referenced. Witnesses, nearly all of whom are now dead, were interviewed and reinterviewed. Thousands of pages of once classified FBI files were obtained through the Freedom of Information Act. Additional thousands of pages were acquired from police departments in Indiana, Illinois, Ohio, and Wisconsin. Court records, transcripts, and the personal files of private detectives and insurance agents were also mined.

The massive and painstaking undertaking, begun in 1945, failed only in the belief that it would temper the colorfully exaggerated aspects of the Dillinger saga. The well-worn cliché that "truth is stranger than fiction" aptly applied.

The dedicated duo uncovered wild bank robberies that were never before reported, bizarre activities of the police and Feds that were covered up, along with intimate details surrounding the fast and furious lives of "The Terror Gang" and their harem of sexy molls. The Pinkston/Smusyn research crackled with excitement from beginning to end.

Poring through the archives, one is left with a greater understanding of how huge John Dillinger really was. Imagine a dashing, ice-cool, Depression-era Robin Hood more famous than anything Hollywood could dream up, running around the country robbing banks, escaping prison, and repeatedly eluding the police in wild chases.

John Dillinger was the Elvis of bandits.

In a little more than a year, he and his gang relieved a dozen banks of close to a half million dollars—$7 million by today's standards—put 75,000 miles on two dozen, state-of-the-art automobiles, made the front page of newspapers hundreds of times, starred in a score of newsreels, and filled the radio airwaves with dramatic accounts of their exploits.

In April 1934, Joe Shepard of the *Indianapolis Star* deftly recorded Dillinger's impact on American society:

> From pillar to post the law has chased John Dillinger. The entire crime-fighting resources of the nation have been united for months against one man, and he has continued to strike and vanish at will with apparent immunity.
>
> Arrested, he walks spectacularly to freedom whistling "The Last Roundup" as he waves a wooden pistol. How is it possible, citizens ask, for one man to flaunt his criminality in the face of the nation and to flout the law at every encounter? How can he disappear so completely?
>
> Every policeman and every school child of the Middle West has Dillinger's facial characteristics

graven in his mind. And yet, John Dillinger is as
loose and as free as ever. Dillinger's ability thus
to "shoot and run away and live to shoot another
day" has led the public to believe that he is a
master mind, a super criminal of brilliant intel-
lect. And in the public mind the police agencies in
comparison consist of a gang of organized nitwits
who fall over each other like a gang of drunken
acrobats in their efforts to keep from meeting up
with this Dillinger person.

The "nitwit" White Hats won in the end—thanks to a Lady in Not-So-Red, and the forgotten Lady in Tan. But what a wild ride it was through a memorable time in American history.

For nearly a half century, it was the dream of Joe Pinkston and Tom Smusyn to have their research whipped into shape and published. It's been my privilege to bring this dream to fruition.

Unfortunately, Pinkston didn't live to see it. Upset over a love relationship gone sour, he followed in the footsteps of one of Dillinger's main hunters—FBI Special Agent Melvin Purvis—and took his own life in 1996. That left Smusyn, and Pinkston's son, Randy, to finish the research and get it into the right hands.

They were successful—and history is the better for it.

—Dary Matera

"I only wish I had a mother to worry over me, but she died when I was three. I guess this is why I was such a bad boy. No mother to look after me."

—John Dillinger

A Tommy-Gun Star is Born

Chapter 1

Nail tough, fiercely determined, and bounding with kinetic energy, the rambunctious ten-year-old reigned over a gang of pipsqueak thugs who stole for profit, including coal they pinched from the Pennsylvania Railroad gondolas. When apprehended, he stood defiantly in an Indianapolis court, arms crossed, cap cocked sideways, chomping on gum. Ordered to straighten up, he moved with deliberate slowness, causing the angry judge to issue the first psychological evaluation in John Herbert Dillinger's illustrious career: "Your mind is crippled!"

As if to prove the judge's point, the unrepentant lad and his crew of dirty-faced blood brothers promptly tied a neighborhood geek to a sawmill carrier and let him progress kicking and screaming cartoonlike until his head was inches away from the massive blade. Hilarious, they thought, a major adrenaline rush.

It was 1913, and the world appeared as one big watermelon patch ripe for the picking. So began the saga of the most notorious felon in American history.

Mathias Dillinger, grandfather of a criminal legend, immigrated to the New World ten years before the Civil War. He set out from his home in Metz, France, when he was twenty, accompanied by his sister and her husband. "Go west, young man" was the trend, so Mathias and crew decided to press forward. The east coast of America, already writing its "Gangs of New York" history, was teeming with immigrants fighting over limited opportunities.

Moving inland was a good life strategy on many fronts. Most of the battles in the pending North/South war would be fought in the coastal states. An American newcomer with no alliances on either side, Mathias didn't want or need to be caught up in the killing. He headed to Cincinnati, hopped a boat on the Ohio River, continued westward to the Wabash River, then hooked north to Terre Haute, Indiana.

Mathias, who pronounced his name with a more musical hard G, "Dil-ling-er," rather than the "Dil-lynge-er" we know today, didn't stay long in Terre Haute. He moved to Indianapolis to work as a farmhand. There, in 1863, he met and married a nineteen-year-old named Mary Brown. They had their first child, John Wilson Dillinger, a year later, eventually adding eight more to the family.

In the summer of 1887, just as the city began to sparkle with electric lights, John Wilson met Mary Ellen Lancaster of suburban Cumberland. Mary Ellen, known as "Mollie," was no stranger to large families, having five sisters and seven brothers of her own. Among her brothers was a strapping man named David who was considered to be the strongest member of the Indianapolis police force, an attribute that enabled him to take command as captain.

John and Mollie married before the summer ended. Expanding upon his agriculture roots, John opened a grocery store near Brightwood in the Oak Hill section of Indianapolis. The new couple's home was right next door.

The quiet young pair enjoyed a more peaceful home environment than what they were used to. Their first child, Audrey, wasn't born until March 6, 1889. Audrey, a redhead, would be noise enough for the next thirteen years. Her infamous brother would not follow until well within the next millennium.

On a steamy July night in 1903, the tiny Dillinger family finally grew by one. The teenage Audrey was thrilled to have a sibling, and christened the moment by composing a fanciful, if somewhat self-centered announcement that she recorded in a personal notebook: "Audrey Dillinger of 2077 Cooper Street has a new arrival at her house, which is a baby boy. He has black hair, dark eyes and is very pretty, the very picture of his papa. It weighs about eight pounds and was born June 22,

1903, on Monday morning at two o'clock. His name we have not decided. It will be either John, Harold, Alfred, Harry, or Theodore."

As in most cases of naming uncertainty, ego ruled the day and the baby became a Junior—only he would be John H. for Herbert.

By all accounts, young John was a happy toddler. Pictures, including some taken in the first automatic photo booths, show a grinning kid who liked to ride carts and wagons, pedal tricycles, and skitter around outdoors. Horses were still the prevalent form of transportation during John Jr.'s early youth, so his infatuation with fast cars wouldn't come until later.

Despite rampant technological advances, medical science struggled to keep pace. Families of the era experienced rapid change from marriage, births, illness, and death. John Jr.'s doting sister Audrey turned her attention to amore and married Emmett Hancock at sixteen, quickly becoming pregnant. Then mother Mollie contracted a lingering illness that would prove to be fatal. Audrey and her husband moved back home so she could help care for John Jr. while John Sr. spent time at the hospital. Mother Mollie never saw her grandchild, dying from a stroke on February 1, 1907. Five months later, Audrey gave birth to a son who died a day later.

That was a lot for a four-year-old to handle.

Audrey recovered and had seven more children, losing an additional two in the process. John Jr. was swept into the new splinter group and became almost like Audrey's son, filling in for the elder child that died. A pianist, Audrey tried to interest her little brother in music, but that wasn't his thing. He was too fidgety.

Mathias Dillinger, the man who started it all, was still around in 1912 to throw one last wrinkle into the American family he started. His widowed son John W. met his second wife, Lizzie Fields, interestingly enough, at Mathias's funeral. The marriage meant more changes for nine-year-old John. Emmett and Audrey moved out of the house next to the grocery store, taking their growing family with them. John Jr. was left to go it alone with the new stepmother—invariably a difficult transition.

Although new mom Lizzie was thirty-two when she married, she wasn't finished having children of her own, giving John Sr. a son and two daughters within eight years.

How all this affected John Jr. remains somewhat of a mystery. Some say his father and stepmother showered him with love and attention, while others portray John Sr. as distant and cold, especially after remarrying. There were reports of John Jr. being tethered to a wagon wheel or locked in the house while his parents worked. Another story has the senior Dillinger throwing an odd fit after catching his son giving a pack of "kiss me" chewing gum to a pretty girl the young boy fancied. John Sr. grabbed the gum from the girl, and bounced John Jr. over a large coffee container. The senior Dillinger would later tell reporters that he came from a "spare the rod and spoil the child" upbringing and raised his kids accordingly.

For whatever reason, John Jr. frequently ran away from home. Was he escaping an unhappy environment, or just suffering from the wanderlust that would inflict him as an adult? The evidence is conflicting, but seems to point toward the latter.

Often, the boy showed flashes of the deviant creativity that would later make him famous. He and some friends tied a rope around a neighbor's rose trellis, then looped the other end to the stanchion of a streetcar. When the car took off, all rosy hell broke loose, which the youths thought was hysterical. The homeowner was not amused. When confronted by his father, Junior spat: "What if I did wreck his roses? The old bastard's mean, anyhow!"

Pop, angry over the defiant attitude, greeted the disrespect with the firm hand he spoke of. "I yanked him out into the kitchen and licked him," he recounted years later. "I turned him across my knee and whaled away 'til my hand stung. But he didn't cry. He just got up and glared at me and then he stomped out. All at once I wasn't mad anymore. I was sick . . . and afraid that my boy would go wrong."

John Junior's teachers remembered him with mixed emotions, noting that he had a good side to complement his mischievous traits. "I can say positively that he showed no inclination to steal," recalled Elizabeth O'Mara, who taught him in grammar school. "Other boys, you know, had stolen change from my desk. But John, although he had ample opportunity to do so, never touched a cent. He was intensely interested in anything mechanical, caring little for academic subjects. It was this indifference to his lessons that caused most of his troubles at school. Of course, he liked to play pranks, yet I must say that, secretly, I found them quite amusing and original."

One of Ms. O'Mara's students saw things differently. "I always remember being frightened of John Jr.," shuddered Violet Lively, a classmate and neighbor who may have gotten the pig-tails-in-the-inkwell treatment one time too many. "His smile was sideways, more like a sneer than a smile, and he was a bully. He and my brother Terrell used to get into fights. Terrell got a broken toe in one fight, and in another his Sunday blue serge suit was torn. Mom (Carrie Lively) went down to see his father, to tell him that she couldn't put up with it, that she would just have to take John to Juvenile Court. The poor, harassed father said, 'Mrs. Lively, if you think that will do any good, go right ahead for I have tried everything.' Mom hadn't the heart to hurt the father, so she didn't do it."

Violet remembers her tormentor making a very prophetic costume choice one Halloween. "John came dressed in his father's derby hat, a turtleneck red jersey sweater, a mask over his eyes, and a gun in his hand.

"One winter," Violet continued, "I made myself a sled . . . When mom wanted to go to the (grocery) store, I took my sled, but knew John would laugh and ridicule it. I went down the alley, intending to hide the crude sled behind the store . . . Just as I was hiding it, I looked up and he was peeping around the corner of the building at me. When he stepped out, he burst into derisive laughter. I could do nothing but feel greatly chagrined."

Striking a blow for women's rights, the chagrined Violet admitted she wasn't above getting even. "One day, John and other boys were sitting on top of the bread boxes under the store's porch roof. (My friend Violet Evans) and I were sitting in her swing, singing. Violet started: 'Oh, Johnnie, Oh, Johnnie, how you can love? Oh, Johnnie, Oh, Johnnie, heavens above. You make my sad heart jump with joy' . . . I joined her. I felt safe, sitting on her porch. We just did not care how mad we made him. We knew he wouldn't come over with her mother around. It did make him angry, and all the boys laughed. I dreaded leaving that porch to go home, but made it without encountering John."

Audrey Dillinger, John's devoted sister, admitted that "I loved him so much I couldn't see any faults in him." Still, she has her memories. "He and another boy got in Mr. Hughs's watermelon patch. Well, Mr. Hughs came with a shotgun and shot it up in the air to scare the boys. When John went to get through the fence, he just ripped his leg along the side. It was rusty barbed-wire, and it got awful sore . . ."

Sunday school teacher Elsa Ellsbury was one of the first to see the bipolar charm that would distinguish the man. "Johnnie was mischievous like the rest of them, but he was such a healthy, normal specimen of a boy that you couldn't help liking him. One thing about him I'll never forget—he always tipped his hat to me."

In his teens, John Jr. crashed an unattended switch engine into a line of coal cars for kicks. He returned to the tracks to steal whiskey from box cars, sometimes showing up at school intoxicated. Sharing the wealth, Dillinger quickly learned the meaning behind contemporary poet Ogden Nash's "candy is dandy, but liquor is quicker" verse, plying adventurous girls with his ready supply of stolen whiskey, and then having his way with them.

Though he was a decent student and got along well enough in school—Violet's memories aside—John Jr. tired of the classroom life by age sixteen. He snagged a job at the same plywood manufacturing veneer mill where he used to terrorize weaker kids, and promptly announced that his homework days were over.

"He came to me the day before he was supposed to start at Arsenal Technical High School," his father recalled. " 'I'm not going. I'm sick and tired of school and I want a job. I'm not going and that's that!'

" 'Someday Johnnie, you'll be sorry,' " I advised.

" 'That's my worry,' John Jr. shot back. " 'I'm not going and I just thought you'd like to know.' "

Being a tough, headstrong teenager, Junior was hell-bent on having his way. John Sr. knew there was nothing he could do.

At the mill, John was a solid worker and had a reputation as a "right guy." He also had ambition, and soon left the dead-end job for the more interesting position as "runner" for the Indianapolis Board of Trade. He soon tired of that and left after four months, taking a mechanic's position at James P. Burcham's Reliance Specialty Company, a machine shop in southwest Indianapolis. John was a good, but spotty worker, choosing to labor three to four months at a time, and then taking long "vacations" until his pockets were empty. During one break, he spent four days as a construction hand for Indianapolis Power & Light Company, pulling down a cool thirty cents an hour. He either quit or was laid off, the "left—laid off" notation in his work file doesn't make it clear. Regardless, with skilled labor in demand, he was always welcomed back at Burcham's, hanging on to that job for four years.

During this period, there was a dramatic development on the home front. In 1920, John Sr. decided to take a step back on the food chain and return to farming. He bought a sixty-two-acre spread in Mooresville, his wife's 1,800-member hometown on the northwest edge of Indianapolis just off State Road 267. The highway, despite its dignified name, was little more than a gravel road linking Mooresville with Plainfield. The move and career change came in tandem with a dramatic religious switch. Stepma and Pa Dillinger started attending Friend's Church, a Quaker worship center located near their corn and chicken farm that was more in tune with Lizzie's family faith.

Although John Jr. was working, he still lived at home and thus made the *Green Acres* trek with his folks, moving into an upstairs bedroom inside the white, two-story frame farm house that sat on a knoll and faced the highway. His half-sister Doris had a room up there as well. John Jr. commuted to town on the Interurban, an electric streetcar that rode the rails into the big city. He sometimes attended the rustic church with his parents, meeting other local teens there.

John Jr., used to the excitement of a big city, didn't take to farm life well. "My people have been farmers for generations," John Sr. explained. "Both on my mother's side and my father's. I liked the land. John never did, said it was too slow. He was born and raised in Indianapolis and I guess the city kind of got a hold of him."

Still, there was one aspect of the country that John Jr. did enjoy. "When he wasn't playing baseball for the Mooresville Athletic Club, he was generally out hunting. He was handy with a gun and a dead-shot," John Sr. noted. "We always had plenty of rabbits, squirrels, and 'possums during the open season. John got his love of hunting from me. There's nothing I'd rather do."

Despite his inability to stay long at the machine shop, John Sr. said his son loved the job. "He was the handiest fellow with a pair of pliers you ever saw. He'd buy old junks of cars and take them apart and put them together again. His hands were always black with grease, and his pants, too. He'd come home from work tired, but he'd spend the whole evening telling us about how good he was getting at running the screw machine . . . We were happy because Johnnie was learning a trade."

Naturally, the mechanically skilled John Jr. quickly put the Interurban in his rearview mirror, first buying and fixing a motorcycle, and then a Chevy, both barely beyond prototypes with model years dating to the teens. As with most young men, John had a hot foot, quickly getting his first speeding ticket. The eleven-dollar fine was nearly a week's wages, but that did little to curb his legendary need for speed. Occasionally, his father would let him drive the family Apperson Jackrabbit sedan, which had a more powerful engine than the Chevy and really let John Jr. air it out.

The teen frequently used his gasoline-powered freedom to visit his sister back in the old neighborhood. During this time, he grew unusually close to his nine-year-old niece Mary.

"We used to go to the little grocery store in Maywood and buy chewing gum at a penny a pack," Mary recounted. "I remember lying flat on the floor, our heads together, trying to see who could chew the most gum . . . We used to play catch when I was seven or eight, because I was a tomboy. We used to Indian wrestle. He was more like my brother than an uncle. He had no violent temper, although he had definite likes and dislikes. If he didn't like some food, he wouldn't try it. He was generous to a fault and had a wonderful smile."

In 1923, the twenty-year-old Dillinger became absorbed with reading books about the Old West outlaw Jesse James. Most were classic "dime novels" that embellished the truth, blending fact with lots of fiction and building the gunslinger to legendary status. Friend Delbert Hobson said John Jr. was struck by James's courage and daring, along with his alleged chivalrous behavior toward women and children—traits Dillinger would strive to match.

Quick to realize that he was a cowboy about as much as he was a farmer, John Jr. took the James persona and melded it with the city gangsters he saw portrayed during the popular Saturday matinees he caught at the Idle Time theater. Soon, he was wearing his hat tilted to the side, and walked with a mobster swagger. Friends noticed that he began to talk tough and take on the air of a hoodlum.

He continued playing baseball in nearby Martinsville, but despite fanciful reports to the contrary, he was never pro or college material.

Although young John had a way with the ladies, even sober ones, he kept his own heart in check until he reencountered his uncle's suddenly mature and developed stepdaughter, Frances Marguerite Thornton. Frances was the epitome of the dark-haired, ebony-eyed pepper pot that he would be attracted to for most of his life. John Jr. was said to be angling to marry Frances, but their families gently cautioned the couple to wait until they were more established. Initially agreeing, John Jr. convinced his dad to name his last child "Frances" in honor of his alluring stepcousin.

The younger Dillinger continued to push to marry Frances, and eventually was rebuffed by his uncle. Angered that she bent to her stepfather's will, he broke off the relationship entirely and refused to speak to her.

Many feel what John did next was due to his rage over the shattered romance. Others say a less public affair with an Indianapolis girl pregnant with his child is more to blame. Whatever the motivation, John stuck a revolver in his pocket on a warm July night in 1923 and headed out for trouble. He stopped long enough to steal a shiny Overland sedan that was sitting outside Friend's Church—an arrogant, almost blasphemous act that signaled his surrender to the dark side. It's not certain what John's plan was that evening, if any, but things nonetheless quickly spiraled out of control. He motored to Indianapolis

and parked the Overland in plain view on the circle beneath the Sol-
dier's and Sailor's Monument. He began walking east into an African-
American neighborhood, stopping at the intersection of Toledo and
Tippecanoe streets.

Sticking out as he did, he was confronted around midnight by two of
Indianapolis's finest, Officers Thomas A. Aulls and Charles L. Hodges.
John gave them a badly ad-libbed phony name, Charles Dillinger,
admitted he was from Mooresville, and volunteered that his vehicle, the
stolen Overland, was four blocks away. It was a bizarre series of self-
incriminating statements from a man who would soon gain a reputation for being ice cool under intense pressure.

Even with the verbal fumbling, the officers would have probably let
everything slide if the standard pat down had not revealed the hidden
pistol. Aulls grabbed "Charles" by the coat collar and marched him to a
police call box on New York Street to summon transportation to the
station. Suddenly, John Jr. slithered away, leaving a stunned Aulls
holding an empty coat. A no-nonsense time in law enforcement history, the two officers thought nothing of pulling their weapons and
firing a total of seven shots at a fleeing young man who had done
nothing worse than having a handgun. Had either Aulls or Hodges
been better shots, John Herbert Dillinger would have been a forgotten
footnote in history.

With his first fugitive status established, Dillinger hid in a nearby
barn. That night, he hatched an escape plan used by many troubled
young men to this day—he decided to join the navy. With his half-
baked alias still providing cover, he made his way to the Federal
Building the next morning and enlisted, giving his complete name but
making up a phony address—916 Bain Avenue. The "don't ask, don't
tell, just sign'em up" Navy recruiters listed him at five-seven, 155
pounds, brown hair, blue eyes, ruddy complexion with "15" hearing,
20/20 vision, and a thirty-five-inch chest that expanded to thirty-
eight—nothing out of the ordinary. Things were a bit more interesting
in the scar department. Hard work and spirited play decorated John
with a half-inch gash on the right side of his face, another half-incher
on his left leg, a "pin" scar on his left knee, a third half-incher on the

ring finger, and a vaccination mark on his left arm. He was given serial number 291-06-76.

The navy was used to taking in wayward youth, and knew time was often of the essence in getting them out of town. They accommodated John by shipping him to the Great Lakes Training Station a mere four days later.

The newly uniformed Dillinger completed basic training on October 4, 1923, and was assigned to the battleship *Utah* as a Fireman, Third Class. His job consisted of shoveling coal into the ship's huge boilers. After twenty-two days of hot, backbreaking labor, he'd had enough. He jumped ship in Boston and went AWOL for a day, probably to cool off. Upon his return, a deck court martial stamped on November 7 was added to his growing rap sheet, along with an eighteen-dollar fine—nearly a month's pay—and a ten-day "bread and water" stint in the brig.

A delay in carrying out the sentence gave Dillinger the opportunity to get into even more trouble. On November 9, instead of laying low, the young man left his duty post "without authority" and in "disobedience of orders." Five days of solitary confinement were tacked on to his previous sentence. The punishment, as his father long lamented, failed to curb his ways. If anything, they made him more rebellious. Weeks after his release, he was in hot water again, failing to return from a twenty-four-hour leave as scheduled on December 4. The navy, noting that he "left with no effects—intentions not known," waited two weeks, then listed him as deserter. They also slapped the first ever bounty on his head, fifty bucks.

A half-century of intense scrutiny has not confirmed what John Dillinger Jr. did from December 4, 1923, until he resurfaced the following March. His family assumed he was dutifully serving in the navy. A friend, however, claims to have solved the mystery. Fred P. Whiteside said he visited John a few times in Indianapolis during that period. Dillinger told Whiteside that he made his way from Boston to New York, then hitched a ride home on the Twentieth Century Limited train. While that seems logical, Whiteside has baffled historians for nearly a century with the rest of his tale. He says he was taken to an

Indianapolis apartment and met a young woman with two babies. Dillinger introduced her as his wife. It was no doubt the same pregnant girlfriend from past unconfirmed reports. Aside from the mother and babies, John seemed equally proud of an assortment of tools he claimed to have stolen from Burcham's machine shop.

Whatever the truth, Dillinger surfaced publicly that March in Mooresville, telling everyone he was honorably discharged due to a heart murmur. There was no mention of a wife and children.

John's fear of the law, civilian or military, apparently vanished during his absence. He went about his business in Mooresville as if nothing had changed, commuting to Martinsville to hang out and chase skirts. One particular skirt, which covered a peppy seventeen-year-old named Beryl Ethel Hovious, caught his attention. He proposed within weeks, and married shortly thereafter, tying the knot on April 12, 1924, at the Morgan County courthouse. The Reverand V. W. Tevis did the honors. Hovious lied about her age, bumping it up to eighteen to get around parental consent laws. Dillinger, obviously, said nothing about a mysterious Indianapolis "wife" and the two babies. In fact, they were never referred to again.

The age and possible marital status deceptions didn't prevent the young couple from taking up residence with Beryl's parents at 249 Eslinger Avenue in Martinsville. They also spent some time at the Dillinger family farm, using his old bedroom as their home before moving to an upstairs apartment at 365 North Main Street, just north of Martinsville's town square. Beryl noted that Dillinger had taken up smoking Bull Durham roll-your-owns, didn't drink anymore, and often stayed out late at night. His career was as spotty as always, bouncing between temporary stints at the unsuspecting machine shop, working as an upholsterer for the Mooresville Furniture Factory, and even spending some time at a haberdashery known as "The Toggery Shop."

However, it was what he was doing during all those late nights out that began to define the man.

Chapter 2

Feeling lonely and abandoned, the teenage Mrs. John Dillinger Jr. began raising a stink about her husband's mysterious late-night activities. Like most women in her situation, she couldn't help but suspect that he was fooling around. While illicit rendezvous might have been part of it, John Jr. was up to far worse. In the summer of 1924, he was busy recruiting his first criminal gang.

John Sr., weary of his daughter-in-law's nagging, queried his son about his incessant night crawling. Junior responded casually that he was usually killing time at the Interurban Barn, a notorious hangout for aimless youth. John Sr. was aware of the transit station's "barn rat" reputation, and knew it was a popular place to stage card games. He wasn't sure what else was going on there, an oversight he'd later lament.

Even if the senior Dillinger had been more aware, it's doubtful he would have been able to prevent his son's next brush with the law. Junior was simply too determined to go bad.

It's not known how many successful missions the infant Dillinger Gang completed before their first bust shed light on their low-brow ambitions. John Jr. certainly wasn't flush with money, nor was he preening around town in silk suits and spats. He was just getting his criminal feet wet, going for small potatoes—almost literally as it turned out.

Ironically enough, in late April 1924, the boy that couldn't be kept on the farm was nabbed for stealing—forty-one Buff Orpingtons to be exact. He and two associates figured they could make a quick buck by hitting the farm of Omer A. Zook, a hardworking Indianapolis poultry man who worked a spread on Route 13, also known as Millersville Road. John Sr. made up for the loss and convinced Zook not to press charges.

It was obvious to all, including John Jr. himself, that if he was going to make a name for himself as a crook, he needed an experienced mentor to teach him the ropes. The man he selected was a distant in-law named William Edgar Singleton, a troubled, hard-drinking father of two who somehow managed to hold down a decent job at an electric light plant in Mooresville. Word was that "Eddie" Singleton had "done time," an accusation that can't be supported by the shaky record-keeping of the era. Regardless, the rumor was enough for Dillinger to seek out Eddie, whom he knew as a baseball umpire as well as a relative of sorts.

Aside from a whispered criminal history, Eddie was known around town for having an embarrassing, but not uncommon, genetic throw-back affliction called syndactyly, or webbed fingers. The enlargement or fusing of the skin between the digits gives a person an amphibious appearance.

On September 6, 1924, John Jr.—already suspected of burglarizing two area gas stations—hooked up with the frog-pawed Singleton and staked out John Smith's barbershop in Mooresville. They were stalking an elderly grocer in his mid-sixties named Frank Morgan. The prover-bial small-town businessman, Morgan had the unfortunate habit of stashing his modest store receipts in his pocket after closing and strolling home. He thought nothing of stopping to get his hair trimmed, or taking care of other errands, along the way.

As Morgan rose to pay the barber, Dillinger and Singleton slipped into Broad Alley, which paralleled Harrison Street, Morgan's route home. Singleton had stashed his Model T nearby at Broad Alley and Jefferson Street, a half block from a Christian church. As they waited, Singleton suggested they exchange hats and coats to confuse anyone trying to identify them. The elder man returned to the getaway car as Dillinger hid in the bushes at the south end of the church. John Jr. was carrying a heavy iron bolt wrapped in a cotton handkerchief. Tucked under his belt was an Iver Johnson .32.

Totally unsuspecting, poor Frank Morgan passed the church and turned south toward his house. Dillinger leaped from the bushes, swung his makeshift weapon, and crashed the bolt on the old grocer's head, crushing Morgan's straw-boater hat and knocking him to his knees. Dillinger let fly again, attempting to knock the victim out. The bolt, while stinging and potentially deadly, didn't have enough weight to render Morgan unconscious. The grocer struggled to his feet and slapped at the gun his attacker was now sticking in his face. The weapon went off, firing harmlessly into the ground, its ear-splitting bang reverberating through the quiet night. Porch lights started snapping on as concerned neighbors fumbled for shoes and shirts in order to dash outside to see what was going on. Morgan instinctively gave the "Masonic Grand Hailing Sign of Distress," hoping someone would recognize the gesture and come to the rescue. (Hands up in the air like a football referee signaling a touchdown, only with the elbows bent to form more of a square.)

Dillinger, unnerved by the turn of events, abandoned the robbery and ran toward the alley. He could hear the Model T crank and fire, but instead of getting louder, the sound of the motor faded! Singleton, the "veteran" crook, heard the shot and beat it in the opposite direction, his young apprentice be damned. John was on his own.

Jittery and discombobulated, Dillinger ducked into a local pool room a few blocks away and ignorantly began to ask people how badly Morgan had been hurt. Nobody knew what he was talking about, but his queries raised suspicions. Some noticed that the nervous young man had bloodstains on his hat and trouser cuff.

Having all but implicated himself in the crime, John Jr. left and began walking toward his pop's farm. It didn't take Sherlock Holmes to track him there. The next morning, Deputy Sheriff John M. Hayworth and Marshal Greeson were pounding on John Sr.'s door. The police told John Jr. to get his hat and coat, because they were taking him to Martinsville, the county seat. John Sr., still oblivious, figured it was probably about some kind of brawl at The Barn.

John Jr. hung tough under the bare lights and rubber hose treatment in the station sweatbox, wary of adding a loose tongue to his growing list of blunders. As would always be his MO, he stayed in full denial, refusing to buckle under the interrogation pressure. The police had enough to hold him without a confession, but figured with time and stress, he'd eventually cave and save them the trouble of a trial.

John Sr. and sister Audrey visited the Martinsville jailhouse on Sunday, September 14, a week later. They were taken to a dank, upstairs cell in the old brick building. It was so dark they couldn't even see John Jr. until he came forward to the bars. His father remembered his face looking cold and hard. Not knowing what to say, John Sr. began rambling about John Jr.'s mother, his wife, the farm, church, whatever popped into his head. John Jr. just listened in silence. Finally, the distraught farmer put his cards on the table.

"Johnnie, if you did this thing, the only way is to own up to it. They'll go easy on you and you can get a new start. You'll be okay, but you've got to tell them the truth."

Simple words, but they got through to Junior. He finally broke down and spilled his guts, implicating his supposed mentor Singleton as well. Morgan County Prosecutor Fred W. Steiger took the confession as Sheriff Lafayette Scott witnessed. Afterward, a warrant was issued for Singleton. He was quickly rounded up and brought in. Faced with John Jr. rolling on him, he confessed his role and asked for a lawyer.

John Sr. believed that making his son fess up was the right move. "I took my grief to God," he'd later explain. "I got down on my knees and prayed for guidance."

On September 15, John Jr. and Singleton were marched to the courthouse—the same place Dillinger had married his teenage bride Beryl six months earlier. Singleton's attorney asked for a continuance and received it. Dillinger, having no attorney, pleaded guilty to conspiracy to commit a felony and assault with intent to rob. Judge Joseph Warford Williams, elected to the bench by Morgan County voters who were now enraged over the vicious attack, was in no mood to cut the local bad sheep any slack. In a stern voice, he sentenced the youth to two-to-fourteen years on the first count, and a whopping ten-to-twenty on the second, meaning he'd have to serve a minimum of a decade in the slammer. Williams gave Dillinger a slight break by making the sentences concurrent, which basically eliminated the first prison term. It was little consolation. John Jr. couldn't believe the harsh sentence. Enraged, he felt that he was sold out by both the system, and his father.

The following day, the angry young man was handcuffed, pushed aboard the Interurban, and escorted to Indiana's newest corrections facility at Pendleton, located twenty-five miles northeast of Indianapolis.

"They whisked my boy off to the reformatory before I knew of the appalling sentence imposed on him," John Sr. said. "The news prostrated me. I rushed to Martinsville to see Judge Williams. I pleaded with him to reconsider the sentences. Judge Williams was sympathetic, but he told me that Johnnie came before him an utter stranger accused of a murderous attempt to rob. 'Under the statutes of the state of Indiana, I had no alternative but to give him the sentence prescribed by the law,' the judge told me."

Williams was probably overstating things. Judges have great leeway in such cases, and similar young robbers had gotten off with little more than a slap on the wrist—although John Jr.'s use of a handgun didn't help his cause.

"I should have got a good lawyer for Johnnie," Mr. Dillinger continued. "I should not have let him face the music alone, depending on the glib promises of a politically motivated prosecutor. Can you imagine my feelings when rumors reached me that there had been talk of turning Johnnie loose because of insufficient evidence until I butted in and persuaded him to plead guilty?"

The prosecutors never showed their hand, but it's likely they indeed pushed so hard for a confession because they didn't feel their case was airtight.

John Dillinger Jr. had no doubt fallen victim to a typical prosecutorial shell game, yet he had no one to blame but himself. Not only was he a repeat criminal offender who used violence for small gain, he was a woefully inept crook who kept getting caught through his own mistakes. The result was getting slapped with a possible twenty-year sentence for a botched robbery of a local businessman in a small town where both he and the victim lived, a town where everybody knew everybody.

Morgan's take that night? One hundred twenty dollars. At best, Dillinger would have come away with sixty dollars after stuffing half into Singleton's webbed hand. Instead, he got twenty years.

Singleton went to trial a month later, October 15, 1924. After a recovered Frank Morgan wheezed out his terrible story, it only took the jury twenty minutes to find Singleton guilty of conspiracy, accessory, and assault charges. He was given two-to-fifteen years, fined twenty-five dollars, and disenfranchised for a year.

Dillinger was further enraged by Singleton's lighter sentence and vowed to keep a promise he made before the verdict that if his accomplice got off easier, "I'll be the meanest bastard you ever saw when I get out."

On the way back to jail after testifying against Singleton, Dillinger feigned indifference. Riding the Interurban, he offered his kindly escort, Morgan County Deputy Russell Peterson, a peach and some candy he was allowed to have. Peterson declined, fearing the treats might be doped. At the Interurban Barn in Indianapolis, Peterson bought John Jr. a soft drink and allowed him to sip it outside at a picnic table, figuring it might be the last such moment the young man would have for ten years.

Deputy Peterson, sitting across from his charge, was about to join a long line of peace officers punished for showing a desperado a measure of mercy. Without warning, Dillinger summoned his rage, braced his feet on the table's edge, and gave it a mighty heave, knocking Peterson backward. John Jr., still in handcuffs, took off west on Washington Street, past the State House, across the lawn, and up a blind alley.

Peterson jumped up and gave chase, firing at the escaping felon with his .25 caliber pistol. They were acting out the same deadly cops-and-robbers game two blocks from where the Indianapolis officers tried to plug the young bandit a year before. Once again, John Dillinger nearly had his historic criminal career end before it started. As before, his uncanny ability to dodge bullets saved his skin.

Although he knew Indianapolis well, the dead-end alley was an unaccommodating escape route. An angry Deputy Peterson quickly cornered him, dragged him back to the Interurban, and continued the journey to Pendleton. The lengthy ride tempered the officer's fury. "I knew John's dad," he told interviewers later. "I thought well of him. Besides, John was just a kid and you can't take ten years out of a kid's life."

Pendleton was a typically bleak incarceration center consisting of assorted tan-colored stone buildings with red tile roofs, thirty-foot concrete walls, and gun towers at each of its four corners. Powerful searchlights swept the premises at night. Inside, a sea of steel doors lead to a maze of corridors and brightly lit, triple-tiered cell blocks.

Oddly enough, the facility housed four commercial factories managed by civilians that took advantage of the cheap, forced labor provided by the prisoners—a popular policy at the time. The businesses made clothing, furniture, tableware, and manhole covers. The prisoners universally loathed the sweatshop concept, particularly Foundry Four, the hot, draining manhole manufacturer. Dillinger, having no seniority, was naturally shoved into that dreaded assignment.

Pendleton, though new, quickly suffered from the overcrowding that afflicts most prisons. Designed to house 1,200 short-term "minors" not yet twenty-one, it soon doubled that number. Dillinger, already over the loosely governed age limit, was fortunate to have been placed there instead of a grislier adult facility. Still, this was no bed-and-breakfast, and oppressive guards, hopelessness, despair, and brutal homosexual rape were as prevalent as the noisy flocks of fowl that swarmed the place. Being older and stronger than most of Pendleton's residents, Dillinger was apparently spared the psychologically scarring sexual aspects.

Superintendent A. F. Miles, a caring man who stubbornly held on to the ideal of rehabilitation, would always remember the almost refreshing frankness of inmate 14395. "I won't cause you any trouble except to escape," Dillinger admitted in his first interview. "I'll go right over the administration building."

The navy, alerted that their missing sailor had been found, filed paperwork for a dishonorable discharge and waived any claim to him.

Physical examinations revealed Dillinger was suffering from gonor-rhea, a sexually transmitted disease that couldn't have been a pleasant gift to his wife if she was so infected. The treatment was fitting punish-ment if he had done so—the painful injection of silver nitrate through the penis into the urethra, a barbaric procedure that would be harkened back to in health classes for decades to come in order to scare high school boys celibate.

The excruciating gonorrhea cure increased the misery of Dillinger's prison life, fueling his already intense desire to flee. Early in his sojourn, even before the Singleton trial escape attempt, he had tried to kick off an exit plan by hiding in a pile of excelsior in the prison's foundry. A sus-picious supervisor loudly announced that he was going to set the highly flammable heap of wood chips ablaze. Dillinger immediately scurried out. Barely thirty days into his sentence, and he'd already earned another six months.

Before Christmas, he was at it again, plotting with two fellow inmates to bust out for the holidays by sawing through the bars. His cohorts had somehow gotten hold of a cherished hacksaw blade, and had made good progress. They showed Dillinger their work. He was confident enough in the failed scheme, as he'd later admit in a written report, that "I told my wife I would be home for Christmas . . ."

The Pendleton officials, wise to the plan, tacked yet another six months onto his sentence. Dillinger had spent only ninety days in prison, and had managed to have an extra year added to his already healthy term. Additional time was added over the coming months for subse-quent misbehavior. At the rate he was going, he'd never be released.

For whatever reason, he stopped the shenanigans in 1927, no doubt having a good measure of his piss and vinegar drained by a nasty case of diphtheria he contracted in March. He also became notably "sullen and morose" when learning that Singleton was paroled on October 30 of the previous year.

The "good John" period ended in 1928 with more reprimands and sentence extensions. Apparently, the concept of being paroled early for good behavior—as Singleton had—was lost on the hothead from Mooresville.

In the early years of his sentence, his family visited about once a month. As is the case with most con families, the time-consuming, unpleasant treks to a depressing corrections facility began to wear the Dillingers down. Their trips became less frequent. Even wife Beryl had enough by 1927 and stopped coming altogether, pleading financial distress. Feeling guilty, she resumed her visits in 1928, one time after selling her sweater for Interurban fare. Touched, John made her a colorful scarf. She refused to wear it.

There were no visits recorded from a mysterious woman with or without two small children, further muddying the waters about those strange but persistent first marriage rumors.

Mary, the favored niece he felt a kinship with, remained loyal, visiting when she could even though the sound of the big iron doors slamming never failed to unnerve her. More important, Mary wrote long letters on a regular basis—a priceless gift to any man in the joint. "He knew when I had my first lipstick and went to my first party and had my first date," she reminisced fondly. "I wrote him every week, ten, twelve, fifteen pages."

In contrast, there's no record of Beryl visiting beyond the summer of 1928. To no one's surprise but John's, she filed for divorce on April 25, 1929. Her attorneys, Vernon & Vernon, emphasized that Beryl was "wholly without fault on her part and she was at all times a true and dutiful wife."

Judge Joe Williams, the man who overruled any confession-based leniency and slapped Dillinger with the harsh sentence, granted Beryl her wish on June 20. A week later, the still attractive, twentysomething Beryl traveled to Martinsville, Illinois, and married a mechanic named Harold C. McGowan.

Dillinger followed his pattern of going into a shell when given depressing news. There were no reports of any antisocial behavior that corresponded with his wife's double whammy. A letter sent to stepmom Lizzie on Mother's Day in 1929, made no mention of his domestic shake-up.

John's last visitors came on July 13, 1929. They were his pop, half-brother Hubert, sister Audrey, and niece Mary. America was on the verge of a dramatic change for the worse—and prisoner number 14395 was about to play a starring role in the New World Disorder.

Chapter 3

John Dillinger came up for parole in July 1929. His chances were slim. The penal parole system is designed to keep prisoners under control. Behave, and you get out early. Act up, and you serve the full term. Repeatedly cause trouble, as John did, and you stay even longer.

The three-member parole board, which included the then-Indiana governor Harry C. Leslie, took one look at Dillinger's thick file and sent him back inside. Hearing the news, the young hopeful merely shrugged and, according to a newspaper reporter, asked to be transferred to Michigan City because they had a "better ball team."

Michigan City was the home of Indiana State Penitentiary, a "belly-of-the-beast" adult facility on the shore of Lake Michigan. The ill-advised request, if accurate, harkened back to Dillinger's bumbling thief days. He was far better off as an older inmate in a semicaring, rehabilitation-oriented juvenile facility than he would be tussling with the grizzled monsters that populated the state pen. In addition, Michigan City was 150 miles to the north, making it harder for his family to visit.

Dillinger scribbled on his release papers that "I was told that I and the three others who came with me were transferred here to play ball, although it wasn't told to me by the Superintendent."

It's more likely that Dillinger, twenty-six, and friends had simply outgrown the youth-oriented Pendleton facility and had graduated to the Big House. And despite Dillinger's wishful writing, he wasn't transferred to play ball. Indiana State had no shortage of bigger, stronger ballplayers. John Jr.'s hopes of making a name for himself on the diamond were once again destined to be dashed. He never even made the team.

As expected, his visitors dwindled down to practically nobody at the distant pen. Even the ever-dutiful Audrey only managed to make it there once during the next four years.

Despite all the negatives associated with the transfer to Indiana State, the one "positive" was that the place harbored a wide assortment of potential criminal mentors. State pens are like colleges for crooks. Experienced thieves, burglars, bookmakers, safecrackers, and other organized crime specialists function as professors, eagerly sharing their stories and expertise to pass the time.

As with Pendleton, Indiana State operated assorted private enterprises inside its confines. Dillinger, now a relatively skilled garment industry drone, was assigned to the Gordon East Coast Shirt Factory— a thriving operation that had expanded westward to take advantage of a captive, cheap labor pool. John's specific assignment was to set collars on Blue Yank work shirts. The job was noteworthy because a trio of new coworkers, Harry "Pete" Pierpont, Charles Makley, and Russell Clark, were convicted bank robbers who would one day make headlines alongside the new recruit.

Pierpont, a Muncie, Indiana, native who moved to Indianapolis with his parents when he was fifteen, possessed chiseled, movie-star features, bright blue eyes, and stood over six-feet-tall. He would inspire nimble-fingered reporters to give him a new nickname—"Handsome Harry." Blessed facially, he unfortunately felt cursed on the other end. His second and third toes were welded together, giving him a duck foot that forever ate at his fragile psyche. Amazingly, John Dillinger's first mentor had webbed fingers; his second had webbed toes.

Handsome Harry was the same age as Dillinger, twenty-six, and his life had progressed similarly—boring dead-end jobs spiced by late-night car thefts, burglaries, and robberies. Pierpont also shared Dillinger's fascination with guns, breaking into a Greencastle, Illinois, hardware store in 1922 and making off with nine shiny pistols.

Although Pierpont had some early criminal success, his initial fall was no less embarrassing than Dillinger's. Attempting to steal a car outside a butcher shop seven years before, the heavily armed felon was bested by an unarmed couple who owned the vehicle. The woman snuck up from behind and clobbered him on the head with a large package of freshly cut meat while he was wrestling with her husband. The fact that Pierpont was carrying four loaded pistols, and fired one three times during the struggle, creasing the owner in the leg, didn't save him from the lady's T-boned wrath. The butchered braining enabled additional citizens to join the fray. They swarmed Handsome Harry and subdued him long enough for the police to arrive.

Locked in a sudden losing streak, he was quickly convicted of assault and battery with attempt to murder, given two-to-fourteen years, and sent to the old reformatory at Jeffersonville, Indiana, just across the Ohio River from Louisville. Thanks to his constantly pestering mother, "Leaping" Lena, he was released in 1924 after thirty-six months.

Pierpont tried to go straight for a while, toiling at his father's sand and gravel business in the exotically named Brazil, Indiana. Poppa Pierpont's operation, however, was no carnival. Handsome Harry quickly tired of the backbreaking labor and instead assembled a gang of ruffians he had met in the joint. The recruits included Earl "The Kid" Northern, Everett Bridgewater, and Thaddeus Skeer. The patchwork mob operated out of Pearl Mulendore's twenty-one-room boarding-house at 718 North Main Street in yet another city with tropical aspirations—Kokomo, Illinois. "Kokomo" Pearl was intrigued by the smooth criminals in her midst, so much so that she eventually married future gang member Dewey Elliott. The pair made a bit of crime history of their own, she as the ubiquitous Pearl Elliott.

At the end of 1924, Pierpont and gang terrorized Indiana, taking down banks in Noblesville, Converse, Upland, Marion, New Albany, and New Harmony, netting anywhere from $3,000 to $10,000 a shot.

In an ironic warning of things to come, it was a lady who put an end to Harry's fast and furious reign—and it wasn't even his lady. After a big score in Kokomo, he and associate Thaddeus Skeer went to Detroit to let things cool off. A lovesick Skeer called his girlfriend back home in Fort Wayne, Indiana, and asked her to visit. The woman's disapproving father, aware of the ruckus his daughter's suitor was creating, squealed to the police. The cops followed the girl to Detroit where she led them right to her boyfriend and his notorious companion. Pierpont was convicted and hit with ten to twenty-one years.

It wasn't long before another familiar figure entered the Michigan City circle, kicking and screaming the whole way. Homer VanMeter was a tall, sinewy fellow who hailed from Fort Wayne. He had a sharp wit that hid an underlying cunningness. To quote an old Frank Capra/Cary Grant movie, *Arsenic and Old Lace*, insanity galloped through his family. An uncle died in an asylum. His father was declared insane before his death. Not surprisingly, Homer hoofed it away from home at age twelve. After years of thieving, he was busted for a train robbery and was given ten-to-twenty-one.

Indiana State teemed with similar characters. Russell "Booby" Clark, Ralston "Blackie" Linton, Frank Bagley, Charles E. Hovious (a distant cousin of Dillinger's ex-wife Beryl Hovious), Charles Makley, John "Three Fingered Jack" Hamilton, Ray Lawrence, and assorted others found their way to the Gordon East Coast Shirt Factory. All were far more experienced and successful criminals than John Dillinger. Few would have wagered that the angry Mooresville farm boy would become the most famous of the bunch.

That amazing transformation to celebrity criminal was still years away. Life at Indiana State at the turn of the decade was little different than at Pendleton. Dillinger kept getting written up for Mickey Mouse offenses like "cooking over fire in cell," in between dispatching cheerful letters to his beloved niece Mary. On Christmas Day 1929, John pitched her on the benefits of education, and spoke of his future beyond the iron bars:

```
If you don't go there are plenty of times you will
wish you had. I'll be out sometime and believe me I
am going to stay out. I know right from wrong, and
I intend to do right when I get out. I suppose that
you think that I do not try to make my time clear
but honey I do try, and a lot of times when I want
to do something or start to do something that might
get me in trouble I think of Sis and don't do it . . .
```

```
I'm not very strong for praying. I think it will
take more than prayers . . . for me to get out of
here. Now don't think I am an atheist for I am not.
I do believe in God, but his ways seem strange to me
sometimes. For if anyone deserves happiness it is
your dear mother [Audrey] who is the sweetest woman
in the world. I will try to pray for Sis not that I
think it will do her any good but I would do any-
thing for her . . . Keep your eyes open for a sweet
girl with plenty of money and ballahoo me up.
```

Despite John's promise to go straight, the truth was that he was eagerly learning at the feet of his new friends.

Dillinger and his array of mentors were pretty much sheltered from the anguish that was going on outside the gates. The party-happy Roaring Twenties they remembered were no more, replaced by the Great Depression that started when the stock market crashed in October 1929. Four thousand banks—including many of those robbed by Dillinger's cellmates—closed due to bad investments, embezzlement, mismanagement, and massive withdrawal runs by a panicked public. Prohibition—America's attempt to outlaw alcohol—combined with the suddenly hard economic times to fuel a ton of anger and anxiety that rivaled what the prisoners were feeling for altogether different reasons. Misery ruled, inside and out. Yet those inside, assured of lodging, heat, and three squares a day, may have actually had it better than many who were free, cold, and hungry. So while the country was going insane, it was merely insanity as usual inside Indiana State.

Slowly smartening up, Dillinger tried harder to avoid petty disciplinary problems. His second parole hearing was approaching, and he wanted to at least have a chance this time. He started doubling his production in the shirt factory, and helped others meet their quotas as well. The bank robbers, Pierpont, Makley, Clark, and Hamilton, were rooting for him, mostly for selfish reasons. It's always good to have a friend on the outside.

By March, 1933, Dillinger was growing increasingly optimistic about his chances of release. He began plotting a strategy he felt might take him over the top, communicating his instructions to niece Mary.

```
    . . . I want Sis to go with Dad before the board
when my case comes up and make a plea for me
and don't take no for an answer. If Sis will
just argue with the board like she does with
Emmett I will be planting my dogs under her table
this Spring. Ha! Ha!
    . . . If I am lucky enough to make it you can all
drive up right away to get me . . . Are you keeping
in practice making coconut cream pie and coconut
cream cake? Oh Boy! I mean is Sis keeping in prac-
tice, not you? I'm not like those beaus of yours
that can exist on love. Ha! Ha!—Love and kisses from
Johnnie.
```

The Dillinger family did a yeoman's job of putting together a parole petition in April, 1933. The main pitch was that John was needed on the farm to help his aging father through the tough times. On top of that, the petition mentioned that his stepmother, Lizzie, was hospitalized with a long, lingering illness. Today, that coincidence might have cast suspicion on John Sr. because he lost his first wife to a similar malady. However, in those days, rural women suffering from "lingering ill-nesses" caused by any number of ailments or diseases were not uncommon.

This time around, the family had learned how to play the parole endorsement game, rounding up a healthy group of movers and shakers willing to lend their support. Those onboard included Morgan County Sheriff Vance Keller, along with the court clerk, auditor, treas-urer, recorder, and assessor. Audrey and crew even squeezed frail grocer Frank Morgan, the victim, into adding his John Hancock to the parole petition. The cherry was getting Hanging Judge Joe Williams to sign on as well.

In all, the Dillingers twisted the arms of 188 people. Among those also putting pen to paper was Chester Vernon, Beryl Dillinger's divorce lawyer. He had taken Judge Williams's seat on the Morgan County bench.

The stars, both literal and allegorical, were lining up. Another Morgan County native, Paul V. McNutt, was Indiana's new governor. Dillinger had yet to serve his ten-year minimum sentence, so his case would be referred to the governor's Clemency Commission in Indianapolis rather than the board of trustees at Indiana State Penitentiary where he had caused all the trouble.

Clemency Commissioner Delos Dean motioned to approve the parole and fellow commissioner Tom Arbuckle quickly agreed. Governor McNutt's secretary, Wayne Coy, had the final vote. For unstated reasons, he abstained. Whatever he was thinking, it was a fortuitous decision as the ambitious Coy—without the stain of approving Dillinger's parole—would later snag the job of Commissioner of the Federal Communications Commission.

Two out of three was enough to set John Dillinger free. The paperwork hit McNutt's desk on May 9. A release order was signed the following day. Despite the importance of the measure to the convict involved, the next step in the process was frequently snail slow. Eleven days passed without word regarding the critical release date.

On May 20, Lizzie suffered a stroke, eerily following in the tragic pattern of her predecessor, Mollie. Hubert Dillinger and Fred Hancock, Audrey's son, rushed to Pendleton to speed the parole process along. Obtaining the last needed signature, they sped 140 miles north to Michigan City, arriving just after 6 P.M. The two young men watched intently as John Jr. changed into civilian clothes, signed various forms, and was handed forty dollars in cash. As they walked away from the dreary building, John stopped, paused, turned around, and gave the hated place one last good-bye gaze. "I'd rather be dead than ever go back in there," he said.

John Dillinger's joyful day was severely tainted by the series of bad breaks that were crushing his father and stepmother. Hubert phoned to announce that John was free. Instead of jubilation, he was greeted by the news that Lizzie was sinking fast. The trio raced south, but had to let up on the pedal when the engine of their vehicle began to overheat. Proceeding at a frustratingly slow pace, they made it down U.S. 31 through Plymouth, Rochester, Kokomo, and Indianapolis before a blow-out added another twenty minutes to the journey. It was 12:30 A.M. when they finally made it to the Dillinger farm.

John walked into his house for the first time in nearly nine years only to be greeted by a wave of grief. "Where's Mom?" he asked.

His father couldn't speak. "I just looked up at him trying to see his face that swam in my tears," John Sr. recalled. The two embraced and wept together. The car troubles had prevented Johnnie from seeing his stepmother take her last breath just before midnight. The tragic moment brings to mind something John Jr. wrote to a friend while in prison. "I only wish I had a mother to worry over me but she died when I was three. I guess this is why I was such a bad boy. No mother to look after me."

Lizzie was buried on Thursday morning, May 25, 1933, in the same plot where Mollie had been laid to rest twenty-seven years earlier. Rev. Charles Fillmore, a family friend who originally married the couple twenty-one years before (and later authored the popular hymn "Tell Mother I'll Be There"), handled the ceremony at Crown Hill Cemetery in northwest Indianapolis.

Feeling melancholy, John left the solemn event and paid a visit to B. Frank Morgan. "He shook my hand and said, 'I want to apologize for socking you that time,' " Morgan recalled. " 'I've turned over a new leaf. I've reformed. I want to thank you for helping get my parole.' He seemed to realize that he had been bad."

While that apology is well known, historians missed a darker event of that afternoon. After making amends with Morgan, John dropped in on his remarried ex-wife, spooking her. "He just wanted to know how I was getting along," Beryl revealed to an interviewer more than a half-century later. "I asked him to leave and he did."

Continuing his rounds, Dillinger met with Mrs. Gertrude Reinier, who, interestingly enough, was the female pastor of Friend's Church. She had received a letter from the Indiana State warden requesting that she look in on John Jr.'s "spiritual needs." Weeks later on Father's Day, with John Sr. and Jr. in attendance, she gave a sermon on the Prodigal Son. "Throughout the sermon, young John sat there beside his father crying," Reverand Reinier remembered. "Afterwards, he came to me and said, 'You will never know how much good that sermon has done me.'"

While Reverand Reinier tried to be supportive after John Jr.'s release, others at the strict Quaker church weren't buying Dillinger's good guy act. Sensing something wrong, Dillinger's Sunday school teacher expelled him from the class and asked him not to come back. Additional parishioners soon convinced Reverand Reinier that Dillinger was anything but reformed. During an "altar call," a Quaker ritual that involves church members kneeling at the altar to support a penitent former bad egg, Dillinger was left to flap in the breeze up front conspicuously alone. Enraged, he spat to Audrey afterward that "I will never go to church again as long as I live." As far as anyone knows, it was one promise John Dillinger kept.

Harsh as the treatment sounds, the Quakers had better insight into Dillinger than his family and friends. While he was wearing the white hat during the day, he was quickly changing into his black hat at night. Within weeks of his release, he was trekking out to Indianapolis at night looking for action.

It wasn't an easy search. America wasn't the abundant place he remembered. The Great Depression produced bread lines, apple sellers, desperate beggars, and boarded-up banks and businesses. Indiana had 100,000 people on relief, and unemployment nationwide topped fourteen million. The new president, Franklin Delano Roosevelt, was struggling mightily to make good on his campaign promise that "happy days are here again!" Roosevelt took America off the gold standard, declared a bank holiday, and phased out the failed attempt to make America a dry nation. All Prohibition had really done was wet the country with the blood of warring bootleg mobs run by the likes of Al Capone. In Chicago alone, there were more than five hundred gang-related murders in the 1920s as unpoliced, unregulated rival factions fought to be the main suppliers of the public's unquenchable thirst for booze.

With legitimate spirits companies preparing to go back in business, the carnage eased up. Unfortunately, with the economic times being what they were, the number of desperados proliferated. In 1932, with John Dillinger safely behind bars, hotfooted bandits would rely upon the development of faster automobiles and better roads to hold up 631 banks, including a whopping 85 in Illinois. Fueling this surge was another invention—the Thompson submachine gun that was popularized by Capone's mob. Boasting either a 20-round .45 caliber magazine, or a brutal 50- to 100-round drum, a single bandit armed with a Thompson could make a platoon of cops drop their woefully inadequate .32 or .38 caliber specials and duck for cover.

Created to perform as a trench broom during World War I, a Thompson set on full automatic could spit an incredible 800-rounds per minute. With its detachable stock, it offered the added benefit of being easily concealed off the battlefield.

Further stacking the deck in the bad guy's favor was the fact that the gun laws were as baffling then as they are today. A person needed a police permit and background check to buy something as tame as a single shot .22 pistol. In contrast, Capone, or anybody else, could stroll into a sporting goods store, hunting shop, or hardware outlet, and walk out with a deadly Thompson simply by plucking down $175. Under the legal statues, a Thompson was considered a rifle and therefore didn't require a permit.

The bad guys had a similar advantage when it came to their getaways. Most police departments were equipped with four-cylinder Model A Fords or six-cylinder Chevrolet "Independence Series" automobiles. Other departments preferred four-cylinder Plymouths, or the newer "Deluxe Six" introduced in 1933.

The crooks gravitated to Ford V8s or the speedy Essex Terraplane Eight built by the Hudson Motor Car Company. These road rockets could hit the proverbial "90 miles an hour," leaving police cruisers in their exhaust. The faster cars weren't perfect, however. The high speed was often more than the suspensions, brakes, steering and engine parts could handle. The heavy vehicles also slurped gas at an alarming rate, offering less than ten miles per gallon. That limited their range to 100 miles between fill-ups.

For bank robbers, it was an acceptable trade-off. The biggest factor in making their getaway was velocity. The initial jump on the posse was critical. The pursuing police were further handicapped by an absence of two-way radios in their puttering vehicles. Those that were equipped usually had only one-way communication, meaning they could take messages from the base, but couldn't send updates back or communicate with other cruisers. It wouldn't be until well into the 1940s that the critical two-way radios would become standard equipment. This "failure to communicate" hindered the quick setup of roadblocks, and stifled the neighboring city and county police tag-teams that would be the bane of future criminals. In the 1930s, however, if a crook could successfully jet away from the scene in their Crazy Eights, they were usually home free.

Even in his dumbest moments, John Dillinger always knew two things—cars and guns. It didn't take him long to realize what had transpired technologically while he was inside, and how the T&T equation, "Thompsons and Terraplanes," favored outlaws to a giddying degree. Toss in the fact that the surviving banks, especially those in rural areas, usually had poor security, and it wasn't hard to see how Dillinger viewed bank robbing as one of the few growth industries in the bleak times.

By chance, John Jr. had spent the past four years learning from the best bank robbers of the time. Not only had the ol' gang back in the shirt shop taught him how to make a score, they went so far as to share their prized "easy jug" list—the names and locations of the most poorly protected banks in the midwest, sitting ducks that could be pilfered with minimum risk.

Dillinger himself was smarter, trimmer, and more muscular than before he went to Pendleton. Maturation had smoothed both his personality and features, making him attractive to women and respected by men. Both enjoyed and sought his company.

In late May 1933, Dillinger brought his knowledge to the "White Cap" gang, a group of young hoods who were staging small stickups in and around Indianapolis. Teaming with a pair of White Cappers, Noble Claycomb and nineteen-year-old William "The Kid" Shaw, the trio decided to stage a job. It was Dillinger's first attempt at crime since his release, and the new and improved Johnnie D inexplicably reverted back to his dumber days. Taken to a weapons broker who offered a wide assortment of handguns for rent, Dillinger reacted like a kid in a candy store, selecting a fancy, long-barreled Colt .32-20. It was some righteous heat—but difficult to conceal.

The preliminary process of stealing a car, and switching license plates to further confuse the cops, immediately involved the newfound partners in two separate police chases. During the second squealing run, the vehicle's rear door was still open when Claycomb floored it. The door slammed into a telephone pole and busted out one of its two hinges, causing it to dangle.

Instead of letting things cool off and calling it a night, the three went right ahead with the planned robbery of City Foods, an all-night grocery at 4609 East Tenth. The ill-advised effort unraveled the moment Dillinger entered the cheerful place. As he and Shaw casually approached the store's office, City Foods clerk Irene Quigley spotted the Colt's elongated barrel poking out of Dillinger's jacket and screamed a warning to manager Walter J. Reeves. Undeterred, Shaw sprang into action, sweeping up $100 worth of bills from a register while Dillinger used the intimidating weapon to force everyone into the rear of the store. An elderly man, frozen in fear, refused to move.

Six days had passed since John Dillinger offered his heartfelt apologies to Frank Morgan, the last old man he tried to brutally rob. His callousness in that instance cost him ten years of his life. Faced with the same situation, Dillinger reacted without a moment's hesitation, clubbing the man across his mouth with the Colt's barrel. The victim proceeded to spit out so many teeth that even a sociopath like Shaw froze in horror. The unrepentant Dillinger had shattered the man's dentures, causing the unnerving spray.

Regaining their senses, the pair backed away and exited the store. This time, Claycomb, unlike Singleton, preformed his duty and swung by to scoop them up.

Despite the numerous flubs, Dillinger viewed the evening as a rousing success. He had put his life on the line, risked another long prison term, and trusted a driver he barely knew—for thirty dollars. In his eyes, it was all good.

The following day, Johnnie D was back in his angel persona, dutifully keeping an appointment with his parole officer. He said he was busy working on the farm with his dad, while at the same time was aggressively seeking steady work.

He was only lying about the first.

Part II: May 1933—January 1934

The Bloody Reign of the Terror Gang

Chapter 4

Johm Dillinger's next criminal adventure would be another duet with Willie "The Kid" Shaw. Wheel man Noble Claycomb wasn't available, so Paul "Lefty" Parker, the White Cap gang's backup driver, eagerly took his place. John Dillinger once again placed his life in the hands of a new getaway man.

The trio headed to Indianapolis's east side where the coincidently named Parker double-parked on Audubon Road near Washington Street while Dillinger and Shaw went into Haag Drug Store at 5648 East Washington. Johnnie D wasn't going to wait for any over-observant clerk to start screaming this time. He and Shaw entered with their guns drawn. Dillinger announced the stickup and began emptying the cash drawer at the soda fountain. Shaw dashed to the back to loot the main register. While in the process, Shaw became uneasy and looked up to see everybody in the place staring at him with their hands raised. He ordered them to pirouette. Seconds later, he glanced up and saw them facing him again. "Turn around!" he screamed, growing angrier. A few moments after that, they were peering at him again. The young robber finally figured out that Dillinger, across the way at the front of the store, was telling the terrified people the same thing. The two bandits were spinning the hostages around like tops.

Outside, the Keystone Robbers story continued. The gun-toting duo was minus a wheelman! Turns out that Parker saw a prized spot open up and decided to practice his parallel parking skills. He wedged the Ford tightly to the curb. Dillinger and Shaw found him, jumped in, and suffered through a few anxious moments of front- and rear-bumper bashing before Parker smashed his way out. They both gave him a fiery tongue lashing.

It's not known how much they netted, probably no more than one hundred dollars—a good chunk of which was turned over to Shorty George Hughes to compensate for the damage to the vehicle they had rented from him.

Never ones to shy away from pressing their luck, the trio decided to ad-lib another hit a few days later. They pulled up to a Kroger store at 3512 North College and cased the neighborhood. Shaw's knowledge of the area made Dillinger suspicious. He asked if the White Cappers had hit that store before. Shaw lied and said no. Truth was, he and Claycomb had robbed the precursor to Kmart less than a month before.

As the pair sauntered into the store, guns drawn, the manager merely sighed and said, "Well, here they are again." Dillinger gave Shaw a withering glance. Shaw shrugged and went to the cash drawer, only to find a few small bills. The glib manager explained that since the last robbery, the company sent collectors in a few times a day to transfer the loot. In fact, one had just left. Ticked, Shaw grabbed a number of cigarette tins as Dillinger backed out of the department store.

Parker was instructed to remain double-parked and not to move an inch until his partners emerged. Spotting Dillinger, he eased forward. Dillinger hopped in the front. Shaw followed and attempted to jump in the back, only to have the door handle elude his grasp. A nervous Parker had hit the accelerator before Shaw could get inside.

A frantic Shaw stood screaming in the middle of College Avenue, his arms overflowing with cigarette tins. He started running after the vanishing Ford. "Hold it! We left the kid behind," Dillinger noted. Parker stomped the brakes, screeching to a stop. He threw the gear into reverse and floored it, shooting the Ford backward. Shaw, still clutching the tins, did his best matador number to keep from being flattened. Finally reaching the door, he jerked it open, dumped the cigarettes into the seat, and slithered inside. Parker slammed the gears back into first and took off.

Dillinger combined his share of the meager profits from both robberies and used it for an oddly altruistic purpose. He handed the cash over as a down payment on an influence purchase from Omar Brown, a former Howard County sheriff said to have juice with the parole board. Keeping a promise made in the Indiana State shirt shop, he was trying to stack the deck at Harry Pierpont's upcoming parole hearing on August 24.

Already growing weary of the nickel-and-dime antics of the White Cappers, Dillinger envisioned a serious gang of veteran bank robbers made up of his mentors wasting away inside the state pen. Homer VanMeter had already done his part, earning a parole on May 19, 1933, the day before Dillinger was freed. VanMeter had returned to the familiar surroundings of northern Indiana, but wouldn't be hard to find when needed. The key to assembling a top-notch team, Dillinger felt, was springing Pierpont, the dapper hood who had been the brains of every gang he'd ever run with.

On June 22—Dillinger's thirtieth birthday—he and Shaw scouted a bank in Indianapolis at Belmont and Washington. The place had already been hit by a bigger force than the White Cappers—The Depression—and was boarded up. Pointing out such closures, Shaw convinced his stubborn partner that his prized "easy jug" list was outdated. The Depression was carving a new landscape across America, and change was occurring rapidly. Shaw suggested that they go back to targeting markets and stores. The takes were smaller, but so were the risks. One such place, Shaw pitched, was known to shelter a number of weapons, including a prized Thompson. That caught Dillinger's interest.

After dinner and a change of clothes, the duo met at 8 P.M. and headed to an open-air fruit market at Tenth and Bellfountain. They parked on Tenth, about fifty feet from the corner, and faced the vehicle west. They entered the market, pulled their weapons, and ordered clerk Claude Priest to hand over the money. He gave them $175. Suddenly, before Shaw could ask about the Thompson, he spotted a child he knew from the neighborhood. "Let's go before that damned kid recognizes me," he whispered to Dillinger. As they scampered to their car, someone threw a milk bottle that shattered on the pavement at their feet. Peeved at the affront, Dillinger whirled and aimlessly fired a round from his ever-present, long-barreled Colt .32-20.

Splitting their small take, the pair ended the day by returning to Shorty George's to return the Colt. Dillinger watched with amusement as The Kid handed over most of his money to cover the cost of a .45 he'd lost in a previous stickup at a thread factory in Monticello.

Dillinger had better ideas for his share. The next time Shaw saw him he could barely believe his eyes. Gone was the cheap, wrinkled prison-issued suit Dillinger had been wearing since his release in order to use his small windfalls to help his friends. Now, Shaw's evolving partner was sporting a stylish number complete with a vest and shiny new dress shoes. The nasty prison "bowl" haircut was gone as well, reworked into a professional tapered trim. Topping it off was a new straw boater hat worn at a crisp angle. Dillinger had rewarded himself with a complete personal makeover.

Shaw, figuring his buddy was, if not dressed to kill, at least dressed to rob, decided they should go out hunting again. On Thursday, June 29, Shaw hotwired a 1931 DeSoto sedan off the corner of Pennsylvania and Washington streets and the dapper duo headed to Eaton's Sandwich Shop, a bustling eatery at 642 East Maple Road. They weren't going for dinner. The robbery went down as smooth as Dillinger's new looks. Shaw merely opened his coat at the counter, flashed his weapon, and motioned for owner Walter Eaton to hand over the bills. While Eaton was doing so, a young waitress came to pick up an order and spotted Dillinger's ever-present Colt. She gasped, put her hand to her mouth, and ran outside, leaning against a doorframe to keep from fainting. The robbers passed her with bemusement on their way out.

Back in the car, they were pleasantly surprised when they counted out the take—$340. It was their biggest score to date. The night was also significant in that it was Shaw's last evening as a free man—so to speak. The following day, he was set to marry Ufah Benitta Hite. Since he'd be busy honeymooning, Dillinger asked if he could take the DeSoto to see a friend in Bradfordsville, Kentucky. Shaw handed over the keys.

The friend was Frank Whitehouse, another Michigan City grad. The plan was to hire some auto-body specialists Whitehouse knew to repaint the DeSoto and alter its engine numbers so it could be used in another heist. While the DeSoto was in the shop, Dillinger offered to treat Whitehouse and his wife to the 1933 World's Fair in Chicago. The couple jumped at the offer and volunteered their car as transportation.

On the way, they stopped in Fort Wayne to drop in on another Indiana State vet, a dangerous fellow named Whitey Mohler. A career criminal convicted of killing a Fort Wayne police officer, Whitey had devised an ingenious way to beat his life sentence. He contracted a mystery illness that turned his skin yellow and made him burn with fever. Baffled prison doctors finally stamped it as tuberculosis and shipped Whitey to a TB sanitarium. There, he made a not-so-miraculous recovery achieved by the sudden lack of shellac in his body. He'd been drinking the potent stuff at the furniture shop in Michigan City.

Newly recovered, and assigned to the loosely guarded sanitarium, he simply walked out the front door and made his way to Fort Wayne. Only a few of the trusted old Indiana State gang knew where he'd settled. Among those was Sam Goldstein, a burglar who put down roots in Hammond, Indiana, after his parole from Indiana State in 1933. Goldstein was next on Dillinger's visitation list. Johnnie D was interested in renewing their acquaintance because it was rumored that Mohler and Goldstein had successfully robbed a dozen midwestern banks, often with the assistance of another name from the past—Homer VanMeter.

After those stops, Dillinger and Whitehouse tracked down a Polish Jewish immigrant turned bootlegger named Fred Brenman, yet another Shirt Shop Boy. Although he was still the least experienced among them, Dillinger sold them all on a grandiose plan of forming a "dream team" of bank robbers. By the time Dillinger finally pulled into Chicago for the fair, he'd received commitments from Mohler, Goldstein, and Brenman. The only one balking was his traveling companion, Frank Whitehouse. He wanted in as well, but was concerned about his wife's reaction.

Dillinger told him not to worry, it would all work out. The three went on to enjoy the spectacular fair. Despite the Depression, the Chicago Fair was one of the few in history to turn a profit, and remains the only one to be carried over into a second year. Dillinger was mesmerized by the sparkling place and visited whenever he was near Chicago.

John Jr. returned to Indianapolis awash in cash from a robbery—either in Kentucky or Illinois—that has never been attributed to him. One can presume that his newly recruited, one-shot Kentucky Gang of Whitehouse, Mohler, Goldstein, and Brenman, may have assisted him. The reunited Shirt Shop Boys apparently got away clean without being recognized or identified. Their target could have been a factory, bank, payroll carrier, or a well-heeled individual. Shaw recalled that his closed-mouth partner carried a briefcase that had to be opened with a knife because of an alleged lost key. Inside were stacks of bills. Dillinger peeled off a few C-notes and handed them to a bewildered Shaw as a wedding gift. He then asked the newlywed where he could buy a car. Shaw cautioned his older friend that thieves were being routinely busted for spreading hot money around, and advised him against the purchase. Dillinger wouldn't hear of it, determined to get some new wheels.

They took Shaw's car to the Mahley Ford Agency. Dillinger inspected the inventory, then picked a maroon 1931 Chevrolet six-cylinder coupe with spiffy red wire wheels. The used vehicle cost $250, down from the $575 it was stickered when new. Johnnie D counted out the cash, then nearly gave Shaw a heart attack when he asked the salesman if it would be difficult getting a driver's license since he'd just been released from prison. The salesman didn't blink, explaining that the process was the same either way.

Odd as that scene was, things were about to get crazier. Three days later, on June 8, Dillinger was back to pleading poverty and wanted in on a job Shaw and Claycomb had been planning. Handsome Harry Pierpont's parole date was approaching, and fixer Omar Brown of Kokomo may have received the rest of Dillinger's mysterious score, leaving him newly broke. Whatever the reason, Shaw and Claycomb agreed, adding Dillinger to their crew. A fourth man, an ex–dirt track race-car driver turned robber named Hilton "Pizzy Wizzy" Crouch, was also recruited.

The target was a redheaded female collector who worked for Haag

Drugs, a chain of pharmacies in Indianapolis. Shaw had been chronicling the redhead's movements for weeks and viewed her as a ripe tomato.

In preparation for the operation, the gang returned to their "free car lot" outside the Apollo Theater where they'd stolen numerous vehicles before. They jumped a brand-new Chrysler Imperial 80 Roadster minutes after its proud owner parked it. The by-now routine theft was notable for the fact that gang's first female member, Shaw's unflappable new wife, Ufah, participated by driving her husband to the scene, then tailing him afterward to a rented garage where they stashed the big Chrysler.

The newly coed gang met at Shaw's on Sunday, July 9, to go over the details. Shaw had learned that every three days, the Haag collector motored around town in her maroon, 1932 Chevrolet two-door, scooping up the dough from twenty-two outlets. The last stop was a pharmacy on Ninth and Pennsylvania. She'd park the cash-laden Chevy on Ninth Street and take a shopping basket into the store to collect the receipts. Her next scheduled round was the following day.

The gang gathered in the morning and drove to the garage to pick up the Chrysler. Shaw advised Crouch that once started, the Chrysler couldn't be turned off for more than a few seconds without burning out the jumper wire used to steal it. Crouch assured Shaw that he was aware of such phenomena.

Dillinger and Crouch climbed in the Chrysler and headed for Ninth Street. Shaw and Claycomb went to Sixteenth and Illinois—the collector's next-to-last stop. When the redhead arrived, they dashed to Ninth to warn their partners she was on the way. Shaw and Claycomb then went back to Shaw's place to let Dillinger and Crouch handle the actual robbery.

A half hour passed and the robbers failed to return. Thinking they may have been double-crossed, Shaw and Claycomb returned to Ninth. They found Dillinger and Crouch standing forlornly on the corner. The red-maned mark had arrived as planned, but they couldn't take her down because the Chrysler had "run out of gas." Since Shaw had filled the car himself the night before, he knew that was a lie. Raising the hood, he quickly determined that the jumper wire had been burned in half. Dillinger sheepishly acknowledged that Crouch had shut the engine off while they were waiting.

Furious, Shaw rewired the jumper and brought the Chrysler back to the garage. He suggested they abandon the Haag job and boot Crouch from the fraternity. Dillinger pleaded his new friend's case for reasons he had yet to let on. He'd been scouting an Indianapolis bank and figured he needed five men to handle it. Even with Crouch, they were still one man short.

Meanwhile, things finally got too hot for Indianapolis' minor league version of Bonnie and Clyde. Tipped that the cops were onto them, The Kid and his bride, Ufah, took the Chrysler and beat it to Muncie, hooking up with a Michigan City vet named Harry Copeland, thirty-seven. Claycomb and Paul Parker made the move with them. Returning to Indianapolis the following day to tie up loose ends, Shaw and Claycomb stole another vehicle, a DeSoto, and robbed a Jewish deli for ol' time's sake.

After settling in, Muncie's newest citizens contacted Dillinger. On July 14, he drove there in his sharp Chevy, meeting with Copeland, Shaw, Claycomb, and Parker at a speakeasy on High Street. Dillinger pitched Frank Whitehouse as a potential recruit, and they traded information on "jugs" that might be worth hitting. Copeland said he'd heard that the bank in Daleville, a small town ten miles west of Muncie, fit the bill. Claycomb, Copeland, and Dillinger immediately went to case the joint. Shaw and Parker stayed behind, drinking beer and gambling. The newlywed Shaw got lucky at both the table and the bar. He was going at it with a pretty lady in the backroom when Dillinger burst in. "Come on, Kid, get your pants on. We got work to do."

They returned to Shaw's apartment complex, where the men had rented a number of separate units, and devised a strategy. Dillinger wanted some heavy artillery in case they had problems with the police. Someone contacted Homer VanMeter, and he set them up with a broker in Fort Wayne. However, before they could make the transaction, the new crew nearly blew apart. Shaw went upstairs and inquired about dinner. "You can get your own damned dinner," Ufah snapped.

Taken aback, Shaw asked her what was up. He was enraged to learn that Parker, drunk and angry over getting fleeced in a card came, had ratted about the backroom girly action. "How the hell am I going to keep you for the rest of my life if I can't keep you faithful for even two weeks?" a tearful Ufah asked. Before he could dream up an answer, Dillinger and Claycomb arrived. Shaw offered to take his ticked wife back to her mom, but she wouldn't budge. Instead, he sent Claycomb to fetch loose-lipped Parker.

"I'm gonna shoot that prick," he said.

Dillinger, leaning on the mantel, smiled and responded, "Kid, if you miss him, I'll plug him." For some reason, that snapped Shaw out of his rage. Instead, they decided to use Parker as cannon fodder in their robberies, hoping the police or security would do the job for them. To satiate his anger, Shaw told Parker as much.

That night, using con illogic, The Kid ordered a shaken Parker to take the still-smoldering Ufah to the movies while the others went to fetch the weapons. Shaw was worried that Parker might rat again, this time to the police, and didn't want him knowing about their weapons contact. The cops were catching on to the White Cappers's activities, so it made sense to tighten the circle. While the odd couple were on their date, the rest of the gang drove ninety-five miles north to Fort Wayne, only to botch the supply connection.

Returning empty-handed, they decided to hit the "Bide-A-Wee Inn," a roadhouse on Burlington Drive and Twelfth Street in Muncie that specialized in barbeque. After pointing out the place, Copeland was dropped off a mile away because he'd dined there before and might be recognized. The robbery went without hitch until they were backing out of the door. Two young couples were coming in, and Dillinger decided to pinch the breast of one of the ladies. Her angered boyfriend lurched forward, and John Jr. struck him across the mouth with his gun barrel. This time, to Dillinger's disappointment, there was no shower of teeth.

The following day, the gang was in the process of rearranging their cars in the complex's garage when several armed men suddenly sprung from the bushes. "Police officers. Get your hands up, now!" The White Cappers had been caught totally off guard.

Luck was with Dillinger. He and Copeland were down the street in the Chevy. Observing what was happening, he shifted the vehicle into reverse and backed away at full speed, leaving Shaw, Claycomb, Parker, and Ufah to face the music. At the police station, Ufah convinced the police she was an innocent spouse who was shocked to learn that her husband was a bad guy. The cops bought it and released her. The others were taken to the Delaware County jail.

Shrugging it off, Dillinger and Copeland decided to go ahead with the bank job in Daleville despite being both undermanned and under-armed. They repainted Dillinger's maroon Chevy green, but left the red wire wheels alone, making the clashing vehicle stand out like a Christmas tree.

With Copeland as the wheel man, it was up to John Dillinger to pull off the bank robbery by himself. At 12:45 P.M. on July 17, he did just that, strolling into the place like he owned it, pulling a pistol from a shoulder holster, and telling teller Margaret Good, twenty-two, "Honey, this is a stickup. Get me the money."

Shockingly, young Margaret was the only person in the bank. The other employees were literally out to lunch. Miss Good raised her hands, but Dillinger calmly told her to put them back down. He didn't want to attract the attention of "citizen variables" outside. Good, with trembling fingers, gathered up the bills from both the teller's drawer and a small money box and laid them on the counter. Dillinger ordered her to open the door that stood between the lobby and the bank's ornately caged working area. Good replied that she didn't have the key. With that, Dillinger gracefully hoisted himself over the six-foot barrier, alighting on the other side. It was the acrobatic move that earned him his first nickname in the newspapers—the Jackrabbit.

A second cage still separated Dillinger and Margaret. He ordered her to open that door, and she complied. The pair then went to the vault. Dillinger scooped handfuls of cash into a sack. He also scored a valuable coin collection, some personal items belonging to cashier J. N. Barnard, and three diamond rings, two belonging to Barnard's daughter Marjorie. The girl had dropped them off earlier for safekeeping while she went to play tennis.

Copeland, watching intently from outside, spotted gas station attendant Lindley Hall stroll inside in search of change. He hopped from the car, pulled his gun, and ushered Hall to a far corner to allow Dillinger to continue his work. Farmer Frank Mowrey and barber Wesley Cox arrived next and were added to the growing pack, as was Miss Good. Finished, Copeland ordered everybody inside one of the cages and closed the door. The robbers then left through the main entrance without further incident and sped off. It's not known how much they totaled, but it was no doubt considerable.

Dillinger and Copeland returned to Muncie with their healthy score. Meanwhile, witnesses were being gathered and police were descending upon Delaware County jail from various parts of the state, eager to close lingering White Capper cases. Claycomb was picked out for the Bide-A-Wee holdup.

Detectives connected Dillinger to Shaw and squeezed The Kid in his cell. Cornered, Shaw began to sing, fingering John "Dellinger" as his partner and tossing in Bill Behrens as well. His tongue further loosening, The Kid confessed to all his stickups. "I was in five jobs and out of the whole mess got only eighty-five dollars," he lamented. "Add to that this prison sentence and well, it doesn't pay."

Shaw was slapped with ten years in a reformatory. Claycomb was dispatched back to Michigan City. Parker, saved from being robbery fodder, was charged with the payroll hit of the Leslie Colvin Construction Company and was sent away as well.

Hearing the bad news, Dillinger tried to give Shaw's mother some cash to compensate. She refused his dirty money, professing to be a Christian.

The arrests spelled the end of John Dillinger's first serious gang. Although he had successfully pulled off a bank job on his own, he knew he needed reinforcements if he was going to continue toward bigger takes. That put him back in the recruiting business.

Chapter 5

J ohn Dillinger and the first wave of Shirt Shop Boys were not
going unnoticed. Newspapers were bannering the colorful
bank robbery stories, often speculating as to who was
involved and playing fast and loose with the facts. A host of criminal
clans were creating boom times for midwest media outlets. There
would be twenty-nine bank stickups in Indiana alone during 1933,
nearly one a week. With one hand, the high-octane scribes were
blowing up the stories and making legends out of sociopaths; with the
other, they were pounding out screaming demands for the good guys
to wake up and start doing something about it.

The man feeling the most heat was Matija Licanin, better known
as Matthew "Matt" Leach. The thirty-nine-year-old Serbian was the
high-strung operational chief of the Indiana State police. As such,
Leach was responsible for keeping his state free of such roving men-
aces. With the newspapers going increasingly wild, few felt he was
doing a good job of it.

Licanin immigrated to the United States with his family when he was
thirteen. His father found work in the Pennsylvania steel mills. The clan
later moved to the gray, mill town of Gary, Indiana.

Matija Licanin worked in the depressing mills for a while, left to
become a wood finisher in Rockford, then joined the army. Tired of
Americans chewing up his name, he changed it to the less tongue-
twisting Matthew Leach. In the military, he helped General John J.
"Blackjack" Pershing hunt down revolutionary leader Pancho Villa in
Mexico. Villa, once a darling of American leftists, incurred Uncle Sam's

ire when he began having trouble distinguishing between the borders. A few bloody raids into New Mexico and other states earned Villa the top spot on the U.S. military's Most Wanted list. General Pershing was given the assignment to teach the mustachioed Mexican legend how to properly read a map. Villa eluded the American efforts, but eventually surrendered and retired in glory. He was later assassinated during one of Mexico's many periods of political turmoil.

When World War I broke out, the veteran Pancho hunter Leach was promoted to sergeant in the 151st Infantry, 38th "Cyclone" Division and was shipped to France. Returning home to Gary after the war, he joined the police force and worked his way up to top dog in the newly bolstered state police. It was a tough, stressful assignment. With a force of less than ninety officers to cover Indiana's ninety-two counties, his men were spread out far and wide. The rash of infuriating bank robberies, combined with the massive traffic jams created by the World's Fair, hammered away at Leach's psyche until he picked up a stuttering tic.

By July 1933, Leach's top detectives had determined that one "John Herbert Dillinger" of Mooresville was responsible for at least part of their boss's disquieting linguistic troubles. They fingered Johnnie D for the Daleville "Jackrabbit" job along with the Bide-A-Wee stickup, and suspected him in others. Swinging into action, they started cranking out wanted posters and spreading them from one end of the state to the other. That kicked off Dillinger's soon-to-explode fame. The initial charges were bank robbery and automobile banditry.

If anything, Dillinger was pumped up by the attention. Two days after Daleville, on July 19, he was back at it again, this time rolling a black, 1933 Plymouth sedan into Rockville to raise a little thrift hell. At 12:50 P.M., Dillinger strolled into the Rockville National Bank wearing a dark brown suit and a light-colored hat. Harry Copeland, wearing a bandage on his uninjured left ear to confuse witnesses, was his accomplice.

Dillinger pointed a hefty .45 automatic at the bank president, A.C. Crays, and gruffly brought him up to speed. "Do as we say if you don't want to get killed. Get down on the floor!" As Crays obliged, Copeland slipped into a back room and returned with the stenographer, Ruth Payne, pushing her down into a chair facing the wall.

Hearing the commotion, Crays's son, Roland, eased out of the anteroom into a hallway and peered through a door into the bank's lobby. Spotting Copeland waving a pistol, Roland Crays pulled a .38 Colt Police Positive from his desk, stuck the barrel through an opening in his door and squeezed the trigger. The slug whistled by Copeland's other ear and smashed into a large plate-glass window.

Dillinger coolly slithered through Roland's door, stuck his .45 in the young banker's stomach, stared him in the eyes, and pulled the trigger. Click. It was a sound Crays would never forget. Miraculously, the point-beyond-blank weapon failed to fire. Instantly reacting, Dillinger knocked Roland to the floor and snatched his .38. Staring at the mortified youth, the bipolar gangster changed his mind about killing him, instead herding the troublemaker to the front door and shoving him outside, causing him to fall on the pavement. After quickly snatching $140, Copeland dashed back to the getaway car, stepping over the guy who had just tried to plunge a bullet into his brain. Apparently, the "no blood no foul" rule applied to 1930s bank robbers as well as basketball players. Copeland let the affront slide.

Dillinger rummaged around inside for three more minutes searching for a better haul. Despite the extra effort, he managed to miss $2,800 sitting in a distant teller's drawer. Frustrated, he exited—passing the now upright but lingering younger Crays—and jumped into the Plymouth. As they squealed away, Dillinger tossed a handful of roofing nails through the vehicle's missing rear window to slow down the expected pursuit.

The only person doing so, surprisingly enough, was the dogged Roland Crays. He grabbed a spectator's car and took off after the deadly bandits, deftly weaving around the nails. Fortunately for the out-gunned vigilante, the auto he snatched was no match for the big Plymouth.

Twelve miles outside of town, Dillinger and Copeland switched the Plymouth for a yellow Chrysler Imperial roadster they'd stashed in nearby Jungle Park. The Plymouth, callously pinched from an Indianapolis priest, was quickly recovered.

A witness questioned after the robbery reported seeing the Plymouth parked in front of the bank minutes before the holdup. She said a woman was in the backseat. If true, Dillinger and Copeland must have been flirting with a local gal as they waited, possibly bragging about what they were up to. The mystery lady subsequently felt no need to come forward and identify herself.

Young Crays, the recklessly courageous banker who peered into John Dillinger's mug for a terrifying moment, described his cold, deadly eyes as being brown. Apparently, the sea of mahogany material that comprised Dillinger's outfit washed over the outlaw's highly reflective light blue-gray irises.

The meager Rockville tally was another one of those financially baffling trade-offs that bank robbers of the time thought nothing about. When the dealing was done, Dillinger and Copeland pocketed sixty dollars each—earned while abandoning a brand-new $900 getaway car. In the minds of 1930s crooks, autos were disposable tools that were easy to acquire, and thus were rarely figured in on the "expense" side of a criminal gang's ledger book.

The following day, the Jackrabbit's thoughts turned to amore. He motored his personal Chevy across state lines to Dayton, Ohio to court Mary Jenkins Longnacker, twenty-three, the dark-haired, willowy sister of robber/killer James Jenkins, a Michigan City lifer. James Jenkins panicked during a store robbery when he was twenty-one and blasted the fifty-year-old owner, Zack Burton, as the man reached inside his cash register. That brief moment of misplaced fear spelled the end of Jenkins's life as a free man.

Mary, orphaned with her brothers by their pitiless father after his wife died in 1917, was married with two daughters of her own. However, she was separated from both her bitter husband, and the children he had snatched and hidden.

With much anticipation, Dillinger parked near Mary's apartment at 228 North Robert Boulevard and scampered upstairs to her place. They talked awhile about James, touched upon her failed marriage, then had lunch downtown at Vargo's Restaurant at 2374 West Riverview Avenue. A second woman, Mary Ann Buchholz, twenty, joined them. During lunch, John wowed them with stories about the Chicago World's Fair.

After dangling the carrot, he offered to take them, his treat. On the return, they could even stop in Michigan City to see James. It was an offer the giddy girls couldn't refuse.

With his comely new galpals aboard the John Dillinger party train, the happy gangster diverted to Mooresville to drop in on his dad for ten minutes, then made a second stop at a gas station in Indianapolis where his half-brother Hubert worked. Hubert wasn't on duty, so John left ten dollars for him with another attendant.

The trio arrived in Chicago at 3 A.M. and checked into the Crillon Hotel under their proper names. Curiously, John scribbled his boyhood address—2053 Cooper Street, Indianapolis—harkening back to happier times. He purchased separate rooms the first night, then adjoining rooms the second. While he showered on night two, the two Marys snuck into his quarters so Mary Jenkins could show Mary Buchholz their sugar daddy's sleek pistol and his thick wallet overflowing with fifties.

The fair, spread out for five miles along the shore of Lake Michigan, dazzled the young women. They snapped five historic rolls of film, mostly of each other. John took the camera at one point and shot a smiling Chicago police officer decked out in a pith helmet. The girls especially liked the elaborate "House of Tomorrow," and baby-talked to the real infants inside wondrous incubators. John was drawn to the huge General Motors exhibit, which included an actual assembly line. (Henry Ford, normally an astute businessman, had declined a similar showcase opportunity, giving GM a huge advantage in the branding department. Ford tried to recoup by displaying his full line of V8s at the 1934 fair.)

Dillinger was especially intrigued by the Hudson Motor Car Company display, particularly the hot new Essex Terraplane Eight. Sitting through a short film, he learned that "on the water, it's aquaplaning. In the air, it's aeroplaning. On the ground, it's Terraplaning!" After the film, there was a demonstration of a bold new idea that was mostly going unnoticed—television. Dillinger was far more impressed by the thought of "Terraplaning" across the state at breakneck speeds.

The fair also boasted an extensive "Crime Detective" display from

Northwestern University—sort of the Criminal Investigations Unit of its time. It's not known if Dillinger took that in.

It's also not known if John Jr. paid any attention to the hot news being splashed in the Chicago papers. A cop from Gary Indiana—Cleo Edwards—had allegedly killed himself in the Sheffield Hotel at 3504 Sheffield Avenue in Chicago. Not all his fellow officers were buying the suicide angle. Edwards had been fired after participating in a drunken brawl at a tavern while waiting to testify in a case regarding a Rumanian whorehouse madam he'd arrested three years earlier. The Feds were trying to deport the madam, Anna Chiolak Sage, but she was furiously fighting it, relying upon her black book of influential clients, a glittery roster that numbered politicians and numerous members of the decidedly corrupt East Chicago, Indiana, police force. East Chicago was painfully close to where Edwards walked his beat in neighboring Gary. Word on the street was that a cunning East Chicago hit squad silenced Edwards to thwart the Feds' case against Chiolak, who was operating under East Chicago's protection. Steve Chiolak, Anna's son, just happened to operate the Sheffield Hotel on behalf of his mother.

John Dillinger knew none of these people at the time. He would soon know them all intimately. A more immediate concern was leaving Chicago and visiting the anti–World's Fair—the dismal Michigan City pen. Before they arrived, Dillinger stopped at a fruit stand and bought an assortment of apples, grapes, oranges, plums, and two bananas. He wasn't particularly hungry. Just before entering the prison grounds, he pulled out a penknife, cut a tiny slit in the top edge of one of the bananas, and slipped in a fifty-dollar bill wrapped in dark paper. He instructed Mary to tell her brother that ten dollars "in the fruit basket" was designated for "certain people," and James could keep the rest. The compassionate ex–Michigan City resident also put fifty dollars in Jimmy Jenkin's account so he could get his teeth fixed.

The Jackrabbit had grown so fond of Mary Longnacker during the trip that when they returned to Dayton, he went to the offices of Pickrell, Schaeffer, and Young and met with a lawyer named Farrell Johnson to help speed along Mary's divorce. Dillinger told the lawyer he would pay for both the divorce and custody case. He genuinely liked kids and had no problem accepting his sweetheart's ready-made family. Returning to Fort Wayne alone, he wrote Mary the next day:

> Honey, I miss you like nobody's business and I don't mean maybe . . . I hope I can . . . spend more time with you, for baby I fell for you in a big way and if you'll be on the level I'll give everybody [the] go by for you and that isn't a lot of hooey either. I know you like me dear but that isn't enough for me when I'm as crazy as I am about you. You may never get to feel the same toward me as I do you in which case I would be better off not to see you very much for it would be hell for me.
>
> . . . I only wish I had you and two or three sweet little kids and was in South America with Jimmy with us. If that lousy husband of yours bothers you anymore, just let me know and he will never bother you again. Well, sweetheart, I guess I will ring off for this time. Love me a little or do you love me a lot? Well baby, ta ta for this time. Hope I hear from you soon.
>
> Lots of love from Johnnie

Mary rarely expressed her feelings other than to giggle to friends that Dillinger was a hit in the sack. A second letter trailed in a week later:

> . . . Baby if I can only get Jimmy out we will get the kids and leave the country . . . How in hell did I know I would fall for you! Honey, I wish you would get your hair fixed up and put on your black gown and have your picture taken especially for me . . .

In Chicago, Johnnie had bought her a floor-length satin evening gown with a floral design at the midriff. Mary kept it the rest of her life.

The threats against his latest beloved's husband were anything but idle. The previous month, he'd driven to Pleasant Hill with Mary, tracked Howard Longnacker to a water pumping station where he worked, and demanded to know where the kids were. Longnacker refused, and the pair began to grapple. The supervisor, Ellis Cecil, ran to get Orth Stocker, the town constable who happened to be working nearby. Stocker and some others broke up the fight, then the unarmed Stocker herded Dillinger back to his car, stood on the running board, and ordered the hot-headed Romeo to drive into town where he was to be arrested. That was certainly a disaster in the making. Sure enough, when they hit Pleasant Hill's main street, Dillinger gunned the car as Constable Stocker hung on for dear life. Outside of town, the bandit skidded to a stop, pushed the shocked lawman off, and sped away. Stocker did pick up some souvenirs for his trouble—Dillinger's hat, and a fountain pen bearing a pseudonymous inscription "D. M. Dillinger."

On July 26, John Jr. returned home to Mooresville only to discover that his parole officer, Frank Hope, was planning to arrest him for his out-of-town travels and various other violations. After a brief visit, the outlaw hit the road. Hope, informed that his charge had fled to Indianapolis, drove to the big city but couldn't catch up. He ordered surveillance on sister Audrey's house, checked half-brother Hubert's gas station, then dashed to Audrey's. Arriving, he spotted a squad car parked under a shade tree a few hundred feet from Audrey's stoop. Both deputies inside were dead asleep. Knocking on the door, Hope discovered that John had dropped off some relatives earlier without disturbing the lawmen's slumber. Fuming, the persistent parole officer raced to the elder Dillinger's farm. There, a weary John Sr., now sixty-nine, said that his son wasn't there, either. John Jr., toying with Hope, snuck by later, staying long enough to present his father with a shirt and tie as a birthday present.

Mooresville's Most Wanted resurfaced in Montpelier, Indiana, on August 4. He and Copeland sauntered into the First National Bank at 2:30 P.M. while a third man, either Cliff Mohler or Sam Goldstein, waited outside in a dark-blue Dodge. The inside men pulled their guns on bank president Merle D. Tweksberry, cashiers H. D. Thornburg and

H. L. Murray, and stenographer Ruth Reynolds. "This is a stickup," Dillinger barked. "All we want is your money. Stand still and you won't get hurt." With that, the Jackrabbit leaped over a guardrail and ordered Tweksberry to show him the money. A calmer and more experienced Dillinger took $6,200 from the vault, then went cage to cage dropping another $3,900 into a large sack. He also pocketed the bank's "security system," a .45 revolver kept for such emergencies. "This was a pretty good haul," he said to no one in particular as another handful hit the bag. It was indeed.

Copeland, chomping furiously on his gum, covered the bank employees with his .38 while Dillinger scooped the money. In mid-robbery, customers Lillie Reeves and Alva Dickerson trailed in and had to join the others behind Copeland's barrel. Dillinger, learning fast, queried Tweksberry about the bank's government bond stash. The bank president explained that they were kept in a safe in Fort Wayne. Accepting that, the two bandits backed out and fled in the Dodge without incident. Slow-reacting Marion and Hartford City police set up the usual ineffective roadblocks while city and suburban residents watched the show from their front porches. Farmer Albert Stoll observed the Dodge stop near his place outside Hartford City so its occupants could change the plates. It then rendezvoused with a green coupe with red wire wheels driven by an unidentified woman.

At dusk, another farmer found the Dodge on County Line Road, five miles north of Medaryville and one hundred miles from Montpelier. The auto was missing a rear window and license plates. Inside was an eight-pound sack of roofing nails, several packs of Camel and Philip Morris cigarettes, some lipstick, and a "git" map with precise directions to a house in Fleetwood. The abandoned Dodge, stolen in Chicago from Isadore Cohn on July 19, had served its purpose and then some. It only had three hundred miles on it when it was taken. It was ditched sixteen days later with an extra three thousand tacked on. Witnesses said the passengers were picked up by a dark coupe with wire wheels and a rumble seat.

The smooth Montpelier job owed itself more to luck than anything else. Three years earlier, three men tried to hold up the same bank. One was shot dead, and the other two were immediately captured due to the fact that the mayor and police chief's shared office was right above the lobby. The pair kept rifles on hand for just such an emergency, and had plugged one of the robbers from the window. On August 4, however, the mayor, Attorney H. L. Kelley, was playing the ponies at an out-of-town horse track. Chief E. R. Coleman was assisting with a road construction project two blocks away. It's possible, but not certain, that Dillinger was aware of those factors.

Thanks to Dillinger and his peers, an ex–Pinkerton detective named Forrest C. Huntington was carving out a solid career tracking robbers for the Indiana Banker's Association. Huntington double-dipped for insurance firms that covered financial institutions as well. Aided by a healthy expense account, Huntington built an extensive file on midwestern bank robbers that was the envy of most police departments. The ex-Pinkerton man was called in by Montpelier officials a few days after the robbery, and hooked up with state police detective Claude Dozier, an old friend and former coworker at the Indiana Bureau of Criminal Identification and Investigation. The duo canvassed the area and struck gold when a waitress at a nearby Barr's restaurant identified Dillinger as having eaten there earlier on the day of the stickup—a curious habit of his. The bank employees then identified the same generously tipping diner as the Jackrabbit who jumped the railings.

Digging deeper, the investigators traced the gang to a local ex-con who admitted he witnessed the robbery from Engle's pool hall across the street. This suspected "point man" may have tipped the robbers regarding the whereabouts of the sharp-shooting mayor and police chief.

Following the trail to Muncie and Fort Wayne, Huntington was given the disquieting news that Dillinger was infiltrating the local police through prostitutes and other loose women both the cops and gangsters shared. Using this sex connection, Dillinger and crew were tipped off regarding attempts to capture them. The gang had also befriended a Fort Wayne gambler named Red Hawkins who was in tight with two influential police detectives.

Unafraid of getting down and dirty, the ever-diligent Huntington went right to the sexy source, grilling the girls at a Fort Wayne bordello operated by Gladys Hill, the former lover of bandit Sam Goldstine, aka Sam Goldstein, aka Sam Goldstien. Hill confirmed that Dillinger and Copeland had been there on July 30, and added that Copeland had taken a shine to one of her girls, Myrtle Dirk, and was making an honest woman out of her. That tip probably solved the riddle of the mystery woman who assisted the men five days later during the August 4 bank job.

The determined private eye continued on to another of Dillinger's old haunts, the Indiana Reformatory at Pendleton. There, inmate Billy "The Kid" Shaw squealed that Dillinger often hid in the Lebanon, Kentucky, area with a contact there named "Whitehouse." The young White Capper added that he'd heard the pair robbed a bank in Kentucky earlier that July, a revelation that would explain Dillinger's fat wallet during his World's Fair extravaganza. Shaw sang for nothing more than having Huntington "put in a word" for him.

Huddling with Captain Matt Leach and the state police, Huntington learned that Hilton Crouch's Indianapolis home was under surveillance, and the postmasters of Mooresville and Maywood had agreed to make tracings of all mail sent to the Dillinger family—civil rights abuses that wouldn't be tolerated today. Further, Ed Singleton, Dillinger's original web-fingered partner, had been brought in by the beak and interrogated, but had nothing to offer. The only thing Johnnie Jr. wanted to do with Singleton was put a slug between his eyebrows.

On August 10, the state police issued an all-points bulletin (the classic APB) for Dillinger, Copeland, and three other ex-cons thought to be associating with them. Two days later, acting on a hunch, Huntington went back to the reformatory to dangle more carrots and see if he could squeeze additional information out of Shaw. Nearly dry but still wrangling, Shaw expanded his sellouts to include Shorty George Hughes, the gun-renting merchant, and detailed the car thefts of the DeSoto and Chrysler. The big score, from Huntington's perspective, was when Shaw tossed in the address of the garage at Thirteenth and Central where the vehicles were stashed.

Following up, Huntington questioned the garage owner. He discovered that a man fitting Dillinger's description rented the place under the name "Monahan" and also went by "Clarence Crews." Both were aliases Dillinger would use again.

The ex-Pinkerton gumshoe was making great strides in tracing Dillinger's past steps. The problem was, the troublesome bandit was hard at work taking bolder new ones.

Elmer G. Romney, the head cashier of Citizen's National Bank of Bluffton, Ohio, was an avid newspaper reader. Even though his institution was perched in a small, obscure town halfway between the equally unremarkable Findlay and Lima, Romney had a hunch that they might be hit by one of the numerous bands of marauding bank robbers plaguing the midwest. He nagged his bosses to put their vault on a time lock, which would render it inaccessible for most of the day. Romney thrust newspaper stories under their cheap banker noses to prove his point. Tales of pistol-whipped store managers and citizens with shattered teeth convinced the bankers that it might be a good idea. Starting in August 1933, Citizens National Bank of Bluffton went on the clock. The vault could only be opened during a brief, designated period.

Romney proved prophetic. Shortly before noon on Monday, August 14, a large green sedan with mud-spattered Indiana license plates pulled up in front of the building, ominously facing the opposite direction on Church Street. Five stern-faced men emerged, leaving the engine running. Acting with practiced precision, two of the men, both dressed in gray suits and cheerful, *Music Man* straw boater hats, entered the bank. Two companions loitered outside. The fifth robber, dressed in a wrinkle-free blue suit, positioned himself just inside the front door.

At the teller's window, one of the two front men asked assistant cashier Roscoe Klingler to change a five, specifying that he wanted three ones, a dollar in dimes and the rest in nickels. Jamming the bills and coins into his pocket, the man smoothly pulled a handgun. Speaking barely above a whisper, he advised Klingler to "stand back," and explained that "this is a stickup." The quiet approach was a departure from the more overt shouted announcements of previous robberies. Obviously, the gang was still trying out different techniques.

The first "unforeseen variable" occurred moments after the Quiet

Man made his announcement. Charles Burkholder, an employee of the Farmer's Grain Company, approached the window. The Quiet Man seized him by the shoulder and pushed him behind the counter to join Klingler. The terrified victims stood with their hands conspicuously raised as The Quiet Man covered them with matching pistols in each hand. The second man, the Jackrabbit, vaulted over the head-high cage fence. Upon landing, he spotted bookkeeper Oliver Locher, and ordered him to lie on the floor with Romney and Burkholder. The leaper then went about emptying the teller's drawers, tossing the cash into a pillow-case-like sack. Angry over the small amount, Dillinger glared at Locher. "You've got more than this. Where the hell is it?" Mortified, Locher pointed to the big vault door. His bony finger was still outstretched when an alarm on the outside wall began to scream.

"They're after us. Let's go," the Quiet Man suggested.

"Take it easy, we've got plenty of time," Dillinger calmly replied as he continued to ransack drawers. A second alarm cut loose—the town's Waterworks whistle—but that failed to shake him either. Finding a locked drawer, Dillinger spat, "Where the hell's the key?" Before anyone could answer, gunfire erupted outside. It was "friendly fire" from the lookout men aimed at keeping the gathering crowd outside at bay. The random slugs shattered the window of Peter Gratz's dry goods store, and sent stone chips flying from the shared wall of Hauenstein Drugstore and Fred Gratz's clothier.

Directly above the gunmen, optometrist Dr. Gordon Bixel was down on his knees peering out of his office window, paralyzed by the wild scene on the street below. Doctor Bixel, armed with nothing more than an eye chart, saw the third man, a "fellow in short sleeves who resembled a movie gangster," wave around a scary submachine gun, but thankfully held back actually shooting it.

Other residents, hearing the Waterworks alarm and subsequent pops, wrote it off as festivities from boisterous legionnaires passing through town for a convention in Lima.

Although the machine gun remained an effective but silent prop, the pistols were still cracking. A bullet crashed through the Hardwick Pool Hall, interrupting the hustles. A second projectile severed the external gas gauge from the rear of Bob Maxwell's mail car. Another whizzed through Patterson's barbershop, scattering the chatty gang that loitered there. Ralph Badertscher of the *Bluffton News* rushed out to cover the event, only to be driven back inside by a ricochet. Reporter Red Biery was already outside when the fun started. He was crossing Main Street when the first gun went off, prompting him to duck behind a parked car. "Good men are scarce," he cracked later. "I decided to preserve one."

Merchant security officer Sidney Garau took a more courageous approach. He ran into Greding's hardware store shouting, "Let's get the shotguns and get them!" Garau's efforts came too late. Before he could arm himself, the bandits had all squeezed into their car, eager to beat town with their disappointing tally—$2,100 and a .32 revolver. Another would-be hero, Postmaster Dode Murray, grabbed a hefty .45 and took shelter behind a brick column in front of the post office. He was going to let the bandits have it as they passed. Unfortunately for Murray's legacy, the green sedan squealed off in another direction, taking Church Street and cutting north on Jackson.

Bluffton's town marshal, Gideon Luginbihl, had been eating lunch at the time of the robbery. Before he could toss back his coffee and rush to the bank, the five-minute stickup was over.

"Reliable" witnesses alternately saw the getaway car as a Buick, an Essex, a Chrysler, a Pontiac, and a Chevrolet. The confusion probably resulted from the machine gun protruding from the rear window that grabbed everyone's gaze. Police went with the Chevrolet, since a knowledgeable gas-station attendant said that was the brand of auto he saw skid around a corner and head down Riley Street.

The robbers were still firing over the heads of the pesky civilians as they motored out of town. One bullet pierced the window of Mrs. Lou Eaton's apartment above the Siefeld bakery and zipped by a chair where she normally sat. Fortunately, she was in Lima for the day.

Lima, on the other hand, was coming to Bluffton—at least in the form of a posse of sheriff's deputies. Allen County's Sheriff Jess Sarber set up roadblocks to the south, while his counterpart in Hancock County, Sheriff Lyle Harvitt, was doing the same to the north. Neither encountered the green mystery auto, which disappeared without further incident.

At the same time Bluffton's "jug" was being knocked over, Matt Leach and his state police detectives were in Kentucky connecting Dillinger with the Whitehouse brothers and scrutinizing the freshly repainted stolen DeSoto from Dillinger's White Cap days. Frank Whitehouse, nabbed for a subsequent stickup, agreed to trade what he knew for the quick release of his brother George, whom he claimed was clean. He told investigators about Dillinger's World's Fair trip, but little more. There was no confirmation of an alleged bank job in Kentucky. Both Frank and George Whitehouse were later set free due to lack of evidence.

Cliff Mohler was pinched in East Chicago, Indiana, and squealed that Dillinger and crew had rooms at the nearby Borland Avenue Apartments. Swarming the place, the detectives, joined by unenthused East Chicago cops, discovered the rooms vacant. Someone, probably the unenthused East Chicago cops, had tipped the crooks off. All they found inside the apartments were receipts for work done on cars. A records check of the listed license plates revealed one of the vehicles was registered to "Fred Monahan," Dillinger's alias.

Interrogated again, Mohler coughed up the Eighth and Madison address of the Beverly Apartments in Gary, Indiana. Nobody was there either, but the female manager said a pair of men named Goldstine and Donavan rented a unit, then vanished. The Beverly tip did uncover information on Dillinger's latest ride, an Essex Terraplane, black on black, with new, seventeen-inch black wire wheels, a "potter's" trunk for luggage, and a straight-eight engine. It was purchased in South Bend at the D. A. Boswell agency by the same Mr. Donavan who rented the apartment—John Dillinger.

A few days later, the big-wheeled Terraplane returned to the complex, but only briefly. Dillinger unknowingly dropped Goldstine into a trap and took off, his magical luck continuing. The manager hit the phone and Goldstine was nabbed. His own recently acquired Terraplane was confiscated and became part of the police fleet.

Before leaving Lake County, Leach and associates, tracking more leads from their pet canary, Mohler, paid a visit to Amy Hiestand, wife of a mail robber doing time at Leavenworth. They found several .45 Colts, holsters, and a sparkling-new Pontiac sedan replete with a ten-pound box of roofing nails, a five-gallon can of gas, and several quarts of oil. The car had been stolen in Chicago nine days before. Mohler sang that it was being readied for a bank job, probably in Findlay, Ohio, scheduled for the next day. Amy Hiestand pleaded ignorance, claiming that a man named Freddie Brenman had rented her garage. The police shrugged and let her off, confiscating the auto and adding it to their growing, gangster-provided motor pool and arsenal. They'd previously acquired a pair of Essex Terraplanes, aside from Goldstine's, and three machine guns.

The Hiestand garage discovery was the kind of nose-to-the-grindstone police investigative success that earned little recognition in the media. The harried Leach and company had prevented a bank robbery, possibly saving lives. Regardless, the pressure raining down on them hadn't eased an iota.

Instead of being lauded, Leach found himself back on the hot seat when six armed bandits looted the People's Savings Bank of Grand Haven, Michigan. During the August 18 hit, the crooks abandoned one of their two cars. Inside was a driver's license issued to "Fred Monahan" the preferred alias of Indiana's favorite son, John Dillinger. While the unthinking slipup pointed a giant finger at Dillinger, the Jackrabbit had no part of the Michigan heist. This production was directed by a tough, arrogant robber named Lester Gillis who was battling Dillinger front page for front page on the publicity front. Gillis, soon to make history as George "Baby Face" Nelson, ran with Eddie Bentz, Charles Fisher, Earl Doyle, Tom Murray, and a "Freddie," who managed to keep his last name secret. Nelson and his crew often hung out in East Chicago and Lake County, Indiana, especially the mean-street, Indiana Harbor area, which was quickly becoming a popular layover for criminals of every ilk.

Fueling the influx of crooks was the word that the East Chicago police had been bought by the cash-fat Indiana Harbor underworld. Dillinger knew Nelson's crew from there, and apparently let them borrow one of his endless supply of stolen vehicles.

Baby Face Nelson had the standard criminal resume—a reform school stint for car theft, then graduation to jewelry-store robberies and bank jobs. Like Dillinger, he boasted a barely legal teenage wife, Chicago resident Helen Wawrzniak, whom he married when she was sixteen. Nelson had better luck than his friendly rival on the domestic front. Helen was devoted and faithful, and the pair soon sired a son, Ronald, and a daughter, Darlene. Aside from marital stability, Baby Face had something else Dillinger couldn't match—a prison escape. The cherubic felon busted out of Joliet prison in February 1932, and had remained free ever since, roaming as far as California to run rum before returning home.

Dillinger had bigger problems than getting tagged with someone else's bank job. With the law enforcement heat starting to increase, and old pal Mohler doing his opera number, he was becoming increasingly cautious. His fears even overcame his pangs of passion. Latest flame Mary Longnacker's letters began bouncing "return to sender." She was itching to tell her man about her new love nest in a three-story rooming house on the western edge of downtown Dayton—a block from police headquarters. She tried again in mid-August, and on August 25, apologized for missing his calls on the 17th and 24th. She was upset regarding an unstated medical problem:

```
I sure am in a fix. But don't want to tell you about
it on paper. It isn't what you think, because I can
just about guess what you are thinking. If you can
come down over Sunday. I want to see you so bad
. . . I had my picture taken, they aren't so hot,
though. I sure don't take a good picture.
```

Trying different addresses, Mary's SOS finally got through. She waited breathlessly for the big reunion. The police were doing likewise. They'd been tipped that Dillinger had a moll stashed in Dayton, but didn't yet have her name or address—324 West First Avenue. They did know that she was the dark-haired sister of James Jenkins, an inmate at Michigan

City. Apparently, Jenkins was decidedly less cooperative than the warbling Mohler. Unfortunately for Dillinger, Mary's literary bent did them both in. The return address on a letter written to brother James pinpointed Mary's spacious new digs.

Dayton detectives Sgts. Russell K. Pfauhl and Charles E. Gross dashed to the west side of town to have a sit down with one Lucille Stricker, Mary's landlady. She allowed the cops to use a room directly below Mary's for their stakeout, and promised to snoop on Mary's mail. She also let them secretly search Mary's quarters. Finding a letter from Dillinger promising to visit soon, the detective's anticipation soared, rivaling that of his lovesick moll. They were planning to stage a big welcoming party for him, complete with silver wrist jewelry and a free trip to their headquarters downtown.

Chapter 6

While the Dayton detectives were sitting on Mary's pad, preparing a spot on their chests for the medals they were sure to receive, the Jackrabbit was busy knocking over a jug in his hometown of Indianapolis.

On September 6, Lloyd Rinehart, assistant manager of the Massachusetts Avenue State Bank on 815 Massachusetts Avenue, was sitting at his desk chatting on the telephone when he heard someone say "This is a stickup! We mean business." It sounded so phony he didn't even glance up or interrupt his conversation.

"Get off that damned telephone," John Dillinger snarled like a crazed monkey from a perch atop a metal cage. Rinehart lifted his eyes and discovered a man pointing a .45 automatic into his face.

Dropping to the floor with the grace of a cat, Dillinger headed to the vault while a new partner, John Vinson, drew down on cashier A. S. Krueger and customers Francis C. Anderson and George Alexander. The citizens were told to stand in the corner with their hands at their sides. Employees were forced to lie on the floor. The jittery Vinson, struggling to keep his handkerchief-mask from slipping down, kept pestering Dillinger to "hurry up," waving his weapon dangerously while his partner danced from cage to cage. The load became especially heavy when Dillinger discovered a cache of 1,000 half dollars. It grew even heavier when the Jackrabbit entered the vault and began flinging sacks of cash over the cage to Vinson. Happily weighed down with money, the pair backed out, hopped into a blue DeSoto driven by Hilton Crouch, burned rubber up Michigan Avenue, and disappeared.

The take, Dillinger's biggest to date, was more than $24,000. The healthy figure owed itself to women's vanity over their gams. The trio had stumbled upon the Real Silk Hosiery Company's payroll.

After leaving Indianapolis, the highly successful mini-gang sped to Chicago without incident. Dillinger divided the loot on the way, then parted company. Although Vinson, Crouch's cousin, had been annoyingly nervous, it wasn't his first bank job. He'd pulled off at least two, along with some lesser hits on stores and crap games. He was arrested in Haines City, Florida, the previous year, but a squabble between police departments in Haines City and Indiana over who would pay the costs of his transportation resulted in frustrated Florida officials kicking him loose.

Surprisingly, it was the cooler veteran Crouch that messed up in the aftermath. Flush with money, he bought a Chicago tavern, then wined, dined, and married a seventeen-year-old girl. By December, the bigspending, highly visible crook was behind bars. In contrast, Vinson took his eight grand and laid so low he was never heard from again.

Meanwhile, Harry Pierpont was hoping the prison circle of life would enable him to offer Crouch his bunk. Handsome Harry's long-awaited parole hearing had finally arrived. Despite the paid-for influence from the outside, his reputation as a jailhouse troublemaker doomed the effort. He was quickly and forcefully denied. Dillinger, rebuffed in his efforts to free his friend by working within the system, now felt it had to be done his way—with guns, violence, and fast cars. All he needed was a plan.

Pierpont, never at loss for ideas, devised one that may have been couched in betrayal. He directed his devoted mother to deliver a letter to Matt Leach offering to track down Dillinger and Copeland for the state police in return for his parole. Set him loose with a single guard, Harry outlined, and he'd be able to lead the posse right to the gang. Nobody can be sure what Pierpont's true plan was, but Leach suspected it was nothing more than a scheme to overpower his shadow and escape. Leach turned him down.

Unaware of the betrayal offer, Dillinger finally formulated a simple scheme that offered a wealth of possibilities, along with an opportunity to spring a group of men at once. Covering all angles, his first step was to make sure his old friends had a place to hunker down once they were sprung. Too many times, he had learned, cons had clever break-out schemes, and then were completely lost once they busted loose. That caused them to be easily rounded up and tossed into the "hole," increasing their misery a hundred fold. No point in that, Dillinger felt. The key was not just escaping, but surviving the first forty-eight hours afterward. To that end, he contacted Mary Northern Kinder, twenty-four, the four-foot, eleven-inch, auburn-haired pepper-pot sister of one of Pierpont's former partners, Earl Northern. Little Mary had taken a shine to Handsome Harry, and had played the dutiful pen-pal girlfriend since she was a teenager. Dillinger visited her in Indianapolis, gave her some of the Massachusetts Avenue cash, and told her to be ready to provide clothing and shelter for as many as fourteen men, including her boyfriend and brother. Thrilled, she promised not to let him down.

With the shelter taken care of, it was time to ignite the escape itself. Harry Copeland, living at 2318 Sunnyside Avenue in Chicago under the name of his girlfriend's imprisoned husband, Arthur S. Cherrington, was recruited to be Dillinger's accomplice in his ambitious scheme. Operating out of Copeland's home, Dillinger purchased three .38 automatic pistols with spare clips and ammunition for forty-eight dollars each. He and Copeland wrapped the weapons individually in Chicago newspapers, bound them with cloth, then covered the packages with roofing tar and rolled them in sand like pieces of batter-fried chicken. They took the movie proplike faux sandstone, drove to Michigan City, parked several blocks from the hated prison, and made their way to the walls on foot. Under the cover of darkness, Dillinger attempted to hurl the stones over the twenty-five-foot wall. It took several tries for each one, but he finally accomplished the task.

Guard William Frehse made his 5 A.M. predawn rounds and failed to spot the earth-toned packs. An hour later, the inmates began filing out to their work stations. An unidentified con found the strange, sticky stones and asked a friend to guard them while he, incredibly, fetched Deputy Warden H. D. Claudy. The DW cracked open the odd rocks. Furious over what he found, he tossed three men into solitary, Danny

McGeoghagen, Jack Gray, and Edward Murphy, all serving time for a bank robbery in Culver, Indiana. Claudy was certain they were behind the potentially deadly escape attempt.

Using the visitor pipeline, Pierpont informed Dillinger of the disappointing fate of the weapons and suggested a more elaborate and less random alternative. While waiting to do it Pierpont's way, some suspect that Dillinger traveled to Farrell, Pennsylvania, on September 12 and lightened the Sol J. Culley State Bank of $15,000. By then, Dillinger was being fingered for every bank job coast to coast. This one was a particularly bad rap because a police officer had been blown apart with a shotgun. What's known is that something occurred, because on September 15, Dillinger was back in Chicago getting his prized Terraplane repaired at a garage at 3034 Lawrence Avenue. For unstated reasons, the fenders had to be straightened and painted, valve tappets adjusted, and the excessively dirty car washed. The bill came to $5.85. He then drove the refurbished vehicle to his gun dealer, purchased three more .38 automatics, and gave them to a designated middleman who placed them in a large thread crate destined for the Michigan City shirt shop.

Seven days later, on the 22nd, Dillinger finally went to Dayton to see Mary. Amazingly, his uncanny luck nearly saved his skin again. After weeks of round-the-clock surveillance, Detectives Gross and Pfauhl chose that same night to take a break, go home, and sleep in their own beds.

John arrived at midnight, parked the Terraplane, and climbed the stairs to Mary's apartment. The nosey landlady, Lucille Stricker, heard him, made out the fancy vehicle, and phoned Pfauhl. Detective Pfauhl notified Gross. By 1:30 A.M., the place was surrounded by uniformed police. Sergeant W. J. Aldredge crouched at the bottom of the stairway while the detectives accompanied Mrs. Stricker up the stairs. Gross, wielding a Thompson machine gun, stood on one side of the doorframe while Pfauhl held a twelve-gauge riot gun on the other. Stricker, armed only with her guile, knocked and announced herself. When Mary cracked the door, the detectives burst inside. "Get 'em up, John. We're police!" Pfauhl screamed. Dillinger was standing in the middle of the room, next to

Mary, looking at photos they'd taken at the World's Fair. He dropped the snapshots and slowly raised his hands shoulder-high, then started to lower them. Pfauhl stepped forward, his big shotgun leading the way. "Don't be a fool. Keep those hands up."

Overwhelmed by the drama, Mary moaned, fluttered her eyes and crumpled to the floor. Fearing a setup, Gross ordered Mary to "Get your butt out of the way, young lady, if you don't want to get shot. Crawl over here on your hands and knees, carefully." The harsh talk angered Dillinger, but he had already been handcuffed and couldn't react. What would have angered him even more was a little fact that the detectives felt no need to reveal—his beloved Mary, the woman who caused his capture, had grown restless during his absence and was sleeping with another boarder, Claude Constable.

Searching the room, the officers found a .38 automatic between the sofa cushions and five pistols inside a suitcase. Dillinger had two more on him. While they searched, Dillinger sat calmly on the couch and offered his perspective on the events. "When you fellows came in, I thought maybe you were part of another gang. I know uni-formed cops, but not you plainclothes guys. I thought you were somebody else."

Outside, the Terraplane was given a going-over. Officers found $2,604 in cash, assorted ammunition, and a sack of roofing nails.

The latest edition of "Typhoid Mary" was raining trouble on all her menfolk that evening. Claude Constable was rousted from his bed and dragged into the police station with her to enable investigators to sort out how deeply the trio was connected. Constable pleaded ignorance, and Mary confessed her two-timing, insisting that Constable and Dillinger had thankfully never met. The cops bought it, releasing them both. If the cops' initial suspicion tipped Dillinger off to his lover's unfaithfulness, he never mentioned it.

Searching Dillinger more closely at the station, they found a dia-gram they couldn't immediately identify. Pfauhl felt it looked like a prison compound, complete with X's over certain areas. Concerned, Pfauhl contacted Matt Leach, thinking it was a break-out plan for Michigan City. Leach blew them off. "You've been reading too many detective novels," he cracked. "This guy ain't that big. They couldn't get out of there if they tried." It was an especially arrogant and negligent attitude considering that it was a pair of stool-pigeon prisoners, not corrections officers, who had just thwarted an almost certain escape by turning in the phony sandstones.

In Dayton, the various interrogators all noted that Dillinger appeared in good spirits and was oddly unconcerned about his sudden misfortune. Admiring the detectives' bulletproof vests while being booked, he asked Gross if they were "any good."

"We don't know, but we feel a little safer with them on," Gross responded. "What do you think?"

"I put three steel-jacketed slugs through one not so long ago," the robber said with a devilish grin as Gross's blood chilled. "Only in practice, of course."

News of the Jackrabbit's arrest spread fast among both the law enforcement and criminal communities. Investigators from Pennsylvania, Indiana, Indianapolis, and Ohio were eager to chat with him. Leach quickly materialized in Dayton with detectives Claude Dozier and Harvey Hire in tow. Suddenly interested in the diagram, he demanded to take it back with him to Indiana—possession being a sticky issue considering that photocopy machines were still decades away from being invented. Dayton's Inspector Seymour "Sy" Yendes was so put off by Leach's arrogance he had him tossed from his office. The more courteous Dozier and Hire were allowed to remain and perform their duties.

Dillinger smartly lawyered up and refused to talk to anybody. Ballistics tests on his weapons failed to match any of those taken from the various robberies, particularly those in which employees, police officers, or citizens were injured or killed.

It was a different story with the lineups. A parade of witnesses dating as far back at the Bide-A-Wee stickup in mid-July were brought in, and most quickly identified Dillinger as the bad guy. That gave prosecutors enough evidence to set his hearing for September 30. Dillinger, still acting like it was all a minor inconvenience, cleverly had his prized Terraplane—purchased legally—turned over to his lawyer, Jack Egan.

The police were forced to hand Egan the cash they found as well, since it couldn't be identified as having come from a robbery.

Ex-Pinkerton man Forrest Huntington arrived in Dayton and was generously given some face time with his longtime prey, getting no farther than anyone else. His disappointment was tempered by the fact that an informant named Arthur "Art" McGinnis had recently reached out to him, offering to lead the private dick to the rest of Dillinger's gang— for a price. McGinnis wanted a healthy reward, along with a piece of the recovered money action. Huntington agreed. The PI had been hired to track down the stolen loot as well as retire the robbers, so finding the gang's hideout was imperative. The deal was cemented when McGinnis showed up at the jail in Dayton accompanied by Hubert Dillinger, John's half-brother. That proved McGinnis's pedigree, and loosened the expense account purse strings of American Surety, the insurance company on the limb for a solid percentage of the stolen money.

On Saturday, September 23, John Jr. was escorted from the Dayton city lockup and moved to a cell at the Montgomery County jail on Ford Street. There, he waited out his hearing, along with the wrangling over extradition and jurisdiction. Indiana was leading the pack on that front. Governor Paul McNutt of Mooresville, the same man who approved Dillinger's parole papers four months before, angrily signed the extradition notice on September 26. It was the same day, interestingly enough, that special agents of the Department of Justice got the drop on George Barns in Memphis. Barns was better known as "Machine Gun Kelly." It was during Kelly's arrest that the certain colorful phrase joined the public lexicon. "Don't shoot, G-Men!" cried Kelly's wife Katherine as she begged her cornered husband, forever renaming government agents, particularly the DI/FBI. (Most crooks, however, stuck with the older nickname "Whiskers," an allusion to Uncle Sam's beard.)

While Dillinger was on ice in Ohio, things were getting very interesting back at his old digs in Indiana. A day or so after his arrest, a two-hundred-pound crate arrived for the Gordon East Coast Shirt Factory inside the prison. It was sent from the Henry Myer Manufacturing Company, 319 Van Buren Street in Chicago. A civilian employee cut a small inspection hole in the container, confirmed that it contained thread, and passed it through. Inmate Walter Dietrich rolled it to the basement storage area. Hip to what was in the works, Dietrich opened the crate, fished out the three carefully wrapped .38s, and hid them in a smaller carton of buttons. Dietrich informed Pierpont, who spread the news to the current crop of Shirt Shop Boys: Charlie Makley, John Hamilton, Russell Clark, James Jenkins, Edward Shouse, Joseph Fox, Joseph Burns, and James Clark. The break was set for September 26.

Earl Northern, Mary Kinder's brother, was penciled in as the eleventh man in deference to his sister, but he contracted tuberculosis and was being treated in the prison hospital.

Jailhouse snitches got wind of the plot, and wasted no time squealing that it was set for the 28th—the original date. Pierpont bumped it up to keep the guns from being discovered, a fortuitous change considering the oppressive number of rats plaguing the joint.

After lunch on the 26th, Dietrich told the clothing shop's civilian superintendent, G. H. Stevens, that there were a couple of men in the basement who wanted to buy shirts. Always willing to make a sale, Stevens took Dietrich to the storeroom. There, he was ambushed by the nine others, three of whom—Pierpont, Hamilton, and Russell Clark—were brandishing .38s. Dietrich went upstairs and informed Day Captain Albert Evans, a man the inmates universally hated, that a jug of wine had been found in the storeroom. Checking it out, he was greeted by a gun in his gut. "I oughta shoot you, you fat sonofabitch," Pierpont growled.

The 300-pound, six-foot, three-inch Evans went white. "No, we can't have the noise," Makley intervened. "Besides, we're gonna need his big lard ass."

Hamilton agreed. "We're going home and you're going to lead us out of here," he informed Evans.

Seconds later, Supervisor Dudley Triplett and five cons walked into the basement. They were all locked inside a heating tunnel leading to the power plant. The fellow inmates received the same treatment as the officers because they weren't part of Pierpont's inner circle and couldn't be trusted.

The plan was that the ten inmates would each grab a pile of shirts, and then march like the sweat-shop drones they were across the lawn toward the gate. Stevens and Evans would lead them, with Stevens in front and Evans bringing up the rear. Any trouble, and the two book-ends would be the first to die.

A couple of inmates had a brain flash and picked up a thick, five-foot steel bar to be used as a battering ram. They carried it between them in the con congo line. Despite that addition, the procession appeared innocent enough, thanks to Stevens and Evans. The group snaked through the yard to the main guardhouse without suspicion.

Officer Frank Swanson already had his key ready to open the door when Russell Clark bolted from the pack and hurried him at gunpoint. The only thing that stood between The Terrible Ten and freedom was a final pair of gates that led to the front office and lobby. Guy Burklow, a guard taken prisoner in an earlier breakout attempt three years before, saw the group and casually began to open the first gate. Once again, instead of going along with the successful deception, a prisoner, this time Hamilton, knocked him back and kicked the door open. Ed Shouse proceeded to deck Guard Fred Wellnitz with a right cross, took his keys, and opened the second door. The Terrible Ten were now in the lobby of the administration office.

The steel bar was no longer needed, so it was dropped on the spot, clanging on the floor. Five cons scrambled across the counter in the chief clerk's office, shouting for employees to hit the floor. Clerk Findley Carson, seventy-two, was slow to move, possibly because he couldn't hear well. One of the trigger-happy ten shot him twice in the right side.

Pierpont confronted the former chief clerk, Russell Bland, demanding weapons and money. Bland explained that Howard Crosby was the new chief clerk and he had the combinations for the various storage lockers. Crosby, however, wasn't anywhere in sight. He was hiding under a desk with a long-cord telephone, trying to whisper an SOS. Hamilton, rounding up the staff, failed to recognize Warden Louis E. Kunkel in the group. That wasn't surprising—Kunkel was a political appointee with no prison experience who preferred to steer clear of the cell blocks, deferring the day-to-day operations to his more experienced deputy, Warden H. D. Claudy. Hamilton did recognize Lawrence Mutch, superintendent of Prison Industries, and ordered Mutch to open the lock to the arsenal. Mutch claimed that he didn't know the combination, either. He was struck across the back of the neck and tossed into a vault.

Pierpont told all the employees to crawl across a counter to the other side. Clara Lamb, Bland's secretary, refused, afraid of being taken hostage. Pierpont threatened to shoot her, but she wouldn't budge. "I can't and I won't climb over that counter!" she insisted. Exasperated, Pierpont let the stubborn woman hide under a desk.

Harrison County sheriff Charles Neel and a friend, dentist Lee B. Wolfe, had just stopped by the administration office to drop off a prisoner before taking a much-anticipated trip to the Chicago World's Fair. Neel was nearing retirement, and had bought a new Chevrolet for just such excursions. The unwitting duo was rounded up as well. A quick-thinking Dietrich snatched the keys to Neel's new car, which was parked right out front in the now-pouring rain. He escorted Neel to it, shoved the elderly sheriff facedown on the rear floorboard, and waved for Burns, Fox, and Jim Clark to pile in. Dr. Wolfe was left alone laying in the mud, and was nearly run over when Dietrich threw the vehicle into gear.

With their friends already on the road, the rest of The Terrible Ten desperately needed their own wheels. Pierpont, Makley, Hamilton, Jenkins, Shouse, and Russell Clark sprinted across the prison lawn to the highway. A Standard Oil filling station just happened to be on the corner of Chicago and Hitchcock streets. One of the men confronted station manager Joseph J. Pawelski as a second jumped on the running board of a suitable auto. "Give us the keys to that car or I'll blow your damned brains out," the con screamed.

"Go ahead, buddy!" Pawelski spat back, taking off in a dead run. Three shots were fired at him, one nicking his shirt. "I guess I'm pretty lucky none of those bullets hit me," he told reporters later. "One grazed my sleeve, but the other two went past my head, or else I outran them!" The reckless Pawelski added that he ran because the convicts "acted like crazy men."

Still in need of a car, a number of the "crazy men" ran back out on Dune's Highway. Herbert VanVolkenberg saw the armed men and, thinking they were police, stopped his Oldsmobile. A con jumped on the running board and ordered VanVolkenberg's wife and her eighty-nine-year-old friend, Minnie Schultz, to get out. The six desperados poured in. "Drive, brother, drive," somebody ordered the baffled VanVolkenberg.

Fifteen miles down the road, the gang decided the feather-footed VanVolkenberg had no future as a getaway driver and bounced him as well. He hitched a ride to Gary in a passing police car and reunited with Minnie and his wife.

Over in car number one, the smaller crew could have used a dose of VanVolkenberg's cautious driving. Dietrich zoomed west on State Road 12 toward Chicago, then turned south on a gravel lane two miles from the prison. It was a road to nowhere. Dietrich tried to swing the Chevy around, instead bogging it down in the mud. That wasn't a good development. Two of the cons jogged to a nearby farmhouse where they asked owner Cecil Spanier to help pull them out with a team of horses. Spanier suggested they join the twentieth century and use his car instead.

Catching on, the perpetually ungrateful cons pulled a gun and barked at Spanier to drive his vehicle back to the site. Instead of freeing Sheriff Neel's Chevy, they all squeezed into Spanier's older model and took off toward Gary. Spanier promptly got lost, and advised that his car was nearly out of gas. The farmer and Sheriff Neel were forced under guard to wait in a ravine while another con drove to Valparaiso to fill up, using money from Neel's vacation stash to cover it. The others nervously waited, hoping their cohort didn't give in to the urge to take off without them.

As both factions of The Terrible Ten struggled to put the miles between themselves and the hated prison, an army of law enforcement types were doing the opposite, swarming to the jailhouse. Michigan City police came with automatics and shotguns. Firefighters arrived for undetermined reasons. A contingent of the Nineteenth Fleet Naval Reserve hit the yard as well, ready to attack. The plan was to quell a possible riot and "secure the prison." Only there was nothing to secure. The ten problem cows, operating alone, were out of the barn. Aside from the added law enforcement presence, the place was back to normal.

The real action remained on the road. After a brief respite, the Dietrich crew hit turbulence again at 5:30 P.M. when a tire blew on the farmer's four-year-old sedan. To make matters worse, they ordered Spanier to keep plowing forward, a decision that caused the entire wheel to sheer off. That forced the impatient gang to abandon the vehicle and head out on foot. Crossing a creek in the rain at dusk, Burns slipped and fell, enabling Spanier to take off. "Shoot him," someone yelled, but nobody had the heart to do it. The farmer disappeared into the darkness, eventually finding his way to another farmhouse two miles away and calling for help.

Following their slower and more anxious start, things briefly settled down for the other half of the gang. Pierpont and company pulled up to a general store in Burdick, just southeast of Chesterton, to replenish their tank. The store's owner, Mrs. John D. Miller, pumped the petrol. She was handed five dollars as payment for the two-dollar cost. The Olds was gone when she returned with the change.

Eighteen miles due south of Michigan City, the six cons turned into the farm of Sally "Sal" Warner, located just north of Wanatah. It was 2:30 P.M. and Sally, a quizzically named man, and his wife were hosting his brother William Warner, William's wife, and their four-year-old daughter. "We're escaped prisoners," Pierpont announced as the gang burst inside. "We're going to be staying here until it gets dark. All of you just sit down and be quiet and no one will get hurt."

On a hunch, two cons were dispatched to the barn to smoke out the ever-present hired hand. Sure enough, they found him, shoving the young man into the kitchen with the others. At four o'clock, the three Warner children came home from school, walked in on the gunmen, and went berserk. Mrs. Warner had to rush over and calm the terrified kids. As the sun began to set, the hired hand pleaded that he needed to bring in the cows. Understanding farm life, the cons agreed, allowing him to do so under careful watch. True to their word, Pierpont and crew left after dark, switching license plates with the Warner vehicle and breaking its gas line. They left with some of Mr. Warner's clothes, two pairs of shoes, a shotgun, and Warner's car keys. The Warners didn't own a telephone.

"Stay in the house for fifteen minutes after we've left," Pierpont instructed. "And you tell the prison men when you see them that we're not going back."

The Warners waited an extra five minutes, then William went to his nearby home and called the local sheriff. By then, the escapees were well on their way to Indianapolis, expecting to be greeted with open arms by little Mary Kinder. They arrived after midnight, only to find that Mary, though happy to see Handsome Harry, was not expecting him for another twenty-four hours. Her three-room home at 930 Daley Street was already maxed out with her mother, stepfather, and sister Margaret. Harry and Mary traded additional bad news. Harry explained that there were five hardened criminals waiting in the car, but Earl Northern, Mary's brother, wasn't one of them. That naturally upset Mary, and would put a serious damper on how the rest of the family viewed the gang. Mary then dropped the twin bombs that she had yet to find a hideout as promised, and that the gang's benefactor, John Dillinger, was in a Dayton jail.

"We gotta get out of here, and fast," Pierpont whispered. "We're counting on you, Mary."

Not knowing what to do, Mary inexplicably led them to the west side home of one Ralph Saffell, a thirty-two-year-old she'd been dating for two months, something she failed to tell Pierpont, before or even then. It was after 2 A.M. when Mary pounded her tiny fist on Saffell's door at 343 McClede. He groggily opened it to let her in, only to discover to his dismay that his cute new girlfriend was leading a pack of six surly brutes. Mary squeaked that they were friends whose car broke down, not bothering to explain why they were all dressed the same. Saffell protested the invasion, causing Pierpont to push him into a chair and threaten him. The Shirt Shop Boys were staying, he informed. Pierpont grabbed Saffell's phone, made a few calls, then ordered everybody to get a little sleep.

Later that morning, two of the cons took Saffell's car to a nearby grocery for supplies. While they were on that mission, Harry Copeland and the buxom Pearl Elliott arrived with a generous bankroll provided by Dillinger. Saffell and Mary were given some of the money and told to go downtown to buy six suits of various sizes. Copeland promised to have a proper hideout ready for them soon in Hamilton, Ohio, just north of Cincinnati.

The cons spent the rest of the day cleaning themselves up, dividing the Dillinger money, and discussing what to do about their benefactor's plight in Ohio. When darkness fell, they pulled out—much to Saffell's relief. Someone tossed a ten-dollar bill on the floor for his troubles.

Across the state, the Dietrich crew could have used a sympathetic sprite with a reluctant, homeowner boyfriend. Instead, they were left to hide in the woods during the day to avoid search planes, and travel on foot during the night. It took forty-eight hours for the four cons and their hostage to reach McCool airfield near Gary. A half-baked attempt to steal a car fizzled when the felons spotted a nearby pay phone and feared someone would drop a nickel. That night, back in the bug-infested woods, they dined on raw vegetables stolen from a garden. The food didn't sit well with James Clark, who suffered from severe ulcers. After consuming green corn and acid-rich tomatoes, he doubled over in pain and cried out that he was dying. Stressed over this latest wrinkle, the remaining cons huddled and concluded they would leave Neel with Clark. The sheriff was told to inform the authorities that the trio had taken off in a car, not on foot. If he didn't, one threatened, they'd show up at his home in Corydon and slaughter his family.

Clark, though in agony, wasn't about to give up. Despite his misery, he still kept Neel under control. They spent the night in a corn shock on a farm near Hobart. After a brief morning encounter with the farmer's startled wife, they continued on to Hobert where Neel bought Clark a properly bland breakfast. Afterward, the two "Stockholm Syndrome" pals took a streetcar to Gary and parted ways.

That evening, Clark waved down a cab in an attempt to get to Joliet. Suspicious of his clothing and manner, the knowledgeable cabbie called the cops. The hapless James Clark was the first of The Terrible Ten to find himself back in custody.

Sheriff Neel, on the other hand, was welcomed like a resurrected hero at the Gary police department. The teletype reports of his death were obviously premature. Fearing his old pals would make good on their threat, he told the Gary detectives that he he'd been tossed out of the getaway car near McCool. Unfortunately, Clark's bust forced him to fess up. The ever-sympathetic Matt Leach made noises about charging the harried, elderly sheriff with "neglect of duty." After slandering Neel in the media, the charges never materialized.

Reunited at Gary police headquarters, Neel gave Clark five dollars and wished him well as the weak-bellied robber was carted back to Michigan City. Neel subsequently canceled his trip to the World's Fair, but recovered enough to go the following summer. His dentist friend who was nearly run over, Doctor Wolfe, never made it to Chicago.

In Michigan City, the typical political infighting instantly broke out among the prison's divided administration. The dramatic escape had thrown gas on the fire of a long-simmering feud between professional corrections officers and apple-polishing political appointees like Warden Kunkel. In this case, the flames were fanned further by politicians and rival law enforcement agencies. Warden Kunkel blamed Deputy Warden Claudy, who had been in his separate office unaware of the breakout until it was too late. Kunkel was even more incensed when he learned that Claudy was given prior word of the escape attempt, but failed to notify him. "I would have had the place barricaded from Sunday on," Kunkel blustered out of one side of his mouth, while admitting out of the other side that his more-experienced underling "had complete charge of the inside of the prison."

Kunkel then grabbed credit for spoiling the previous escape plan when his loyal inmates found the sand-wrapped weapons, which he claimed were theatrically dropped by a low-flying airplane. Claudy had wrongfully punished three non–Shirt Shop prisoners for that, and now Kunkel insanely ordered that the same three stooges should be sent back into the hole again. Warden Kunkel concluded his bizarre press conference by noting that it was the first-ever escape from Michigan City through the front gate, as if that was significant. Reporters reminded him that three men had escaped through a side exit on

Christmas eve, 1931, and two more had scaled the twenty-five-foot wall the following April.

At the governor's office, Parole Secretary Wayne Coy was quick to accuse the guards of being in on the scheme despite no evidence to support his slanderous claim.

Matt Leach stammered his own wild speculation. He told reporters that The Terrible Ten were part of a gang headed by John Dillinger, now under wraps in Dayton. According to Leach, Dillinger had orchestrated the escape, and the escapees would thus be obligated to free their boss once he was back in Indiana. Although some reporters snickered, figuring the stressed-out, stuttering Leach had a "Dillinger fixation," the Indiana State police chief was dead on the mark. It proved to be a rare moment of insightful clarity. Leach was back orbiting the ozone when he blamed Dayton officials for not giving him the maps and notes in Dillinger's possession that he felt outlined the plot. Inspector Seymour Yendes shot back that Leach had been privy to every document they had. The squabble, mostly political hot air, did have the effect of interfering with Dillinger's extradition. Sure enough, a home field court in Dayton remanded Dillinger to authorities in Allen County, Ohio, to stand trial for the Bluffton bank job. Forrest Huntington cringed when he heard the news. He figured the small-town "easy jug" jail was exactly where John Dillinger wanted to be.

If it was any consolation to the exasperated ex-Pinkerton man, something happened that wasn't what Dillinger wanted. With her gangster boyfriend safely behind bars, the troublesome Mary Longnacker moved in with her housemate, Claude Constable. They married not long after. They divorced not longer after that.

Dillinger, of course, had bigger problems at the moment. Still, his timing was once again uncanny. His loyalty to his imprisoned friends assured that help, however slowly, was on the way.

That is, if his friends could keep from getting popped. Two days after the cons left Mary Kinder's perturbed boyfriend's house, the VanVolkenberg Olds was found abandoned near Brownstown, Indiana, seventy miles south of Indianapolis. It was abandoned on an old logging road in the Hoosier National Forest. Inside were Makley and Shouse's prison jackets, along with five pairs of state-issued pants. Witnesses reported that the felons were picked up by a second car, then headed east toward Seymour on U.S. 50. They arrived in Terre Haute at 9 P.M. There, they stole a pea-green Franklin sedan from Frank M. Radcliffe, fifty, outside a vegetable stand. They grabbed Radcliffe's watch and took off, closely followed by a second car.

The conspicuous, air-cooled engine Franklin was spotted at 8:45 A.M. on U.S. 40 near Brazil, but police were unable to catch it. The crooks, unhappy with its unusual color, dumped it on the banks of Deer Creek, just south of Greencastle, and continued on toward Indianapolis in another Oldsmobile.

At the west edge of Indianapolis, the Olds was intercepted by state troopers equipped with a souped up, armor-plated Studebaker President sedan with steel louvers across the radiator, and gunports that could accommodate two Thompson machine guns, two .30-30 rifles, and a number of .12-gauge riot guns. Sgt. Bert Davis pulled the juiced Studebaker behind the Olds and gave chase, red lights flashing and siren blaring. Any doubt whether the cops had the right car was dispelled when the muzzle of a Thompson appeared from the rear window. Roaring forward at 85 mph, Davis figured there was no time like the present to test the Studebaker's newly installed bulletproof glass.

The Olds driver, sensing a weakness in his pursuer, suddenly locked the brakes, forcing Davis to jerk the wheel to avoid a thunderous rear-end collision. As the overweight cop car lumbered by, the more nimble Olds careened south on High School Road, skidding around a corner and striking a utility pole. The rear door flew open, and one James Jenkins was spit out like a fur ball from a coughing cat. Jenkins, Mary Longnacker's brother, rolled to his feet and limped away into the darkness, his troubles just beginning.

Bystander Edward Watts, a local jeweler, pulled a pistol and took a pot shot at Jenkins before he vanished. The bullet whizzed over his head. Hearing the shot, the crooks in the Olds sped off, leaving Jenkins to fend for himself.

The flubbed state-police intercept enraged the Indianapolis cops. The city force, also tipped that the crooks were on the way, had set up a trap at Mickleyville, just east of where Davis blew by the Olds in his steroid-fed Studebaker. The two forces continued to tussle as both agencies were hot on the trail of the isolated Jenkins, whom they now viewed as the gang's weakest link.

Chapter 7

Victor Lyle, twenty-four, had just dropped off his date and was about to step inside his car at the corner of Morris and Fruitdale in Indianapolis when a disheveled stranger approached with a wild story. James Jenkins—once in line to become John Dillinger's brother-in-law—begged the young man for a lift, saying he'd been in a fight "over on Washington Street" and was being hunted by an angry mob. Lyle played Good Samaritan and told him to hop in. The new friends drove east to Lynnhurst and turned south, attempting to avoid the alleged gang.

Jenkins said a car was waiting for him on State Road 67. Reaching the drop-off point and finding no such vehicle, Lyle was in no mood to go farther out of his way. Jenkins responded by pulling his revolver. He confessed that he was actually in a much bigger "jam" and needed to keep going. Lyle motioned to the fuel gauge and pointed out that he was already on empty. The desperate con ordered him to keep pushing forward until the tank ran dry.

Operating on fumes, they made it to Jimmy Davis's Marathon gas station in Nashville, Indiana. It was nearly 3 A.M. and Jenkins left the vehicle to rouse the proprietors from their sleep. At previous stops, Jenkins had taken the car keys with him. This time, he forgot. Lyle jumped at the opportunity, stepping on the starter and praying that he had enough gas left to blow out of there. His prayers were answered as the vehicle fired up. He raced to Bloomington where he told the authorities about his disquieting ordeal.

At daybreak, an army of state and local police began combing the area for the elusive Jenkins—whom they had now identified thanks to Lyle. The search proved fruitless. At dusk, Jenkins was still very much free, but didn't seem to have a plan. He knocked on Leander Zody's door near Georgetown (now called Beanblossom) claiming to need auto parts. Zody's suspicious son-in-law slipped out back and sprinted to McDonald's Grocery Store, where he informed Herb McDonald and customer Ivan Bond that the fugitive the police were looking for had just been at Zody's house.

Jenkins, unaware that he'd been made, was loitering just north of the store trying to convince another resident, Alva Schrock, to drive him to a garage. She refused, but was kind enough to give him a glass of water.

Next door to Alva, Paul Kanter, thirteen, burst in on his family's dinner and shouted, "That convict's outside!" Paul's easy-going pop, Benjamin, grabbed a .20-gauge double-barreled shotgun and lazily said, "I'd better go out there before someone gets killed."

Confronted by the senior Kanter, Jenkins repeated his car trouble story. Another son, Victor Kanter, fifteen, proceeded to grill him about the phantom vehicle. A car buff, Victor wasn't satisfied with the stranger's answers, so much so that he raced inside and begged his mother to give him a .45 automatic pistol. Hallie Kanter wisely refused. Outside, Ben Kanter invited the youthful Jenkins to spend the night and said they'd worry about the car the next morning. He wasn't buying the story, either, but figured Jenkins might drop his guard inside and would be easier to disarm. Jenkins declined the generous offer and started to walk away.

A few moments later, he found himself facing grocer Herb McDonald, and his customer Ivan Bond. The pair were sitting in McDonald's Model A Ford blocking the fugitive's path. McDonald was armed with a shotgun.

Jenkins stuck to his car problem story. McDonald said if that was true, they'd be glad to help—but they'd have to search him first. With that, Jenkins pulled his revolver and promptly shot McDonald in the right shoulder. Suddenly remembering that Ben Kanter and his big scattergun were still in the vicinity, he spun around. The soft-spoken farmer was standing right behind him! Jenkins hastily rang off another shot, but missed badly. Kanter raised the .20 gauge so fast the barrel struck Jenkins's head. He fired—and missed as well, his point-blank aim thrown off by the collision. Knowing that he couldn't afford to miss again, the farmer lowered the muzzle and squeezed off the double-barrel's second and last shot. This one blew off a chunk of Jenkins's skull and dropped it to the road. The escapee collapsed, his bright red blood gushing from the gaping hole in his head, painting the white, crushed-stone road red.

A fourth armed resident rushed over and was preparing to plug Jenkins where he lay to make sure he was dead. Ben Kanter moved in the way to stop him, saying the damage was done. Ben then calmly shooed his children back to the supper table where he insisted they finish their dinner. "What a nice-looking young man. I hope he doesn't die," Kanter eulogized. He then turned to his three strapping teenage sons. "See what can happen when you get mixed up in crime, boys." The stoic farmer never mentioned the incident again, and refused to comment when anyone else did.

Despite his gruesome injury, the street-tough orphan hung on until he was finally taken to Dr. Louis Crabtree's office in adjacent Nashville. Turns out Ben Kanter had nearly missed with his second shot as well. The glancing shotgun blast, even with the dramatics of the flying skull fragment, wouldn't have been fatal. The red flow road-painting act, combined with the delay in getting treatment, sadly were.

The Terrible Ten was now down to the Crazy Eight.

In an ominous foreshadowing, John Dillinger's swooning over the fickle "Typhoid Mary" Longnacker had resulted in his capture and imprisonment, along with indirectly leading to her brother's violent death. One cannot imagine Dillinger receiving a better education on the dangers of falling for sexy dames—or messing with the alluring sisters of his cohorts.

Thanks to Jenkins's association with Dillinger and the dramatic jail-break, an astounding 5,000 people filed past his casket at the Bond Funeral Home in Nashville before it was shipped out. Back home in Bedford, another 8,000 poured through the Roach Funeral Home to gawk at the young robber. Jenkins's death had given the nation its first grassroots indication of how famous Dayton's favorite incarcerated felon was becoming. Even lesser lights like Jimmy Jenkins were drawing the crowds like flies.

Jenkins's blue-steel .38, property of Indiana State Prison, somehow made it out of the Brown County police department and was put back into circulation. It was sold, stolen, then sold again. The final buyer, Theron "Tubby" Clark of Nashville, didn't know its significance. When he later found out, he gave it to grocer Jack McDonald—the man Jenkins shot with it years before.

Others in Nashville were reminded of the incident in more sinister ways. Although Ben Kanter wouldn't speak of Jenkins again, he couldn't escape the fallout from what he'd done. He was warned that every two-bit bandit in the midwest might come gunning for him as a way of getting in good with John Dillinger. The gentle farmer took to wearing a .45 at all times, and rearranged his children's rooms so their beds wouldn't be near the front walls in case a bad guy with a Thompson appeared. Arming himself proved to be a smart decision. He had to pull the .45 that October when two strangers in a black Ford coupe suddenly appeared at his farm. Seeing the weapon, the driver took off. Victor Kanter memorized the license plate, which was traced to the October 14 robbery of the Hamilton-Harris Tobacco Company that resulted in a shoot-out with the police. An officer, Charles Hodges, was hit in the firefight but survived. Kanter's visitors were obviously up to no good.

John Dillinger would have preferred having a ringside seat to the jail-break havoc he showered over his home state at the end of September. Instead, he had to catch bits and pieces of news as he languished in his cell on the second floor of the Montgomery County jail in Dayton. Sheriff Eugene Frick instituted a news blackout, isolating Dillinger from visitors and interviewers so he wouldn't find out about the Michigan City escape. The law enforcement types clamoring for his attention still harbored hopes of getting him to confess, and didn't want him hardening up in anticipation of being rescued.

He was allowed to leave his cell to stand in lineups or sit behind windows so the never-ending trail of witnesses could pin various crimes on him. Carl Enochs, cashier of a bank in New Carlisle, Ohio, was pushed to the head of the line because Ohio officials wanted to keep their prize in-house. Enochs hedged, saying he couldn't be positive but Dillinger "resembled in every respect" one of the masked bandits who had recently robbed their establishment. The vain Dillinger, reveling in his growing status, had never been known to wear a bandana to conceal his features.

The Indiana escape that Ohio officials didn't want Dillinger to know about nonetheless caused them to move up his hearing two days, to Wednesday, September 27. After various witnesses had their say, Dillinger instructed his lawyer, Jack Egan, to plead guilty to the Bluffton job. It was an unexpected maneuver that spoke of a secret strategy nobody could figure. Dillinger was remanded to the Allen County jail in Lima.

There, he penned a remorseful letter to his pop—possibly because he was aware that those controlling his fate would be reading it:

> . . . Maybe I'll learn someday, Dad, that you can't win in this game. I know I have been a big disappointment to you but I guess I did too much time for where I went in a carefree boy I came out bitter toward everything in general. Of course, Dad, most of the blame lies with me for my environment was of the best, but if I had gotten off more leniently when I made my first mistake this never would have happened . . .
>
> I preferred to stand trial here in Lima because there isn't so much prejudice against me here and I am sure I will get a square deal here. Dad, don't believe all that the newspapers say about me for I am not guilty of half the things I'm charged with and I've never hurt anyone . . . Just wanted you to know I am well and treated fine.
>
> From Johnnie

The note, sincere or not, deeply affected John Sr. "I smiled for the first time in years because maybe he'd won after all. When Johnnie was just a kid we took him to church and we tried to teach him the difference between right and wrong. A man doesn't forget what he learned as a boy. We'd proved that now. Johnnie hadn't forgotten and now he was going to go straight. I knew from his letter and from the way he talked to Hubert that Johnnie wasn't a goner and that all he needed was another chance."

On October 4, Johnnie put pencil to paper again, this time writing his old pen pal, niece Mary.

```
 . . . About the only time I get any letters from
you is when I am in jail. Ha. Ha. . . . I wanted to
take you and Hubert and some of the kids to the fair
a week ago last Sunday but someone had other plans
for me . . . I sure would like to have seen the
World's Series. I was intending to drive to New York
and see the first two games then go to Washington
to see the rest . . . Well, honey, so long for this
time, come and see me if you get a chance.
                    Lots of love from Uncle Johnnie
```

Mary wasn't the only one contemplating a visit to Lima. Handsome Harry Pierpont had taken Makley, Shouse, Russell Clark, and Hamilton to his parents' farm near Leipsic, Ohio—just twenty-eight miles from where Dillinger sat. They cautiously moved between the house and barn, staying on the lookout while waiting for things to cool off. During the stay, they all agreed that the first item on their new freedom agenda was to return the favor to John Dillinger.

Despite the obvious hideout location, and its disturbing proximity to Lima, the cops inexplicably failed to track them to Leipsic.

Harry Copeland arrived on October 1 to announce that the Hamilton, Ohio, hideout was ready to go. The house at 1052 South Second Street was owned by Stanley Wagner, father of Naomi Hooten, who lived next door with her husband. Naomi was the sister-in-law of

Russell Clark, and had previously been married to Bob Kolker, an inmate at the federal pen in Atlanta. Hamilton, Ohio, was 125 miles south of Leipsic. Between the cities sat Lima. Traveling in two cars, Pierpont and gang took the time to slowly cruise through Lima, paying special attention to the jail.

At the new hideout, everyone huddled and decided to hit a bank in St. Mary's, Ohio, to get some seed money. The gang retrieved Dillinger's black Terraplane 8 from his attorney, and had Copeland's new Oldsmobile as well. They also had a diminutive new partner— Mary Kinder. She volunteered to drive the backup Olds for a share of the loot.

Pierpont's younger brother, Fred, teamed with Naomi Hooten to stock the Hamilton hideout with food and other supplies, which would then be carted to a remote fishing campsite ten miles southwest on the Miami River. Naomi rented it from farmers George and William Erd.

At 2:40 P.M. on October 2, Pierpont, John Hamilton, and Russell Clark eased into the Pauck Building on South Front Street in St. Mary's. The job went off without incident and the newly freed bandits pocketed $15,000, more than enough to keep them going. The robbery stuck a fork into the already teetering First National Bank of St. Mary's. It was done.

In Indiana, a seething Governor McNutt wanted to reopen the investigation into The Terrible Ten escape. He wasn't satisfied with the accurate report that cited a shortage of guards, and the haphazard way outside material was brought in. McNutt requested $4,000 from the legislature for an armored car like the ritzy Studebaker (on loan from another prison), along with additional squad cars equipped with red lights, sirens, and guns. Other organizations, including the Indiana Banker's Association, were banding together to raise the $60,000 necessary to establish a statewide, interagency police radio system like the one already in use in Michigan.

While a beefed-up force would no doubt help stem the state's criminal tide, it remained debatable if such expanded power should be allowed to fall into the hands of the state police captain, Matt Leach, a man whose behavior was becoming increasingly bizarre. Leach ordered his troopers to squeeze the still-trembling Ralph Saffell, the unwitting boyfriend of Typhoid Mary II, little Mary Kinder. A near-hysterical Saffell argued that he was a hostage, not an accomplice. An unsympathetic Leach tossed him behind bars anyway, dubbing him a "material witness." Leach then had his personal goon squad rough up Kinder's parents and sister Margaret. Angry over the bullying, Margaret clammed up, earning the nickname "Silent Sadie." Leach charged her with vagrancy and tossed her into the slammer with Saffell.

Captain Leach was coming unglued.

The Dillinger and Pierpont gangs had always been equal opportunity employers, and the new merger incorporated the trend—despite all the trouble the fairer sex was causing. On October 10, Mary Kinder was sent on a very special mission—fetch John Dillinger's "other" girlfriend from Pearl Elliott's place in Kokomo. The existence of such a woman—a stunning, brown-eyed vixen who was one-quarter Native American—could explain why the Jackrabbit wasn't ruffled by Mary Longnacker's betrayal. The Kokomo beauty, also named Mary, owed her exotic looks to her French father and a half-French, half-Indian mother. Mary Evelyn "Billie" Frechette, was born twenty-five years earlier on the Menominee Indian Reservation at Neopit, Wisconsin. She grew up there with her two brothers and two sisters, attending the reservation's Catholic mission school. Her father died when she was thirteen, and Billie was sent to the government school in Flandreau, South Dakota.

Three years later, she moved in with her aunt in Milwaukee, working as a "nurse-girl", that is, a nurse's aid, as well as a waitress. Attractive and accepted because of their strong Anglo features, Billie and her sister Frances often performed Native American skits at local churches. Two in particular, "Little Fire Face" and "The Elm Tree," were big hits. Buoyed by the reaction, the teens took to calling themselves "The Indian Players," and often served their delighted audiences parched corn and wild rice.

Despite her church work, Billie was a hot-blooded young lady with a tight, shapely body who was known to be a skilled, enthusiastic, and passionate, if indiscriminate, lover. By seventeen, she had earned herself a "bad reputation." By eighteen, she cemented it, finding herself pregnant and unmarried. Part of her problem in that area was attributed to insecurity over facial blemishes left from a childhood bout with smallpox, a self-perceived defect she learned to hide with makeup and overt sexuality.

Questioned by social workers, she listed four men as the possible fathers. She was directed to the Beulah Home and Maternity Hospital at 2144 North Clark Street in Chicago, where she gave birth to a son, William, on April 24, 1928. She left the child with the home's operators, a self-taught "Reverend" named Edward L. Brooks, and his wife, whom the pregnant girls called "Ma." Unencumbered by motherhood, Billie moved back to Neopit, her girlhood home. While there, her orphaned son "Billy," along with eighteen other babies, died at what the media called "the death farm" in Beulah, Michigan, the place where the unwanted children were being shipped. Many had been poisoned, while others succumbed to violence. William Frechette died at five months, apparently from syphilis handed down from his mom.

The whacked-out Brooks, who steadfastly denied any wrongdoing, were never prosecuted.

Billie, who didn't know about the fate of her son until years later, moved to Chicago in the Spring of 1932 and snagged a job as a waitress and hat-check girl at a popular north Chicago nightspot. There she met a bosomy blonde dancer named Patricia Young who also had Native American blood despite her Nordic looks. Patricia, like Billie, had a sister named Frances. In 1922, Patricia's Frances married a man named Russell Lee Clark, a troublemaker destined to be a Shirt Shop Boy and a member of The Terrible Ten.

On August 3, 1932, Billie and Pat had a weird double wedding, marrying a pair of sad-sack mail station robbers named Arthur Cherrington and Walter Spark who patronized their club. Ten days later, both husbands were on their way to Leavenworth Prison to serve fifteen years. The girls, possibly overcome by romance and pity, married the duo despite knowing their pending fate.

Pat continued to dance while Billie frequently traveled back to the Neopit reservation. In the summer of 1933, Pat was shaking her stuff at the Island Queen Cabaret at Ninety-second Street and Harbor Avenue in South Chicago when Harry Copeland waltzed in. He took an immediate shine to her, and they soon became lovers. Copeland not only grabbed Arthur Cherrington's girl, he stole the man's identity as well, helping himself to a ready-made alias. Harry and Pat then introduced John Dillinger to Billie, who was back in town working at the now-forgotten predecessor to the Royal Palm Show Lounge at 1015 North Clark Street inside the Olympic Hotel. Johnnie Jr., who always had an eye for dark beauties, was immediately smitten. He introduced himself as "Jack Harris" and Billie had no reason to believe otherwise—not that it would have mattered, since Billie had already married one crook. Dillinger was a major upgrade.

Following the introduction, the two couples were frequent companions, often traveling to Kokomo to party at Pearl Elliott's gambling, entertainment, and whorehouse Meccas. Dillinger trusted the larger-than-life Pearl to such an extent he often left large sums of money—$25,000 to $30,000—in her care.

After Mary Kinder fetched Mary Frechette from Kokomo and all but gift wrapped her at the hideout in Hamilton, the stage was set for Pierpont to pay his IOU.

Prior to Pierpont's planned intervention, there were rumblings that Dillinger attempted to bribe his way out with the help of his old fixer pal, Omar Brown. Omar mysteriously appeared in Lima and was promptly given an audience with "his client." The local sheriff was said to be listening, but reportedly wanted more than Dillinger was willing to pay. Brown allegedly contacted Pierpont and gave him the news that Plan A had failed.

On Wednesday, October 11, Pierpont and Clark rolled into Lima inside Dillinger's Terraplane. Driving behind them were Makley, Shouse, Copeland, and John Hamilton. Pierpont got out and scouted the brick Allen County courthouse and jail, and noted that the high-priced sheriff, Jess Sarber, had his residence there. Pierpont returned to the cars ready to charge in and blast Dillinger out on the spot. Makley advised caution, arguing that they needed more information on the internal layout. He suggested that they send in one of the molls to case the place. Pierpont reluctantly agreed. The gang caravanned north twenty-eight miles to the farm in Leipsic to rethink things.

On Thursday, October 12, Columbus Day, Sheriff Sarber told Cora Jones to take a break from playing the jail's organ that evening during the worship services. The jail was holding a dangerous criminal and he didn't want to get any of the church volunteers hurt. It was a prophetic decision.

Pierpont and Clark left Leipsic in the Terraplane at 4 P.M. Makley, Ed Shouse, Hamilton, and Harry Copeland were set to meet them outside the Allen County jail at six. Pierpont spent the extra time trying to convince local attorney Chester M. Cable to act as bag man in a new bribe attempt. Cable declined, insisting that Sheriff Sarber couldn't be bought. Cable reportedly called Sarber to warn him about the visit, and added that Pierpont was trying to slip a female visitor inside under the guise of being Dillinger's sister. The balding, 240-pound, forty-seven-year-old sheriff thanked him but took no precautions other than to cancel the evening's organless church services.

When the second car arrived, Pierpont was ready to enact Plan B. He, Makley, and Clark would enter the jail, while Hamilton and Copeland kept the cars ready. Shouse was the designated lookout. It was 6:30 P.M.

Inside the brick building, Lucy Sarber and a domestic helper were finishing the dinner dishes while her husband sat at his office desk reading the *Lima News*. He was in short-sleeves, and his .38 was inside one of the desk drawers. When the dishes were finished, the helper left. Mrs. Sarber sat in a chair near her husband and began deciphering a crossword puzzle. Deputy Wilber Sharp, thirty-two, off-duty and in civilian clothes, sat on the couch playing with Brownie, the Sarbers's dog. His service revolver and holster were on the desk where Sarber sat.

Just down the hall, Dillinger was playing pinochle on a large dining table in the cell block he shared with prisoners Art Miller, Claude Euclid, and George Young. Miller was awaiting appeal on a second-degree murder conviction. The others were petty thieves.

Sarber glanced over his paper and saw three well-dressed men enter the building through the east entrance. They made their way to his office. Asking their business, Sarber was told by Pierpont that they were from Michigan City and were there to take custody of John Dillinger. Sarber raised his eyebrows and requested some credentials and a transfer order.

Pierpont stopped short of saying "we don't need no stinkin' credentials," instead whipping out a .38 and uttering the less colorful "here's our credentials."

"Oh, you can't do that . . ." Sarber responded, his hand inching toward his drawer. Pierpont's weapon exploded, spitting a bullet into Sarber's left side that tore through his abdomen and deflected into his thigh. He fell over on his back, blood spurting from a severed femoral artery. The unexpected shooting so unnerved Russell Clark that he accidentally discharged his weapon, grazing the finger on his left hand before sending the slug harmlessly into the wall. The sheriff struggled to rise, but Makley went around the desk and cracked him over the head with the butt of his revolver. The blow had such force it split the cop's scalp to the bone and caused the weapon to fire into the door.

"Give us the keys to the cells," Pierpont demanded. When the stunned sheriff didn't respond, Pierpont fired twice more, but both shots missed, possibly intentionally. He then turned the weapon and cracked Sarber over the head again.

"Don't kill him," Clark pleaded, but a frenzied Pierpont clubbed him again, even harder. Deputy Sharp rose to his feet, but Makley got the drop on him. "Take it easy, boy," he warned. The trio assumed Sharp was an inmate-trustee, and spared him the brutal treatment. Pierpont raised his weapon a third time over Sheriff Sarber.

Lucy Sarber, sensing this would be the death knell, stood and screamed, "Don't hit him again! I'll get the keys." Pierpont followed the sobbing woman to a hall cupboard where the keys dangled from a nail. He took them and started toward the cell block, then stopped, remembering the sheriff's movements. Pierpont had already taken the deputy's pistol that was on the desk, but a brain flash warned him that Sarber hadn't reached for that one. Returning, he searched the drawers for the weapon he suspected the sheriff was going for, quickly finding it. As he buried the snub-nose revolver into his pocket, he jerked the telephone wire from the wall.

Dillinger, hearing the shots, returned to his cell to get his suit coat, then patiently waited at the card table.

Walking to the nearby cell block, Pierpont used the keys to unlock the first set of double-doors. When he failed to open the third, he fetched Sharp and forced him to do it. Dillinger immediately appeared. Pierpont handed him Sarber's pistol.

By then, other prisoners began moving toward the open door. Pierpont blasted a shot down the hallway, the slug whistling by Sharp's ear while the sound nearly shattered his eardrum. "You other bastards get back in there!" Pierpont screamed. "We just want John."

The Jackrabbit walked out and headed to the office. There, he recoiled when he saw Sheriff Sarber sprawled in a pool of blood, his hysterical wife kneeling beside him. "Men, why did you do this to me?" Sarber moaned. Then, turning to his wife, he said, "Mother, I believe I'm going to have to leave you." Dillinger had grown to like the hefty, personable sheriff, and didn't want it to happen this way.

Pierpont herded Deputy Sharp and Lucy Sarber into the cell block and locked the doors. Lucy begged to be allowed to stay with her severely injured husband, but cold-blooded Harry refused.

Outside, an elderly couple, Mr. and Mrs. Fay Carter, were passing by on foot when the first shots were fired. Shouse materialized and volunteered to check out the ruckus. He ran over, opened the door, then returned, saying it was only a file drawer dropped from a desk. As he spoke, a third shot rang out. "There goes another drawer," he cracked.

"Well, there's so darned many crooks around nowadays, when you hear a noise you don't know what to think," Mrs. Carter offered. Acting fast, Shouse changed the subject to the activities at the nearby Moose Lodge where he suspected the couple were going, then offered to escort them there. Just as the Carters were out of sight, Dillinger and Pierpont emerged from the kitchen exit. Clark, and Makley came out through the front. They all climbed into the Terraplane. Copeland drove to the second car where Hamilton and the returning Shouse waited. Copeland jumped in that vehicle, leaving Dillinger, Pierpont, Clark, and Makley in the Terraplane. The cars then took different routes back to Hamilton.

Inside the Terraplane, Dillinger was still fighting to control his anger over what happened to the friendly sheriff. He was thankful for the rescue, but didn't understand the excessive violence. Choosing his words carefully, he turned to Pierpont and Makley. "Did you have to do that?" Neither man answered. Sensing that Pierpont might have unleashed some long-repressed rage over his webbed-foot deformity, Dillinger let it drop.

Shortly after the assailants left, Jess Sarber's son Don returned home from a trip to Columbus where he had purchased tickets to the upcoming Ohio State versus Northwestern football game. Realizing what had occurred, Don, a deputy himself, swung into action and rushed upstairs to the bedrooms where there was a second phone. He called the Davis Miller and Son Funeral Home for an ambulance (no paramedics back then), then rang a number of other officers and citizens. He ran back downstairs to see if he could free his mother and Deputy Sharp. Don and his fellow officers battered down the first set of doors, but the third had to be burned through with an agonizingly slow acetylene torch. Don Sarber handed that job off and left in the ambulance with his dad. His father was conscious, and told his son he had been attacked by big men he hadn't recognized.

At 8:05 P.M., Sheriff Jess Sarber died at Lima Memorial Hospital as a result of blood clots in his brain caused by the totally unnecessary pistol whipping. What could have been a colorfully dramatic rescue in which no one was seriously hurt had turned decidedly ugly. Six posses raced from Lima, most filled with bloodthirsty vigilantes, but none had any success. At midnight, a swarm of cops finally did the obvious and raided the Pierpont farm in Leipsic, irritating Lena and arresting her son, Fred, when he couldn't explain why the new Olds in the garage was full of gas but had no plates. Fred was later released when the Olds turned out to have been legally purchased.

The newspapers, naturally, went nuts. Not only were the Crazy Eight on the loose, but they were adding members and had transformed back into The Notorious Nine. However, even the entertainment-hungry citizens who secretly admired the bandits cringed over lurid descriptions of how the popular sheriff was savagely beaten to death. John Dillinger Sr. was asked for his response and wearily admitted,

"Well, I don't know what to think but it's pretty bad." The mood in the law enforcement community was more than "pretty bad," as most police officers in the midwest felt overwhelming fury combined with renewed determination.

Two days later, another heavily armed police squad exploded into the Dillinger farmhouse in Mooresville to search the place. "If John was here, I didn't see him," John Sr. offered.

John wasn't there. He was too busy getting passionately reacquainted with his hot-blooded welcome-home present—Billie Frechette. By all accounts, the two were carnal soul mates who could match each other fiery stroke for fiery stroke. The sizzling reunion in Hamilton rocked the hideout to the extent where the others worried that their animalistic mating cries might bring the cops down on them.

In Lima, the air was filled with screaming of a different nature. Jess Sarber was buried as 2,500 angry residents paid their anguished respects. Don Sarber was sworn in as sheriff, becoming, at twenty-one, one of the youngest in the nation to ever hold such an office. The county commissioners announced they were offering a whopping $5,000 reward for the killers, a considerable sum in the depressed times.

As anger over the killings faded, and the gang—aside from the overheated Johnnie and Billie—kept quiet in Hamilton and at the fishing camp, the newsmen once again began building the Dillinger legend. Follow-up stories painted him as a gang leader so beloved and respected that his underlings would resort to killing cops to set him free. In truth, it was the cruel and heartless Handsome Harry Pierpont who clearly led the gang. The breakout was a payback for the thread-box weapon shipment that enabled the Shirt Shop Boys to escape Michigan City. Regardless, the new "cold-blooded cop killers" image of the roving mob of hardened escapees acted to terrify the public and put Dillinger's name on everybody's tongue coast to coast. He was Dracula, Frankenstein, and the Wolfman rolled into one.

And worse yet, he was growing bolder by the minute.

Chapter 8

Dillinger and Pierpont were climbing the walls in Hamilton, itching to get back into the bank robbery business. But first, they staged a preparation raid that would be one of their most shocking to date.

On the evening of October 14, the reunited escapees waltzed into the Auburn, Indiana, police station at Ninth and Cedar streets, confronted the two officers holding down the fort, and announced a stickup. The stunning statement made sense to the crooks—they were looking to boost their arsenal. Given the keys to the taxpayer-funded gun lockers, the pair scooped up a Thompson submachine gun, two .38s, a .30-caliber Springfield rifle, a Winchester semiautomatic rifle, a shotgun, a .45 Colt automatic, a Smith & Wesson .44 revolver, a .25-caliber automatic pistol made in Spain, a 9mm German Luger, three bulletproof vests, and a large supply of ammunition.

Charlie Makley, covering the door, helped load the weapons into the getaway vehicle. The bewildered cops were locked in their own holding cell, giving Dillinger and Pierpont a brief moment of satisfying revenge.

In Indianapolis, Capt. Matt Leach was fuming and stuttering more than usual. He'd been tipped about the unprecedented plot, but insisted the informant said Aurora, not Auburn. It's possible the snitches heard it wrong. It's also possible Leach's hearing was no better than his eroding speech. Whatever the foul-up, while Dillinger, Pierpont, and Makley were doing their thing in Auburn, Leach's men were 160 miles due south brushing away gnats outside the sleepy Aurora police station.

To cap off the bad day, Leach stormed from his office only to discover that an enterprising thief with a strong sense of irony had stolen the Indiana State police captain's car.

The newspapers, naturally, went berserk over the Auburn raid. The strike against the police themselves had a chilling effect upon the public psyche. It was as if nothing could stop John Dillinger.

Matt Leach begged to differ. His painstakingly recruited network of plants, snitches, and rats, though frustrating at times, were still in business. He had even tapped into Forrest Huntington's prized pigeon, Art McGinnis, a man with a penchant for playing all the angles. One of the informants was certain to pay off.

A solid one came from Fred Pierpont, of all people. Given the bare light and rubber-hose treatment during his short jail stay, the weak link relative cracked, coughing up the gang's Hamilton hideout on South Second Street. Leach sent Detective Walter Mentzer and Butler County Chief Deputy Sheriff Art Lincoln to check it out early on the morning of October 14. Seeing the house lights on and cars in the garage, they summoned a hundred-strong, multicounty task force to crash in at 7:30 A.M. By the time they got the blue mob organized, the early-bird criminals had beat it. The only thing left was a single car, a Ford V8 that had been stolen from Chicago on October 6.

Angry law enforcement officials suspected that the felons, whoever they were, had been tipped, possibly by crooked cops in the pocket of local gambling houses.

Acting on another tip, again from the loose-lipped Fred Pierpont, the law regrouped and swarmed the fishing camp on the Miami River. Nobody was there, either. They did find a note on a table that said, "Thanks, Dillinger, for the new coat." Next to the note was a receipt from Rollman's of Cincinnati for a lapin jacket. The receipt was actually the best tip yet. Dillinger and Pierpont had taken their pint-size girl toys and moved south fifteen miles to Cincy's Locust Hill Apartments at 825 Taft Road, a three-story complex near Peebles Corner that was across the street from a grammar school. It was here, Mary Kinder would later say, that she and Handsome Harry finally found the time and privacy to consummate their long-term pen-pal relationship.

Russell Clark had also tagged along, sans wife or moll. Dillinger soon found that five was a crowd. He and Billie put a sixty-five dollar deposit on a rented room at 3532 Pape Avenue, a quiet residential section known as Oakley. The owner and landlady, Elsa Waterman, thought the man introduced as "John Dietz" was charming, but looked down her nose at his dark mongrel "wife" in her "cheap fur coat." Possibly because Billie sensed Waterman's disapproval, the couple never returned.

Captain Leach responded to the latest disappointment by creating a six-member "Mobile Dillinger Squad" that roamed the state 24/7 searching for the elusive felon. The media dubbed Dillinger "Public Enemy Number One," and referred to his crew as "The Terror Gang." Reporters watched with great amusement as Indiana and Ohio officials, including Governor McNutt, traded barbs over who was responsible for the latest escape. Indiana claimed that if their hometown bandit had been turned over to them as requested back in September, Sheriff Sarber would still be alive. Incensed Ohio politicians responded that Indiana should have captured "The Hoosier Hellcat" long before it ever came to that.

Leach poured more fuel on the fire when he told reporters that Dillinger had led twenty-four successful bank jobs in two months, covering Indiana, Ohio, Michigan, and Illinois. It was a wildly exaggerated, unfounded claim, but Leach was only getting started. "This man Dillinger is more deadly than Machine Gun Kelly ever dreamed of being . . . It was a foregone conclusion that an attempt would be made to free Dillinger [in Lima]. We tried to make the Ohio people realize it, but they wouldn't believe us . . . Dillinger belonged to Indiana . . . We would have taken adequate precautions against any attempt to liberate Dillinger."

Ohio officials were quick to shoot back that Leach failed to take "adequate precautions" to prevent Dillinger from "liberating" Pierpont and his nine friends. Brushing the criticism off as unprofessional and insensitive, Leach sidestepped by building up the legend of his prey. "When all of the known facts about Dillinger are dragged into publicity, it will be found that no desperado in America can approach this bad man's record." To prove that he meant business, Leach revoked the Jackrabbit's parole from Indiana State Prison.

A few days after Leach's dizzying pronouncements, Dillinger and Pierpont walked into the Peru, Indiana, police headquarters just after 11 P.M. and got the drop on two cops, a security guard, and a nightshift cook who had wandered by to chat. Pierpont, seemingly on the same alien wavelength as Captain Leach, snarled, "I haven't killed anybody for a week now. I'd just as soon shoot one of you as not. Go ahead and get funny!" While the duck-footed Pierpont was perfecting his madman act, Dillinger calmly emptied the gun cabinet, dumping the weapons in a large robe spread on the floor. The haul included two fully loaded Thompsons, a tear-gas gun, three rifles, two sawed-off shotguns, a .12-gauge automatic shotgun, a .32-caliber automatic pistol, a .45-automatic pistol, five .38 Special revolvers, 9 bulletproof vests, 10 magazines of machine-gun bullets, 3 badges, 2 boxes of shotgun shells, and a pair of handcuffs—perhaps for more bedroom fun with the awaiting Marys.

Asked what was behind a locked door, patrolman Eldon Chittum stammered that they kept confiscated liquor there. "Well, forget it then," Dillinger said. "I don't drink."

Dillinger and Pierpont, working the high wire without the net of a wheelman, returned to the parked Terraplane and vanished down U.S. 31.

Beyond the obvious arming of the Shirt Shop Boys for further bank robberies, the motive for the highly publicized police station hits was not known. Some speculated that the pair were trying to take some of the starch out of the police and the increasingly meddlesome citizen vigilante groups. The Terror Gang wanted everyone to know the firepower that would be involved should they find themselves cornered.

Leach was putting his money on a new spate of robberies. He began wracking his hyperactive brain and squeezing his snitches to try and determine where the next job would occur. Knowing where the gang was bedding down would have been a good place to start. The ever-trustworthy Pearl Elliott had prepared their latest hideout in Terre Haute, seventy miles southwest of Indianapolis near the Illinois border. Settled into their new home, Pierpont suggested they take the bank in Greencastle, a town of 4,600 located thirty miles northeast of Terre Haute. He'd once worked at a sand and gravel plant in Ferndale, twelve miles west of Greencastle, and knew the area.

The rest of the crew liked the idea. What they didn't like was Pierpont's crazed plan of attack. He wanted to kidnap five or six of Leach's finest state troopers, steal their uniforms, and wear them during the heist. When his partners balked at the risky scheme, pointing out that the uniforms would only help momentarily, Pierpont grew violent, arguing that his associates were narrow-minded cowards. He was finally placated by an even more preposterous plan pitched by Russell Clark, apparently for no other reason than to distract his explosive friend. Clark proposed that after the bank job, they should go to Michigan City, kidnap the hated Deputy Warden Harry Claudy, tie Claudy to the bumper of a car, and drag him down the streets of Chicago. Pierpont loved it, putting in a rider that they'd also assassinate Matt Leach and Forrest Huntington on the same trip.

The insane idea lost some steam when it was announced, four days later, that Claudy and the equally detested Albert Evans were fired by the governor for "gross negligence" in the escape of The Terrible Ten. Leach piled on by announcing that he was still convinced the cons had bought their way out, further shaming the innocent Claudy and Evans.

On Monday, October 23, a day after a rousing "Old Gold" homecoming at nearby DePauw University, a big, black Studebaker double-parked facing south on Jackson Street outside the Central National Bank of Greencastle. The license plates—Ohio A63-167—had last been seen on John Dillinger's Terraplane.

At that exact moment, elderly security guard Len Ratcliffe, feeling a bit chilly, climbed down from his perch inside a new steel cage constructed over the front door to combat the likes of The Terror Gang. Without missing a beat, Ratcliffe ventured even lower, descending into the basement to stoke the furnace. Four men emerged from the Studebaker just as Ratcliffe abandoned his post. Three of them hooked around a corner and entered the bank through its Washington Street doors. The fourth, Russell Clark, peeled off and stood by the front entrance.

Insurance agent Gordon Sayers, manning his father's desk, saw the trio and thought to himself that their topcoats were too bulky. He watched with interest as Harry Pierpont walked to a teller's cage, pulled out a twenty, and asked the assistant trust officer, Ward Mayhall, if it was real. "Take it to window number two and ask Mr. West," Mayhall said, barely glancing up. Feeling a bit put off, Pierpont dug into his coat, pulled out a .45 Colt automatic, and announced, "This is a holdup. Don't anybody press any alarm."

The bandits in the lobby, Dillinger and Makley, swung open their coats with dramatic flourish and produced dueling stockless submachine guns. The customers in the relatively crowded building gasped as one, their eyes riveted to the deadly barrels. The robbers motioned for them to gather in manageable clumps.

Makley had things under control, enabling the Jackrabbit to perform his signature act, bounding over the three-foot-high railing into the loan officers' area. Handsome Harry, satisfied with his own narcissistic nickname, joined him by simply walking through a gate. Smashing a lock on the mesh door leading to the tellers' cages, the pair began dumping money into sacks. Aside from the easy-to-tote bills, they swept up $400 worth of half dollars, $200 in quarters, and eighteen silver dollars. They didn't bother with the nickels and pennies.

Clerk Edith Browning was near her desk on the bank's mezzanine, checking stock certificates for an elderly customer. Heading downstairs to retrieve some additional documents, she spotted the armed crooks from the top of the stairway. "They looked up at me," she recalled. "I guess I didn't appear too dangerous because nobody ordered me down." Backing away, she walked to a window and sure enough saw the big black gangster's car her imagination had conjured up waiting out front. She figured somebody was inside because "In all the holdups I'd read about, somebody always stayed with the car." This time, she was wrong. The Terror Gang had decided that wheelmen were an unnecessary luxury.

Browning returned to her desk and whispered to her customer that there was a robbery in progress downstairs and it was best that they appeared busy. Staying out of sight, Edith and the mortified gentleman missed seeing the infamous John Dillinger stick a pistol into Ward Mayall's ribs and order him to open the vault. Cashier Harry Wells stepped forward, explaining that the combination was finicky and his coworkers had problems with it under normal circumstances. Machine guns at their heads weren't going to make navigating the stubborn dial any easier. Wells volunteered, and nailed it the first time.

In the lobby, a customer, Hugh Hammond of Sinclair Oil, walked in and deposited $300 into Makley's pocket. Postal clerk Elmer Seller followed and unhappily donated $400 to the same cause. Distracted by the unexpected cash flow, Makley missed seeing bank employee William Styles slip to a rear door, trot down to the basement, and exit the building through a small side door. Once outside, Styles tried desperately to find some nails to put under the driverless Studebaker's tires. Had he been more up on the news, he would have known precisely where to look—the backseat of the car itself. If such a flash of insight had occurred, the Terror Gang might have spent the rest of their days in small cells reconsidering their "wheelman as an unneeded luxury" theory.

Styles, unable to locate any puncturing devices, found a phone instead and called the Greencastle police. He was told to remain where he was. Oddly enough, neither Styles nor anybody else thought to alert the county sheriff, who was sitting in his office at the courthouse right across the street.

Backing out of the bank, Dillinger, in "boisterous spirits" witnesses would recall, said, "Boys, take a good look at me so you will be sure to know me the next time you see me!"

Leaving through the front door, the trio encountered grocer Rex Thorlton on his way in. Lost in thought, Thorlton reached into his back pocket for the cash he was planning on depositing. Pierpont thought he was going for a gun and cracked him in the head with a pistol. The grocer staggered to his feet, stumbled back to his A&P store a block away, and collapsed.

With that "threat" alleviated, the three robbers entered their vehicle, pulled up to the crossing, and picked up Clark, who had wandered from the door to keep the growing crowd at bay. The Studebaker leisurely headed down Washington Street, then turned south on State Road 43 toward the railroad tracks. A snail-like, lumbering train blocked their path, giving them a classic "oh sh* - - ." moment.

The sheriff and townsfolk had figured their bank was safe for that exact reason—two sets of tracks crisscrossed nearby, cutting off the main escape route whenever a train thundered by. Astute bandits, they surmised, wouldn't gamble with the unpredictable schedules and frequent appearances. Although startling, the locomotive turned out to be a minor inconvenience as the gang detoured west on a dirt road, reached the city limits, and headed south down to Manhattan. Poolroom operator Charles Crawley, obviously unaware of the recent police arsenals heists, gave chase in his car. Luckily for him, he was easily outrun.

Catherine Tillotson, oblivious to what had just happened, proceeded to enter the bank to deposit receipts from the DePauw College treasurer's office. She was spared, by minutes, the opportunity to make a substantial contribution to the Charlie Makley pocket fund.

Down the road, the Studebaker slowed down long enough to gas up in Ferndale. The young attendant stared with amazement at the carload of gangsters right out of central casting, complete with machine guns on their laps. One was using expensive binoculars to scope the countryside through the rear window.

"What the hell are you waiting for? Fill it up!" Pierpont growled, startling the youth into action. Before roaring away, the thunderstruck attendant was handed two dollars to cover the $1.70 bill.

In Indianapolis, Matt Leach got wind of the robbery and headed out on the road with detective Claude Dozier. Demanding an instant personnel accounting, he stammered a bitter curse when he discovered that only a single pair of his troopers had been in the vicinity. The 24/7 "Mobile Dillinger Squad" was on the other side of the state.

Investigators, attempting to sort things out, initially identified Walter Dietrich and Harry Copeland as Dillinger and Pierpont's costars. Dietrich was eventually dropped, but Copeland, who resembled Russell Clark, made it all the way to being indicted by the Putnam County grand jury. (He'd later gladly confess to the job to avoid being sent to Lima, Ohio, to stand trial for Sheriff Sarber's murder.)

The Greencastle heist was the first to kick off what would soon became a disturbing double-whammy for insurance companies and government regulators—thieves robbing banks and crooked bankers grossly inflating their losses. The Central National Bank first reported that The Terror Gang made off with $1,760.28, along with an unspecified quantity of bonds. The bonds were later said to be worth a whopping $56,300. The bankers similarly boosted the lost cash number to $18,428. The subsequent indictment against Dillinger, Pierpont, Makley, and Copeland jumped the loss to a nice, round $75,000. An amused Dillinger told intimates the take was closer to $32,000.

Grilled by journalists on the multiple accounting discrepancies, bank president F. L. O'Hair kept his response short: "We are not seeking any publicity in connection with our experience with Mr. Dillinger." Such stonewalling fueled rumors that the hit, completed with the missing security guard, was a setup between the gang and the bankers aimed at covering previous losses and widespread embezzlement. The accusations were never proved.

The story of the brazen robbery, however, exploded out of the midwest and led most national news reports. Forty years later, a fictional television family living in the Blue Ridge Mountains of Virginia in the 1930s, *The Waltons*, would be shown gathered around their radio listening in hushed silence to a report that "John Dillinger has just robbed the Central National Bank at Greencastle, Indiana."

Lost in the hoopla of Greencastle was a smaller bulletin coming out of Brainerd, Minnesota. Baby Face Nelson had chosen the same day to rob a bank there. He would not be featured on *The Waltons*.

The following day, the Western State Bank of South Bend, Indiana, was relieved of $5,000 by three gunmen. Everybody screamed "Dillinger" until the trio, along with six other members of their sloppy gang, were arrested in Peoria, Illinois. Two more stickups followed on October 25 in Fillmore and Modoc, but the small takes, $130 and $400, appeared to rule out The Terror Gang. The increasingly paranoid Captain Leach feared a wave of copycats and Dillinger wannabes were on the loose.

A more astute and calmer state police captain would have been counting his blessings. With each new robbery, the Indiana legislature opened its treasury, giving Captain Leach pretty much anything he wanted. His troopers received beefed-up cars, submachine guns, and steel vests—all thanks to John Dillinger. In addition, a law was passed empowering all Indiana sheriffs to deputize anyone willing to arm themselves against The Terror Gang. This created a rash of dangerous, rag-tag roadblocks across the state, every single one doing nothing more than scaring children and hassling the innocent. The highly recognizable Pierpont boasted that he passed through such yahoo operations more than thirty times.

Captain Leach wasn't the only one milking hyperventilating politicians. Marion County Sheriff Buck Sumner filled the jumpy legislators with visions of massive, violent jailbreaks orchestrated by Dillinger to enable the famous outlaw to build an army of new members. Sumner quickly received the funds needed to reinforce the Marion County Jail with sheet steel, add an armored cage at the entrance, and put a machine gunner inside. Indianapolis police stuck their hands out and received enough cash to arm their entire, single-gun force with a second weapon. A subsequent infusion of money enabled them to customize a cruiser into a machine gun–equipped, armor-plated, John Dillinger fighting machine!

Not to be outspent, the fledgling, statewide radio communications center at Willard Park was surrounded by barbed-wire and bulletproof glass to keep The Terror Gang from putting them off the air—something the crew never even remotely considered.

Fearing the army of cutthroat felons Sheriff Sumner was fantasizing about, the city of Marion armed its fifty-member fire department and swore them in as "special" policemen. Marion's mayor Jack Edwards asked the Board of Public Safety to give him the money needed to turn the police station into a "fort." Back where it all started, at Michigan City, Warden Kunkel used his sudden cash flow to form an elite, fifteen-guard unit armed with tommy guns. Kunkel placed them on immediate, around-the-clock duty.

Uncle Sam was tossing the federal bucks around as well. The biggest deployment came from the United States military. On October 26, a force of 765 National Guard marksmen were stationed at armories throughout Indiana and placed under the command of the state police.

The Guard promised to stand by with troops, tanks, poisoned gas, and airplanes. Feeding off his boss's paranoia, Leach underling Al Feeney requested that Halloweeners refrain from costumes and activities that might lead them to be mistaken for gangsters—as if a three-foot version of Johnnie D was going to confuse Indiana's crack law enforcement agents.

The police hysteria, seen in dozens of historically preserved memos exaggerating The Terror Gang's activities, numbers, and strength, was not universally shared by the public. In a time of bank closings, mortgage foreclosures, and thrift scandals, many people were rooting Dillinger on.

Devious newspaper reporters, aware that Leach was heading over the edge, couldn't help taunt him by sending notes and letters purportedly from Dillinger, most of which ridiculed the efforts to catch him. Leach would invariably release the letters to the press, completing the circle of manufactured news. One reporter even sent "Kaptain Leach" a book entitled *How to Be a Detective.* Leach went to his grave thinking it came from Dillinger.

The thirty-year-old object of all this attention quickly tired of backwoods Terre Haute and headed for the nightlights of Chicago. The gang decided they would attract less attention—and have more fun—by splitting up and blending into the bustling big city. Johnnie and Billie moved into flat number 311 of the Parkside Avenue Apartments complex at 150–154 North Parkside Avenue, a quiet neighborhood a half-mile east of Oak Park. Harry Pierpont and Mary Kinder took up residence next door in unit 312. Most of the others found similar accommodations scattered around the city.

Russell Clark, suddenly a cash-laden, suit-wearing, successful bank robber, managed to woo back his ex-wife Francis, aka Bernice, aka Opal Long, aka the sister of Harry Copeland's busty girlfriend Pat. Even independent-thinking Shirt Shop Boy Homer VanMeter was living large at the Lincoln Park Arms, shacked up with a slender brunette moll named, what else, Mary—Marie Marion Conforti.

The Terror Gang insulated themselves mobster-style by communicating through Arthur "Fish" Johnson and Jack Perkins, associates of

Baby Face Nelson. The duo could usually be found at a poolroom at 3925 North Sheridan Road, or a bookie joint nearby at 3939. They functioned as the gang's answering machine and messenger service.

Dillinger and Pierpont selected the Parkside Avenue complex to isolate themselves from their associates. They soon discovered that while such distancing was a good hide-out strategy, it made operating their lucrative bank-robbing business too unwieldy. The pair huddled, then decided to hit the road again, this time moving back to the north side. They selected a ritzy complex at 4310 Clarendon Avenue that came complete with bellboys to fetch their cash-heavy luggage. The men, giving fake names for both themselves and their "wives," shared a spacious, fully furnished, two-bedroom unit that had a large sun porch. The building was a half mile from Lake Michigan, and had a deli on the first floor, the Mary Ann Food Shop, where the Jackrabbit liked to buy newly legalized Schlitz beer and frog's legs.

Settled in as successful city folks, Dillinger and Pierpont let their Terror Gang comrades pretty much go their own way and make their own mistakes. It was different with the women. The boys set down rules for both Billie and Mary, insisting that they eschew flashy dresses and "movie star behavior" that might attract attention. Dillinger told them which places to steer clear of, and asked that they avoid drinking too much, which might loosen their pretty lips. To set an example, both Dillinger and Pierpont took to wearing conservative, three-piece suits and matching fedoras—effecting the dignified, conformist image of the bankers they robbed. In fact, the two were becoming such solid citizens Pierpont gave Mary $1,000 and told her to open a bank account under an assumed name, "Fred Ross." Handsome Harry, unlike others at the time, apparently hadn't lost his trust in the institution of banking.

The two new roommates got along well enough in the apartment, but clashed over social activities. The tall, handsome, emotionally volatile, and more conspicuous Pierpont wanted to stay home with the girls and lay low. Dillinger wasn't a hole-up kind of guy, especially with his new prosperity. He shopped, mostly for designer clothes, took in sporting events, and hit the town nearly every night. The easygoing Dillinger tried to coax Harry to join him, mostly to no avail. When John and the girls, who were always eager to go out, planned a big day at the World's Fair in early November, Harry took a pass. The happy, souvenir-laden trio didn't return until late in the evening. "Our pictures are in every newspaper and you're out gallivanting around the fair!" Harry raged. "You're gonna get us all sent back to prison!"

Dillinger, who had learned to let Harry's rantings roll off his back, merely flashed his crooked grin and said, "Well, you gotta take chances now and then." It was an exasperating response from Pierpont's perspective, considering that his bipolar partner hid in the bathroom whenever delivery boys showed up with groceries.

The ladies, although friends, began to clash as well, mostly over "girl stuff." Feisty Mary didn't feel Billie was doing enough in the kitchen. Billie admitted as much, adding that she more than pulled her weight, and other things, in the bedroom. That hardly calmed Mary down. She nagged "Harried" Harry, who reluctantly took it to John. "I'm not much of a cook," Billie shrugged. Weary of the bitching, John ordered Billie to "do your share." When she failed to comprehend what exactly her share entailed, Dillinger ended up covering for her, doing the dishes and house-cleaning himself. The Jackrabbit obviously appreciated her bedroom contributions more than the others.

During this domesticated period, the four kids from the wrong side of the tracks took the opportunity to have extensive dental work performed by an accommodating dentist in Chicago's Loop district. Johnnie would often wait patiently in the lobby during Billie's lengthy procedures, reading *Popular Mechanics*, or updating himself on all the newspaper stories about the gang. He was particularly amused by the distant bank jobs he was being accused of orchestrating.

Occasionally, Billie's generous beau allowed the girls to splurge. Billie was treated to a $150 fur coat, a huge extravagance for the Depression era, but a lovingly applied sheet of psychological armor even a disapproving, clothing-conscious landlady couldn't penetrate. A tipsy Patricia Cherrington did Billie one better, spending $190 of Harry Copeland's hard-stolen money for a watch from the snooty C. D. Peacock Jewelers on State Street.

With such expenditures, The Terror Gang knew they'd have to start thinking about going back to work. They toyed with Homer VanMeter's ambitious plan of teaming with Baby Face Nelson's crew and Tommy Touhy's gang for a big train robbery in Terre Haute. Dillinger and Pierpont eventually quashed the idea. The two top guns saw themselves as the biggest fish in the gangland ocean. A flood of new men with no personal loyalty to them might prove suicidal. If something went wrong, these strangers might be more than willing to cut sell-out deals to save their skin. No, it was better, they decided, to stick with their trusted associates, their plans, and their territories—Indiana, Ohio, and Illinois. Michigan, despite news stories to the contrary, was avoided because of the police radio network, a strong state trooper force, and fewer rural roads.

The two gang leaders, for all their caution and rapidly acquired personal sophistication, were still trapped by providential thinking. Toying with the Matt Leaches of the world, they had no inkling of the specialized heat Uncle Sam was about to lay on them.

Initially, they had no reason to worry. Both President Herbert Hoover and his successor, Franklin Delano Roosevelt, were against the establishment of a national police force. They weren't, however, opposed to occasionally loaning out some federal muscle if a need existed. The previous year, Treasury Department bean counters had brought down the "untouchable" reign of Chicago crime boss Al Capone. They slapped the bewildered wise guy with a then unique federal income tax evasion charge.

Despite that success, President Roosevelt was reluctant to send his forces after the roving bands of bank robbers ravaging the midwest. The president was naturally more concerned with the collapsed economy and high unemployment rate. Roosevelt, a liberal Democrat, put such a low emphasis on fighting crime that he selected a seventy-four-year-old figurehead as Attorney General, Montana's senator Thomas Walsh. The Big Sky politician was so enfeebled he wouldn't even get a chance to be harassed about John Dillinger. He died on the way to the March 2, 1933 inauguration. Roosevelt went back to the political payback well and replaced Walsh with Homer Stille Cummings, sixty-three, the little-known former mayor of Stamford, Connecticut.

Cummings, surprisingly, took the job seriously. Keenly aware of the bank robbery plague in voter-rich Middle America, he picked an ambitious, mob-busting Ohio prosecutor named Joseph B. Keenan as his assistant. That summer, Cummings also announced that the intense and determined head of the Bureau of Investigation, J. Edgar Hoover, would be staying on for another term. At the time, the Bureau of Investigation worked cases for the Justice Department, mostly policing the White Slavery Act, the Mann Act (taking females across state borders for immoral purposes), the Dyer Act (stolen cars across state lines), and Native American Reservations. Hoover however, unlike his presidents, felt that was only the beginning of what his troops could do. He envisioned a *Metropolis*-like army of nameless and faceless agents that gathered information for Washington and operated completely in the dark, prohibited by directive from ever speaking to the press. In 1933, Hoover had a force of 266 such clandestine special agents, along with 60 accountants. His men, in keeping with their underground profile, had no right to carry firearms or make arrests.

That oversight changed on June 17, with the infamous "Kansas City Massacre." Attempting to return a Leavenworth escapee named Frank "Jelly" Nash back to his cell, a team of local police and FBI agents were set upon by three men with submachine guns, one of which was Charles Arthur "Pretty Boy" Floyd. An agent and three cops were killed, as was Nash himself—apparently because the rescuers didn't expect that he would be driving. The agent sitting behind him, in the spot where the prisoners normally were stashed, was unscathed.

Hoover used the shocking attack to successfully push for legislation that would beef up his forces, arm his troops, and give them the power to make arrests. Prior to that, on July 30, the name was changed to Division of Investigation, and money was appropriated for two hundred additional agents. (It wouldn't be named the Federal Bureau of Investigation until July 1, 1935.) The following summer, Congress finally gave Hoover the right to arm his men and authorized them to haul in the bad guys. At the same time, Congress passed a law that made robbing a federally insured bank a federal crime. That placed it under the jurisdiction of Hoover's newly empowered agents.

These changes were not fully in place during the fall of 1933 when John Dillinger and Billie Frechette were busy playing Ozzie and Harriet, getting their teeth polished, and buying suits and furs. But a stronger law enforcement was coming, and both Assistant Attorney General Joe Keenan and J. Edgar Hoover were preparing to hit the ground running. A special agent was dispatched to Lima after the Dillinger breakout, and the G-Man's reports were being dropped right on Hoover's desk. Law enforcement's most legendary chief would be on Dillinger's tail from that point on.

Even so, a federally funded lion in faraway Washington couldn't match the effectiveness of a spaniel with his nose to the trail in Indiana. Forrest Huntington was still on the job, and his pet snitch, Art McGinnis, remained the closest thing anyone had to a mole inside The Terror Gang's organization. Trouble was, too many people were trying to tap into that mole. Huntington threatened to pull McGinnis out when he got word that other agencies, including a force led by the untrustworthy Matt Leach, had compromised his cover. Huntington's fear was that a crooked cop on Dillinger's payroll would expose his rat.

McGinnis, still craving the insurance companies' reward money, assured Huntington he could dodge the bullet. To prove that he was too valuable to cut loose, McGinnis dropped a bomb. Dillinger, Copeland, and Terrible Ten member Joseph Burns, posing as Oriental rug salesmen, had recently gained access to the Fort Harrison military base in Indianapolis. The trio spoke with the base commander, Colonel Robinson, and the chaplain, Alfred C. Oliver, then cased the place for a munitions raid. Apparently, robbing police stations had lost its thrill.

McGinnis explained that the gang wanted to tap into a supply of army uniforms, heavy machine guns, and mortars—armament for a planned assault on the Pendleton reformatory. The motive was said to be recruiting, but others suspected this was pure revenge for the cruel treatment Dillinger always believed he suffered there. Wild as the story was, it checked out. Three men who fit the descriptions of Dillinger, Copeland, and Burns had indeed appeared at the base trying to sell rugs. Warned by Huntington, Colonel Robinson doubled security and began checking all cars entering the government facility.

On November 3, Pierpont, Hamilton, Copeland, Shouse, and Joe Burns were indicted in Lima for Sheriff Sarber's murder. Burns had nothing to do with it, but got tagged anyway. If the five weren't already desperate enough, the indictment sealed their resolve. No point being taken alive if the electric chair awaited.

Under accessory laws, prosecutors could have charged Dillinger as well, but the statutes were muddy then, enabling him to escape.

Governor McNutt, to his eternal chagrin, continued to take heat for signing Dillinger's parole six months earlier. No one could have predicted that the inept, small-time Mooresville delinquent would, in a few short months, transform himself into Public Enemy Number One. Regardless, politics being what it is, McNutt's political enemies and opposition wasted no time using that routine parole paperwork to their advantage, blasting the governor at every opportunity. Instead of sticking to his guns, McNutt, reeling from the attacks, mentally staggered and confessed to the press that it was a mistake. That only made his enemies push harder.

Dillinger was busy pushing harder as well. Instead of learning from the gratuitously violent Lima incident and counting his lucky stars, he allowed his all-consuming need for vengeance to cloud his thinking. The man who played the devil-may-care, affable good crook to Pierpont's psychotic killer suddenly did a role reversal. A seething Dillinger showed up in Dayton in early November and boldly went to the homes of Detectives Pfauhl and Gross, pretending to be a lawyer. Fortunately, neither man was home. Billie Frechette would later confirm that her boyfriend's intention was to shoot them both. He did not, however, pay the same visit to Mary Longnacker and her new live-in paramour. Apparently, in Dillinger's twisted mind, a personal betrayal from a friend or lover wasn't as bad as an impersonal law enforcement officer simply doing his job.

The chilling visits also followed Dillinger's odd habit of attempting such vengeance only once, then letting it go regardless of whether the mission was successful. It was as if the attempt itself, and the enduring fear it caused, was enough to cure what was eating him.

After that trek into homicidal madness, Dillinger decided to tempt fate further by transforming himself into Johnnie Jr. and returning to Mooresville. Late one evening in early November, he slipped in through the unlocked back door of Audrey's house in Maywood, nearly causing his beloved niece Mary to jump out of her skin. Mary, up late studying, let out a scream that woke Audrey and her husband. The family quickly settled down enough to have a pleasant visit. Johnnie was traveling with Russell Clark, and Clark joined in as well. Eager to go home, John Jr. convinced Mary, a student at Butler University, to head over to the farmhouse in Mooresville with him. Tossing the obvious danger aside, Mary hopped in the car and raised no objection as Clark raced to Mooresville at ninety miles per hour, a speed once unheard of.

The two relatives chatted about her school and ambitions, then grew more playful. Mary was allowed to caress the infamous machine guns. At one point, the studious college coed lifted one up and pretended to fire away, imagining herself a famous bank robber. "It was silly. Kid stuff, as one is apt to do," she explained later.

At the farm, they visited with John Sr., who promptly went to bed early despite the rare appearance of his prodigal son. John Jr., Mary, and Clark tossed some wood into the furnace and talked for a couple of hours before returning Mary to Maywood. "We stayed away from what they had been doing—it wouldn't have done any good to talk about it," Mary recalled. After saying good-bye, John Jr. and Clark drove off to parts unknown.

On November 12, Forrest Huntington went to Chicago to confer with the Chicago Police Department's "Secret Squad," an elite force assigned to special, high profile cases. Their latest mission was to break up "The Dillinger Gang." Headed by Lt. John Howe, one of their best tactics was the innovative technique of bugging the phone lines of criminals and their associates. Using the crude but workable technology of the time, they were wiring up everybody they could smoke out that was remotely connected to the outlaws. Lieutenant Howe admitted they were doing so by shadowing Art McGinnis, Huntington's pet snitch. McGinnis had led them to a former Shirt Shop Boy named Fred "Happy" Meyels, aka Fred Meyers. "Happy," who lived at 4147 Irving

Park Boulevard with his wife, had unhappy health problems that prevented him from taking an active part in The Terror Gang. A sympathetic Dillinger tossed him a bone every now and then and farmed out minor jobs.

Irritated anew by all the police in bed with his source, Huntington extracted a promise from Lieutenant Howe to withdraw his shadows. "You better keep an eye on that bird," Howe advised in return. "He's slippery as snot on a doorknob."

McGinnis was indeed slippery, but he was the best thing the law enforcement agents had going. He was about to prove his worth yet again by repeatedly delivering Public Enemy Number One on a silver platter. Yet, because of the greed and egos of all involved—snitches, private dicks, and cops—it was a dish served cold.

Chapter 9

Despite all the detectives, secret crews, wiretaps, G-Men, and 24/7 state police "Mobile Dillinger Squads," the Jackrabbit strolled uncontested into Happy Meyer's house the next morning to meet with the slippery Art McGinnis about fencing eight, World War I, thousand-dollar Liberty Loan bonds. Pierpont, Dillinger added, was in Milwaukee trying to do the same with fifty-six more—all from the Greencastle job.

After Dillinger left, McGinnis phoned Huntington, informed the exasperated PI of the visit, and said not to worry about the missed opportunity, they were scheduled to meet again that afternoon at a parking lot in The Loop. McGinnis refused to say exactly when and where until Huntington promised that nobody would try to apprehend Dillinger there. Huntington, still after the money more than an empty-handed gang leader, explained that he had to run it up the flagpole. He called Lieutenant Howe at the Chicago police department. Howe had to run it up his big pole—to the police commissioner. After more calls, Lieutenant Howe was advised to use his discretion. He agreed to McGinnis's "paws off" terms. The PI and cop were then informed that the meeting would be 2 P.M. at 222 State Street.

Huntington stationed himself in a second-floor cafeteria across the street. Lieutenant Howe, in plainclothes, loitered at a newsstand. Sure enough, Dillinger appeared, accompanied by a second, unidentified man. The pair spoke with McGinnis for a few moments, then rounded a corner and headed into the Lauer Bar on Lawrence Avenue. The crook-friendly bartender warned them that some of Chicago's finest were across the street staking out the place. They weren't Lieutenant Howe's men. The Lauer Bar was a known hoodlum hangout, and the felons had simply wandered into somebody else's stakeout. Dillinger and McGinnis tipped the bartender and left, reconvening inside Dillinger's black Terraplane 8, Illinois license plate 1-269037.

During the leisurely drive, Dillinger suddenly queried McGinnis about his relationship with Forrest Huntington, saying he'd heard they were relatives. McGinnis, struggling to stay calm, responded that they were distant in-laws. "He ever ask you about me?" Dillinger asked.

"Yeah, a time or two," McGinnis cleverly replied, figuring a total lie would cause suspicion. "But I didn't tell him nothing and he let the matter drop."

Dillinger was naively satisfied with that, his ego blinding him to the possibility of being betrayed. He went on to jabber to the snitch that Copeland, VanMeter, and Burns were also in Chicago, while John Hamilton and Walter Dietrich had gone to St. Louis. Dillinger threw in that he'd been casing a bank in Antioch, Illinois, just north of Chicago, but didn't like the security and layout. A second bank, this one in Paris, Illinois, was now at the top of their list.

After being dropped off, McGinnis met with Huntington and unloaded the gold mine of information. Better yet, he would be meeting Dillinger again that evening for dinner after doing some gun-running for him at the Lauer Bar. The snitch had also set Dillinger up with a doctor to treat the outlaw's sycosis condition, a chronic inflammation of the hair follicles also known as "barber's itch." The appointment was with Dr. Charles Eye, a dermatologist with a second-floor office at 4175 Irving Park Boulevard, a block from Happy Meyers's house. McGinnis renewed his steadfast request that Dillinger not be arrested. The snitch was working on commission, which included a percentage of the recovered stash; a $1,000 bonus for the capture of Dillinger, Pierpont, and Copeland; and $500 each for any other gang member. He thus had little motivation to snatch Dillinger alone.

The Chicago cops, eager to capture the whole gang as well, once again agreed. A subsequent briefing included state police detectives, who naturally ran to their agitated boss. Captain Leach, for all his emotional problems, saw this one clearly. He couldn't fathom the "whole ball of wax" plan the others had agreed to and wanted Dillinger immediately caught or killed. He spent the next hour spitting into a telephone, arguing his case with Huntington and Lieutenant Howe—all to no avail. Howe's only concession was to include ISP Detectives Gene Ryan and Chester Butler on the observation team. It's not known if the rabid Leach ordered his men to plug the bandit at the first opportunity.

Huntington, Howe, Butler, and Ryan stationed themselves in an unmarked car outside Doctor Eye's building that evening. At 7:15, Dillinger cruised up in the Terraplane, complete with an added bonus—Handsome Harry Pierpont cuddling with Mary K in the back-seat! Had Captain Leach known, he'd have no doubt been absolutely ape-spit apoplectic. Pierpont, an escaped felon wanted for the brutal murder of a sheriff among other things, should have been arrested on the spot.

He wasn't. Huntington and Howe kept their promise to their oily snitch and did nothing but peep. Dillinger, his itchy head tingling from the soothing prescription ointment, emerged from the physician's office fifteen minutes later and sped off.

The following day, Dillinger missed a scheduled meeting with McGinnis, but was set to see the doctor again for a follow-up treatment. By now, a Lima police inspector was in town and shared Captain Leach's bafflement that Dillinger and Pierpont weren't shot full of holes the night before. Lieutenant Howe finally agreed that the plan to round up most of the gang at once was too ambitious. Over Huntington's stren-uous objections, the order was given that Dillinger and whomever came with him would be popped that night. Three squads of detectives were rounded up to do the honors.

Among the sixteen officers and four unmarked cars stationed around the doctor's office was the Essex Terraplane 8 the ISP had recently con-fiscated from Sam Goldstine. Huntington and Lima's Inspector Rooney were in the back of the Terraplane, with an ISP trooper, Art Keller, lit-erally riding shotgun. One of Lieutenant Howe's "Secret Squad" detec-tives, John Artery, was at the wheel.

At 7:25 P.M., Dillinger rolled up in his matching Terraplane. This time, only Billie was with him. Dillinger received his scalp massage from a nurse, then sauntered out around 7:45. Scanning the street, he may have recognized the Goldstine Terraplane, a vehicle he probably helped purchase. Although the autos were assembly-line productions, Dillinger, as was his habit, no doubt requested subtle, customized features that his trained eye would have immediately noticed. For whatever reason, instead of going south down Keeler Avenue as expected, Dillinger threw his Terraplane into reverse and backed onto busy Irving Boulevard. The unexpected maneuver caught the cops completely off guard. The only vehicle able to recover and remotely keep up was the aforementioned Goldstine Terraplane. Pulling beside Dillinger, Captain Leach's boy Keller cut loose with five shotgun rounds into the bandit's door—and, he thought, the front tire. The big black vehicle didn't even slow down. Officers Rooney and Artery emptied their revolvers as well, but Dillinger floored it and pulled away. He killed his lights, then careened south on Elston, spun around to Barnard Street and vanished.

Johnnie and Billie eventually made it to Russell Clark's apartment, where a party was in progress. Pierpont, Mary K, Shouse, Copeland, Bernice Clark, and Pat Cherrington were all dancing to the big band sounds on the radio when their harried friends rushed in with their tale of woe. Because of the unmarked and strangely familiar Terraplane, Dillinger thought he'd been set upon by another gang. Confused, Pierpont and Makley drove Dillinger back to the scene to hunt for clues. Nothing jumped out at them.

While the cops fumed and blamed each other for the latest flub, the Chicago newspapers had a field day, weaving tales of a miraculous escape in a "speedy armored car as dozens of shots rapped harmlessly on the bulletproof glass." Another paper described a machine gunner blasting away from a porthole in Dillinger's Terraplane "shattering the windshields of police cars" while Johnnie D's "blonde girl companion joined in, handling her revolver like an expert." Truth was, the shattered windshields came from the cops shooting through their own windows. There was no mystery machine gunner, and neither Dillinger nor his nonblonde, sexpot sweetheart fired a single shot. The Jackrabbit didn't even go for blondes!

Whatever his secret instructions, ISP Det. Art Keller admitted he aimed low into Dillinger's door because he feared a fiery crash involving both vehicles had he raised the weapon and taken the bandit's head off. Keller also failed to accomplish the simple task of blowing out one of the Terraplane's balloonlike tires. His biting blasts splattered into his own arching wheel-well.

Stung by the taunting headlines, the Chicago police slapped a $10,000 reward on Dillinger's head, and added that he and his men, now called "The Savage Seven" were to be shot on sight.

Leach, of course, was beside himself.

The next day, on November 16, Dillinger's cherished Terraplane was found at 7600 Greenview Avenue in the far north side. An examination revealed that none of the pellets or slugs penetrated the sturdy Terraplane's sheet metal. Not a speck of blood was found anywhere. Lab technicians did find a receipt for the Buena Park garage at 4132 Clarendon—two blocks from Dillinger's ritzy digs. Despite a dizzying array of tags, registrations, and phony addresses, the vehicle was successfully traced to the Clarendon Avenue suite, and a second residence at 2847 West Washington Boulevard. Police raided both locations, along with Harry Copeland's Montrose Avenue apartment, and came up empty on all counts. Remarkably, Dillinger remembered the receipt and moved the entire gang to a backup hideout at 150 North Parkside Avenue.

A nosey neighbor told police that three men and two women left the area at dawn in a maroon Plymouth after failing to start a stubborn Buick. The witness, Carlyle J. Woeffler, wrote the license plate number down. The Plymouth was registered to Pearl Elliott. The uncooperative Buick, left behind, had been stolen a few days before.

The morning newspapers gave the still-confused gang the true picture of who was after them. The police was indeed in Goldstine's Terraplane. Reading between the lines, Dillinger was convinced that it was an undercover goon squad out to assassinate him, no questions asked, because they'd never properly identified themselves. It also finally dawned on The Savage Seven that Art McGinnis was the snitch—although Art himself was in denial and wanted to stay in the game.

The fury of McGinnis's puppet master, Forrest Huntington, now rivaled that of the unstable Captain Leach. In one fell swoop, Huntington's mole was exposed, his plans were shattered, and the gang was driven underground. In return, the good guys captured no one, recovered not a dime, and Huntington was back to square one. The peeved Pinkerton vet funneled his anger at Captain Leach and his men for impatiently pushing the confrontation at the wrong time.

Fed up, Huntington convinced McGinnis that the gig was up and he needed to blow out of the Windy City ASAP. Huntington was also unnerved over reports he was getting of a wicked collusion between Dillinger and crooked bankers all but begging the infamous bandit to hit their institutions in order to mask their own thefts. Private papers recovered from ISP Detective Gene Ryan three decades later would include transcripts of wiretaps on Happy Meyer's phone that indicated such made-to-order robberies had indeed occurred. The callers, however, were smart enough to cloak the individual banks and officers.

With the exposure of at least one rat in their belfry, The Terror Gang's age of innocence had ended. Dillinger knew he had some internal housecleaning to take care of before a repeat performance of the Doctor Eye incident. In mid-November, the gang was lightened by two charter members. Harry Copeland was expelled because of his excessive drinking. Ed Shouse slipped off on his own after being warned by Russell Clark that Dillinger was about to plug him because of his overt lust for Billie Frechette, which the overheated Billie failed to discourage. Shouse repaid Clark for saving his life by stealing Clark's new Terraplane and leaving Chicago on November 18. The following day, a wasted Copeland was arrested in front of the Rainbow Barbeque at North and Harlem avenues. The much sought-after Public Enemy was waving a pistol and loudly arguing with a prostitute who had ripped him off the night before.

Although shrouded with aliases, Copeland's fingerprints exposed his true identity. He was taken under heavy guard back to Michigan City for a long period of forced rehab. Leach had him temporarily transferred to Marion so he and other officers from around the midwest could grill the longtime Terror Gang member for information. The proverbial parade of witnesses were bussed in to identify him and clear various cases. Copeland, sucking up the attention, was nonetheless not very forthcoming. The forced sobriety returned his senses, and he had enough working brain cells left to know which jobs to cop to, and which to vehemently deny—that is, the ugliness in Lima that promised a direct route to the electric chair.

While the media viewed the Copeland capture as a major victory and swarmed to Michigan City and Marion, Captain Leach scoffed, correctly speculating that he'd been spit from the gang for being a dangerous drunk.

Shaking their heads in "I told you so" disgust, Dillinger and crew read about Copeland's bust from their new hideout in Racine, Wisconsin—provided by yet another Pearl Elliott connection. While there, they decided to hit the American Bank and Trust Company, possibly with the full approval of the struggling bank's top officers. The institution, which had changed names numerous times, had a disquieting history of embezzlement arrests.

Unlike past hit-and-run operations, the Racine scheme was precisely calculated in advance, complete with maps of both the bank's inside, and the subsequent escape routes. Yet with all the advanced planning, the gang selected an uncharacteristic getaway vehicle—a black Buick Auburn with jump seats and bright yellow wire wheels. It was not the type of car that would go unnoticed.

The Savage Seven, now reduced to The Furious Five, had changed their mind yet again about the no-wheelman theory. They had a mysterious new recruit at the helm who was responsible for implementing an experimental manpower delivery system. The Buick's driver motored by the bank twice, dropping two men off each time to draw less attention. He then parked the vehicle out-of-sight behind the building, leaving the engine running. The four operatives, decked in stylish suits, hats, and topcoats covering stockless Thompsons, entered the bank in pairs through the Main Street entrance. One of the men, Pierpont, was carrying large rolls of paper under his arm. Inside, he unveiled two cheerful Red Cross posters, which he pasted, with the nodding approval of curious customers, on the large, plate-glass window facing the street. The posters obscured about 80 percent of the unusually open view into the bank. Once shielded, Dillinger and Makley approached the tellers' cages, while Russell Clark took his customary spot by the entrance.

The head teller, Harold Graham, thirty-four, had his back turned counting money when Makley approached his closed window and said, "Hands Up!" An annoyed Graham thought it was a joke. Without turning, he was about to tell Makley to get his rump to an open window when the robber repeated his demand. "I said, hands up!" Graham spun around to face the speaker to see if he knew him, forgetting to lift his hands as ordered. Panicking, Makley squeezed the trigger of the murderous weapon and bounced a hot slug off of Graham's elbow that burned through his belt and buried into his right hip. Makley fortunately had the Thompson on "single fire," otherwise Graham would have been blown into the back wall.

Clerk Helen Cespkes heard the ear-splitting bang and nearly went through the roof. "That first shot sounded so loud and it was so near to me that I jumped and screamed."

Graham fell to the floor—right next to the silent holdup alarm. With tingling fingers, he pushed it, notifying the Racine police. "The next thing I remember, I looked up and saw the blood and knew I'd been shot. Through the grill of the sliding door, I saw Dillinger and Pierpont dashing for the back of the bank. Then one of the robbers came in [to his cage] and took the money. He gave me a kick and said, 'You will press the alarm, will you?' It wasn't a hard kick, not a savage kick, not a swift kick. He opened the drawers and threw the money into a bag, then went on to the next cage. It took him about a minute."

The robber, probably Makley, missed $50,000 in thousand-dollar bills that Graham had stashed behind a pile of deposit tickets for safe-keeping. Instead of reaping that windfall, Makley, remembering the bonus loot from the Greencastle heist, relieved customer Barney Cowen of $170 he was preparing to deposit.

Clerk Janette Williams could see and hear what was going on in the backrooms from her position under a desk. ". . . Harry Pierpont, he was the glamour boy of the outfit, a gentleman type," she editorialized, having not seen Psycho Harry in action before. "Pierpont went in the vault . . . I can remember [teller] George Ryan saying 'For God's sake, mister, point that [machine] gun the other way!' Pierpont laughed and said 'As long as you're a good boy, you don't have to worry.' "

Dillinger then appeared and tried to get rookie teller Don Steel to open the vault, but Steel said only the officers had the combination. Judging the claim reasonable, Dillinger walked to the front and fetched Grover Weyland, the bank president who was a vain, prissy man with a superior attitude, along with Weyland's more personable junior officer Loren Browne. Walking back to the vault, Dillinger accidentally stepped on the finger of teller Harold Anderson. "I didn't even say ouch," Anderson recalled. "We all used to talk about what we'd do in case of a holdup . . . but when the chips were down none of us did anything . . . When you look down the barrel end of a .45 it looks like a cannon!"

Weyland, cigarette dangling from his lips and acting annoyed by it all, opened the vault with Browne's help, as it was a two-man operation. His odd, fearless behavior led rise to suspicion that he was in on it, an accusation, like all the others of its kind, that was never proven.

L. C. Rowan, an assistant cashier, was more concerned with saving his own skin than observing his boss' questionable behavior. Fearing being taken hostage when the cops arrived, he jumped at an opportunity to duck into a stairway leading to the basement. On the way down, he stepped on another floor alarm, this one connected to an external bell outside the bank that immediately began to scream. Rowan continued to a rear door and spilled out—only to find himself looking smack into the rear of the getaway car. He slipped right back inside.

Rowan wasn't the only person desperate to distance himself from the stockless Thompsons. A visiting bank examiner locked himself inside the bathroom. Bookkeeper John Schmitz tried to hide in a closet in the director's room, only to find two other cowering bank examiners in there already. A customer, Mrs. E. C. Wilson, preferred the hide-in-plain-sight technique, sitting patiently in a safety deposit booth until the ruckus was over.

For the first time, the police arrived during the middle of a Dillinger heist. Officer Cyril Boyard, Sgt. Wilbur Hansen, and Patrolman Franklin

Worsley, hearing the silent alarm a police headquarters, shrugged and casually responded. The faulty siren had been going off for weeks, and the men were frankly getting tired of it. On the way out, Sergeant Hansen grabbed a Thompson submachine gun that was a gift from a local gun expert, William J. Pearman. He figured it would make a nice prop to entertain the bank's customers while checking out the presumably false alarm. Turning on Fifth from Lake, the three cops blew right past the gaudy getaway car without being tipped to the danger that awaited them.

Lumberman Garrett Veenstra absentmindedly preceded the policemen through the door, thinking only that the cops were making a bigger racket than usual that day. Although the bank's outside alarm was engaged, and the cops arrived with sirens blaring, the chainsaw operator, obviously used to loud noises, never put two and two together. Inside, Veenstra found it strangely quiet, "like a bank holiday." He put his deposit on the teller's cage and was surprised when the wide-eyed man made no effort to take it.

Officer Boyard followed Veenstra and instantly felt a barrel dig into his back. Russell Clark grabbed the cop by his Sam Browne belt and pulled him out of sight. Makley emerged Jesse James–style through a pair of swinging doors in the middle of the bank just as Sergeant Hansen walked in with his Thompson hanging limply at his side.

"Get the cop with the machine gun!" Clark shouted. Makley lifted a pistol and fired twice. The oblivious Veenstra heard the shots, turned, and saw Sergeant Hansen go down, crashing hard to the floor. Seconds later, a female customer nearby fainted. Her fall was followed by a large vase toppling over. Veenstra finally awakened from his bliss. "I was scared as I could be," he said. "I had my hands up. I was near a big post in the middle of the bank and I never saw a post that looked so good in my life."

Veenstra glanced toward the big window and saw dozens of eyes peeking around the posters, eager to catch the action. "I thought they were dumb. I thought, 'If I could only get out there I'd be on my way!'"

Makley stepped over Sergeant Hansen, approached Officer Boyard, and tried to remove the cop's service revolver from a new leather holster. When it wouldn't budge, he jerked the whole belt off and ordered Boyard to lie on the floor.

"No, we want to take him with us," Pierpont shouted from across the room. Makley nodded, leaned over Sergeant Hansen, and scooped up his unfired Thompson.

The outside alarm was starting to beckon an even larger crowd of gawkers. O'Connor and Goldberg Shoe Store manager Leo Krause and his assistant, Edward Kirt, ran toward the noise and pressed their noses to the window. Boyard recognized the pair and motioned for the footwear hawkers to take off. They did, but only to Fifth Street where they climbed on a ledge to try and see into the lobby. Makley spotted them and fired a blast from the Thompson over their heads, shattering a window and raining sharp glass on their faces and shoulders. Some of the bullets bounced off the cement frame and zipped across the street where they smashed the window of Joseph Mezine's second-floor photo shop. Right below Mezine, Wilbur Hansen's wife was shopping in a dime store, unaware that her husband was bleeding on the floor of the bank across the street.

Dillinger and Pierpont finished gathering the cash and looked out the back window of the bookkeeping room. The two-story drop to the pavement was deemed too steep to exit that way—even for the Jackrabbit. "We'll have to shoot our way out the front," Dillinger said with a shrug. Pierpont smiled and grabbed the snooty Weyland to use as his shield. Dillinger scanned the room for his protection. Never one to miss a pretty lady, he spotted a trio of comely young women huddled under a marble counter. "All right, you, come out of there."

"Oh, do you mean me?" Janette Williams squeaked.

"Who the hell do you think I'm talking to. Get up and get out of there!"

Helen Cespkes and Ursula Patzke were under the counter as well and were ordered to fall in line with Williams. "We were the last to leave," Cespkes recalled. "When the fellow guarding us (Dillinger) stopped to load his machine gun, that's when I was sick with fright. The click of those bullets going into the gun was horrible."

Like a snowball rolling down a hill, Dillinger and Pierpont accumu-
lated additional hostages as they moved across the lobby to the exit.
Officer Boyard was added to the fattening pack near the entrance.
Customer Wally Nelson and off-duty cop Lawrence Keyes were swallowed in tandem the instant they walked through the front door.

Weyland, his annoyance growing, suddenly felt the need to mouth
off. "You wouldn't be so brave if you didn't have that gun!" he hissed, as
if he could have overpowered the burly robbers in a fair fight. Wham!
The finned-barrel of a Thompson crashed across his face, jamming his
eyeglasses into his nose and drawing blood. Veenstra, for one, couldn't
believe the starched banker's risky banter. "I worried about that remark
afterwards, while Weyland was gone (as a hostage)." Wising up, the
money man restrained himself from offering any further observations.

Exiting the bank inside their human cocoon, the gunmen forced
their way through an unruly mob. Pierpont somehow spotted two
armed detectives, Rudolph Bergerson and Lester McEachern, running
down the sidewalk across the street. He alerted Makley, who squeezed
off several bursts from his Thompson, now switched to automatic
mode. A fog of masonry dust exploded from the storefront walls as the
slugs dug in. Bergerson ducked into Wylie's hat shop where he found
Elsie Delenbach crouched on the floor in near shock. One of the bullets
had seared through the brim of her hat before destroying a mirror
behind her. Bergerson crouched behind the store's radiator and shouted
for his trailing partner to "Get back. Get back!" As he screamed, something popped him on the hip. Reaching down, he picked up a warm,
flattened .45 slug that had ricocheted from points unknown.

Detective McEachern veered into the Venetian Theater and searched
for a phone to alert headquarters. He couldn't find one. Frustrated, he
slipped out a back door where he met up with his like-minded partner.
Both detectives concluded that not only were they badly outgunned,
but they couldn't even return fire due to the womb of hostages and
thrill seekers surrounding the bandits.

Racine resident Kenneth Lee, drawn to the commotion, had just
parked his car on the curb across the street when another of Makley's
errant shots cut through his fender and punctured a tire. "I ran back

toward Main Street to get out of range and watch the holdup men leave. While they were walking toward the car there must have been a crowd of between fifty and one hundred people following them down the street with their hands up in the air. It was the funniest thing you ever saw. Nobody tried to stop them, but the crowd seemed to want to get as close as possible."

As the bizarre mob rounded the corner to Fifth Street, they spilled down an incline leading to the parking lot behind the structure. Helen Cespkes and Janette Williams lagged back enough to vanish into the swarm. Noticing the clever move, Wally Nelson and Lawrence Keyes followed suit. Ursula Patzke tried to do likewise, but Pierpont spotted her loud outfit. "You, in the red dress, come with us!"

"You mean me?" Patzke asked incredulously.

"Yes. And be quick about it."

The fashion betrayal burned so deep into Patzke's psyche that she would never wear red again for the rest of her life.

At the Buick, Dillinger climbed behind the wheel. Makley grabbed shotgun, and Pierpont, Clark, and the original wheelman piled in the back. The three remaining hostages, Patzke, Weyland, and Boyard, were stationed on the running boards, with Patzke and Weyland on Dillinger's side, and Boyard on the opposite. Makley clung to Boyard's belt to keep the cop from hopping off.

Grover Cleveland Lutter, a 245-pound ex-football player turned Racine police chief, arrived on the scene at that moment after sprinting six blocks from the station house. His motor pool was barren, leaving him no other option but foot power to cover the distance to the bank. Catching his breath, he bolted upstairs, found an overlooking window, and took aim. As with his detectives, he couldn't lob a single shot because the hostages were effectively shielding the occupants.

The Buick, a lumbering, but commanding twelve-cylinder, headed east on Fifth and made a sharp turn at Lake Street. There, the car passed Lt. Arthur Muhlke, kneeling with a sawed-off shotgun, and Officer Franklin Worsley, wielding a carbine. Once again, the highly effective human shields prevented either from ringing off a shot.

Dillinger turned west on Seventh Street past the Hotel Racine, riveting the attention of all who watched. "I was wondering what they were advertising," a Milwaukee salesman thought as they blew past. The Buick rumbled onto Wisconsin, turning again on Eighth, skidded west on Marquette, and north to Sixth. The sharp turns in the city traffic were so tight that Patzke's troublesome red dress brushed a passing car. A motorcycle cop saw the running-board riders, thought it was indeed a quizzical site, but zipped on by.

Hooking west on Lafayette, a traffic jam slowed them to an unnerving crawl. At Sixth and Lafayette, Boyard was ordered off, possibly to lighten the load. "It all looked like a movie," he would reflect later, thankful to be alive.

Patzke and Weyland were yanked inside to diminish the attention. Patzke squeezed in next to Handsome Harry, while Weyland was shoved into the jump seat with Clark, their feet resting rather appropriately on the money bags. Speeding toward the country, the mystery man called out landmarks as Makley announced the odometer readings. The vehicle stopped twice so the bandits could change license plates— ignoring the fact that the bright yellow tires could be recognized from a dirigible, much less on the ground. During one such pit stop, the money was transferred from the bags to suitcases. Spotting a large number of one-dollar bills, Makley accused Weyland of "pulling a fast one," and suggested holding him for ransom—making a Grand Canyon–sized leap of faith that someone in Depression-torn, banker-hating America would actually pay to have the financial prima donna returned. Weyland rolled his eyes and explained that the larger bills were further back in the stacks. "Just keep counting. We're a small bank. You took all we had."

Makley let fly some choice obscenities, but Pierpont cut him off, reminding him there was a lady in the car. Keenly aware of that fact, Dillinger discussed some hideout possibilities and asked Patzke if she could cook. "After a fashion," she said truthfully, causing the men to wince, laugh, and goad Dillinger about his continuing lack of luck in that department.

The good humor was interrupted by a line of cars on the road ahead. The bandits tensed and raised their weapons. It turned out to be a harmless funeral procession. Shortly afterward, a second cluster of cars gave them pause, but it was just a farm auction.

Sensing Patzke shivering, Pierpont gave her his topcoat. The vain Weyland then lapsed into the bizarre again, this time displaying a more human side. His dignity ruffled, he asked the rough-and-tumble gunmen if he could remove a silk handkerchief from his pocket and tie it around his head glad-rag style to keep his bald spot from being exposed by the buffeting wind. An understanding Pierpont simply handed him his own fedora.

An hour after exiting the city, the Buick turned onto Highway X, a secluded road between Routes 83 and 59 near Saylesville that functioned as a local lover's lane. Dillinger eased down Highway X for a mile, then turned into an overgrown trail and cut the engine. One of the bandits grabbed a gas can hidden in the bushes and filled the Buick's tank. Pierpont ordered the hostages out and marched them into the woods, stopping to allow Ursula to tie her shoe. She and Weyland were told to face each other on the opposite side of a large tree and join hands. "Time for ring-around-the-rosy," Pierpont teased, removing some shoelaces from his pocket. "You'll be a little late for supper."

"How long do you want us to wait? Ten minutes?" Weyland asked, anticipating easily breaking loose from the wrist ties.

"Better make it twenty," Pierpont responded, retrieving his coat from Patzke. That act stabbed her with fear. She figured they were goners. When Pierpont walked away, then briskly did a pirouette, she was certain they were about to be shot to death. The indignity of being killed tied to a stuffy banker was as paralyzing as her fear.

Pierpont reached for Weyland's head. "Sorry mister. I'll have to have my hat back." Patzke sighed in relief as Handsome Harry vanished for good.

The odd couple didn't attempt to free themselves until the allotted twenty minutes had passed. Weyland annoyingly counted down the minutes to the second based upon his wristwatch—which the bandits had failed to snatch. As the banker expected, they quickly freed themselves from the flimsy shoelaces, then headed toward the sound of agriculture machinery. Observing the well-dressed city slickers approaching, farmer William J. Klussendorf, cutting corn for his silo, figured they were "holy rollers" come to preach to him and/or solicit funds. As they drew nearer, he picked up on a series of oddities. "His right hand was tied to the woman's hand. They had no overcoats and they were shivering," Klussendorf noticed. Weyland outlined what happened and asked if Klussendorf could drive them back to Racine. The farmer, no doubt having stood in one long bank line too many, said he'd be happy to—as soon as he finished his work. He suggested they wait at the house and sample his wife's coffee and "special cake," which they did.

His job completed as the sun set around 6:30 P.M., Klussendorf kept his promise and drove the ex-hostages thirty-five miles back to Racine where a frenzied mob of newsmen were waiting. *The Chicago Tribune* promptly paid Ursula, the latest "lady in red," twenty-five dollars to pose for exclusive photographs.

Harold Graham, the man Makley shot in a panic, wasn't privy to a similar media bonanza. He was off being treated at the local hospital. "You don't feel the darn thing for the first few minutes. But I was sure feeling it by the time those ambulance boys came." Shot in the wrist and side, he would recover.

After the bandits left, the clerk Don Steel ran and bought a three-dollar pint of illegal whiskey, which he and his fellow coworkers quickly polished off. At closing time, they went out for more drinks and oysters before returning to their respective homes. Steel recalls being strangely calm that evening, thanks, no doubt, to the booze. "I didn't begin to feel the effects until two or three days after the holdup. Then I trembled so I could hardly stand up."

Chief Grover Lutter, taking a cue from his peers in the big city, was quick to use the incident to get the funding necessary to bolster his force with radio equipment.

As additional dust cleared, it was determined that Det. A. N. Devoursney, assigned to investigate bank robberies for the Wisconsin Banker's Association, had missed a chance to observe one in progress because he was in Winnipeg attending a canary show.

Forrest Huntington, a driven man with no such distracting hobbies, was, by sheer coincidence, in Wisconsin at the time. Traveling with ISP Detectives Verne Shields and Gene Ryan, the trio had come to Milwaukee to follow the money trail. They were attempting to discover where Pierpont was trying to unload the $56,000 in stolen bonds. They quickly hooked up with Racine County officials and went through the mug books, picking out Dillinger, Pierpont, Makley, and Joe Burns, who may or may not have been the fifth mystery man. Russell Clark was identified the next day.

Milwaukee detectives determined that the twelve-cylinder Buick Auburn was purchased from a "sub-dealer" for a whopping $1,965. The buyer, "John Stanton," bought it with $2,000 worth of Liberty Loan bonds, one for $1,000 and two for $500. The sub-dealer, Albert Cunningham, acquired the vehicle from Fleisher Buick Sales, which accepted the bonds as payment after checking their numbers with New York. Cunningham made a cool $363 for brokering the sale. He also pulled a last-minute substitution, switching a $1,000 Liberty Loan bond for a more valuable and easier-to-move $1,000 Treasury note the customer originally offered. Since the shady buyer was paying with stolen paper, he obviously didn't care about Cunningham's larcenous cut or financial shuffling.

Cunningham escaped scrutiny because his brother was the police commissioner of nearby Burlington. That's where an ex-con tavern owner had hooked him up with the bond-rich buyer. Spreading around mug shots, Huntington determined that "John Stanton" was the now-incarcerated Harry Copeland.

Huntington's targets had also made it to Milwaukee, splitting up their loot not far from where he was conferring with local law enforcement officials. The take came to $27,000. Each man took $5,000, and Dillinger put aside $2,000 in freshly printed, easy-to-trace ones to exchange for larger, older bills. A few days later, in Hamilton, Ohio, Leroy and Naomi Hooten, busy packing up to leave town, paid off a debt to a neighbor with twenty crisp one-dollar bills.

The Furious Five stayed on the move, returning to Chicago immediately after cutting up the money. They were in great spirits, razzing Handsome Harry for loaning his coat to the pretty clerk, and harassing his girlfriend Mary K because she didn't have the radio on to monitor their progress. She was too busy doing laundry. "They didn't say nothing about any shooting," she recalled, referring to the returning bandits.

Two days later, Dillinger appeared at the Logan Square Hudson-Essex Motors dealership at 2506 Milwaukee Avenue in Chicago. Perusing the lot, he plucked down $813.96 for, what else, a new Terraplane 8 sedan, black on black.

The following day, Chicago police arrested a Dillinger gang errand boy named Leslie Homer at Ohio and LaSalle streets. Homer was carrying a black satchel with a pistol, two clips, and $511 in brand-new one-dollar bills—$300 of which was designated for Hubert Dillinger in Indianapolis. Grilled, Homer initially gave up little information of any use. He told the cops that the gunmen were long gone, and professed to be an uninformed fringe player. Little by little, he began to open up, eventually transforming into a fountain of news. Handsome Harry, he squealed, had dyed his blond hair brown, frequently wore glasses to mask his bright-blue eyes, and preferred gray suits and hats. Top moll Mary Kinder had similarly dyed her flaming red hair to a more muted black. Homer gleefully noted that they were a kinky Mutt-and-Jeff couple, with Mary standing under five feet, while Harry towered over six.

Homer gave similar updated descriptions covering the rest of the crew, specifying who had gained weight, who had lost weight, what color hair each sported at the moment, and so on. Dillinger, Homer noted, was pretty much the same as his pictures, with the prominent cleft in his chin a sure way to identify him. He described Billie as "almost Jewish in appearance" and noted her "coarse" facial skin. Bernice "Opal" Clark had red hair and was "homely," while sister Pat, the stacked cabaret dancer, had dyed her red hair black.

The gang, Homer went on, used secret rings and knocks to allow entry into their various apartments. Racine officers attempted to paint Homer as the mysterious fifth man, but witnesses failed to clearly identify him. He denied it, then later confessed. Officials didn't know what to believe, but eventually stuck him with the Racine job. Most suspected he copped to the crime in order to be sent to prison in Wisconsin, far away from The Furious Five he'd just ratted out.

Before heading northwest to serve his time, Homer said the gang was looking to clip the rat Art McGinnis, and were probably after him as well.

Aware that their underlings were starting to drop like flies, and would be angling to cut deals, Dillinger and Pierpont decided to take separate vacations. Johnnie and Billie went to Hot Springs, Arkansas, for Thanksgiving. Handsome Harry and Mary chose Houston, Texas.

It was a relaxing, if temporary, respite from their dangerous lives.

Chapter 10

On December 5, 1933, the failed attempt to make the United States a dry nation mercifully came to an end. The taps had been flowing all along, with speakeasies thriving, and bootleggers making fortunes. John Dillinger and crew were never into that aspect of organized crime, preferring to go directly to the cash source. Those who were, however, found themselves out of work. With the unemployment ranks sky-high for both legitimate and illegitimate activities, fears that The Terror Gang was planning a militarylike recruitment assault against a prison began to fade. It was a buyer's market for manpower.

That was good news for Dillinger and Pierpont because attrition continued to eat away at the ol' gang of theirs, whittling down their nicknames from The Terrible Ten to The Notorious Nine to The Savage Seven to The Furious Five with each new killing or arrest. If that wasn't disturbing enough, those who remained found themselves in increasingly hotter and deeper water.

On December 14, John Hamilton joined the intensely hunted ranks of cop killers after Chicago police tracked him through his green, Auburn cabriolet convertible. Acting on a tip, the police staked out a body shop where he'd dropped off the sporty vehicle for a five-dollar fender repair. When Hamilton and his plump girlfriend, Elaine Dekant Dent, thirty-two, arrived at Tower Auto Rebuilders, 5320 Broadway, to retrieve the car, they were set upon by a decorated but impatient officer. Sgt. William T. Shanley was briefly operating alone in the body shop's office due to a badly orchestrated shift change. A struggle ensued, and

Hamilton shot Shanley in the chest. Hamilton and Dent immediately took off on foot. Frightened out of all sense of chivalry, the desperate con quickly abandoned his slow-footed lover because she was dragging him down. Sure enough, the bewildered Dent was quickly scooped up by responding officers. The swifter Hamilton escaped through the maze of city streets. Fifteen minutes later, Sergeant Shanley, forty-three, died at Edgewater Hospital.

The incident fueled extra large, screaming headlines because Sergeant Shanley was a hero who had received a highly publicized award from *The Chicago Tribune*. He was glorified for entering a dark store and single-handedly apprehending a pair of safecrackers. It's likely that Sergeant Shanley was thinking of similar accolades when he acted alone in trying to arrest the armed and dangerous fugitive. Regardless, the death of the popular, devout father of four, who ushered every Sunday at St. Gertrude's Church, enraged Chicago's heavily Catholic community.

"His eyes moved when I took his hand," Mrs. Shanley sobbed to reporters. "I was planning a happy Christmas. I was going to go shopping for presents today. But there will be no joy with Bill gone."

As was the case in those days, the death not only came as a staggering emotional blow for the family, it stripped them of their breadwinner and tossed them into instant poverty. A small insurance policy from the Policemen's Benevolent Association barely got them into the new year.

The enraged police initially thought the killer was Pierpont. However, when Dent mentioned that the assailant only had three fingers on one of his hands, they turned their attention to Hamilton. Dent, who never knew her boyfriend's real name, thought he was a wealthy heir fallen from the clouds who was going to lift her out of her bleak, waitress existence. "Once, he showed me seventy thousand dollars in thousand-dollar notes," she lamented. ". . . My folks thought he was a great catch and encouraged me to marry him. He was awfully nice. He used to take two baths a day and never used curse words!"

Twenty-four hours later, after being arraigned as an accessory to murder, Dent changed her tune. "If I ever get out and he tries to get in touch with me, I'll put the button on him," she spat in her best 1930s moll talk. "I'm accustomed to meeting gentlemen . . ." Prosecutors determined that Dent was too dim to know the difference, and eventually ordered her release.

The Chicago police, a commanding, six-thousand-member department, once again spoke openly about executing Dillinger and his gang on sight. "We hope, although their trails are cold, to be able to drive them out of town—or bury them. We'd prefer the latter," announced Capt. John Stege, using language that wouldn't be tolerated today. To back up his threat, he organized a handpicked squad of marksmen, put them on the critical night shift, and assigned the deadly crew to Sgt. Frank Reynolds, an accomplished assassin who had already killed twelve crooks at that point in his career.

Dillinger, back in Chi-town from his Hot Springs vacation, sensed the heat coming. He quickly launched into nomad mode, vacating two housing complexes on Humboldt Avenue—the Aldort Apartments at 1742, and the Humboldt Apartments at 1850—just days before massive police armies raided the places. The cops learned about the locations through the ongoing tap on Happy Meyer's telephone. The crucial information well was capped on December 18 when scoop-crazed Chicago and Milwaukee newspapers got wind of the bug and ran with the story—an editorial decision that infuriated the police.

Briefed in Washington, J. Edgar Hoover jumped in and named Dillinger "The Number One Criminal At Large" a precursor to the FBI's famous "Ten Most Wanted List." Chicago dusted off their Al Capone dictionaries and followed Indiana in naming Dillinger "Public Enemy Number One."

Oddly enough, his status was all due to guilt by association. Dillinger, who had yet to kill anyone, was in no way responsible for Hamilton's behavior. Regardless, it was his picture on the front of the nation's newspapers the following day, and his name on the tongues of Hoover and the Illinois police.

On December 19, ISP troopers cornered Ed Shouse and two attractive female companions in front of the France Hotel in Paris, Illinois. Shouse, still driving Russell Clark's Terraplane, was hemmed in by officers who blocked his escape. The police opened fire after the felon tried to bolt from the car and flee on foot. In the confusing crossfire, Lt. Chester Butler accidentally blasted rookie Trooper Eugene Teague, twenty-four, in the head with a .32 caliber, double-ought buckshot slug, instantly killing the six-foot, four-inch cop. Shouse and the ladies, all unhurt, were pinned down and captured, but Lieutenant Butler was shaken to the bone, so much so he required medical treatment. Cleared of any wrongdoing and nameless in the official medical examiner's report, Butler nonetheless took full responsibility. "Regardless of what anybody says, I'm the man," he confessed to reporters. "My God! He was my friend and I killed him." Unable to shake what happened, Lieutenant Butler resigned from the force.

Captain Leach, of course, blamed John Dillinger. "It will cost the lives of more officers before we get them. I may be the next to pay, just like poor Eugene Teague . . . It was an unfortunate, unavoidable occurrence."

One of the women in the car, Frances Colin, twenty-eight, wasn't so accepting. "They ought to hang that copper for killing another policeman," she said. "But he's a copper, that makes a difference."

The second woman, a stunning redheaded California "model" named Ruth Stewart, eagerly posed for newsmen, offering to do so in a bathing suit if they desired. Regarding Shouse, she feigned a pout, puffed on her cigarette and announced that she was "crazy about him" and that they planned to marry. Turned out she was a prostitute he'd met three weeks before in San Diego. Colin was a woman of unstated background that they picked up "enroute to Chicago" for "company." Both ladies were held through Christmas, then released.

Interrogated in Indianapolis, Shouse, twenty-eight, would only say that he'd broken with the Dillinger gang and no longer knew anything about them. He was shipped to Michigan City to serve out his original, twenty-five-year auto banditry term. He was not charged with complicity in the death of Trooper Teague because such laws weren't in place yet.

Shouse opened up at the dismal state pen, telling Chicago police and Mrs. Machine Gun Kelly's "G-Men" much of the same things Leslie Homer had already ratted. A new nuance he revealed was that whenever there was a knock on a hideout door, even if it was the proper code, The Savage Seven would grab their guns and go to designated defensive stations. He also said the men sometimes slept in their stolen bulletproof vests, and talked incessantly about killing cops. "They're all kill-crazy. That's why I left them," Shouse claimed.

The dapper ladies' man failed to mention that he'd actually run off because Dillinger's hot-bod moll, Billie Frechette, was sex crazy and he found her irresistible despite the tremendous danger such a forbidden liaison presented. Instead of spreading that self-destructive news, he spoke of a lavish hideout on the thirtieth-floor of a building at 188 West Randolph Street that housed the private Steuben Club. He also revealed that the $56,000 in stolen bonds had finally been unloaded at .435 cents on the dollar with the help of a middleman named Jim Murray.

His tongue further loosening, Shouse let on that the planned robbery of a Muncie, Indiana, bank a few months earlier fell through when driver Harry Copeland missed a turn and had to circle back. By the time they reached the place, it had closed. Pierpont wanted to shoot Copeland on the spot, but Dillinger dissuaded him.

Lamenting his own fate, Shouse said, "I wish the cops had put a bullet right in the middle of my forehead. The others, too, would rather die than be returned to Michigan City. You might as well be dead as be there!"

On December 21, a Chicago police goon squad headed by Captain Stege and Sergeant Reynolds took Ed Shouse's words to heart. They burst in on three Jewish felons holed up at 1428 Farwell Avenue and shot them all dead. No officers were injured, and it was questionable whether the robbers and suspected cop killers, falsely rumored to be part of Dillinger's gang, even had time to reach for their weapons—if they had any. Armed or not, Louis Katzewitz, Charles Tattlebaum, and Sam Ginsberg were all spared Shouse's gloomy fate, and Sergeant Reynolds added three more notches to the butt of his .38 Special.

District Attorney Tom Courtney, far from investigating the bloody incident, told reporters that the shooting proved that the Chicago police "do not lack courage and bravery."

Captain Stege, in a newspaper interview that naturally focused on

Dillinger, chillingly predicted that when the famous outlaw was finally taken, it would be through his "women friends."

On December 23, Stege and company staked out an apartment at 420 Surf Street and arrested a resident named "Bob Price," who owned a car on their suspect list. Price turned out to be Hilton Crouch, a Dillinger associate who participated in the Massachusetts Avenue bank job in Indianapolis the previous September but had since fallen out of touch. Crouch, aware of Captain Stege's murderous reputation, thanked his lucky stars that his alias confused the Stege death squad long enough to prevent his instant execution. Crouch, hit with a fresh twenty-year sentence, joined Copeland and Shouse at Michigan City.

Captain Stege and company were picking off the weak links and fringe players, but they still weren't burying the high-ranking Furious Five members they craved. The gang was smartly on the road again, this time heading toward the uncharted territory of the southeast.

At 3 A.M. on December 14, a caravan of three gleaming new cars filled with Public Enemies and their sexy molls pulled out of Chicago. Johnnie, Billie, and the red-hot, three-fingered John Hamilton were in the new Terraplane sports coupe, squeezed together in the front seat. Harry, Mary, and Makley were behind them in Harry's more spacious Studebaker. Russell Clark was at the wheel of a Ford V8 Deluxe four-door he'd bought the day before. His wife, Bernice, and sister-in-law, Pat Cherrington, were with him. Leaving the city via Michigan Avenue and Lake Shore Drive, they hit Indiana 41 and split up as planned, intending to rendezvous in Tennessee three days later. The leisurely pace was designed to enable Dillinger to visit his half-brother Hubert in Indianapolis, his sister Audrey in Maywood, and various other relatives. At each stop, he played a combination of Robin Hood and Santa, joyfully dropping off a host of Christmas presents without being spotted by cops or G-Men. He then detoured to Kentucky to visit the Whitehouse brothers in Lebanon before rolling into Tennessee.

Clark and his wife had a much rougher time. Approaching the Kentucky-Indiana border, their new Ford skidded on the rain- and snow-slicked road and broad-sided a truck. Bernice was knocked unconscious, a deep gash rutting her forehead. Clark and Pat were uninjured. When Bernice came to, she was being loaded into an ambulance. She regained her senses enough to fret over the gun-packed suitcases, and the $4,000 stuffed in her shoes. Staying cool, Clark, posing as a tourist complete with a slouch-hat and pipe, accompanied the police back to Evansville. There, he piled his cash and machine-gun-laden suitcases in the police station's lobby. Accepting all responsibility for the accident, he paid the trucker up front to settle the damages, and was subsequently viewed as an all-around great guy. It was an Academy Award–worthy performance, considering that in 1926, Clark had been busted in Evansville for a holdup, and was hunted down by many of the same cops buzzing around the station at that moment.

Clark took a cab to the hospital and discovered that his feisty wife and sister-in-law had successfully fought off all attempts to remove Bernice's shoes while being treated. Taking one for the gang, Bernice also refused ether and endured the pain of having her head stitched up sans painkillers for fear of jabbering under the effect of the drug. Clark pressed to have her released, and the trio spent the night at a local hotel. The next morning, they chartered a private plane to Nashville.

In the future Music City, the gang turned into the Keystone Robbers, harkening back to Dillinger's early days as a hapless gangster wannabe. The plan was to reunite at the Grand Hotel. Trouble was, the Grand Hotel was in Chattanooga, not Nashville. Bernice, her stitched head still smarting, phoned every lodging establishment in the county until "Frank Sullivan," Dillinger's road-trip alias, turned up on a registration. She finally struck pay dirt at the Hermitage Hotel. The others, she learned, were also in the city.

Hamilton, possibly suffering from stress, had a mental meltdown that nearly proved costly. After registering in the Hermitage that morning, he went for a walk. He didn't return until nine that evening. He'd forgotten both his room number and the alias he used to register. He had spent the day trying to remember, at one point standing outside staring at the rows of windows, desperate to spot one of the gang. Giving up, he finally checked in again, this time using a different alias. Throwing caution to the wind, he described Dillinger to a bellboy, who helped him find his "friends."

In the midst of all the hand wringing, he managed to visit the Hippodrome Motor Company and purchase a new Ford V8, paying the happy salesman with a stack of hot fifties.

Harry and Mary weren't exactly laying low, either. They waltzed across the street where Harry made up for all the aggravation of the frequent moves by buying his pint-sized moll a $500 diamond ring along with an $85 gold wedding band. The delighted jeweler sized the rings extra small and delivered them the next day.

John and Billie, now traveling alone, left Nashville early on Sunday, December 17, and made it to Jacksonville, Florida, where they burned up the sheets of another hotel. They completed their long journey the following day with an easy, ninety-mile hop to Daytona Beach. There, they rented a colossal, three-story, seventeen-room, oceanfront mansion at 901 South Atlantic Avenue for a thrifty $100 a month. "Frank Kirtley" told realtor J. M. Green that they would probably stay three or four months—typical of wealthy midwestern snowbirds—and were expecting to be joined by friends.

A fly in the luxury beach house ointment was Edwin Utter and his wife, a couple who had previously rented an apartment over the mansion's detached garage. Edwin Utter made the new arrivals—four couples—as Chicago gangsters right from the get go. However, since they were quiet enough and didn't have a lot of visitors, he and his missus kept it to themselves, good neighbors being hard to find and all.

Although the "three to four months" was actually only two weeks, the gang's girls—Billie, Mary, Bernice, and Pat—agreed that it was the best time of their lives. They swam, sunbathed, and rode horses along the white sand beach during the day, then played cards, shot craps, and attended movies at night. Charles Makley felt comfortable enough there to start dating a local girl. John Hamilton, using the name Art Morton, licensed his new Ford in Florida.

Dillinger bought clothes and spent his days monitoring radio and news reports, chuckling over the latest robberies he was being accused of back in Indiana and Illinois.

Unfortunately for the blissful vacationers, snitches back home tipped the police that the gang had either gone to Texas or Florida.

Captain Leach sent photographs, fingerprints, and other information to the Miami, Miami Beach, and Dade County police departments, warning them that these were very dangerous men, heavily armed who "will not be taken alive." Once again, Captain Leach was inches away from greatness, overshooting his guess by 260 miles.

That Christmas, the guys showered their molls with expensive baubles. Harry gave Mary a diamond watch to add to her growing collection. Billie was given a Boston Bull puppy, an unusual choice for a band on the run, along with the more understandable array of sexy silk underwear—a gift John's friends playfully teased was more for himself than his doll. Stung by the accusation, he slipped Billie $1,000 to make up for it.

The cuddly behavior and generous presents conflict with accounts from previous books and stories that describe John and Billie as having a violent fight on Christmas eve regarding her flirtation with Ed Shouse. Dillinger was said to have blackened her eyes and shipped her back to the reservation in Wisconsin. None of the girls, who were destined to sell their stories for extensive newspaper reports, confirmed that tale. What is known is that on December 26, Dillinger, aka Frank "Kirtley," visited a notary public named D. R. Beach and signed the Terraplane over to Billie "free of all encumbrances." Interestingly, Dillinger used his alias—which Beach misspelled—but listed his "sister" as "Evelyn Frechette of Neopit, Wisconsin" to assure that the deal would be legally legit.

On the same day, the banner headline of the *Daytona Beach News Journal* screamed "Police Warn Against Kill Crazy Gangsters." The Associated Press story was taken from the alarmist ramblings of Ed Shouse, and didn't specify where the deadly crew was hiding out.

Pierpont, never one to save news clippings, was more interested in a story about the new 1934 cars that were coming out the next day. Excited about models with "knee-action" suspension, he phoned the Carter-Sawyer Buick dealership in Jacksonville and wired $1,600 for the first one they received. He gave his name as "J. C. Evans," using the surname of one of the most hated guards at Michigan City. The next day, he sent Mary K to Jacksonville to fetch the vehicle.

The gang was subsequently shocked to discover that the dealership made a big deal over the arrival and sale of their initial 1934, alerting the local paper. *The Jacksonville Times Union* sent a photographer to snap the vehicle, and popped a second shot of sales manager O. B. Gannway accepting the $1,600 from a Western Union representative. The story said the vehicle had been purchased by Mr. J. C. Evans of Indiana, who was vacationing in St. Augustine, Florida. Although the spread gave them all a start, nothing came of it. Captain Leach apparently didn't subscribe to *The Jacksonville Times Union.*

Surviving that scare, Dillinger and Pierpont drove to Tampa to check out an estate advertised for $15,000. Liking what they saw and ready to close the deal, they had to back off when the owner asked too many questions, including a request for references.

As the new year approached, the gang decided to hit the movies, only to find that all their choices—*Charlie Chan's Greatest Case* with Warner Oland, *White Woman* with Charles Laughton and Carole Lombard, and *I'm No Angel* with Mae West, Cary Grant, and Edward Arnold—were sold out. Reluctantly returning to their mansion, they broke out the drinks and watched a pre–New Year's Eve fireworks display over the ocean. Not a regular drinker, Dillinger became overly tipsy and decided to add his own contribution to the ceremonies. He took a Thompson from a locked closet, walked out on the beach, and fired a full drum over the Atlantic, flames blazing from the searing barrel.

Three curious young boys, the Warnock brothers, lived next door. They heard the unusual sound and rushed outside to see what was causing it. They spotted Dillinger with his trusty Thompson, a fearsome sight that caused them to scurry back into their home.

Coming to his senses the next morning, Dillinger decided that his reckless act spelled the end of their splendid Florida vacation. They packed, split up, and waved good-bye to Daytona. Billie tossed the puppy, the underwear, and the $1,000 into the Terraplane and headed for Wisconsin to visit her mother. Afterward, she'd reunite with John and the gang in a location to be determined.

Footloose and fancy-free, Billie flipped the speedy vehicle on an icy road near Port Washington, Wisconsin, but didn't injure herself or the puppy. She was arrested, probably for driving under the influence, fined a dollar, and released. She phoned a friend in Neopit named Vivian Warrington, and Ms. Warrington drove down to pick her up.

Sisters Bernice Clark and Pat Cherrington picked up Clark's repaired Ford in Evansville and headed for Detroit. Pat, afraid she'd be identified as Harry Copeland's moll, wore a blonde wig. Clark and Makley drove off together, probably in Pierpont's Studebaker, and headed west.

According to Mary K, she and Harry decided to go further south, touring West Palm Beach, Miami, and the Florida Keys. Interrogated by investigators and newspapermen months later, she claimed Dillinger and Billie went with them. That was apparently part of an elaborate ruse to cloak their whereabouts and distance themselves from a Chicago-area bank robbery in which a police officer was slain. In truth, Billie was long gone, and Dillinger and Hamilton had headed north in Hamilton's new car, stopping off at the Palace Cafe in South Bend, Indiana, for a brief meeting with Pearl Elliott, now going by Pearl Applegate. (Despite the heat on her, she couldn't part with her cherished first name.) Pearl told friends and investigators afterward that she was terrified of Dillinger because the South Bend police had recently squeezed her and she spilled "all she knew about the gang." More likely, that was just another in a long line of Pearl stories designed to get the cops off of her well-cushioned back.

Mary Kinder's South Florida excursion might have been a phony cover as well. Numerous witnesses placed the couple in Indianapolis on January 3, and then at the farm of Mr. and Mrs. Bert Orcutt between Gaston and Muncie a few days later. Mrs. Orcutt was Harry's aunt on his father's side.

On New Year's Day, 1934, John stopped long enough wherever he was to pen a letter to niece Mary:

```
    . . . I see in the papers where I'm robbing cabarets
and most anything that comes along but you know
that's a lie don't you honey? When I steal anything
it isn't going to be a few hundred dollars. They
```

```
blame me for most everything now a days but it
doesn't make any difference for its all free now
. . . Tell Bud (Hubert) I found out he lied to me
about not getting that three hundred dollars, and
for lying to me he won't get a new car. I was going
to buy him a new Ford V8. I guess I will buy Emmett
and Sis one soon for they need one.
                        Love to all. Johnnie
```

Dillinger's "it's all free now" phrase referred to the fact that he was charged with, or accused of, so many crimes that adding new ones didn't matter anymore. The $300 given to Hubert wasn't the stack of mint fresh ones that got intercepted with Leslie Homer's arrest, but another $300 John had previously sent to put a down payment on a car. For unknown reasons, possibly because of law enforcement scrutiny, Hubert was denying that he received it.

Makley and Clark made it all the way to Tucson, Arizona, without incident, registering at the Heidel Hotel in early January under assumed names. Makley was now the oddly spelled J. C. Daviess, and Clark picked the alliterate L. L. Long. They stayed a few days, then backtracked east to Texas. Obviously in a West Coast frame of mind, Makley sent a telegram to "Frank Kirtley, 901 Pacific Street, Daytona Beach, Florida." Despite scribbling in the wrong ocean, the telegram was delivered. Both Dillinger and Pierpont, however, were long gone. The telegram said simply "Look for me sometime Monday. J. C."

On January 6, Capt. Dan Gilbert of the Illinois state attorney's office received a tip regarding the whereabouts of Walter Dietrich, one of the Terrible Ten escapees. Gilbert dispatched two squads of officers to 619 South 24 Avenue in Bellwood, a suburb in west Chicago. Dietrich was lathered up and shaving when the cops exploded inside, grabbing him without resistance. Dietrich, subsequently returned to Michigan City, marked the fourth of the ten to be recaptured.

On a hunch, Captain Gilbert kept the house under watch. Three hours after they snagged Gilbert, another man pulled up. When officers ordered him to surrender, he went for a gun and was shot dead with a

Thompson. The corpse turned out to be "Handsome Jack" Klutas, the leader of a gang of thugs known as the "College Kidnappers." Klutas had no connection to Dillinger.

Billie stayed on the reservation in Neopit until January 7. Hitching a ride with her friend Vivian, they went back to Port Washington to pick up the wrecked but drivable Terraplane, then caravanned to Milwaukee and checked into the Hotel Jackson. Billie traded the wrecked Terraplane 8 for a used 1932 Essex Terraplane 6 coupe, giving the Braemar Sales Corporation $220. The dealer knocked $175 off the $395 sticker as consideration for the trade-in. Their dealing done, the reservation girls left Milwaukee on the 11th.

The long-hauling Makley and Clark were back in Florida by January 10, taking in the "All American Air Races" in Miami. One of the youthful aviators they watched was a budding entrepreneur named Howard Hughes. Pierpont and Mary were with them, motoring down from Indiana instead of going straight from Daytona Beach as Mary later claimed.

While Billie was trading cars and the others were watching airplanes, Billie's beau was being hung with another crime, this one the January 9 kidnapping of a farmer's wife in Hannibal, Missouri, that resulted in a running gun battle with the police. The unharmed victim, Mrs. Roy Carpenter, identified John Dillinger as one of her abductors. On January 17, four men robbed the bank at Nauvoo, Illinois, sixty miles north of Hannibal. Fingers were again pointed at Dillinger. Five days later, the four were arrested by Chicago death squad Capt. John Stege. One of the men, Lloyd Lohraine, thirty-five, was described as a "dead-ringer" for Dillinger. Lloyd was no doubt the man who nabbed Mrs. Carpenter. The Dillinger spottings prompted *The Chicago Tribune* to unleash a biting satire:

```
Mr. Dillinger was seen yesterday looking over
the new spring gloves in a State Street store
in Chicago; Negotiating for a twelve-cylinder car
in Springfield, Illinois; Buying a half-dozen
sassy cravats in Omaha, Nebraska; Bargaining for
```

```
a     suburban   bungalow   at    his   home   town   of
Mooresville,  Indiana  .  .  .  Drinking  a  glass  of
soda  water  in  a  drug  store  in  Charlestown,  South
Carolina;  and  strolling  down  Broadway  swinging  a
Malacca  cane  in  New  York.  He  also  bought  a  fishing
rod  in  a  sporting  goods  store  in  Montreal,  and
gave  a  dinner  in  a  hotel  in  Yucatan,  Mexico.  But
anyhow,  Mr.  Dillinger  seems  to  have  kept  very
carefully  out  of  London,  Berlin,  Rome,  Moscow  and
Vienna.  Or  at  least  if  he  did  go  to  these  places
yesterday,  he  was  traveling  incog!
```

The Illinois and Indiana police were not amused.

It wasn't happy days for Art McGinnis, either. His cover blown by inept police before he could reap the expected financial bonanza, he no longer had any value and was being callously abandoned by both the Illinois and Indiana law enforcement communities. The one-time vital mole inside The Terror Gang was now being cast off as "a nuisance" and a "waste of time and money." To complicate matters, he had a Savage Seven bounty on his head to boot. Such is the woeful life of a snitch.

As McGinnis had tried to warn them, Dillinger soon resurfaced in both Illinois and Indiana. Inexplicably, on January 15, Dillinger and Hamilton returned to the exact thirty-square mile area on the planet where they were the most wanted. The pair, and a third man, were going to add insult to men-in-blue injury and take down the First National Bank of East Chicago at Chicago Avenue and Indianapolis Boulevard—a mere twenty-five miles from the heart of the Windy City. (Despite the blur of confusing names, East Chicago is located just over the border in Indiana. It's not a suburb of its more famous Illinois namesake.)

The targeted bank was across the street from Alice's Delicatessen, 719 West Chicago Avenue. The eatery was run by the sister of Freddie Brenman, a Shirt Shop Boy and Lake County, Indiana, underworld figure. Investigators believed that Brenman suggested the hit and cased the place for the two Johns.

At 3:45 P.M. that Monday, Dillinger and Hamilton stepped out of a new Ford V8 Tudor sedan with Ohio license plates and walked briskly toward the bank. The wheelman, never identified, waited behind, double-parked on the wrong side of the street facing east. If that wasn't obvious enough, the vehicle was also blocking the South Shore commuter tracks.

Dillinger was carrying an oblong, black leather valise as he and Hamilton maneuvered through two sets of double doors before reaching the lobby. In full view, Dillinger put the valise on the floor, unsnapped its duel catchers, and lifted out a stockless Thompson. Then, as mortified customers watched, he calmly inserted a fifty-round drum and walked to the desk of cashier James A. Dalton. "This is a stickup! Everybody put your hands up."

There were twenty-plus regulars in the big city bank. Hamilton shooed the women and children from the open lobby area to a safer corner. Dillinger suggested that a lady pushing a baby carriage station herself behind a teller's cage. The male hostages were lined against a wall, a massacre position that no doubt terrified them. Dillinger, Thompson in hand, stood watch while Hamilton worked the drawers with his eight fingers.

First National Vice President Walter Spencer was at his desk talking on the phone when the deal went down. On the other end was Joseph Walkowiak, an official at Union National Bank in adjacent Indiana Harbor. "We're held up, Joe!" Spencer whispered. As he placed the receiver down, Spencer slid his foot over the silent alarm button that was wired directly into the East Chicago police headquarters, a block and a half away.

As usual, the police reacted with annoyance over the faulty "crying wolf" technology. "There goes that damned alarm again," someone cursed. "Guess we'd best walk down and check it out." Det. Sgt. William Patrick O'Malley buttoned up his coat and motioned for the patrolmen Hobart Wilgus, Julius Schrenko, and Pete Walen to go with him on what they were certain would be nothing more than a frigid afternoon stroll.

Approaching the bank, their initial impression was reinforced by the tranquility of the scene. No crowd or commotion, no blaring alarms.

Business as usual. Dropping their guard, they entered the bank in single file. The lead officer, the uniformed Wilgus, walked through the second set of doors and found himself staring down the barrel of John Dillinger's machine gun. Wilgus froze, his eyes like saucers. Sergeant O'Malley peered around him, saw what was happening, shut the doors on his underling, and pulled backward, piling up the forward moving Schrenko and Walen. Recovering, they spun around and dashed back into the cold.

Officer Schrenko ran into a nearby Walgreen's drug store to phone for backup. Sergeant O'Malley pulled his .38 and stationed himself against the limestone facade between the bank and Newberry's Five and Ten Cent Store. He pulled back the hammer of his weapon and waited. Patrolman Whelan drew a bead on the bank's side door. Schrenko ran over from Walgreen's just as a squad car pulled up carrying Capt. Tim O'Neill, Capt. Ed Knight, and Officers Nick Ranich and Lloyd Mulvahill. Parking the cruiser around the corner on Forsythe Avenue, the cops spread out and took cover, ducking below the high curb and crouching behind parked cars.

Not a single officer thought to check for the getaway car—sitting big as life across the street facing the wrong way.

Inside, Dillinger took Wilgus's service revolver, snapped open the cylinder, and dumped out the six cartridges, causing them to ping and dance on the floor. He notified Hamilton that the "heat" was outside, but ordered his accomplice to take his time and make sure he scooped up all the money. Hamilton nodded and went about his business, emerging a few long minutes later with a sack stuffed with more than $20,000.

Dillinger ordered Wilgus and Spencer to walk in front of them toward the foyer. Spencer, noting the icy weather, asked if he could get his coat. "You're not going that far," Dillinger assured. Abandoning the expensive leather gun case, the gangsters marched their human shields into the cold January wind just as the clock struck four.

Spotting the hostages, the cops outside held their fire. Neither robber saw Sergeant O'Malley flattened against the stone face of the building ten feet to Dillinger's left, his .38 aimed directly at the notorious bandit.

Instead of ordering Dillinger to halt, Sergeant O'Malley addressed his officer. "Wilgus!" The patrolman darted to the side, leaving O'Malley with a clear shot. Without hesitation, the veteran detective fired, sending four slugs directly into John Dillinger's chest in bursts of two. Startled, Dillinger staggered back, dust flying from his protected torso. Like a horror movie monster, Dillinger regained his balance, swung his finned barrel, screamed, "You asked for it," and squeezed the trigger. In an instant, eight slugs hammered into O'Malley's body, one slicing through his heart. The heroic Irish sergeant went limp, crumbling to the pavement in a puddle of blood.

John Dillinger had now joined his friends Harry Pierpont, Charles Makley, and John "Red" Hamilton as a fellow cop killer.

Despite the shock of what he had just witnessed, Officer Wilgus got his legs back and took off. Not thinking, Hamilton started after him, emerging from the protection of the one remaining hostage. He took a few steps, heard some distant gunfire, dropped his pistol, and fell wounded to one knee. He had been hit so many times from an assortment of single-shot weapons that seven slugs penetrated his body in areas not protected by his bulletproof vest.

Like a Hollywood stuntman, Dillinger ran over, grabbed Hamilton under the shoulder with his left arm while simultaneously firing short bursts from his Thompson with the right. He half-dragged his wounded companion across Chicago Avenue toward the getaway car. Miraculously managing to keep the police force pinned down, the crook-who-wouldn't-die made it to the vehicle, shoved Hamilton into the front seat, and jumped down into the rear. The mystery driver popped the clutch and the Ford took off squealing. The unlatched passenger door bounced open and nearly sheered off as it hit a parked car—an unwelcomed replay of a prior getaway.

A pair of Indiana game wardens, just passing by, heard the shots, spotted the Ford, and gave chase, firing at the felons as they fled east to Olcott, veered to 150th Street, then swung back west. Certain they'd hit the vehicle, the poacher hunters nonetheless lost them on Hammond.

Outside the bank, Sergeant O'Malley remained prone on the pavement, covered in glass from the shattered dime-store window above him. Women's purses were scattered around, a mystery quickly solved by inspecting the store's display. Dillinger's errant shots had knocked over a row of purses like ducks at a country fair. O'Malley, forty-three, married with three daughters, died on the street. His body was carried directly to Fife Mortuary, a few doors down from the bank.

Acting fast to shore up already low public confidence, the bank announced that by 8 P.M. that evening, their losses had been covered by the Fidelity and Deposit Company of Maryland, and the bank would be open for business as usual the following day.

It was business as usual for the Terrible Two as well. From the escape route they selected, the East Chicago cops guessed that they were heading to Chicago—from the frying pan to the fire.

Wanted: Dead or Dead —The End of a Wild Era

Chapter 11

Clad in a steel vest stolen from a distant police department, John Dillinger had weathered the storm of .38 slugs and returned fire with a fifty-shot, .45-caliber machine gun on a police sergeant wearing little more than a cloth coat and armed with a five-shooter. It was one of the most vivid examples yet of how the deck was stacked in favor of the outlaws.

Although Dillinger benefited from the decided advantage, he wasn't happy about the outcome. The more he learned about O'Malley's grieving wife and daughters, the deeper in denial he plunged. Quick to hide behind the ready excuse that the police were blaming him for everything, he steadfastly insisted to his family that he was not part of that deadly job. He'd later admit to his attorney that O'Malley "had it coming. He stepped right out and started throwing slugs at me. What else could I do?"

Plenty, according to the O'Malley girls. They would grow up bitter that Dillinger's name lived on in infamy, while their hardworking, salt-of-the-earth father was instantly forgotten. Even in accounts of the robbery back then, he was often referred to as "a policeman."

Further embittering the family and community were the rumors that again swirled regarding the possible sordid nature of the tragic event. Word quickly filtered down to the financially battered public that the East Chicago robbery had been another "made-to-order" production arranged by sleazy bankers to cover their embezzlement. As always, the accusations were never proven.

Anger over O'Malley's death ignited new talk about John Dillinger being wanted "Dead or Dead." The *Gary Post-Tribune* captured the mood in a story published the week of the shooting:

> As they spread their dragnet for the Hoosier youth who has shot his way into the position of being America's most feared bandit, police moved but with a single thought—that gunfire would attend Dillinger's capture and that he would never be taken alive.

Dillinger was busy living that precise life-and-death scenario as the reporters were still formulating such concepts in their heads for the next day's paper. Foolishly escaping to the familiar comfort of Chicago, he was standing in Pat Cherrington's hotel room a half hour after blasting his way out of East Chicago. Hamilton remained downstairs in the getaway car, sprawled on the backseat bleeding from multiple bullet wounds. Pat hustled to the rescue and played nurse, attempting to comfort Hamilton as best she could while Dillinger frantically searched until nearly midnight for an underworld doctor he could trust. They were finally directed to Dr. Joseph P. Moran, thirty-nine, whose office was on Irving Park Boulevard. Still clinging to the last threads of his respect, the alcoholic MD had stooped to specializing in illegal abortions and gunshot wounds—the last retreats of a troubled doctor on the way down.

Convicted of performing a botched abortion on a LaSalle, Illinois, girl who subsequently died, he was sentenced to ten years in prison. Too valuable to society to serve more than two, he was released and began practicing again. Another unpleasant abortion experience in Depue, Illinois, resulted in a parole violation and eleven more months inside. During both jail tours, he befriended high-level criminals who suspected they might one day need his services. Among those were members of the Barker Gang, to which Moran had become essentially the house doctor.

Doctor Moran determined that Hamilton had taken six shots in his shoulders and left arm, and one just above his pelvic bone. Frowning, he callously told John and Pat that their friend had lost so much blood it was doubtful he would make it. Dillinger told him to dig in anyway. Doctor Moran removed the slugs, dressed the wounds, then hit Public Enemy Number One with a whopping $5,000 bill—equivalent to $67,000 today. The doc had made himself a full partner in the robbery.

The mummified Hamilton was carted back into the dinged-up getaway car and taken to the apartment of Hazel Doyle in the always-popular Lincoln Park Arms Hotel. Doyle, a hostess at the 225 Club, was the wife of Earl Doyle, a Baby Face Nelson associate doing time for an August 1933 job on a bank in Grand Haven, Michigan. Hazel, ever the businesswoman, put Hamilton up for five days at $100 a day. It was a lofty price considering that the seventeen-room, oceanfront mansion in Daytona Beach cost only $100 a month.

After that costly stay, Hamilton was moved to a house at 5740 Homan Avenue owned by the aunt of Dillinger's imprisoned associate Arthur "Fish" Johnson. The fee there was a more reasonable $75 for five days.

Feeling stronger, Hamilton was then taken to Fort Wayne and placed into the custody of his half-sister and her husband. He would remain there until fully recovered—a fortunate stroke of fate, as things turned out.

As if simply being in Chicago wasn't bad enough, Dillinger abandoned the Ford V8 on January 16 at the intersection of Byron Street and California Avenue. Chicago police had figured he was long gone and had called off the dogs. The discovery of the blood-soaked getaway car convinced them he was still in town, intensifying their hunt.

If Dillinger was searching for any good news in all this misery, Billie provided it. On January 17, she filed for divorce from Walter Sparks, stating the she had "conducted herself as a true, kind and affectionate wife" for a whole fifteen days until he was imprisoned. The jailing, in the legal brief, was viewed as "desertion." To celebrate, Johnnie and Billie took the 1932 Terraplane to Mooresville, where John visited his aging pop for thirty minutes. The loving couple had reunited, according to Billie, on a bridge in St. Louis at a designated date and time in mid-January following their cross-country separation. Billie cooed that when she drove up, her Most Wanted beau was there waiting.

John, not particularly happy with Billie's auto-buying skills, decided to purchase yet another new car during their return to St. Louis from Indiana. Since the 1934 Terraplanes downgraded to six cylinders, the high-octane Dillinger had to switch to the bigger Hudsons. There weren't any on the Essex lot, so the eager salesman escorted John and Billie to the St. Louis automobile show at the Mart Building. With his choices limited to display models, he selected a "Bison Brown" Club sedan for $1,229, minus $275 for the Terraplane.

While waiting outside, Billie's puppy slipped its collar and ran loose on the front lawn. Dillinger came out and started chasing it. A police officer saw him and lent a hand. For five minutes, Public Enemy Number One and one of St. Louis's Finest teamed up to catch a lady's puppy.

When the auto show ended that Sunday, John and Billie hopped into the showroom Hudson and took off for Tucson, the specified location of the next Terror Gang convergence. They figured the sleepy, old-west town would be a good place to lay low for a while and enjoy another vacation.

Makley and the Clarks arrived first, hitting Tucson on January 21, 1934. After a fire chased them from the Congress Hotel, they rented a house at 927 North Second Street to await the others. Makley had been to the desert city before, and had various friends there. He killed time catching up.

Handsome Harry and Mary K wheeled in on the 24th in their Buick and checked into the Arizona Tourist Court at Sixth Avenue and Nineteenth Street. Billie arrived by cab a short while later, telling them that John had stopped off at a local smoker to watch a boxing match. Her boyfriend had also, no doubt, laid eyes for the first time on his nick-namesake. Long-eared jackrabbits were abundant in Tucson.

The next day at noon, Dillinger, Pierpont, Makley, and Clark met two miles outside of town near the Veterans Hospital to discuss their next, unspecified robbery. Following the short get-together, they split up.

Despite Makley's assurances, Tucson was not a good choice for a rendezvous. The midwest gangsters in their big new cars stood out, and people were starting to buzz. A firefighter recognized Clark from a *True Detective* magazine story and went to the police. A pair of traveling salesmen had a few drinks with Makley and Clark at a local watering hole and began trading stories about what neat toys they owned. One of the salesmen bragged that he had some dynamite. Clark, not to be outdone, blabbed that they had machine guns. The salesmen sobered up the next day and ratted their new friends to the cops.

Piecing things together, Tucson Police Chief C. A. Wollard figured some bad hombres had blown into town. Investigating, he was informed by Congress Hotel officials that the men in question had moved to 927 East Second Street. Detectives Dallas Ford, Chet Sherman, and Mark Robbins were assigned to check the place out, taking along Officers Jay Smith and Frank Eyman. They staked out the property, hiding in the bushes. In the driveway, they noticed a brand-new tan Studebaker, which Makley had purchased in Jacksonville during his return trip to Florida.

Makley and Clark were inside with Bernice and a woman named Madge Ritzer, Makley's latest local girlfriend. As the officers watched, Makley and Ritzer exited the house and took off in the vehicle. The cops followed them to the Grabbe Electric and Radio store downtown where Makley had gone to pick up a shortwave radio he'd left there to be fixed. Detective Sherman, in civilian clothes, followed him inside. He waved over a clerk, identified himself, and asked the man to check if the customer had an index finger missing on his left hand. The clerk did as told, confirming the absent digit. Sherman signaled for Ford, Eyman, and Robbins to join him. Confronted, the unarmed Makley claimed he was J. C. Daviess and asked to be taken back to the house to prove it. The wary officers took him and Madge to the station instead. There, Madge also gave a phony name, May M. Miller, and was eventually released.

Detective Sherman was convinced that Makley's associate was indeed Russell Clark from the *True Detective* spread. He returned to the house with Eyman, Ford, and officer Kenneth Mullaney, parking in an alley half a block away. Mullaney and Eyman went to the rear while Detective Ford covered the front from across the street. The short, slightly built Sherman then went to the entrance, using an envelope as a prop to pretend he was searching for an address. Sherman rang the bell and Bernice Clark came to the door. Sherman said he had a letter for Mr. Long from Mr. Daviess that he needed to deliver in person. A few moments later, Clark appeared next to his wife. The detective seemed "too young and too small to be a cop," so Clark relaxed.

Sherman tried to pull his gun and make the arrest, but Clark grabbed it and the two began to wrestle, a dangerous battle that spilled into the house. Detective Ford sprinted over to help, but Bernice slammed the door on him, breaking his finger. The wrestling match moved through the living room into the bedroom, with Bernice Clark pecking away at the officer as well. Clark was trying to get to a pistol stashed under the pillow, unaware that his wife had moved it.

"We wrestled down onto the bed and while we were there someone hit Mr. Clark on the head with a gun," Detective Sherman recalled. "When Mr. Clark was hit he wasn't hit hard enough to knock him out. He turned and looked over his left shoulder and saw Dallas Ford standing there. When he saw Ford he let go of my gun and had only one hand on it. I got the gun (away) and hit him on the head with the barrel and that was about all."

Ford had broken through the front door to assist his partner. The other officers rushed in via the back as planned. The Clarks were cuffed and arrested.

The Tucson cops, learning on the fly, made the mistake of failing to keep a watch on the house after the arrests. They missed an opportunity to grab Pierpont when he appeared an hour later. Finding the door open and nobody home, Pierpont went inside. The bloodstains and toppled furniture told him all he needed to know. He rushed back into his car and sped to the Arizona Tourist Court. Although he'd rented his own house at 725 North Third Avenue, he and Mary had not yet moved in.

Harry and Mary scrambled to pack and beat town—a smart move considering that a neighbor scribbled down their license number while Harry was at Clark's place and had called the police. Shooing Mary to the car, Pierpont stopped long enough to phone local attorney O. E. Glover and hire him to represent "Long" and "Daviess," whom he correctly assumed had been pinched. The call delayed the escape long enough to allow the Tucson police to catch up. The department knew where Harry was staying because he'd run a stop sign when he first arrived in town, and talked his way out of a ticket, explaining that he was a tourist from Jacksonville staying at the resort on Sixth Street. The officers readily remembered him because of the 1934 Buick, the first they'd ever seen.

Pierpont was heading out when they pulled in. The cops, Jay Smith, Frank Eyman, and Earl Nolan, hooked their car around and fell in behind Pierpont, motioning for him to stop. Pierpont obeyed, burying a .45 between his legs just in case. Smith and Norlan drew their weapons but stayed in the car as Eyman, falling into a bumpkin, "howdy partner" persona, approached and explained that tourists needed an Arizona inspection sticker. Pierpont handed him a driver's license identifying himself as John Donovan of Indianapolis. Eyman suggested that he ride with the couple to the station where he'd personally take care of getting the proper sticker. Pierpont, suspecting nothing, agreed. Eyman hopped in the back and sat on a pile of luggage. Noticing Pierpont adjusting his rearview mirror to keep watch on the trailing patrol car, he quietly pulled his weapon and had it ready.

The unlikely trio made it to police headquarters without incident. There, however, Pierpont spotted Makley and Clark's luggage inside Chief Wallard's office and freaked, reaching for his pocketed gun. Eyman stuck his weapon into Pierpont's ribs and took the tall robber's pistol. In a flash, Pierpont drew a second pistol from a shoulder holster, but Eyman, Chief Wollard, and Jay Smith were all on him. In the struggle, Pierpont's rimless eyeglasses were knocked to the floor and shattered. He was subdued and cuffed, but remained furiously angry. Spitting that they were "small-town hick cops," he threatened, "I'll get you . . . and you . . . and you," his burning gaze burrowing into each officer. "I can get out of any jail and I'll not forget!"

Patting him down, the Tucson cops found two more weapons— including Sheriff Jess Sarber's .38—Pierpont, in one of his less intelligent acts, was carrying the service revolver of the cop he'd murdered. During his booking, the police noticed something in the famous hood's mouth. After another struggle, they retrieved it. It was a note, but the ink had smudged, making it unreadable.

Outside, waiting in the car, Mary was arrested without a struggle. During her booking, she was relieved of her prized diamond watch, three rings, necklaces, and $3,118.95 in cash. Pierpont had only been carrying $94.81. The cops had previously taken $7,264.70 from Makley and Clark, most of which had been stuffed into the zippered linings of their money belts.

Across town, John and Billie remained in the dark. They'd rented a house that morning, this one at 1304 East Fifth Street, and ordered a load of coal for the furnace to get them through the chilly desert nights. Intending to stay a while, they went into town and stocked up on groceries. Later that evening, they drove to Pierpont's place and found no one home. Thinking nothing of it, they headed over to Makley's.

Catching on, the Tucson police now had Officers Kenneth Mullaney and Milo Walker hiding inside Makley's living room, while Officer James Herron watched from his car across the street. Dillinger strolled up the walkway while Billie and the puppy waited in the Hudson. Herron approached as the Jackrabbit reached the porch. "Who are you looking for?" Herron casually asked.

"I'm at the wrong house," Dillinger responded, starting back toward the Hudson.

"Oh, no, you're not," Herron said, pulling his weapon. Before Dillinger could react, Mullaney and Walker came flying through the front door, guns drawn. Dillinger protested that he was Frank Sullivan, a businessman from Green Bay, Wisconsin. Frisked, his .45 suggested otherwise. Billie was ordered out of the Hudson and told to put her hands on her head, a command that elicited a strong objection from her protective boyfriend. The couple and the puppy were taken to headquarters where Dillinger was relieved of the $6,875 he was carrying. Billie had only $67.97. John was allowed to hang on to a rabbit's foot charm he'd recently purchased.

"That's one time your rabbit's foot didn't work, boy," one of the officers quipped.

"That rabbit was a lot luckier than I was," Dillinger responded with a grin, taking it all in stride.

The puppy gave the officers great pause. It was wearing a weird pair of doggie goggles that a fast-talking salesman had pawned on Dillinger, saying the animal needed them to protect its eyes from the desert sand. The cops, fearing it was some kind of gas mask, were momentarily braced for a sudden chemical attack.

Fingerprint technician Mark Robbins confirmed what everyone already knew—the Tucson police had nabbed the great John Dillinger. Despite the ID, Dillinger held on to his Frank Sullivan alias until Robbins pointed to the distinctive scars on his left wrist and upper lip. Knowing the gig was up, the Jackrabbit confessed.

Following the mug shots, Officer Eyman handed Dillinger back his glasses. "You can have them," Dillinger cracked.

"What, you don't need them?" Eyman asked in mock surprise.

Searching the bandit again, another $200 was pulled from the lining of his coat. In the Hudson, the officers found two Thompsons, 500 rounds of ammunition, and two shortwave radios. At the East Fifth Street house, they confiscated $6,500 from a suitcase, $1,000 from a locked closet, and two modified Winchester .351 rifles fitted with custom fore grips and Maxim silencers. Impressed, police technicians fired the weapons and reported that they sounded no louder than BB guns.

The Makley house produced three Thompsons—two .45 caliber and one modified to fire .351 cartridges—a pair of steel vests, two .45 Colt automatics, assorted ammunition, handcuffs, and brass knuckles. It was enough armament, the *Arizona Daily Star* would write, to supply "three Mexican revolutions."

Incredibly, in a matter of hours, the "hick town" Tucson police had captured John Dillinger and his entire inner circle, seized their weapons, and confiscated $27,000 of their stolen money. It was the kind of devastating coup d'etat that eluded the embarrassed law enforcement armies of Indiana, Illinois, Ohio, and J. Edgar Hoover's G-Men. To pile on the humiliation, the Tucson cops had done it without firing a single shot.

Once the news was announced, the national media flocked to Tucson. Motion picture cameramen from Pathe, Movietone, and

Universal Newsreel lugged their heavy equipment to the desert and joined the mob of print journalists and photographers. When Pierpont tried to shield his face from the flashbulbs, a pair of muscular cops grabbed him and forced a pose.

After their highly publicized bookings, the gang was handed off to Sheriff John Belton and the Pima County jail. The ladies, Mary, Billie, and Bernice, were elevated to the "penthouse," the top-floor women's section, while their men languished below. A routine search at the jail uncovered $2,000 in Dillinger's belt, causing one lawman to observe that every time the bandits were shaken down, they "rained money."

Some of that green rain would prove to be especially damaging. Serial numbers on 200 five-dollar bills were traced back to the First National Bank of East Chicago. Dillinger may as well have been carrying slain Sgt. William O'Malley's revolver.

Fully aware of what he was dealing with, Sheriff Belton isolated Dillinger from the others, and beefed up security. Heavily armed guards were stationed throughout the facility, and shotgun-toting deputies walked the corridors. Border patrol agents were bussed in for additional manpower. The no-nonsense Belton told each crook that if anybody tried to break them out, they'd be the first to die. "You're worth just as much to me dead as alive, and I don't intend to get a bunch of good men killed just to see you get away."

A special APB went out nationwide for John Hamilton, the only remaining inner-circle member still at large. If there was going to be a break-out attempt, the still-recovering Hamilton would have to lead it. A similar APB was sent for Hilton Crouch until Indiana officials notified Tucson and the G-Men that he was safe and sound at Michigan City.

Friday morning, it seemed like half of Tucson showed up for the arraignment, filling the courtroom pews and corridors and covering the lawn outside. Thirty armed deputies lined the courtroom walls. The four infamous men were brought in manacled together as the crowd gasped, gawked, and pulled back in fear. The molls, not so much as a cuff on their dainty wrists, followed. The ladies in the crowd commented on their every hairstyle, nail color, and bra size. A swarm of

newsmen interviewed the arresting officers hundreds of times and pho-
tographed the cars, money, and weapons.

Justice of the Peace C. V. Budlong ordered the men to stand and sit
on command, and tolerated little disrespect. Pierpont, ever recalcitrant,
made a series of smart remarks and laughed audibly when Billie was
referred to as "Ann Martin."

"There ain't no such animal," he cracked.

The gang's quickly hired attorney, John L. VanBuskirk, pleaded them
not guilty, then objected to his clients being held without bail, arguing
that under Arizona law, that could only be done to those committing
crimes in Arizona. Justice Budlong, scanning the array of machine guns
on display, made his own law, slapping each man with a $100,000, get-
out-of-jail bill. The ladies could free themselves for a mere $5,000. The
robbers weren't allowed to use the confiscated cash because bank officials,
attorneys, and insurance companies were already laying claims. To slow
the reclamation process down, the gang signed the money and their cars
over to VanBuskirk, who promised to fight to keep it all as his legal fee.

Dillinger unintentionally delighted the gawkers when he leaned
over and gave Billie a kiss. A reporter who observed the tender moment
was moved to write: "He has none of the look of the conventional killer.
Given a little more time and a wider circle of acquaintances, one can see
Dillinger might presently become the central figure in a nationwide
campaign, largely female, to prevent his frying in the electric chair."

That afternoon, the giddy Tucson police swarmed the Makley house
with guns drawn after neighbors reported that another man had rolled
in. The visitor turned out to be a crafty real-estate agent. He figured the
gangsters wouldn't be using the places they'd paid for, and was already
renting them as "historical sites" for a larcenous profit. The couple who
snatched the Dillinger residence was allowed to enjoy the freshly
bought food as well.

The local Hudson dealer, with no new 1934s to hawk, somehow got
hold of Dillinger's vehicle and immediately put it on display under a
ten-foot banner that proclaimed DILLINGER CHOOSES THE 1934 HUDSON FOR
HIS PERSONAL USE. Dillinger was not paid for his ringing endorsement.

In Mooresville, John Sr. faced the reporters once again. "I kind of hoped John would get out of the country before he got caught, but maybe this way is best. I was so afraid that when they tried to close in on him he would shoot somebody or would get shot. Someway I couldn't bear to think of that."

With the Fearsome Four under lock, things progressed with startling speed. The following day, a Lake County, Indiana, grand jury indicted John Dillinger for the murder of Sgt. William Patrick O'Malley, a charge that came with a mandatory, death-by-electrocution sentence if convicted. Lucy Sarber, widow of Sheriff Jess Sarber of Lima, filed a $50,000 civil suit against Dillinger, Pierpont, Makley, and Clark for the loss of her husband's services.

The two salesmen who ratted out their Tucson drinking buddies filed a claim for what they estimated would be $30,000 in rewards. Not so fast. The *True Detective* firefighter staked his claim, as did many of the arresting officers. Greed was quickly tarnishing Tucson's heroic image.

Allowed to speak to the media on the 27th, the gang mostly ranted, denied, and threatened their jailers. Dillinger lamented, "You're framing me for crimes I never even read about!" Then barking like Pierpont, he added, "You can't keep me in any two-by-four jail like this . . . I'll get out and kill you all."

The newsmen, being fed quotes better than anything they could make up, barely contained their excitement. Warming up, Dillinger filled their notebooks. "I'm an expert in my business. I can play tag with the police anytime. They just dodge around the old trails like hounds that don't know what's going on. And the dumbest ones in the world are the Chicago kind. Right now, none of those smart-aleck coppers have got a bit of evidence that I killed anybody or robbed any bank. And they can't keep me penned up anywhere—here, Atlanta, Leavenworth, or Alcatraz Island—anymore than they could keep my men in Ohio or Indiana."

After hearing these remarks, Walter Naughton of the *Chicago Herald and Examiner* chilled his vast audience from the opening line: "John Dillinger is as tough an individual as your reporter has ever seen, and I have looked many a tough one in the eye."

Addressing an *Indianapolis News* reporter, Dillinger softened for a moment when asked about his dad. The reporter, William L. "Tubby" Toms, relayed the quote about John Sr. being glad his son was taken alive. "That's fine of dad. He's a great scout. I'm sorry I've caused him so much worry but, well, that's just how life goes. We can't all be angels." The outlaw reached into his pocket and gave Toms his rabbit's foot. "Here. You may as well have this. My luck's running out anyway."

Dillinger ended the interview sessions by asking the assembled reporters to urge their readers to "vote for Sheriff John Belton in the next election." The reason for the endorsement was no doubt to polish the apple that controlled his immediate fate. The flattery worked. Belton beamed when he heard about it and dropped his tough guy act a notch.

In the "penthouse," Billie was allowed to entertain the press hounds as well, fawning over her "dashing Romeo" who she described as "gentle as a lamb." Even the officers noted that he held her hand and cuddled her in the car as they were brought in to be arrested, assuring her that they'd been in tougher jams and would survive to make love again. "Isn't he grand?" Billie sighed. "He's always that way, rain or shine. You can't help but love a man like that."

Arizona Governor B. B. Moeur, knowing a photo op when he saw one, arrived at the cell block on the 27th. Most of the guys and molls treated him coolly, but Makley, always the rapper, agreed to come out of his cell and shoot the breeze. They chatted like old friends about the weather, Tucson, business conditions, along with a surprising number of mutual acquaintances the two shared in both Phoenix and Indianapolis. "When I get out of here I'll be hotter than ever," Makley told his new friend. "I may get out. I've gotten out before."

Loosening up to kill the boredom, Handsome Harry told reporters that Dillinger's favorite movie was *The Three Pigs*, an award-winning cartoon, and portrayed himself as a valuable member of the gang because of his "indelible memory." When asked why he was carrying Sheriff Sarber's revolver, that indelible memory suddenly went blank. "I can't remember."

Mellowing further, Pierpont praised the Tucson cops and took back his "hick town" comments. He lauded Officer Frank Eyman for his ruse of taking him in for the Arizona license sticker, saying the cop's politeness and calm demeanor totally fooled him and made him put away the .45 in his lap. "I think you're a swell fellow not to shoot me," he said, addressing Eyman directly when the officer appeared to let the boys play with Billie's dog. "We hold nothing against you officers. You're on one side and we're on the other."

To prove there were no hard feelings, Pierpont told Eyman he could have his .38 Colt super automatic. Dillinger similarly signed over his pistol to Det. Chet Sherman. "They're paid for and on the level," Dillinger assured. Moved by the sudden spirit of giving, Makley presented Officer Dallas Ford with his amethyst ring.

As the cops and crooks were staging their love-in at the county jail, the usual political machinations were going on in Illinois, Indiana, Ohio, Missouri, and Wisconsin, with Hoover sticking his nose in as well. Captain Leach wanted Dillinger shipped to Indiana to stand trial for the O'Malley murder. He generously deferred to Allen County, Ohio, regarding Pierpont and Makley, figuring the Sarber killing was their quickest route to the electric chair. Clark, Leach said, could go to whatever jurisdiction had the best case.

The other states had their own ideas, including Johnnie-come-lately Missouri, which was still trying to hang Dillinger with the silly farm-wife kidnapping he had nothing to do with.

The Racine, Wisconsin, police department filed a claim to have a tommy gun recovered that was stolen at their bank, serial number 3363. Tucson police telegrammed back that they indeed had the weapon in their stash. Harrison County, Indiana, Sheriff Charles Neel, the hostage in the Michigan City jailbreak, asked to have his .38 Colt Police Positive, serial number 46,645, returned. An Indiana detective reminded Neel that the bandits caught in Tucson were not from the same splinter group that had grabbed him.

Tucson officials, reveling in the attention, perched themselves on the catbird seat and let the bidding war for the gangsters begin.

"This stamps out the so-called Dillinger gang," Captain Leach told newsmen as he boarded a train for Tucson with Detectives Harvey Hire, Verne Shields, Gene Ryan, and Don Wynn, along with Fingerprint Clerk Marie Grott. "That's all of them. We have the two important characters, Dillinger and Pierpont. The curtain closes down on them."

Justice Budlong, becoming nervous over rumblings that Dillinger might make bail, oddly reacted by raising the bond on Mary and Bernice a whopping $95,000, giving them full, six-figure equality with their men. There was more head scratching when he kept the price on Queen Moll Billie Frechette's pretty head at a bargain basement $5,000.

From the Fearsome Four's perspective, the parade of law enforcement officials into their cell block was a minor annoyance. Even when East Chicago officer Hobart Wilgus dramatically pointed a bony finger at Dillinger and identified him as the man who killed Sergeant O'Malley, the robber merely glared and paced. That all changed with the arrival of Captain Leach. The moment he set foot on the cell block, Harry Pierpont went nuts. *Indiana Star* reporter Joseph Shepard witnessed the explosion:

> An infuriated tiger, Harry Pierpont, caged but untamed Indiana desperado, leaped like a mad man to the bars of his cell here today when he glanced into the eyes of the man he hates worst in the world— Captain Matt Leach, chief of the Indiana State Police. The glance lashed him into insane rage in the fraction of a second. His eyes glared wildly, veins in his neck stood out like purple vines and saliva dripped from his lips. He mouthed only futile impotences as he tried to form words.
>
> Then words came, torrents of blasphemy and oaths. Accusations and invective, screeched at the top of his lungs, petrified the little group of officers who had escorted Leach for his first peep at the men he has hounded for months. The spectators drew back, leaving Leach alone and silent standing at the bars.

The talented Shepard couldn't quote Pierpont directly in the family newspaper, but others were happy to. "You rotten son-of-a-bitch . . . I have only one regret and that's not killing you when I had the chance."

Pierpont's rage was based on his belief that Leach had arrested his mother in Terre Haute, and threatened his brother as well. Leach shrugged and said other police agencies had made those arrests. "Pierpont also is bitter toward me because I've kept this whole Dillinger gang thing hot," he explained to the media. "There was one chance for them to get to safety and that was to have the whole case die out, the public to lose interest, and the police get cold. I saw to it that the case was kept hot . . . I'll take no chances with this gentleman as we go back . . . These men have been my babies for so many months that I've figuratively eaten and slept with them, and fight or not fight, I'll bring them back."

Dillinger refused to say anything to the hated cop, but did shake his hand through the bars. Makley looked around Leach and cracked to his jailer, "Can't you do something about these bunks to get rid of these bugs?"

While the jurisdiction wrangling raged, Sheriff Belton took the unusual step of opening his jail to the public to allow "woman voters" to gawk at the superstar felons. Four hundred women and men came the first Saturday, parading through in groups of fifteen. On Sunday, Belton woke up to find another 1,100 people waiting to do likewise.

Pierpont, infuriated by the zoo act, put on his usual show, chilling and thrilling the crowd with his obscene tantrums. Dillinger mostly ignored the onlookers, then flipped when he spotted a spectator he was certain was from Indiana. "I can tell you damned Hoosiers," he snapped. "Those other people stop and look, but you just stand and gape!"

The circus ended when Leach waved a telegram from one of his lieutenants back home reporting that two car loads of heavily armed men were seen in Illinois speeding westward. For security reasons, Sheriff Belton felt it best to end the tours.

When things quieted down, Pierpont asked for a word with Sheriff Belton. Claiming that little Mary was pregnant, he wanted to know if they could get married. Always looking for a story, Belton agreed. He summoned Court Clerk Elizabeth Oney, much to her horror. The quiet woman was barely able to scribble down the information on the required license because her hands shook so in Handsome Harry's presence. She noted that Pierpont was thirty-two, and Mary was twenty-five. Mary, during her interview, conveniently left out the fact that she was already married. Belton kicked in the two-dollar fee, but had it boomerang when Justice Budlong refused to perform the ceremony. A Catholic priest declined as well, scuttling the idea. Billie and Bernice, munching on candy bars sent by compassionate locals, comforted a disappointed Mary. "Gee, but I love that man" Mary wailed.

Rebuffed in matrimony, the gang now worked on their major agenda—getting remanded to Wisconsin. As with Lima before, they figured their best chance of escape was in the frigid state. In addition, no one had been killed in the Racine robbery, so they wouldn't be facing the chair. Their attorney, VanBuskirk, played up to the Wisconsin delegation, and the Fearsome Four were on their best behavior when the Wisconsin officials visited them. "I want to go back with you fellows," Dillinger told Racine Police Chief Grover Lutter, the former football player. "You look more sociable."

On January 29, the four signed waivers of extradition to Wisconsin. Tucson Police Chief Wollard and Justice Budlong agreed to the deal—if Wisconsin paid the reward money. Wisconsin readily showed them the money, $6,000 to start, and tossed in that they would pay to have the Tucson arresting officers escort the prisoners to their fine state. Naturally, that put the Tucson police squarely in Wisconsin's corner.

When news of the move leaked, the other agencies were naturally beside themselves, pushing every political button they could—including governor-to-governor chats—to keep the deal from going through. Captain Leach, armed with extradition papers signed by Arizona's Governor Moeur, pushed his way to the head of the blocking line. Somehow, teaming with Illinois and Ohio officials, Leach managed to get Wisconsin's Governor A. G. Schmedeman to cave in and backstab his own delegation. Schmedeman agreed to waive all claims to Dillinger.

Shortly thereafter, Sheriff John Belton and four burly deputies burst into Dillinger's cell. "You're shanghaiing me!" he screamed as he tried to brace himself against the bars. The deputies jerked him free and slapped on the cuffs.

"They're putting you on the spot, Johnnie," Pierpont called out. "You're not going back to Indiana!" Kicking and struggling the whole way, Dillinger was dragged down a back stairway to a waiting car and whisked to the Tucson airport. There, with only the clothes on his back—slacks, white dress shirt, and a vest—he was stuffed inside a Bellanca Skyrocket, a high-winged private monoplane owned and piloted by "Smiling" Dale Myers. The battered outlaw was forced to squat at the feet of East Chicago Police Chief Nick Makar and Lake County Chief Deputy Sheriff Carroll Holley. Handcuffed to the frame of the pilot's seat, the Jackrabbit spat, "Hell, I don't jump out of these things."

The sleek aircraft immediately took off, followed by a "chase" plane piloted by Charles Mayse, a well-known World War I pilot. East Chicago Officer Horbart Wilgus and Lake County Prosecutor Robert Estill were inside with Mayse. Both planes landed an hour later in Douglas, 100 miles southwest of Tucson near the Mexican border. Dillinger was taken to the Douglas police station, forced to change clothes, then, under heavy guard, was put aboard an American Airways commercial flight headed for El Paso, Texas. That leg went smoothly because there was only one other non-law enforcement passenger on the twin-engine Curtis Condor airliner. When the Condor set down in snowy El Paso, Estill placed a spare jacket around Dillinger's shoulders, surprising the outlaw with his humanity.

Word quickly spread in Tucson that Dillinger had been spirited away. A crowd gathered in the street below the Pima County jail. When Terror Gang girls appeared at a window, the crowd began to cheer. "Where are we going?" Mary Kinder called out. "Wisconsin. Wisconsin," the knowledgeable crowd chanted back. Hearing that, the girls squealed and hugged.

The subsequent outrage of attorney VanBuskirk over his client's kidnapping was matched only by that of the Wisconsin delegation. All pointed the finger at the universally loathed Captain Leach. Racine prosecutor John Brown didn't hide his feelings during a bitter news conference: "Indiana, a state which turned these mobsters loose on the Middle West, has Dillinger in custody again. It's hoped that the negligence of the officers of that state will never be repeated."

Despite the hostility and revulsion, Captain Leach wasn't finished. Bolstered by the appearance of Indiana Attorney General Phil Lutz, and waving a fistful of signed extradition papers, the pair appeared before Superior Court Judge Frederick W. Fickett and successfully wrangled legal possession of the rest of the gang. Leach and six officers rushed Mary Kinder and the heavily manacled men into a waiting car. Makley, passing a pack of furious Wisconsin officials, said, "I'm sorry you lost."

The coed quartet was taken to the Southern Pacific railroad terminal and placed inside a Pullman car named "Camp Pike." A crowd of 1,500 watched as thirty-five machine-gun-toting deputies ringed the loading platform. When Det. Chet Sherman and other Tucson officers tried to follow the prisoners inside, Under Sheriff Maurice Guiney barred their passage.

The Tucson officers were foaming because Captain Leach pulled off the coup by offering nothing more than $300 in rewards. The cops were expecting about $2,500 each from Wisconsin, and rumors swirled that the gang itself was going to funnel another $60,000 worth of stolen bonds to Tucson and Wisconsin officials—washed spic-and-span through their attorney. Seeing it all fall through his fingers, little Chet Sherman grabbed Leach by the collar and shouted "You're everything Pierpont said you were! A double-crossing rat."

Leach offered no reply. At 10:55 P.M., the Golden State Limited chugged its way out of the terminal.

"Tucson Sighs As Gangsters Leave Arizona," the *Arizona Daily Star* screamed the next day. "They brought a lifetime of tension and excitement to the Old Pueblo," wrote Fred Finney. "Tucson was on the map of the country's front pages, but Tucson also had the tiger by the tail, and the tiger was a sinister animal."

Amid all the hoopla, the "Ann Martin" and "Opal Long" aliases of Billie Frechette and Bernice Clark slipped through the cracks. The women were released as unwitting moll bimbos. They gladly accepted the insult and hopped a bus out of town. Before leaving, Billie reclaimed her puppy.

"The Dillinger gang has come and gone," a reporter lamented. "Even to the dog."

Chapter 12

The Terror Gang's Tucson disaster flew in the face of the standard "if you can't stand the heat, get out of the kitchen" theory of criminal hideouts. The problem was, thanks to John Dillinger's immense fame, the entire nation had become a blazing hot oven.

Capt. Matt Leach, extremely pleased with himself, was moved to gather the fawning reporters steaming with him on the Golden State Limited. He waxed philosophical about his grand moment. "They were a long way from home out here and they had plenty of money. They wanted to rest up and have a good time. It seemed to them a perfect hideout. They had used up every disguise of glasses and dyed hair back in the middle-west, so had to run out where they were supposed not to be known."

Leach also shed light on why tiny Mary was dragged on the train while the other ladies walked. "Mary Kinder has a record a yard long. Her brothers, Earl and Charles Northern, are both in the Indiana prison for bank robbery, and her husband, Dale Kinder, is in on the same charge. So's her brother-in-law, Behrens. Kinder was the makeup artist for the troupe. She painted up the men so they couldn't be recognized . . ."

Both Leach and Pierpont, high-strung polar opposites, slowly mellowed during the long train ride. Leach allowed Mary to sit with her beau, which had the desired effect of calming him further. Handsome Harry returned the favor by telling newsmen that "Matt Leach wasn't such a bad fellow after all."

Resigned to his dismal immediate fate, Pierpont's mind was nonetheless already sowing the seeds of a future escape. He made it a point to tell the newsmen that John Hamilton had died from his East Chicago wounds and had been tossed into the Calumet River, a statement that would send police dragnet boats and divers into action. Hamilton, in truth, was alive and getting well, and would therefore be expected to lead the break-out charge.

Pierpont also began to work the potential jury pool by playing up Robin Hood comparisons. "I stole from bankers. They stole from the people." As usual, however, the calm merely preceded the storm. "In the last few years of my life there's never been a day that some incident hasn't happened to make me hate the law. I suppose I'm what you would call an abnormal mental case. Maybe I am, too, but once I was normal."

The Con-rail express thundered through Arizona, New Mexico, and Kansas, attracting huge crowds at every stop. Pierpont, Makley, Clark, and little Mary were *almost* the biggest things going—almost, because the biggest thing going was getting the VIP treatment in the skies above.

Actually, the plane carrying John Dillinger made a stomach-churning four stops in Texas alone, adding layovers in Abilene, Fort Worth, and Dallas, to the one in El Paso. Although Charles Lindbergh had crossed the Atlantic in 1927, air travel was still in its maddening infancy. The tag-team of commercial jets ferrying Dillinger topped out at 100 mph— barely outrunning a gangster's Terraplane. The aircraft did offer something Dillinger's hot rods could never provide—a leggy stewardess. The Dallas–to–Little Rock–to–Memphis leg came with a chatty, twenty-two-year-old named Marguerite Brennan who handed out gum to combat altitude pressure, cotton balls to battle the noise, and the usual assortment of beverages. "I felt sorry for him," she observed. "He looked like a little puppy with his tail between his legs."

In Memphis, the "little puppy" was escorted to a Ford, three-engine, high-winged Trimotor. Its deafening corrugated metal cabin accommodated eleven passengers balanced on wicker seats used to lessen the weight.

In St. Louis, a clever *Chicago Times* photographer named Sol Davis bought all four remaining tickets to block his rivals, then pestered the weary felon to pose for a series of historic photos. "All right, kid, what the hell, go ahead and shoot." As he flashed away, the "kid" peppered Dillinger with questions.

"How'd this happen, John?"

"Oh, some dumb cluck slipped up."

"The breaks aren't coming your way, eh?"

"These bastards won't give me a break. I was supposed to be brought before the Tucson judge, but those Chinamen hustled me out! When those pricks nabbed me, I wish I'd had five seconds."

"Why five seconds?"

"If I'd had those five seconds, they wouldn't have taken me that way."

As Davis persisted with the conversation, the media-savvy Dillinger realized he was wasting his time. "I thought you was a cameraman! What the hell's the use of me answering all these questions over again? Go away and let me sleep!"

Davis skittered off, his prized photos secure. "I served a long stretch in the army and I met plenty of tough guys," he'd say, "but I don't think I ever met a tougher one than Dillinger."

Death Squad Captain John Stege was given the honor of leading the 150-officer detail responsible for greeting John Dillinger at Chicago Municipal Airport and transporting him to the three-story, Lake County jail at Crown Point, Indiana. Two squads of Illinois state troopers and six squads of Indiana troopers rolled in to fatten the pack further. "Enough policemen to scare hell out of Japan," a scribe wrote, noting the island nation's aggressive rumblings in the Pacific.

Because of the huge crowds of media and gawkers, along with the competing law enforcement agents, Stege wasn't able to execute Dillinger on the runway, as he so ached to do. He would also find it impossible to pull over to the side of the road enroute and blow the bandit away during a manufactured escape attempt. Dillinger, fully cognizant of these factors, was thankful the otherwise annoying press hounds were around—even if it meant surviving to face a murder rap.

Ironically, the Jackrabbit's predicament wasn't foreign to Captain

Stege himself. At fifteen, the future decorated cop killed his stepfather, claiming the hated parent was violently abusing his mother. The youth was convicted as a juvenile and served a short sentence handed down by a sympathetic judge. He joined the Chicago police force by lying about his name, birthplace, and background. He was on the job for twenty-seven years before it came back to bite him, but by then, he was too dangerous and powerful to be shown the door.

After stepping down the metal stairs into the cold winter nighttime air, the Jackrabbit was shoved into a big Lincoln police car. Welcoming him inside was one Frank Reynolds, Stege's chief goon. Sergeant Reynolds itched to add the superstar robber to the growing list of those he'd unceremoniously planted. "Just start something," Reynolds growled. "You'll be the first dead man!"

The massive law enforcement caravan included lead cars equipped with blinding spotlights used to sweep the shoulders and ferret out possible hidden bands of compatriots intent on busting Dillinger loose. The task was complicated by the thousands of onlookers standing along the route, braving the winter cold to catch a glimpse of the famous outlaw. If the 150 officers weren't enough, detectives and patrolmen from Hammond, East Chicago, and Gary fell in line at the Indiana border.

Dillinger, suffice it to say, wasn't sharing in the excitement. Despite all the national and international headlines, he'd only been free for eight whirlwind months. Now he faced either a lifetime behind bars, or the electric chair. Either way, it appeared doubtful that he'd ever spend another night of throbbing passion with Billie. That ate at him the most.

In Mooresville, John Sr. fretted over having to leave the farm and make the long trips to the Crown Point jail. The double-widower told reporters that he didn't have any clean shirts for such a trip. "Of course . . . I could buy a shirt."

Dillinger arrived at Crown Point at 7:35 that evening. The possibilities presented by the small-town jail immediately lifted his spirits. The brick facility was set in a Lima-like borough of only 4,000 residents located a quiet fifteen miles from the more populous East Chicago, Gary, Indiana Harbor, Whiting, and Hammond.

Among those greeting Dillinger at the prison was a tall, slim, dark-haired lady named Lillian Holley, forty-three, the high sheriff of Lake County. She was thrust into the job just months before when her dentist husband, the elected sheriff, was shot to death in Ross, Indiana, by a local crackpot. That left her in charge of the couple's three separate farms, along with his law enforcement duties. Taking the job seriously, she had become proficient in using firearms, including a machine gun. To be cautious, she had already sent her twin, nineteen-year-old daughters to a finishing school back east even before Dillinger descended upon her jail.

Instead of wearing a uniform, Sheriff Lillian met Public Enemy Number One in a mulberry dress with a white angora jabot flowing in layers from her neck. She greeted the lawmen with sandwiches, coffee, and a half-barrel of beer. Dillinger, not allowed to share in the party treats, was taken to an isolated cell, then was retrieved twenty minutes later to hold a press conference. He appeared dressed in dark pants, a white dress shirt open at the collar, and a dark vest. A pencil jutted from one vest pocket, while a comb protruded from the other.

Goaded by reporters and photographers, Prosecutor Robert Estill was talked into putting his arm around the notorious bandit's shoulder, his hand dangling in front. The pair, sometimes joined by others as well, smiled for the cameras. One of the photos, published on the front page of the nation's newspapers the following morning, caused an uproar that would doom Estill's ambitious political career. Not only was Estill shown buddying up to the bad guy, but Dillinger was leaning on the prosecutor's shoulder smiling like he was in total control. Further, the outlaw appeared to be making the classic thumb and forefinger gun sign, viewed as message to his supporters to take Estill out.

During the wide-ranging interviews, Dillinger kept to the story that Hamilton was dead, fingered Art McGinnis as the rat in the Doctor Eye scenario, complained that his Tucson attorney took "everything I had," repeatedly denied any connection to the deadly East Chicago robbery, admitted he owned five machine guns, said he was planning to leave the country "next summer," inflated his first grocery store robbery to $500, threw his support to President Franklin Roosevelt and the Bank

ABOVE: Audrey Dillinger was left to raise her little brother, John Herbert Dillinger, after their mother died when he was three. She loved him like a son. (Courtesy of 7ony Stewart) RIGHT: John Dilliinger's parents, John Wilson Dillinger and Mollie. John Jr. often lamented the loss of his mother and felt things might have turned out differently for him had she not died. (Courtesy of 7ony Stewart)

CLOCKWISE FROM TOP LEFT: John Dillinger Jr. at 3 1/2 years old. A sad, little motherless child. (Family photo) • Adapting to the loss, Johnnie Jr. grew up happy and well cared for. Pictured here in 1913 at age 10. (Family photo) • Wild and untamed, Johnnie, 14, was a force in neighborhood gangs. (Family photo) • Dillinger's first and only known wife, Beryl. (Courtesy of 7ony Stewart)

TOP: The Dillinger home in Mooresville. (Family photo) **ABOVE LEFT:** John Sr. with Hubert Dillinger, John Jr.'s half brother. (Defunct newspaper photo) **ABOVE RIGHT:** Dillinger's weakness for dark, exotic women would repeatedly be his downfall. Girlfriend Mary Longnaker was both unfaithful and the cause of his September 22, 1933, capture in Ohio. (Family photo)

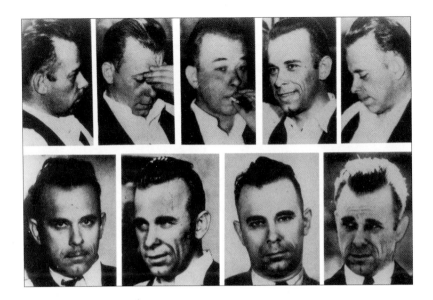

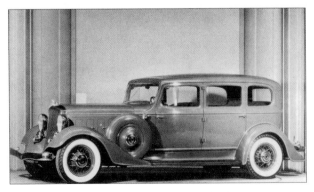

TOP: The Many Faces of John Dillinger—G-Men and local police from coast to coast were ordered to memorize his image. (FBI photos) **CENTER:** A Boy and His Toys—Dillinger's crime sprees provided the ambitious young man with the five things he coveted—cars, guns, clothes, exotic women, and nights on the town. His favorite set of wheels was the 1933 Hudson Terraplane Eight. (Author's collection) **BOTTOM:** Dillinger bought more new cars in a single year—a Great Depression year at that— than most folks own in their lifetimes. The state-of-the-art 1933 Hudson Eight provided more luxury than the Terraplanes. Either vehicle could blow away anything the cops had. (Author's collection)

ABOVE LEFT: The love of John Dillinger's life, Evelyn "Billie" Frechette, a hot-blooded blend of French and Native American. Dillinger longed to run away to South America with Billie and start a family. (Family photo)

ABOVE RIGHT: Queen of the Mollettes—As with her famous boyfriend, Billie always looked good during her arrests. She was the one lover who was loyal to the end. (Defunct newspaper photo)

RIGHT: Little Mary Kinder, Handsome Harry Pierpont's feisty long-time love, points out one of the gang's hideouts at 4310 Clarendon Avenue in Chicago. (*Chicago Herald & Examiner* photo)

John Dillinger   13225

Harry Pierpont   11014

Charles Makley   12636

Russell Clark   12261

John Hamilton   11963

Edward Shouse   13915

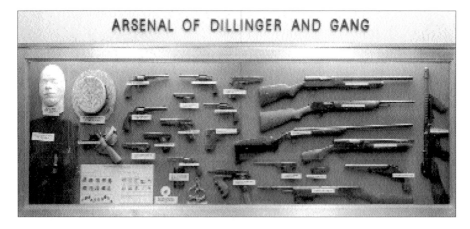

ARSENAL OF DILLINGER AND GANG

TOP (FROM LEFT TO RIGHT): The Savage Seven Shirt Shop Boys—John "the Jackrabbit" Dillinger, Handsome Harry Pierpont, Charles Makley, Russell Clark, John "Three-Fingered" Hamilton, Edward Shouse, and Homer VanMeter, next page. (Police mugs) **BOTTOM:** More Toys for the Boys—Dillinger and company had the best weapons stolen money could buy. The gang was always able to outrun or outgun the police. (FBI photo)

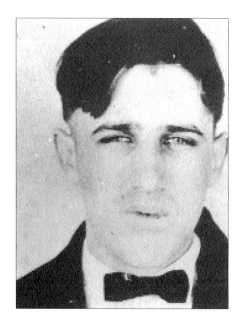

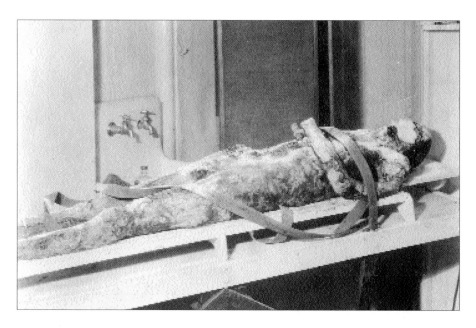

TOP LEFT: Homer VanMeter went the back-alley plastic surgery route with Dillinger in an attempt to disguise his distinctive looks. (FBI photo) **TOP RIGHT:** Baby Face Nelson, with his wife, Helen, and infant son, Ronald. The crazed bantam accounted for three of the first six DI/FBI agents ever slain in the line of duty—an inglorious body-count record that still stands. (Defunct newspaper photo) **BOTTOM:** After escaping a massive Federal dragnet at Little Bohemia, Wisconsin, John Hamilton was shot in the back during a harrowing car chase with the police in St. Paul, Minnesota. Following a slow, agonizing death, an emotional Dillinger buried his friend in a gravel pit in Illinois. The Feds later dug him up. (FBI photo)

TOP: Indiana State Police Captain Matt Leach (third from the left) was consumed with capturing Dillinger. A high strung, tempermental sort, he developed a pronounced stutter during the sensational hunt. (Defunct newspaper photo) **BOTTOM:** A different angle on the famous photo of an ice cool Dillinger posing with police and prosecutors at the Crown Point, Indiana, jail. The "lovey dovey" picture ruined bespectacled prosecutor Robert Estill's political career. Dillinger promptly escaped. (Courtesy of the late photographer Stu Thomson)

Recovery Act, admitted he smuggled in the guns that set off the Michigan City escape, dubbed Sergeant Reynolds "my worst enemy," and offered this classic comment on his personal habits. "I don't drink much and I smoke very little. When you rob banks, you can't very well do a lot of drinking. I guess my only bad habit is robbing banks."

Leaving the press wanting more at the end of the show, he remarked, "Now you see fellas, I ain't such a bad guy at heart. I try to be right."

Many in the crowd agreed. "It was difficult to realize that here was one of the most ruthless killers in the country," wrote a charmed newspaperman. "The whole thing seemed to be a joke to him."

Another writer, Robert J. Casey of the *Chicago Daily News,* viewed it more seriously. "Looking at him for the first time [one] can hardly realize that in a very few days, a month or two at the outside, this cheery, affable young man will probably be a corpse—and a very good one. For, though the finger is definitely on Mr. Dillinger, he still rates in the eyes of calloused observers as the most amazing specimen of his kind ever seen outside of a wildly imaginative moving picture."

Such a specimen needed an equally impressive mouthpiece. Some of Dillinger's old Michigan City cellmates suggested flamboyant Chicago defense attorney Louis P. Piquett, a man not afraid to break the law for his own benefit. Often described as looking like a lightweight ex-boxer who had "gone fat," Piquett, fifty-four, sported a vertical mop of curly hair, and could always be counted upon to put on a good show in court. A scrapper with political connections, he never attended law school, gaining his legal license by passing the bar exam on his fourth attempt in 1920. He later became a prosecutor, and was part of the law enforcement cartel that often attended banquets thrown by mobster Al Capone. Indicted for being part of a group of politicians accused of taking rake-offs from coal sales to schools, he escaped when the prosecution stalled. He switched sides and became a less-scrutinized defense attorney in 1922.

Piquett befriended a suave stock-and-bonds salesman named Arthur O'Leary who helped him run his law practice. As with Piquett, O'Leary never let meddlesome legalities interfere with business.

As the Dillinger circus paused to catch its breath, the rest of the gang swept into the state and jumped into their respective rings. On Thursday, February 1, Pierpont, Clark, and Makley arrived at Chicago's LaSalle Street terminal. They were given a similarly overwhelming police escort to Michigan City. Approaching the hated prison, Makley turned to Sergeant Reynolds, the noted assassin, and said, "Shoot me through the head so I won't have to go back in there!" Reynolds had to restrain himself from obliging.

Makley had good reason for his trepidation. He and his partners were stripped to their underwear, tossed into solitary, and fed bread and water. The shivering, starving monotony was occasionally interrupted by intense interrogation sessions.

Mary Kinder was spared such treatment. She had been taken off the train in Kansas City the day before. After an emotional parting with Pierpont, she was diverted to a gentler women's facility in Indianapolis. There, she complained that the Tucson cops had confiscated her diamonds, along with her entire seven-suitcase wardrobe.

Unlike Kinder and Dillinger, who were set to stay a while at their locations, the Michigan City men had more heavily guarded roadtrips in their future. Meeting with Ohio officials, Leach promised he would turn the trio over to Lima authorities to stand trial for murder as soon as they had been thoroughly grilled.

Photogenic Prosecutor Estill, weathering intense criticism from such far off detractors as an outraged J. Edgar Hoover in Washington, stuck to his guns and hung on to the case. "It seems that some people would want me to glare at Dillinger. I believe such a pose would be sheer hypocrisy. A prosecutor should not cease to be human. Dillinger acted like a gentleman with me and I was duty bound to treat him likewise . . . There is no affection between us. He respects me and knows that I will show him no leniency . . . I will do everything in my power to send Dillinger to the electric chair for the murder of detective O'Malley . . . He knows he probably will die for the shooting. There is no reason why he should not be treated humanely, and that I propose to do while fulfilling my duties as prosecuting attorney."

Estill deftly tried to divert attention from himself by ripping into everybody's whipping boy, Captain Leach. Raining mud on Leach's parade, Estill claimed the selfish police chief spent most of his time in Tucson drunk and partying, leaving everybody else to cover for him.

Leach responded with typical sputtering rage that defied physiology. "I have never been drunk in my life! I take a drink, who don't? But I have never been intoxicated. I'll let my friends pass judgment on the charge I was liquored up while on duty. They didn't even know in Tucson that Estill was there. I had to shoulder all the responsibility."

The skunk fight was still brewing when a Chicago newspaper leaped into the ring. On February 5, a scoop-happy journalist identified the finishing school where Lillian Holley had stashed her daughters—the Mary Baldwin School in Staunton, Virginia—and mentioned that both girls had been threatened with being kidnapped and exchanged for Dillinger. If Dillinger's supporters didn't have the location, or even the idea, the newspaper had just handed it to them. Sheriff Holley naturally hit the roof. "That newspaper ought to be blown into Lake Michigan . . . I think the story is heartless and whoever wrote it didn't have much consideration for the heart of a mother!"

The press wasn't having much consideration for the heart of a father, either. They continued to interrupt John Sr.'s farm chores to pester the seventy-year-old for exclusive interviews. "Look at his mother's picture up there on the wall," he wearily told one persistent scribe. "Thank God she's beyond knowing of this disgrace. I don't uphold what John has been doing. No, I don't do that. But I love him and I would do anything I could to get him a lighter sentence . . . I feel responsible in a way for the trouble he's in now. When he was first in trouble I didn't have the money, fifteen dollars, to hire a good lawyer. Yes, I was to blame. I didn't know then what I do now."

It may have given John Sr. a small measure of pride to learn that at Crown Point, Dillinger's fellow inmates showed their new bunkie the ultimate respect by unanimously voting him in as the judge of their kangaroo court.

It would not have given John Sr. any pride if he had seen the condition of his son's beloved Billie that morning. The French/Native American beauty showed up at the Chicago airport at 2 A.M. on February 8 blitzed out of her pretty head, and two hours late for a chartered flight on Blue Bird Lines to Indianapolis. She insisted on taking the co-pilot's seat, yapped incessantly, swigged whiskey from a bottle, flashed a fat roll of cash, cussed like a sailor, claimed to be a skilled, high-speed Essex Terraplane getaway driver, and bragged about being John Dillinger's girl. Upon landing, it took the pilot, Oscar Hanole, a full fifteen minutes to rouse her from her stupor and get her off the aircraft. She stumbled away to parts and missions unknown.

Dillinger's heavily guarded arraignment was held on February 9. Defense Attorney Piquett performed as advertised, infuriating Estill and Judge William J. Murray while at the same time delighting the reporters, spectators, and forty armed guards. He went particularly ballistic when the prosecutor asked to have the trial start in ten days. Piquett had requested four months. "Could it be that a political campaign is approaching? That man's life is at stake," he shouted. "There's a law in Indiana against lynching and to go to trail so soon would be legal murder. The defense must have more time!"

Judge Murray peered down at the frenzied bantam before him and launched the ultimate threat. "You'd better watch out, or the prosecuting attorney will have his arm around your shoulder next thing you know." The courtroom, including Estill and Dillinger, roared with laughter. "Ten days is not enough time and one hundred twenty days is too long a time to consider," the judge continued when the chuckles subsided. "It's my desire that the defense and the state reach an agreement on the trial date." The judge then made the decision for them, scheduling it for March 12.

Piquett next demanded a list of all the state's witnesses—always a sticky situation when dealing with a notorious gangster with a wealth of deadly associates. Deputy Prosecutor Frank Underwood promised to provide the list.

"All of the state's witnesses?" Piquett clarified.

"Not necessarily all," Underwood danced. "But all you're going to see."

Piquett jotted it down as a protest card to play later. The hearing ended and Dillinger was taken back through the "Bridge of Sighs" that connected the jail to the courthouse. Spectators swarmed around until he was out of sight.

Estill wasted little time telling reporters that in the judge's chambers, the feisty defense had offered to plead guilty in exchange for life. It was the kind of surrender any prosecutor would leap at today. Back then, things were different. Justice was speedy and capital punishment was viewed as a major deterrent. Estill, his mind set on frying his Polaroid pal Dillinger in the chair, refused the deal.

Piquett, of course, denied making the offer, reserving all his defense options.

At Michigan City, Warden Louis Kunkle was disappointed that Estill was taking such a hard line. Kunkle wanted Dillinger back under his thumb and promised he would be stripped naked and tossed into the hole with his old buddies.

In the center of the state, Indianapolis was enjoying their part of the legal circus as well. Mary Kinder, somehow acquiring new threads, showed up for her arraignment dressed in an ankle-length black "Morticia" dress, black fur-collared coat, black hat, and veil. Judge Frank P. Baker set her bail at $25,000, a $75,000 discount over Tucson. Angered over fanciful reports that the flea-like Lady in Black was the brains of the gang, Judge Baker took it upon himself to lash out. "She's a dumb girl who ran around with dumb men who carried machine guns." When Mary's attorney suggested such prejudice was cause for the Judge to remove himself from the case, Baker spat, "Then I'll see that you never get a judge less tough."

Mary, unable to make bail, was sent back to her dungeon.

The next day, Pierpont, Clark, and Makley signed waivers of extradition for their return to Ohio. The willing signatures spoke volumes about their hatred of Michigan City. They faced the death penalty in Ohio, but preferred that fate over serving out their original sentences in the noted Indiana hell hole.

Prosecutor Estill was growing increasingly nervous about Dillinger's less-hellish Crown Point accommodations, preferring that he was stashed in Michigan City. Estill's anxiety increased when he began hearing ugly rumors that Piquett was spending more time orchestrating Dillinger's escape than preparing for a trial. Judge Murray denied Estill's transfer request, saying it would be an insult to Sheriff

Holley, women everywhere, and Lake County. Holley responded to the concerns by announcing that on top of the multitude of armed guards and volunteer vigilantes, she was calling in the Indiana National Guard's 113th Engineers. The soldiers would be stationed at the jail with precision engineered Browning automatic rifles "capable of firing 120 bullets a minute, and of easily piercing bulletproof vests now commonly worn by gangsters."

Holley also announced that she was personally reading all of Dillinger's mail, and that Piquett would not be allowed to bring any scheduled or potential witnesses into the prison to meet with his client. Piquett loudly squawked that "Mrs. Holley has, it seems, taken on herself the duties of the Supreme Court!" The issue was critical to Piquett's defense because he needed witnesses to identify Dillinger in order to testify that the gangster was sunbathing in Florida on the day of Sergeant O'Malley's murder in East Chicago.

Piquett, throwing fuel on the "no visitors" fire, showed up on February 14 with a sober Billie Frechette in tow. Sheriff Holley, all but turning her nose up at Billie's latest fur coat, refused to let her in. Piquett gave the press a long, bitter oration on how the civil rights of his client were being trampled upon, and insisted that a change of venue was needed.

Then, titillating the reporters with his flair for the dramatic, Piquett announced that a professional race car driver would be hired to try to drive from Florida to East Chicago in the time the prosecution claimed Dillinger had traveled the same distance. The driver, of course, would be expected to lose the 1,150-mile race to the clock, failing to make it in the allotted twenty-three hours.

After discussing this stunt during a privileged meeting at the prison, Dillinger handed Piquett a note for Billie. Assuming it was a love letter, the attorney couldn't resist sneaking a peek. He was aghast at what he discovered—an elaborate escape plan that involved dynamiting the southwest corner of the jail, cutting through the steel cage with a torch, and engaging in a massive, machine-gun battle with the guards. The note also included an accurate floor plan of the prison building. Afraid of Dillinger's reaction if he didn't present the note, Piquett did as ordered, hoping to convince Billie of the plan's futility.

Fearing a change of venue, Sheriff Holley and Judge Murray caved in to Piquett's demands and allowed Billie through the gates on the 16th. In her report, Holley stated that Billie was intoxicated, spoke "with a great deal of slang," and was wearing a black broadcloth coat with an imitation caracal fur collar, a black crepe dress, and a "cheap black turban." No matter how hard she tried, poor Billie couldn't get any respect from the fashion police.

The whole ensemble hit the floor when Billie was forced to strip buck-naked and submit to a cavity search. Sheriff Holley guessed her nationality as "part Indian, Italian or Mexican."

Communicating through a wire-mesh screen, the reunited lovers mostly spoke in code regarding the escape plan. Billie reported, truthfully or not, that the recovering John Hamilton viewed it as too risky and preferred a straight-ahead assault similar to the one in Lima.

When Piquett continued to have trouble getting others inside to see Dillinger, he threatened the change of venue again. This time Holley and Murray agreed to his demands that family, friends, and potential witnesses could be escorted through the Bridge of Sighs to see the famous felon.

Unknown to Piquett, however, was the fact that Billie's girlfriend Pat Cherrington was secretly huddling with G-Men and blowing away his whole Florida defense. Cherrington laid out the post–East Chicago scenario, complete with the frantic search for the costly underworld doctor. The still-married Cherrington added that she was no longer in love with the imprisoned Harry Copeland, but had transferred her fickle affections to John Hamilton, whom she'd been nursing back to health. Despite cozying with the Feds, Cherrington refused to give up the whereabouts of her new lover.

At the end of February, some good news was given to at least one Terror Gang member. Judge Frank P. Baker was forced to sign an order releasing Mary Kinder for lack of evidence. Seems the prosecutors couldn't prove that she was a full-fledged participant as opposed to a "dumb girl." Once again, playing stupid was the smart move.

Dillinger himself was playing dumb, passing himself off as just another intellectually challenged crook hopelessly trapped in a cage.

That carefully crafted facade was exposed in dramatic fashion on March 3.

Prison handyman Sam Cahoon, sixty, went about his normal routine that morning, working the various dials controlling the maze of doors that allowed prisoners to file into the dayroom for breakfast. While the cons were at large, Cahoon then did something he had never done before in his six years at the jail. He opened the main cell-block door while the prisoners were out of their cells in the walkway. The normal procedure was to wait until they were locked down in the day room.

Suddenly, John Dillinger elbowed aside two African-American trustees, Charles Lewis and Ernest Walker, and appeared at the opened door. The gangster pushed Cahoon against the control box and shoved a pistol under his chin. "I don't want to kill anyone, so you just do what I tell you," Dillinger said, shifting the weapon to Cahoon's stomach. "If you want to live, get in the cell block and be quick about it!"

"What's the matter, John, haven't we been good to you?" Cahoon blurted.

"Never mind."

Guard Wilfred Bryant, standing a few feet away in shock, noticed Dillinger struggling to keep his grip on the weapon, at one point grabbing it with both hands. Bryant didn't know what to make of that—not that he had a lot of time to think about it. Herbert Youngblood, an African-American inmate charged with murder, approached Bryant wielding a toilet plunger handle. He asked Bryant if he had a gun. The petrified guard responded that he was unarmed. Youngblood then ushered Bryant and the trustees, Lewis and Walker, into the number-two cell. Cahoon started heading there as well, but Dillinger stopped him. "Not you, you stay out here. I have use for you. You're gonna take me outta here."

Dillinger and Youngblood pushed Cahoon through the cell-block door and ordered him to work the levers that locked down the cells and day room. "How many guards are there out front?" Dillinger asked.

"I don't know," Cahoon answered. "I guess ten or twelve."

Keeping Cahoon in front, Dillinger moved along the platform, down four steps, crossed a landing, and climbed the four steps on the north side. Hiding behind Cahoon, he scoped a long corridor and spotted Ernest Blunk, a familiar fingerprint technician. "Call Blunk back here." Cahoon hollered as instructed. Blunk left prisoners Orville Throgmorton, Thomas Evanter, and Mike Garrity in the receiving room and walked down the corridor toward the rear of the jail. He spotted Dillinger behind Cahoon. The gangster flashed the barrel of his pistol, then quickly returned it to Cahoon's back. "Do as you're told and nobody gets hurt. Get up here and no funny business." Blunk searched for a possible escape route to his right, but found himself staring into Youngblood's snarling face.

Blunk was ordered into the cell block, and Cahoon sealed him into a cell. There, Blunk asked the other prisoners about Dillinger's weapon and was told it looked like a .45 automatic. "They'll kill the son-of-a-bitch now for sure," he observed.

Moving into a foyer where two corridors met, Dillinger told Cahoon to call for the warden, Lou Baker. "I'm sorry John, but this has gone far enough," Cahoon would later claim to have said. "Shoot me if you have to, but I've done all I can do for you." Youngblood moved toward the reluctant handyman, but Dillinger stopped him.

"None of that," Dillinger cautioned. "I'll handle this." He shoved Cahoon back up the stairs to the control box. "I've never killed anybody, but I'm getting out of here," Dillinger insisted.

"They'll kill you before you get halfway down the hall," Cahoon warned.

"Watch me," Dillinger replied.

Back on the cell block, Dillinger switched Cahoon for Blunk then returned to the foyer. "How many guards up front?" the outlaw repeated to the new hostage. Blunk claimed ignorance. Dillinger asked about weapons and car keys, and Blunk responded that they were probably in the warden's office. "We'll see. Call Baker back here."

Dillinger turned Blunk loose and allowed him to walk alone down the 100-foot corridor to fetch Warden Baker. Instead of ducking through the steel doors near the warden's office, he did as told. Baker responded that he was busy and would be there in a second. A few minutes later, the warden appeared and had trustee John Kowaliszyn open the steel doors. Again, Blunk could have slipped through at this moment, but he wasn't even near the entrance! He was already halfway back to Dillinger, waving Baker to follow him. Thinking nothing of it, Baker strolled down the pathway whistling. Reaching the foyer, he started up the steps and was grabbed by the collar by someone crouching on the opposite stairway.

"Make any dumb moves and I'll blow your head off!" John Dillinger warned to Baker's horror as the famous felon jammed the weapon into the man's back. The warden was taken up the stairway, down the platform, and was shoved into another cell. Calmly sitting on a bunk, he shrugged and asked his fellow prisoners, "Anybody got a cigarette?"

Still manipulating Blunk, Dillinger had the technician close the cell-block doors yet again. When that task was completed, the three men stepped into the landing. Dillinger asked his hostage if there was a door that led from the trustee cell block to the kitchen. Blunk said there wasn't. Miffed, Dillinger had Youngblood check. The con returned with the news that Blunk was telling the truth. "Then I have been misinformed," Dillinger noted, his mind already working on a new angle.

Dillinger directed Blunk into a small recess near the penal farm section, swept up volunteer guard Matt Brown, seventy-seven, and repeated the cumbersome task of pulling levers, opening doors, and adding Brown to the growing group inside the hostage cell.

Deputy Kenneth "Butch" Houch was next to fall to Blunk's siren call. Unlike the others, he resisted, grabbing for Dillinger's wrist. Houch was quickly overpowered by the two murderers and packed into the cell. Guard Marshall Keithley, ignoring warnings from Gatekeeper John Kowaliszyn that "something must be wrong back there," was nabbed as well.

After locking Keithley down, Dillinger asked Warden Baker where the machine guns and car keys were.

"Out there," Baker replied.

"Out where?"

"Out in the office."

"Where in the office?"

"Just in the office."

"Let's go," Dillinger said to Blunk.

Retracing their steps for the umpteenth time, Dillinger now penetrated further down the corridor toward the receiving room. He and Youngblood stood behind a door as Blunk motioned for Kowaliszyn to open the steel gate. Dillinger and Youngblood darted behind Blunk through the passageway, then shoved Blunk and Kowaliszyn into the now accessible warden's office. The hostages were ordered to stand against the opposite walls with their hands above them. Dillinger smiled as he spotted two fully loaded Thompson submachine guns sitting in the windowsill. He grabbed one and gave the other to Youngblood. "How does this thing work," the African American asked. Dillinger gave him a quick lesson.

Kowaliszyn was peeled off the wall and marched through the corridor into the hostage cell. Facing Warden Baker again, Dillinger, armed with the Thompson, asked why there were no car keys in the office as promised. Not waiting for an answer, he asked for directions to the prison garage. Baker responded it was in the rear.

"We've got to be going," Dillinger said, almost as a good-bye. Then he looked toward the day room. "We're wasting too much time. Any of you want to come along?" Dillinger's cellmates Fred Beaver and Leslie Carron, both charged with grand larceny, immediately jumped forward. James Posey, a robber in an adjoining cell, asked to go as well. Dillinger ordered Blunk to set them free.

Once his new gang had been recruited, Dillinger pulled the pistol from his pocket and raked it across the bars in front of Warden Baker. Instead of the expected clang of metal on metal, there was only a dull thud. "This is what I did it with," the outlaw said with a huge grin as he displayed the half-finished, wooden pistol. "I carved it out myself. If you don't believe me, come here and frisk me."

"I'll take your word for it, John," Sam Cahoon responded for the group. The narrow "weapon" was missing a handle, explaining Dillinger's struggle to hold on to it.

Dillinger and crew exited the cell block for the final time. Blunk went through the familiar routine, but this time failed to seal the day room or cell doors. Realizing they wouldn't be coming back, he then gave his keys to the outlaw. On the landing, Blunk balked and pointed to Youngblood. "This guy doesn't know how to use that 'Tommy' and I ain't gonna walk in front of him while the safety's off." Ignoring the complaint, Dillinger nudged Blunk forward.

The pack traversed the familiar corridor with Blunk in the lead, the trio of opportunistic crooks behind, and Dillinger and Youngblood directing from the rear with their deadly weapons. Passing through the open doors, Dillinger came to the kitchen. Prison chef William Ziegar was standing near a steam cooker. Two vigilantes, John Thomas and Guy Surprise, were sipping coffee at a table. Dillinger slipped inside. "You two, on your feet!" The men laughed, assuming a fellow vigilante was playing a joke. "Get off your butts and get your hands up!" Dillinger repeated. This time they did as told. The outlaw waved the others inside, and had Blunk take Thomas's .45 Colt.

"Where's your gun? Youngblood asked Surprise.

"I don't have one."

Youngblood frisked him and discovered that he was lying. After being disarmed, the pair was ordered to join the cook in a tiny kitchen closet. When they didn't fit, Dillinger changed his plans and took them along. As they exited, Dillinger spotted some raincoats and hats in the closet. He and Youngblood put them on. The hostages were then directed to pass through a barred door that led to a twenty-foot-wide courtyard. Hidden by the seven-foot brick wall that ran the length of the jail, they made their way to the rear of the building.

Trustees John Hudak and Bub Chandler were inside the garage working on a 1931 Nash touring car. A Model T Ford, a 1930 Hudson sedan, and three motorcycles were parked nearby. Hudak was bent over a fender when he felt something touch his back. He turned to find two men in raincoats wielding machine guns. "Get in and drive," Dillinger commanded. Hudak looked at Blunk. "Do what he tells you, John, and you won't get hurt," the fingerprint man assured. Hudak stammered that none of the cars had keys. Dillinger's eyes flashed rage. "Then Baker, the son of a bitch, lied to me. I oughta go back and kill him! Whose this car belong to?"

"It's the sheriff's," Blunk explained.

Ticked, Dillinger ordered the three kitchen hostages into a blanket storage closet and left Youngblood to watch them. Then, incredibly, he walked the length of the courtyard back through the kitchen door.

Up on the cell block, trustee Ernest Walker managed to pry the heavy but unlatched cell door open enough to squeeze through it. Warden Baker and the others followed into the walkway and began to scream and rattle the barred cell-block door. A floor above, Irene Baker heard the racket and dashed to a closet where a peephole had been drilled. Peering through, she saw her husband in the walkway below. Sprinting out, she snatched a telephone and called the switchboard. Nobody answered. Panicking, she ran to the front of the jail and down the stairwell to the first floor to get help.

Sam Cahoon looked out of a barred window and saw a mailman below sauntering down the sidewalk. Pointing him out to Baker, the warden pounded on the high-impact glass and screamed as loud as he could. The postman stopped, looked up, squinted in the sun, then kept on walking. It was going to be a long morning.

Chapter 13

I t was approaching 9 A.M. when National Guardsman Ward Hile heard the jail's entrance bell ring. Curious, he knocked on the steel door that connected the warden's living quarters to the office. There was no answer. Hile walked to the front porch and headed south, turning into the same courtyard Dillinger had just traveled. The guardsman entered the building through the kitchen and discovered it strangely empty. He crossed the hall to the warden's office and found it barren as well.

Perplexed, he opened a window and yelled, "Something's wrong," to a fellow guardsman stationed next door in the law library of the criminal courts building.

The alert Hile let the oblivious mail trustee, Joe Golek, in through the front residence door, then walked back outside, through the courtyard, and reentered the kitchen. This time, three men were there: Ernest Blunk, trustee John Hudak—and a figure in a rain slicker with a cap pulled over his eyes holding a machine gun.

"Do you know where the keys are?" Blunk asked.

"What keys?" Hile answered.

Before Blunk could explain, vigilantes Mike Miller and Phillip Schreiber walked in. Dillinger got the drop on them with the big Thompson, forcing the local tough guys to immediately surrender. Blunk again collected the weapons, two .45s and a .38. Dillinger was quickly stockpiling a new arsenal.

Hile, Miller, and Schreiber were locked inside the receiving room. Figuring they'd caught a break, they dashed into an overlooked stairway at the rear that lead to Chief Deputy Carroll Holley's second-floor apartment. Holley, already alerted to the trouble, was busy changing into his uniform.

Downstairs, Dillinger ushered Hudak and Blunk back through the courtyard into the garage. Noting the large number of employees who lived on the premises, he asked where the personal cars were kept. Blunk answered that there was a second facility two buildings north, just beyond the criminal courts.

Prison matron Mary Linton, Irene Baker's mother, returned from an errand and walked into the garage. She took one look at Dillinger and fainted. Hudak had to carry her into the blanket room. Seconds later, Irene Baker herself burst inside screaming "Dillinger's out! Dillinger's out!" The object of her hysteria stepped from behind a post and grabbed her arm. "My God, it's you!" she shrieked before being dumped inside the blanket closet with her unconscious mother.

Still behaving like he had a wealth of time, Dillinger told con Fred Beaver to disable the motorcycles by ripping apart their ignition wires. Hudak was instructed to ground the Hudson and Nash. Figuring he'd have to fix them later, he gingerly began to pull their spark-plug wires. "Hell, that's not the way," Dillinger growled, nodding toward a nearby hammer. "Give me that." In a flash, the outlaw smashed the porcelain plugs and pounded holes in the carburetors. Pleased with his more-effective technique, he used the same hammer to break the padlock on the large garage door. Shouting for Hudak to bring him a pinch bar, he was miffed to see the nervous trustee instead dash through the small side exit. Hudak ran across the courtyard and hid in the kitchen. Dillinger shrugged and forgot about him.

Inmates Beaver, Carron, and Posey, cognizant of the minutes that had elapsed coupled with their leader's unnervingly unhurried pace, decided that they, too, would return to the jail. The trio was certain the cavalry had gathered outside and they'd be blown to bits the moment they showed their faces. Dillinger didn't much want them dragging him down anyway, so he let them go.

Now more streamlined, Dillinger, Blunk, and Youngblood walked through the garage-door opening that faced the rear of the building, turned left on East Street, made it past the criminal court building, and slipped inside the Main Street Garage through a storeroom entrance. Mechanic Ralph Wright was working in the back when he heard a noise. Looking up, he saw three men easing their way to the front. Edwin Saager, a night mechanic, was preoccupied with the generator of a Chevy and barely glanced at the intruders as they passed. The fact that two were carrying machine guns didn't phase him because everybody was packing heavy artillery at the time.

Robert Volk, a young mail carrier, happened to be hanging around the busy shop chatting with his friends. Unlike the others, Volk was armed. He had a .45 Colt automatic slung across his shoulder, issued to guard against mail theft. Eying the Thompsons, the postman knew he was no match and ducked behind his vehicle.

"What's the fastest car in the place?" Dillinger asked. Saager, figuring Dillinger for a vigilante, nodded toward a black Ford V8 four-door sedan. "Call that guy in the back," Dillinger ordered.

"There's something wrong up here, Ralph," Saager yelled. Wright stopped what he was doing and came forward to assist his coworker.

"Just stay quiet now, boys, and everything will be all right," Dillinger assured. He turned to Saager. "Let's get going."

"I can't go!" the mechanic protested. "I'm working on a car." Dillinger tapped the tommy gun's barrel on Saager's leg. "I said let's go!"

Saager and Youngblood climbed in back, Blunk took the wheel as directed, and Dillinger got in beside him. The savvy outlaw rolled down the window, hung his Thompson out, and kept watch on Wright. If he noticed, or even cared, about Volk and his .45, he didn't let on. Blunk hit the starter, causing the car to roar to life with a distinctive throaty rumble.

"Open the doors," Dillinger said to Wright. Nobody moved. Lauren Raber, another employee, volunteered to do the honors. Blunk accelerated through the opening, turned left onto East Street, rolled to the end of the block, then turned west on Joliet. Told to ignore traffic lights, Blunk nearly collided with a car traveling north on Main. "If we hit somebody, I'll plug you first," Dillinger threatened. "Keep it at forty and watch what you're doing. We don't want a speeding ticket."

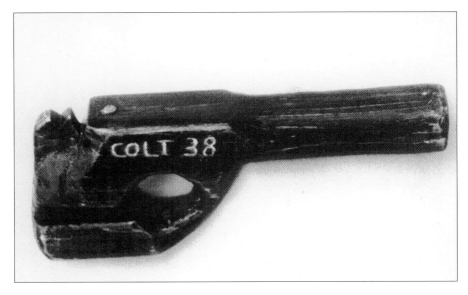

TOP LEFT: Crown Point Sheriff Lillian Holley—a rare 1930s lawwoman—had the most famous felon in the world dropped into her lap. Unfortunately, he didn't stay there for long. (Defunct newspaper photo) **TOP RIGHT:** Future DI/FBI boss J. Edgar Hoover (left) and star special agent Melvin Purvis. The pair feuded over the Dillinger fallout—and the subsequent credit. Both rode Dillinger's coattails to personal glory. (FBI photo) **BOTTOM:** The fake gun Dillinger allegedly carved from a washboard slat and painted black with shoe polish. It enabled him to walk unmolested out of the heavily guarded Crown Point jail. (Courtesy of 7ony Stewart)

TOP: Adrenaline junkie John Dillinger staged bold robberies of police department arsenals. The Cleveland, Ohio, police—among others—used the bank robber's image on their firing range targets. (Defunct newspaper photo) **BOTTOM:** The lodge at Little Bohemia. Quick-triggered G-Men nearly derailed the infant DI/FBI after panicking in the inky darkness and blasting a civilian vehicle. (FBI Photo)

TOP: The Feds opened fire on a Chevy containing three locals who had been drinking at the Little Bohemia bar. One man was killed, and his friends were injured. Dillinger and pals escaped. The Feds should have known the old Chevy wasn't the Jackrabbit's kind of ride. (FBI Photo) **BOTTOM LEFT:** Despite an intense, nationwide manhunt, Dillinger managed to sneak home for a visit in April 1934. He playfully displayed his cherished Thompson machine gun, along with the wooden pistol from the Crown Point jail escape. (Family photo) **BOTTOM RIGHT:** John Dillinger's famous crooked smile. (FBI photo)

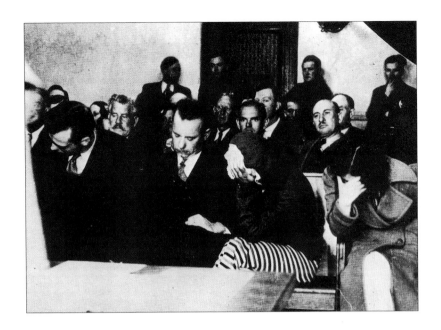

TOP: Dillinger, Pierpont (front left), and their molls Billie Frechette and Mary Kinder try to hide from the photographers during their hearing in Tucson. (Defunct newspaper photo) **BOTTOM LEFT:** Robbing banks wasn't all fun and games. Terrible Ten member Russell Clark shows the scars of hand-to-hand combat with the Tuscon cops. (Defunct newspaper photo) **BOTTOM RIGHT:** Double Trouble—The infamous "Lady in Red" Anna Sage (right) and her minion, the Billie Frechette clone Polly Hamilton. Sage served up Dillinger to the Feds for cash and a promise not to be deported to Rumania. (Defunct newspaper photo)

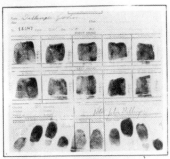
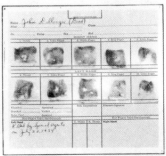

FEDERAL BUREAU OF INVESTIGATION
UNITED STATES DEPARTMENT OF JUSTICE
★ ★ ★ John Edgar Hoover, Director ★ ★ ★

Identity of John Dillinger Confirmed by Fingerprints

37-41

ABOVE: FBI "Wanted" poster of John Dillinger. (FBI photo)
RIGHT: Seeing Red—The cops took most of Anna's reward money, then she was betrayed by Uncle Sam. Welshing on their promise to end her deportation troubles, the Feds booted her out of the country. Nobody likes a rat. (Defunct newspaper photo)

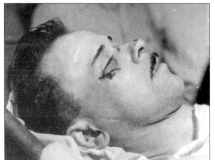

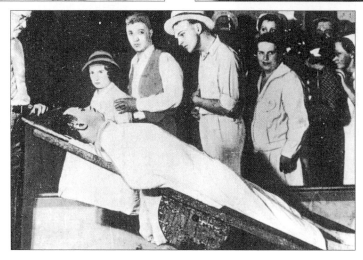

TOP: The Biograph Theater in Chicago where Dillinger was betrayed by his ladies. Clark Gable was on the screen—while a huge G-Men/East Chicago Police assassination squad sweated outside. Dillinger had no chance. (FBI photo) **CENTER LEFT:** Die young and leave a pretty corpse. Dillinger after being betrayed and assassinated. (FBI photo) **CENTER RIGHT:** Left profile of the slain Jackrabbit. The release of such gruesome photos was common in Dillinger's days. (FBI photo) **BOTTOM:** Death of a Superstar— Huge crowds, 15,000 people a day, queued up for hours to see the displayed corpse of America's first celebrity criminal. Many newspapers, like this one, took photographs and airbrushed out a rise in the outlaw's midsection caused by his arm that fueled the enduring legend that Dillinger possessed a huge sexual organ. (Defunct newspaper photo) [See the original photo at: www.snopes.com/risque/penile/dilling.htm]

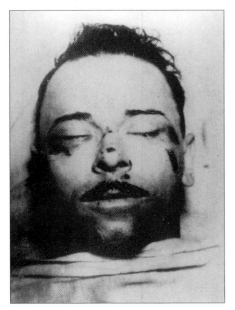 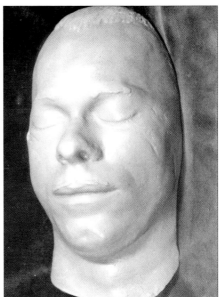

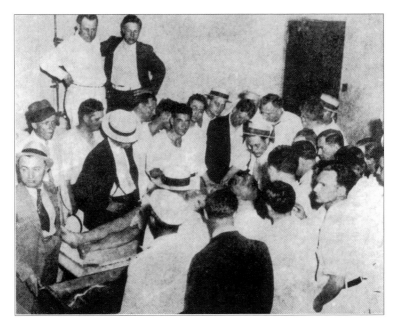

TOP LEFT: Straight shot of the slain Jackrabbit. The public couldn't get enough of Dillinger—dead or alive. (FBI photo) **TOP RIGHT:** One of the many death masks taken of John Dillinger. This one was on the wall outside J. Edgar Hoover's office until the famed FBI boss's death. (FBI photo) **BOTTOM:** Everybody wanted to see the body. Dillinger was the Elvis of crooks. (Defunct newspaper photo)

TOP LEFT: Within minutes of Dillinger's death, word spread and crowds thronged to the death scene. Many dipped clothing, handkerchiefs, or newspapers into the bank robber's blood. (Courtesy of 7ony Stewart) **TOP RIGHT:** A roguish John Herbert Dillinger—America's first celebrity criminal. His fame will probably never be equaled. (Police/FBI photo) **BOTTOM:** Gone but not forgotten. Nearly 70 years later, a little girl points out the spot where John Dillinger took his last breath. (Smusyn family photo)

The unmolested Ford passed the Lake County courthouse, swung around a bus double-parked in the street, and went north by the First National and Commercial Bank. Dillinger considered making a quick withdrawal, but figured that would be pushing it. Instead, he instructed Blunk to turn west on State Road 8. The fingerprint man explained that they'd already missed the entrance.

"Well, go west on the first road you come to."

"There's no road between here and the Lincoln Highway [U.S. 30]," Blunk informed.

"Then make one."

The first opportunity to do so came at a Clark Oil station just past the Pennsylvania Railroad tracks. A small dirt road headed west to the next intersection, then curved south. Blunk weaved to the Old Jackson Highway and then swung north through Spring Hill Grove, crossing the tip of St. Johns, Indiana. Checking the glove box, Dillinger found several 12-gauge 00 buckshot shells and a set of handcuffs, indicating that it was a police car. He signaled for Blunk to stop. Saager was sent out to twist off the bumper-mounted red fog lights that identified it as a law enforcement vehicle. The harried mechanic returned to his seat, lamps in hand. What Dillinger didn't know, and Saager wasn't saying, is that he had stolen Sheriff Holley's vehicle!

Continuing west, the four men crossed the border into Illinois—a minor event that had the dramatic legal effect of allowing J. Edgar Hoover into the game. Dillinger, flushed with freedom, couldn't care less. He began to hum and sing, fixating on "The Last Roundup," a western tune with the stretched-out refrain, "git along little doggie, git along." It was an odd choice for a man who'd found the west so inhospitable. In between verses, he asked his car mates if they'd like to see St. Louis. Blunk responded that they were in no position to quibble.

Back at the prison, mail carrier Robert Volk found himself playing the role of Chicken Little. He first tried to alert the Gary police via telephone. The dispatcher promised to check out the prison escape report when he found the time. Frustrated, Volk sprinted from the garage to the prosecutor's office in the court building. Several vigilantes were idling about. "Dillinger's escaped!" the postman gasped.

"You're nuts," one of the volunteers snapped, shooing him away like an annoying gnat. "Get out of here."

Flabbergasted, Volk spotted deputy prosecutor Floyd Vance walking to his office. "Dillinger's escaped!" Volk cried again.

"Is that right?" Vance asked skeptically. A bit more concerned, Vance walked to the jail. No one answered his knock. Concerned but not alarmed, he searched for another route inside.

Meanwhile, John Hudak, the escaped hostage, skittered from the kitchen to Lillian Holley's quarters above the jail and woke up the sheriff. The overburdened woman had been working around the clock since Dillinger's arrival, and had chosen that Saturday morning to catch up on her sleep. Hudak waited until she'd collected herself, then gave her the news. Sheriff Holley took it like a .45 butt to the head. Crying and nearly hysterical, she called the escape "too ridiculous for words" and hissed, "If I ever see John Dillinger, I'll shoot him through the head with my own gun!"

Glancing through her window, she cringed at what she saw below. The media was already swarming in for the kill.

The sheriff's nephew and chief deputy, Carroll Holley, continued the comedy of errors when he notified the state police, but gave them the wrong plate number—679-929—for the sheriff's stolen car. That tag belonged to a Mrs. M. C. Mayes of Hammond. The multifaceted mistake occurred when Deputy Edward Rogers was dispatched to the garage to record the numerals on an Auburn patrol car with a number that was one higher than Sheriff Holley's Ford. Nobody could remember the sheriff's number, so they planned to figure it out by means of subtraction. The deputy, Edward Rogers, failed to notice that there were two Auburns in the garage. He picked the wrong one, then transposed its numbers, turning 697-930 into 679-930. That led to 679-929—and poor Mrs. Mayes's Hudson.

Holley's notification, correct number or not, came twenty minutes after Dillinger fled. The delay was blamed on the time needed to summon the Holleys, free Warden Baker and the others, and have Rogers fetch the plate number. By then, the Jackrabbit was in Illinois.

The rain began to fall as Dillinger and company continued to distance themselves from Crown Point. The gangster stopped singing and stiffened as they approached a group of parked cars on the shoulder up ahead. He reminded Youngblood to lay low with his rain hat pulled down over his face because a salt-and-pepper team of escapees would be easy to recognize. The vehicles turned out to belong to road workers.

The rain made the muddy street slick. Blunk struggled to stay on course. "Put it in second gear," Dillinger suggested. Blunk hit the erratic mechanical brakes instead, sliding the V8 into a water-filled ditch twenty-three miles west of Crown Point, and twenty-five miles south of Chicago. Dillinger, still displaying his extraordinary cool, asked if there were chains onboard. Saager fished a pair from the rear floorboard. He and Youngblood stood in ankle-deep water and labored for a half hour to get the chains around the seventeen-inch rear wheels without the benefit of a jack.

As they worked, Dillinger further enlightened the men regarding his original weapon. He had used a razor blade to whittle it from the top rail of a washboard. The barrel was the handle of a safety razor. The wood was blackened with shoe polish. The crafty outlaw was quite pleased with himself. (For alternate theories on the origin of the famous wooden gun, see Source section, Chapter 13.)

The chains did the trick and the quartet was back on the road, heading for Peotone. "I suppose you'll be going to Lima to bust your men out of jail?" Blunk asked.

"They'd do as much for me," Dillinger replied.

As they passed a landmark known as Lilley Corners, Dillinger looked up and noted that telephone poles no longer lined the road. He told Blunk and Saager to exit the vehicle. "I'd probably get a better start if I shut you two up right here," he threatened, giving them a moment of terror. "But I never killed nobody, especially that cop, O'Malley, and I don't wanna start now. You guys do whatever you have to do, but I can tell you that's the last jail I'll ever be in."

With that, he fished in his pocket and handed them each four dollars— money he'd lifted from the warden and guards at the jail. "This'll get you to a town. It's not much but it's all I can spare." Blunk declined, but Saager grabbed his share. Dillinger shook their hands and grinned.

"Maybe I can remember you at Christmas time?" He climbed behind the wheel of the Ford, told Youngblood to lie on the back floorboard, and sped over a rise toward the south.

Blunk and Saager hitched a ride with a local farmer named Ed Rust. They were dropped off at the drug store in Peotone. Flagging down a deputy sheriff, they relayed their story. The sheriff rushed them back to where they'd been dropped off, then followed the distinctive chain marks until the rain obliterated the tracks. "I don't know what we would have done if we'd caught up with him anyway," Saager mused, noting how outgunned the ambitious sheriff was.

By early afternoon, news of the stunning escape was leading every radio broadcast from coast to coast. Most afternoon newspapers slapped the story in huge headlines on their front pages, with similar banners following in the morning papers that Sunday. The clever nature of the escape—using the fake gun colored with shoe polish—along with the getaway in the sheriff's own car, shot Dillinger's fame to previously unheard-of levels. The headlines and radio broadcasts crossed both the Atlantic and Pacific and made the airwaves and front pages around the world.

Locally, Prosecutor Robert Estill's chance of redeeming himself for the embarrassing photo was instantly dashed, his political career in smoking ruins. Sheriff Lillian Holley found herself being pilloried in an unapologetically sexist manner. A quickly produced film documentary claimed she was in the kitchen baking pies when the escape occurred. It was a lie, but the truth that she was sleeping, or dressing for work as she claimed, wasn't exactly vindicating. Her city was being referred to nationally as "Clown Point" even though it was the county facility, and not the city jail, that had been breached. Rival politicians suggested that Holley's Democratic party should dispense with the donkey and use a wooden pistol as their new symbol.

Hard-line conservatives called for her immediate ouster in order to hire a real—that is, male—sheriff. A letter sent to a local resident addressed to "Wooden Gun, Indiana" was delivered without delay. In Indianapolis, wooden guns were passed out at a Republican fundraising dinner, while speakers spoke of "wooden-headed" Democrats in the state.

Mrs. Holley, like others in the Dillinger saga, stopped speaking of the incident after a few weeks and would never mention it again the rest of her life. That was saying something, considering that she lived to age 103, passing away in 1994.

Of a more immediate concern was the health and welfare of the nation's bankers and bank employees. Dillinger was free and in need of funding. He no doubt would rectify that situation at the first opportunity. The nation's banks were put on a security alert, which plunged virtually everyone in the battered thrift industry into a state of fear and paranoia.

If the bankers were quaking, one can imagine the mood at the jail in Lima. Dillinger, now a mythical figure, was sure to be heading their way. The National Guard, already on the scene, bolstered their troops in nervous anticipation. Reports filtered out that Pierpont, Makley, and Clark had changed into their street clothes and were waiting to be liberated.

The gang, however, was all dressed up with no place to go. Dillinger was in Chicago, not Lima, cruising the city in the getaway car, passing scores of newsstands that already carried his picture. Off-duty police detective Lorimer Hyde was driving home to his apartment at 3020 North Broadway when he spotted a black Ford with Indiana license plates being driven by a man that appeared to be John Dillinger. The plate had a different number, thanks to the foul-up, but Hyde's instincts were screaming. The Ford pulled over to the curb at Broadway and Belmont Avenue. Hyde stopped 100 feet behind and exited with his gun drawn. Dillinger spotted him, jumped back into his car, and vanished west on Belmont. Hyde called in the troops, but Dillinger was gone.

The wave of fear spreading across the country wasn't lost on former Terror Gang member Hilton Crouch. "A couple of more jail breaks like Dillinger's, and you guys will all be dead of heart failure," he crowed as the Marion County jailers prepared to ship him to Michigan City for safer keeping.

Crouch wasn't exaggerating. Bridges and tunnels in New York City were being blockaded despite the fact that the confirmed Hoosier had never been there before. Pennsylvania state troopers were given copies of the escapee's mug shot and were ordered to pin it to their visors. Reports of ghostly Dillinger sightings came from Youngstown, Ohio; Buffalo, New York; Jacksonville, Florida; El Paso, Texas; and throughout Michigan, Missouri, Indiana, Illinois, Iowa, and Ohio.

John Sr. was in Mooresville getting supplies when Margaret Moore, the wife of *Mooresville Times* editor Everett Moore, gave him the news. "What?" he asked, stunned. "Escaped how? Is he all right?" Mrs. Moore told him what she knew. "Well, it makes a fellow feel a little better, but of course, they may catch him . . . Guess I'll start listening to the radio again now. When he was out before, that's all I did when I wasn't working."

Wayne Coy, Indiana Governor Paul McNutt's hatchet man, was answering four letters from people asking to witness Dillinger's execution when he heard the news. His boss, still reeling over the fact that he'd signed Dillinger's parole order, wasn't expected to take the news well. The "don't kill the messenger" job fell upon Indiana Attorney General Phillip Lutz. "This is the most fantastic jailbreak that has ever been called to my attention," McNutt exclaimed. As the day wore on, he was calling it a "disgrace" and joining, if not leading, the mob that wanted to hang Sheriff Holley by her frilly angora jabot.

Matt Leach took the news better than expected, possibly because he was still recovering from partying in Gary the night before. He zipped over to Crown Point to take personal command of his troops, using the opportunity to make a renewed pitch for better communication. "If we had police radios in our department, we'd probably already have Dillinger in custody." He also couldn't help but hammer the final nail in Estill's coffin. "That picture deprived the jail guards of their fear . . . Love-making between prosecutors and notorious criminals is shockingly out of place!"

In Washington, Hoover wasn't above casting a large smear net as well. "It's a damnable outrage," he decreed. "Someone is either guilty of nonfeasance or malfeasance. Either negligence or corruption must be at the bottom of this!"

While the fingers were being pointed at Holley and Estill, the authorities failed to take a hard look at one Louis Piquett—even after Dillinger appeared in Chicago near the attorney's office during the fugitive's encounter with Detective Hyde. Piquett, with advanced notice of what was about to go down at Crown Point, was sitting behind his desk at 7:15 A.M. to monitor the news. Arthur O'Leary was there as well. At eight, night owl Billie Frechette waltzed in. Meyer Bogue, an ex-con who had put Piquett and Dillinger together, sprung out of bed as well.

Carefully waiting until the news hit the radio at 9:30, Piquett phoned Warden Baker for a confirmation. Billie shrieked in delight as Piquett signaled that it was true. Sent to fetch the late-morning newspapers, Bogue returned with party supplies, the ingredients for making "gin-rickeys." By 11 A.M., Billie was comatose on Piquett's couch.

No doubt having celebrated a bit too much himself, Piquett lapsed into a brain snag worthy of a Crown Point deputy. He decided to use the apartment of a former employee and girlfriend, Esther Anderson, as Dillinger's hideout and love nest. He asked Esther if she'd mind putting up a "couple" for the night at her north-side flat on 434 Wellington Avenue. Thinking more George and Gracie than Johnnie and Billie, Esther agreed. A regular radio listener and newspaper reader, Esther was struck with fear when she heard that Dillinger had escaped. Could he be part of Piquett's couple? She brushed it off as paranoia. The paranoia became a terrifying reality when Piquett materialized with a tipsy Billie Frechette, whom Esther instantly recognized from newspaper photos. Esther became hysterical and refused to allow Billie inside, much less her notorious boyfriend. Scrambling, Piquett parked Billie in the building's lobby and ordered her to wait there until her beau appeared. The lawyer then went to rendezvous with his client, a meeting scheduled for 4:30 at Broadway and Belmont.

After shaking Detective Hyde off his tail, Dillinger circled back, spotted his attorney's car, and motioned for the lawyer to follow him down Belmont. They parked, and Piquett slipped into the famous get-away car. He nodded to Youngblood still sprawled in the back, gave Dillinger $300, and told him where to find Billie. Piquett would, of course, deny all of this to investigators, instead claiming that Dillinger owed him money and he never expected to see the bandit again.

The lovers' reunion on Wellington was passionate and emotional.

Billie, never one to be discreet, threw herself into her beau's arms, tears flowing down her cheeks. Dillinger herded her to the car and raced off. At a streetcar stop on Western Avenue, he gave Youngblood $100 and said good-bye.

Finally alone together, Billie cooed to John that she was staying with her half-sister, Frances "Patsy" Frechette Schultze, twenty-eight, at 3512 North Halstead. He was welcomed to crash there. Dillinger wheeled the unmarked cop car around, headed east on Belmont and then north on Halstead.

Detective Hyde, who lived nearby, had given up the hunt and was heading home when he incredibly spotted the Ford again. The addition of Billie did nothing to throw him off track. Dillinger spotted the pesky Hyde and the chase was on, cop and robber weaving through the heavy traffic. Up ahead, a streetcar stopped to discharge its passengers. Detective Hyde slid to a stop, but his prey swerved into the oncoming traffic, wheeled around the obstruction, and kept going, not so much as scratching Sheriff Holley's Ford. Hyde cursed his fate as the world's most famous felon eluded him a second time.

Undeterred, Dillinger pulled behind the apartment house at 3512 North Halstead and entered the building through a side door. He went to Patsy's second-floor apartment while veteran speed driver Fireball Billie took the Ford and parked it three miles away in front of a home at 1057 Ardmore. She walked back to Broadway and hopped a southbound streetcar to Patsy's. Billie's sister and her roommate, Marge Edwards, shared the only bedroom, leaving John and Billie to quietly consummate their grand reunion on the more public couch. In between doing so, they had an hour-long meeting with Piquett and O'Leary. Dillinger was informed that a one-armed attorney his father had briefly retained for $500, Joseph Ryan, had not passed the money to Piquett as ordered.

"Get that sonofabitch on the phone, Mr. Piquett," Dillinger snapped. "Tell him I said he'd better cough up that dough and quick!"

Ryan happened to be in Chicago the following day. Piquett located him and summoned the attorney to his office. Shaken, Ryan promised to get the money. Instead, he left town without bothering to check out, pay his bill, or retrieve his bags from the Hotel Sherman.

As Ryan headed for the hills, Ira McDowell, Chicago's acting police commissioner, was issuing the familiar death threats. "If Dillinger sticks his head inside Chicago, he'll be shot on sight. Those are my orders!"

Dillinger, of course, was already in Chicago, sticking his head in many familiar places. Captain Stege, suspecting as much, bitterly reactivated his Dillinger Death Squad. "What's the use of arresting Dillinger if we can't keep him in jail? I'm sending squads all over the city to nab him . . . But even if we do get him, it will probably be the same thing all over again. I'm disgusted. If we do find Dillinger, he'll never go back to Indiana—except in a box!"

The tough talk wasn't limited to Indiana and Illinois. Assistant United States Attorney General Joseph Keenan echoed Stege's sentiments. "I don't know when or where we will get Dillinger, but we will get him—and I hope we get him under such circumstances that the government will not have to stand the expense of a trial."

Not everyone shared such vengeful emotions. Dillinger, still viewed as a man of people, was being lauded in letter-to-the-editor sections of newspapers nationwide. Concerned citizens begged the governors of Indiana and Illinois to give him a pardon and leave him alone. Others elevated his importance to society over that of those trying to catch him. A Martinsville farmer, acknowledging the inevitability of another robbery, summed up the feelings best: "As tough as times are, John's doing the country a favor by getting the money out of the banks and back into circulation."

Spectators flocked to Crown Point, overloading the city and snarling the roads around the prison for weeks afterward. An estimated 1,500 cars, mostly from Illinois and Michigan, arrived on the first Sunday alone. Mobs literally wore a path between the rear of the jail and the back of the Main Street Garage, retracing Dillinger's historic steps.

Despite the hoopla, hysteria, and frenzied hunting, Sheriff Holley's Ford wasn't discovered until 2:30 P.M. the following Monday—two days after Billie had abandoned it. A Crown Point vigilante's .38 was found in a map pocket. The discovery set the volatile Captain Stege off again. "I told them this would happen! I pleaded with Governor McNutt's secretary [Coy] to have him held in a state prison. How in the name of common sense can a prisoner go through six barred doors to freedom?"

Mrs. Holley took no joy in having the already legendary vehicle recovered. "I am a broken woman. The courage I am trying to show is but exterior . . . I tried to make good but I just couldn't make it. And I wanted to be the ideal woman sheriff, too." After some rest and reflection, she returned to her feisty self, fighting for her job and forcefully denying that it was "too big for a woman."

As happens, one woman's loss was another woman's gain. John and Billie left Chicago on March 4 and headed for St. Paul, Minnesota. Two days later, at the behest of Indiana Deputy Attorney General Ed Barce, hostages Ernest Blunk and Sam Cahoon were charged with assisting a criminal to escape. The evidence was flimsy, and it reeked of scapegoats, but Cahoon and Blunk's actions that morning were indeed suspicious. Cahoon had opened the cell-block doors with the prisoners loose, and the highly cooperative Blunk had missed repeated opportunities to escape. Old-timer Cahoon wasn't phased by the potential problems, pointing out that all the lawmen could do was incarcerate him inside the same jail where he already lived. Blunk, thirty-two, stood to suffer the most from the smear.

Judge Murray was incensed by the arrests, calling them the result of "a bad case of hysteria." He refused for a week to suspend Blunk from his job, pointing out that the mild-mannered, unarmed county employee was a fingerprint expert, not a law enforcement agent or corrections officer. Murray would subsequently come under attack and investigation himself for refusing to transfer Dillinger to Michigan City as Sheriff Holley had originally requested.

Piquett, who was guilty as sin, was busy painting his client as something akin to an angel. Responding to a fan letter that expressed concern for the outlaw's well-being, he described Public Enemy Number One as a Christian who was touched by the hand of God, and promised that he had seen the light and wouldn't rob any more banks. Dillinger, according to Piquett, was going to "travel the path of righteousness" and intended to "give the balance of his life in this world to God."

In truth, Dillinger was giving his all to Billie, not to God, and was hanging with felons instead of church folk. John Hamilton and his new girlfriend, Pat Cherrington, had picked up the couple in Chicago that Sunday evening and had taken them to St. Paul, where Hamilton was now living. The double-talking Cherrington had ditched her G-Man chaperones and was squarely back in The Terror Gang fold.

St. Paul was a popular place for hoods, thanks to a police force eager to be greased. The Barker-Karpis gang, Tommy Carroll, Homer VanMeter, and Baby Face Nelson were all hiding out there, among others. In fact, on the day John and Billie arrived, Baby Face was busy chasing down and murdering an ammunition dealer named Theodore B. Kidder, thirty-four, who had rubbed him the wrong way. Kidder was shot in his car in front of his screaming wife and mother-in-law.

The wild Minnesota city was certainly a happening place, but it was a bit too noisy and bloody for Dillinger. He sent Billie to adjacent Minneapolis where she rented unit 106 of the Santa Monica Apartments on 3252 Girard Avenue. She peeled the forty-five-dollar monthly fee from a fat roll of stolen money. Dillinger, Hamilton, and Cherrington arrived shortly thereafter, brought in the luggage, and wired down the window shades. Billie and Pat were dispatched to Stillman's Grocery at Thirty-first Street and Hennepin, the same store where the Barker-Karpis gang had been getting their grub. Homer VanMeter, using the name John L. Ober, was hiding nearby as well, at 3310 Freemont, shacking up with Marie Conforti.

The two Shirt Shop Boys staged a small reunion on Monday, March 5. VanMeter told Dillinger that he, Nelson, and Eugene "Eddie" Green were planning to hit a bank the next day in Sioux Falls, South Dakota, 170 miles away. Dillinger was naturally cut in.

The following morning, a Packard sedan containing six men pulled up in front of the imposing Security National Bank and Trust Company at Ninth and Dakota Avenue in Sioux Falls. A young bank clerk saw them through the window and instantly tensed, telling those around him that the strangers looked like a pack of holdup men. Cashier Don Lovejoy hovered his finger above the alarm button as he watched four of the men get out, hats pulled low and collars upturned. They were Dillinger, Nelson, VanMeter, and Green. Three-fingered John Hamilton stayed with the car, and Tommy Carroll, hiding a tommy gun under his topcoat on the chilly, thirty-degree day, positioned himself at the front door.

Nelson, VanMeter, and Green also held concealed machine guns. Dillinger, leading the group and sporting a mustache, was packing light, a .45 automatic pistol. He walked to teller Robert Dargen's cage as the extroverted Nelson whipped out his Thompson and announced the holdup. Patrolman Peter Duffy, in the bank on personal business but in uniform, turned and was knocked to the floor and disarmed by VanMeter and Green. Seeing more than enough to confirm his fears, Lovejoy hit the button, flashing a signal to a central telephone operation and setting off a small alarm inside the bank. Dillinger ignored the din and began scooping the money from Dargen's cage. Nelson, more high-strung, began screaming threats. "I'd like to know who the hell set off that alarm. Which one of you bastards did that? If you wanna get killed, just make another dumb move!"

Hearing the noise, bank president China R. Clarke stepped out of his office. "You got the combination to the safe?" Dillinger asked. Clarke responded that he didn't. Dillinger gave him a swift kick to the butt. "Then get me someone who does!" Clarke fingered teller Dargen, who was waved over to successfully perform the task. VanMeter ducked inside and swept up $13,000. Spotting a second vault door, Dillinger nodded for Dargen to open that one. Dargen explained that it was on a time lock, and only contained bonds. VanMeter didn't buy it and forced Clarke to make an attempt. The trembling president tried and failed.

A block away at police headquarters, the desk sergeant took the call from the alarm company reporting trouble at the bank. The dispatcher failed to specify what kind of "trouble." Chief M. W. Parsons and Detective F. C. White left to check it out.

Officer Homer Powers was standing near the Power City Drug Store when Carroll walked over and took him prisoner. A. R. Reesler, a local cashier at the nearby *Argus Leader* newspaper building, observed Powers being walked toward the bank at gunpoint. "The bank's being robbed!" Reesler exclaimed. A dozen pressman, editors, and reporters stuck their heads out of various windows to watch the show, which was just getting good. Motorcycle cop Hale Keith ran down Ninth, ready for action. The diminutive Baby Face spotted him, jumped on a desk for a better vantage point, and squeezed the trigger of his Thompson, blowing out the window and dropping Keith with slugs to the stomach, right thigh, elbow, and wrist.

A citizen, C. A. Wikle, crawled to the fallen officer. "How bad are you hurt?"

"Pretty bad, I guess," the still-conscious Keith gasped, dragging himself toward the street.

Inside, the half-crazed Nelson was up on a marble countertop pacing like a bantam chicken. "I got one! I got one of 'em," he proudly crowed. Dillinger ignored him.

Police fingerprint technician Roy Donahoe pulled up out front. Carroll greeted him with a single shot to his tire. Chief Parsons and Detective White arrived behind Donahoe and were taken prisoner by Carroll as well. The efficient "doorman" lined the hostages against the bank wall as the crowd of spectators watching from stopped cars and surrounding buildings swelled to over a thousand.

"Everything okay out there?" one of the robbers shouted from inside. Carroll yelled back that he had things under control.

Ted Ramsey, a photographer for the *Argus Leader*, flashed the action from the steps of the Modern Plumbing Shop, fighting with the crowds to keep from being bumped. He was so excited he forgot to switch the film three times, overlaying the images.

At the Minnehaha County courthouse, Sheriff Melvin Sells received a disturbing phone call. "Bring all of your guns to Ninth and Main!" a breathless voice said, immediately hanging up. Sells grabbed a Thompson and a riot gun, ran to his car, and raced toward the bank. At Main and Sixth, he picked up court reporter H. M. Shoebotham. "Stick a couple of loads into the shotgun," Sells ordered.

"I don't know how!" a fumbling Shoebotham confessed.

At Ninth and Main, the pair saw the huge crowd, their 2,000 eyes glued to Carroll. The lone bandit was in the middle of the street waving his Thompson in an attempt to smoke out more cops. Sheriff Sells backed his vehicle into an alley between the Ritz Cafe and Lincoln Hotel and jumped out, the nervous court reporter in tow. They ran through the hotel lobby and were about to climb a stairway for a vantage point when they heard someone say, "They've shot a cop!" Another voice cried, "There they go. They're getting ready to leave."

"Get my car and bring it around the front," Sells barked to Shoebotham. The warning was premature. Dillinger and crew were still inside sucking up the money, $46,000 and counting. As they dumped the bills into sacks, local resident Gus J. Moen, lost in thought, ambled down from an upper floor and strolled through the lobby, completely oblivious. Nelson shouted for him to stop but the words didn't register. Never one to need much of an excuse, Baby Face fired a burst into a window above the former banker's head, showering him with glass. Finally tuning in, Moen dropped his briefcase with a startling smack and joined the others.

Carroll had four cops under his control when his cohorts emerged, protected by a giant cocoon of forty customers and bank employees. At the Packard, clerks Mildred Boswick, Alice Blegen, Emma Knoback, and Mary Lucas were spread out on the running boards. Teller Leo Olson was forced on as well. After Carroll hopped inside, the robbers rolled down the windows and grabbed the arms of their human shields.

"Don't be afraid," one of the bandits said. "We don't intend to hurt you."

Patrolman Harley Chrisman arrived on foot just as the vehicle was preparing to take off. Thinking fast, he ran ahead, ducked into Maxwell's hardware store, commandeered a hunting rifle, and slammed in some cartridges. He dashed to a basement stairwell, took aim, and fired a hefty slug into the Packard's radiator. The big car rolled 300 yards and paused for a moment in front of Modern Cleaners. The gang considered hijacking another vehicle, then thought better of it, turning west on Thirteenth Street and again on Dakota. They slowed to pass a horse-drawn milk wagon, continued south to Twenty-ninth, then swerved to Minnesota Avenue.

Sheriff Sells and Shoebotham were hot on the crippled Packard's trail, as were Chrisman, Deputy Sheriff Lawrence Green, and U.S. Marshall Art Anderson. The police cars met at Minnesota Avenue for a quick strategy session. Sheriff Sells jumped in with the other law enforcement officers, leaving Shoebotham on his own.

At Forty-first Street, Leo Olsen was told to get off—right in front of radio station WNAS. "Good-bye, Shorty," one of the bandits cracked. "We don't need you anymore." Dillinger chuckled and tossed out a handful of roofing nails.

The women, none of whom was wearing a coat, took the opportunity to complain bitterly about the cold. "Get in the car then," Dillinger instructed. The girls hurried inside, propping themselves on the laps of the grinning crooks.

Wilson Service Station attendant Bill Conklin saw the smoking and hissing Packard, grabbed a fire extinguisher and ran into the street to help. "Get back in there," one of the gang snapped to the Good Samaritan as the vehicle roared by.

Spotting a police car in the rearview window, Hamilton stopped to let his associates deal with it. They sprayed the chase vehicle with lead, exploding its windshield, crushing its headlight, and vengefully puncturing its radiator. The cops were forced to retreat, unable to shoot back because of the women inside the getaway car.

A half mile further, Hamilton saw rural mailman Bert Hester making his rounds. The gang considered taking Hester's old Chevy, then decided they were better off in the Packard, busted radiator or not. The faithful car made it another four miles before seizing up. Hamilton had just enough time to jackknife it across the road, blocking the way of farmer Alfred Muesch's Dodge. While the men were making the switch to Muesch's vehicle, Mrs. F. H. Farragher puttered up in a Chevy coupe. "You girls will catch your death of cold out here without coats," she scolded.

A bandit materialized from behind the Packard. "How much gas you got in that car?" he asked. Told that it was less than a quarter tank, he brushed her off and went back to transferring the Packard's gas to the farmer's Dodge. Mrs. Farragher started her Chevy and pulled forward.

"Where the hell you think you're goin'?" one of the crooks yelled.

"Just turn around and go back the way you came," one of the female hostages suggested. Attempting to do just that, the prim and proper lady was ordered to kill the engine and stay put.

Dillinger came over and told the girls that the Dodge wasn't big enough to stuff them all inside so they were free to go. The fast friends all said their farewells, then the girls watched as the charming, well-dressed robbers drove away. Mrs. Farragher, perturbed by the interruption, chugged off as well, failing to offer the stranded young women a lift.

The Dodge swung east to Shindler, crossed into Iowa, then back to Minnesota. All along the way, they left a trail of irate motorists waving their fists by their nail-flattened tires. Two airplanes shadowed the robbers from above, but lost them when they transferred to a black Lincoln they had stashed. That vehicle was spotted in Worthington, Currie, and Lucan before vanishing completely.

Sheriff Sells and the others gave up near Luverne. Guessing that the crooks were heading for St. Paul, Chief Parsons alerted the locals.

"Don't worry," an officer responded. "They won't get by us."

Chapter 14

By early afternoon, small, squeaky voices began overloading the Sioux City hospital's phone lines. They all asked the same question, "How's Officer Keith?" The young motorcycle cop had been a fixture at area school crossings, and his little charges were overwrought with concern.

The good news was that despite the four bullet wounds, including the critical one to the gut, the popular Keith pulled through. Surgeons patched him up, then released bulletins on his recovery that were posted at the schools.

"Boy, it was a tough one," he told reporters when he was able to talk. "I wish I could have got into action before they got me."

In Indiana, Capt. Matt Leach was in denial. "Dillinger hasn't had time for that job, or I'm badly fooled. That job sounds to me like the work of a Minneapolis gang. His ace holdup men—Pierpont, Makley, Clark, Shouse, Copeland, and Crouch—are all in prison. He'll have to have time to mobilize another bad gang. If the Sioux Falls job had been pulled next week, I might have suspected Dillinger."

Humorist Will Rogers wasn't buying it. "They had him surrounded in Chicago, but he robbed a bank in Sioux Falls that day," Rogers cracked in his syndicated column. "So, they was right on his trail. Just three states behind!"

If the Minneapolis gang's destination wasn't clear enough, investigators found a map in the Packard that had the route from St. Paul to Sioux Falls marked in crayon. Not far from the waxy line's point of origin, the returning bandits gathered inside Eddie Green's apartment and divided the loot. Baby Face, reminding everyone that it was his job, not Dillinger's, counted it out. That was fine with John. He was a sociable sort who always fit in well, and never seemed to be bothered by the eccentric behavior of his loosely wired associates.

Thanking Nelson for the opportunity, he announced that he would use most of his $7,000 share to pay for Pierpont, Makley, and Clark's attorneys. After he left, Bessie Green whispered to her husband that living so close to such a notorious felon wasn't smart. She vowed to hunt for a new apartment the next morning.

There was no need to rush. By Thursday, March 8, John and Billie were right back in Chicago, visiting friends and dropping off $976 to Piquett. That same day, Harry Pierpont's murder trial began in Lima. With Brigadier General Harold M. Bush on the scene commanding a force of twenty-three, stoic Ohio National Guard soldiers, Dillinger knew that busting his pals out at that time would be futile. General Bush went so far as to turn the Hotel Norval into a fortress and command post, moving Judge Emmitt E. Everett, Prosecutor Ernest Botkin, and their families into the heavily secured building. The jury was stashed there as well—three farmers, two tool makers, a pair of merchants, a real estate agent, a bee-keeper, a church janitor, and two housewives.

The Allen County jail had a similar military feel, surrounded by sandbags, wire, temporary wooden walls, and armed soldiers. Pierpont's lady lawyer, Jessie Levy, protested to deaf ears that the overt security and oppressive leg irons convicted her client before the proceedings started. Prosecutor Botkin merely had to drop the "D" word to convince the judge that all the security and restraints were necessary.

General Bush, trying to think like Dillinger, immediately saw a kink in the armor—the increasing number of "special deputies" recruited by young Sheriff Don Sarber. Figuring Dillinger and friends could slip in under the guise of these unknown plainclothes deputies, he cracked down, limiting their ranks and access. Rumors swirled that Pierpont had offered $1,000 to any deputy who provided him with a weapon. Subsequent rumors had some interested parties holding out for $5,000. Shortly thereafter, one of General Bush's men relieved a deputy of a .38 in the cell block.

General Bush himself didn't expect Dillinger to act until things quieted down, terming the bandit "a very careful and methodical planner."

A parade of witnesses identified Pierpont as one of Jess Sarber's killers. Handsome Harry displayed little emotion until a heavily manacled Ed Shouse took the stand and ratted the entire crew in unwavering detail. Pierpont glared and mumbled death oaths as his ex-partner buried him. Pierpont's fate was sealed when Tucson officer Jay Smith testified that he took Sarber's .38 Colt Detective Special from the tall gangster when he was arrested out west.

If there was any hesitancy in giving Pierpont the chair, it was erased when Lucy Sarber testified how Harry locked her in the cell block and refused to allow her to care for her dying husband.

Levy put up a good fight, but she couldn't overcome those sledgehammer blows. After a three-day trial—the norm in those simpler times—Pierpont was found guilty of first-degree murder.

Politicians and law enforcement agents in six states celebrated by keeping their eye on the ball. It was announced that Illinois, Indiana, Ohio, Minnesota, Michigan, and Wisconsin were each ponying up $1,000 as a bounty on John Dillinger's head. The $6,000 total was sure to tempt the dubious loyalties of those in and around the criminal underworld.

The following Monday, March 12, the glib Charles Makley had his day in court. The judge immediately ratcheted up the tension by announcing, "We've received direct word that John Dillinger is on his way here with armed men." The scare, which wasn't true, was the judge's way of quashing all change-of-venue requests based upon the military presence and circus atmosphere. General Bush reacted to the judge's statement by situating guardsmen at the Ohio governor's mansion in Columbus, and assigning others to act as bodyguards. The stone-faced soldiers shadowed the governor and his daughter, Mary, wherever they went.

In Crown Point, a grand jury was impaneled that same morning to investigate the escape. Media hounds in Indiana and Ohio looking to dominate the news were soon disappointed. The object of their fears and investigations was about to trump them once again.

The First National Bank of Mason City, Iowa, boasted to a nervous public that their cash reserves were in excess of $240,000. The big bank in the small town—25,000 residents—was perched twenty-three miles south of the Minnesota border. A few days before the planned heist, Eddie Green, on a reconnaissance mission, dropped by the home of the assistant cashier, Harry C. Fisher. Green used the ruse of searching for a nearby address so he could make a mental sketch of Fisher's face. The purpose was to be able to quickly identify the cashier during the robbery because inside sources leaked that he was the one who had the codes to the vaults.

Homer VanMeter assisted Green as part of the scout team. Arriving for the actual hit that Tuesday were Dillinger, Tommy Carroll, John Hamilton, Baby Face Nelson, and John Paul Chase. The five joined Green and VanMeter in a large, blue Buick that had been stolen in Chicago from Charles Williams on October 13, 1933.

The packed Buick rolled into Mason City at 2:20 P.M., turned west on State Street, and double-parked behind the bank. Chase, armed with a state-of-the-art "Monitor," a commercial version of the military's Browning Automatic Rifle, stayed with the car as the others exited.

Marching toward the bank, Carroll saw independent filmmaker H. C. Kunkleman standing behind a movie camera across the street. Kunkleman was filming an unrelated feature on small town America. "Hey you, put that damned thing away!" Carroll ordered. "If there's any shooting to be done, we'll do it." Kunkleman's eyes froze on Carroll's Thompson, then moved to Nelson who was in the street waving a similar weapon. The startled cameraman quickly folded up his equipment.

With Carroll and the volatile Nelson positioned outside, the remaining four headed down Federal Avenue, turning north into the bank. Dillinger, smartly clad in a gray suit, dark fedora, matching overcoat, and striped muffler, had the entranceway duty and carried the appropriate Thompson. Demonstrating the inclusive nature of the new gang, it was the lesser lights—Green, Hamilton and VanMeter—who were assigned the critical inside work.

It may have been democratic, but it wasn't very wise. The excitable VanMeter approached bank president Willis G. C. Bagley, brandished his weapon, and yelled like a madman. Thinking he was deranged, Bagley sprung from his chair and ran to his nearby office. VanMeter followed, sticking the barrel of his .45 Colt into the doorjamb as Bagley tried to slam it shut. For a moment, the pistol was trapped and VanMeter was unarmed. He frantically jerked it loose, then fired through the wooden obstacle, creasing Bagley's vest and splintering wood into the banker's sleeve. The rattled thug pulled the trigger again but the weapon misfired. Bagley seized the opportunity to lock his door. Secured, he tried to call the police but couldn't get an outside line. Peeking through his window, he saw people with their arms raised. Realizing it was a holdup, and that his attacker had accomplices, Bagley ducked behind his desk and remained there.

First National's telephone operator, Margaret Johnson, was walking from her desk to the bank lobby when she saw the crooks and heard the shot. She did a pirouette and scooted back to her switchboard on a rear mezzanine balcony. She plugged in an outside line—then froze in fear. She failed to complete the SOS because she was afraid the robbers might overhear.

VanMeter's premature shot prompted Harry Fisher and assistant cashier Ralph E. Wiley to drop behind their cages. Hamilton saw the move and shouted, "Get the hell out here with everybody else!"

An ominous security feature at the bank may explain why Dillinger and Nelson instinctively chose to remain outside. An enclosed guard tower had been constructed that offered a commanding view of the lobby. It was equipped with bulletproof glass, tear-gas ports, and rifle slits, which enabled someone to fire a Winchester semiautomatic in total safety. Green and VanMeter failed to notice or recognize the tower while casing the joint.

Security officer Tom Walters promptly shot a gas projectile that slammed Green square in the back, nearly knocking him over. "Where's the son of a bitch who shot me?" a furious Green demanded. Finally spotting the offending tower, he raised his finned Thompson barrel, screamed, "Get that guy with the gas!" and squeezed the trigger. The massive assault pocked the resistant glass, launching stinging shards into Walters's ear and chin. As blood dripped on his hands, Walters fumbled with his weapon, desperately trying to extract the swollen gas cartridge from the chamber. He whipped open his pocketknife, but the blade quickly broke on the hot metal.

Green grabbed customer F. A. Stephenson and used him as both a shield and source of quick information. "How many guards are in that thing and how do you get into it?" he demanded. Stephenson, surprisingly enough, knew both answers. One guard entered via a ladder.

The inside men, along with everybody else, were now suffering from the gas attack that burned their eyes, nose, throat, and skin. "We'd never have come in here if we'd known you had that damn thing up there," VanMeter choked to Wiley, admitting his own preparation mistake. The dark-haired, narrow-eyed crook's misery was about to double. Tom Barclary, an assistant auditor, grabbed a second tear-gas canister from a cabinet near his balcony office, pulled the pin, and heaved it like a hand grenade over the railing. The smoky can bounced near a customer lying on the floor. The man kicked it away. Another prone customer booted it right back. Mortified, the first man coughed, put his hand over his searing eyes, and swiped at it a second time, sliding it in a different direction. Someone else sent it spinning off from there. Until it was spent, the hated canister bounced around the lobby floor like a pinball.

Outside, Nelson was similarly darting about, fiendishly laughing, randomly firing his thunderous weapon, and threatening everyone in sight. He blasted a new Hudson sedan that approached, causing the terrified driver to back the whole way down the block.

Spectators were both excited and dangerously confused. Many had noticed the big movie camera being set up earlier and thought it was a scene from a film. A citizen, John Kelroy, observing real bullets destroying real property, took it upon himself to try and wake everybody up from their Hollywood dream. "Movie men don't act like that!" he warned the star-struck crowd, mostly to no avail.

The spectators weren't the only ones lost in a fantasy. R. L. James, the secretary of the local school board, strolled down the street deep in his own world, heading for the bank's back door. Baby Face shrieked at him, then promptly shot the man twice in the leg. Riffling through the bleeding man's briefcase, he exclaimed, "You stupid bastard, I thought you were a cop!"

Any remorse Baby Face may have felt was dashed when he stood and fired a second burst at Tom James, R. L. James's son, who was rushing over to help his injured father. The younger James wasn't hit.

On Federal Street, an agitated motorist tried to pass a line of stopped cars. Dillinger, still holding the Thompson, pulled a .45 with his left hand and adroitly fired a slug into the aggressive motorist's radiator.

Police Chief E. J. Patton was on his way to the courthouse when he heard the shooting. He ran through "Central Park," a small wooded area in front of the bank, surveyed the scene, then continued to the second floor of the nearby Weir Building where he stationed himself at a window that offered a decent vantage point.

Patrolman James Buchanan popped out of the trees a few moments later. Armed with a sawed-off shotgun, he took cover behind a small boulder placed there as a memorial to the Grand Army of the Republic veterans organization. As with Chief Patton, Buchanan couldn't fire for fear of hitting bystanders. Dillinger didn't harbor such fears. Still using his left hand, he disrespectfully smacked a .45 bullet off of Buchanan's historic rock, sending the chips flying. "Come out from behind there, you son of a bitch!" Dillinger challenged.

Buchanan didn't take the bait. "There isn't any question that bird was an artist with a pistol," he'd later remark.

Mason City had a few such artists of their own. John C. Shipley, an elderly judge, looked down from his third-floor office in the bank building and observed Dillinger threatening the pinned-down Buchanan. Judge Shipley grabbed a Wyatt Earp—era six-shooter, took aim, and fired. Dillinger grabbed at his right shoulder and searched the windows for the offending party. He spotted some movement and returned fire Gatlin-gun-style. Shipley, no fool, had quickly backed away, avoiding the rain of deadly bullets and stinging glass.

Realizing they were on the verge of being surrounded, Dillinger sent word that it was time to move out. VanMeter relayed the news to Hamilton, who was at the vault trying to prod Harry Fisher to spin it open. "Get a move on!" Hamilton ordered, kicking the cashier in the behind. Fisher opened the vault, but there was a second, barred gate between the outside and the safe. Fisher astutely ducked inside and let it slam behind him. He then protested that the tear-gas fumes were blinding him, and he couldn't open the safe. Hamilton raised his weapon—that miraculously cleared Fisher's vision. He opened the safe on the first try. Digging again into his bag of tricks, Fisher claimed that he couldn't unlock the barred gate that was keeping Hamilton from reaching the money. Instead, Fisher began to slowly pass packs of small bills through the openings between the bars. "Hand the big bills out here or I'm going to plug you!" Hamilton fumed. After a few more minutes, VanMeter signaled that it was time to go. Hamilton cursed at Fisher, then grabbed Francis DeSart, a savings department clerk, to use as his shield.

Green, VanMeter, and Hamilton herded a pack of hostages outside. As the group walked south, Judge Shipley peeped out of his shattered window and decided to take a chance. He aimed the classic weapon and fired a second time, hitting the perpetual slug magnet John "Three Fingers" Hamilton in the right shoulder. Hamilton wheeled around, couldn't find the mystery attacker, and continued on. As they prepared to enter the Buick, Dillinger saw R. L. James lying in a pool of blood on the sidewalk. "What the hell did you do that for?" Dillinger asked. Baby Face just shrugged.

The hostages were stationed on the running boards and bumpers as usual—only this time there was an astounding number. Thirteen bank employees, customers, and bystanders formed a flesh-and-blood fence around the vehicle. Stephenson, Green's personal shield, complained that he was totally blind from the gas. "You've done your part," Green said compassionately. "Get out of here."

Ralph Wiley tried to join Stephenson. "Get on there you bald-headed bastard," Nelson insulted, pushing Wiley to the rear bumper where four others were already hanging on for dear life.

Like an overstuffed clown car, the Buick crept slowly to the corner, turned north on Federal Street, angled to Second Street, hooked west to Adams Avenue, then south to First Street. Wheelman John Paul Chase wound his way to Clear Lake Road, passed a snooty country club, and then turned south again. Chief Patton and two officers closed in, then veered off, realizing they had no chance against the impenetrable human shield.

On the passenger-side running board, Mrs. Jack Leu's hat blew off, exposing the hostage's head to the bitter cold. She rectified it by boldly burying her head through one of the open windows. "Nice police department you've got here," an amused Baby Face told her. "They'd best quit following us or we're gonna shoot all of you."

Clarence McGowan was out for an afternoon drive with his wife and five-year-old daughter when he saw what looked like a one-car parade. He edged forward to check out the festivities. Baby Face tried to blast him, but was having trouble shooting around druggist Carroll Mulcahy's flapping lab coat. "Button that damned thing! It's in my way," Nelson ordered.

"If I let go to do that I'll fall off," the petrified druggist screamed.

"Then I'll just shoot through it!" Despite the multiple hindrances, one of Nelson's slugs ripped through Mulcahy's gown, pierced the metal of Clarence McGowan's vehicle, and sent splintered .45 fragments into McGowan's abdomen and knees. The injuries were painful but not life-threatening.

With McGowan out of the way, Nelson had a clearer shot at the trailing cop car. When Chase reached the city limits, the trigger-happy Nelson ordered him to stop so he could get out and take even better aim. The patrol car anticipated the assault and ducked into a driveway. Frustrated, Nelson haphazardly threw a handful of roofing nails on the street, some of which rolled back near the Buick's tires. Dillinger pointed it out and Baby Face kicked them in a huff. Then, with a crazed look, he offered a suggestion. "Let's fight it out with 'em here!"

"Get in!" Dillinger ordered, vetoing the idea.

As they continued on, one of the bandits noticed that hostage Bill Schmidt was clinging to a paper bag in his free hand. Schmidt was forced to fork it over. Fishing inside, the crew was delighted to discover that it was filled with freshly made sandwiches from Killmer's Drug Store where Schmidt worked. The outlaws helped themselves. Schmidt would later refuse to pay for them, claiming he never legally received the large lunch order.

After crossing Highway 65, the Buick stopped and set the railbirds free. Two others inside the car, Mrs. William Clark and Mrs. Frank Graham, were let go a short time later. Asked by reporters if she would be able to identify her captors, Mrs. Clark hissed, "I sure would! Especially the one who winked at me!"

The winker and friends ditched the Buick in a sandpit four miles from the city and took off in two separate cars stashed there. Roadblocks were set up, but as always, they failed to deter the bandits.

Thanks to Fisher's clever tactics, the robbers only came away with $52,000. Fisher's subtle defiance and bravery saved his employers and customers $157,000. Both Johns—Dillinger and Hamilton—paid for their share in blood, catching a pair of Judge Shipley's prized bullets with their right shoulders. Back "home," the two were taken to a St. Paul gangster physician, Dr. Nels G. Mortensen of 2252 Fairmount Avenue. Mortensen, raising his eyebrows over the near identical injuries, advised his late-night patients to come to his office the next day where he would be better equipped to double check for lingering slugs. Neither showed, preferring to take their chances.

The *Mason City Globe Gazette* pulled out their biggest headlines to announce the robbery the following day. One story paid the fairer sex a left-handed compliment from a bygone era. "All the women concerned in the holdup acted calmly. None of the fainting and hysteria attributed to the sex were evident during the exciting moments."

That same day, a similar brand of excitement struck Port Huron, Michigan. Herbert Youngblood, twenty-nine, the African American who broke out of Crown Point with Dillinger, was surrounded in a store after being betrayed by a self-serving friend. A sheriff and three deputies tried to take him peacefully as he shopped. After one officer relieved him of the .38 Dillinger had given him during the breakout, Youngblood suddenly pulled a backup .32 Savage automatic and blasted the sheriff and two of his men. They returned the favor, riddling Youngblood's sturdy body with ten slugs before managing to subdue him.

Youngblood, given woefully half-hearted treatment, died four hours later. Medical examiners discovered that he had used burned cork to cover identifying scars on his forehead and hand. Deputy Sheriff Charles Cavanaugh also died, despite being furiously worked on by emergency room doctors while Youngblood bled to death in the waiting room. Sheriff William L. Van Antwerp and Deputy Howard Lohr survived their injuries.

The ever-present Matt Leach, who just happened to be in Detroit, rushed into town and identified Youngblood as Dillinger's Crown Point accomplice. Leach dashed all thought that the Jackrabbit was in Port Huron as well. The captain, always ready to get in a dig, claimed that Dillinger was languishing in Chicago alone and broke, deserted by his gang because he was too hot.

On Thursday, March 15, Dillinger was indeed back in Chicago, but he wasn't alone or broke. He met with Arthur O'Leary and asked if they could speed up Billie's divorce from imprisoned Welton Sparks so they could get married. Piquett, already in deep enough, declined, saying his firm didn't handle divorces. Meeting with O'Leary again, Dillinger had another request. He wanted to find a discreet plastic surgeon. O'Leary promised to beat the bushes for such a creature.

Billie showed up at O'Leary's apartment the next morning bearing a stack of green gifts. She gave him $2,300, specifying that $1,000 was for Dillinger's legal account, with a second $1,000 designated to fund Pierpont's appeal. Scrapper Meyer Bogue was to receive $200. The remaining $100 served as a tip for O'Leary. Billie then went to the Stockyards Inn at Forty-second and Halstead and wired $100 to "Ann Jackson" aka Pat Cherrington, with the message to come to Chicago at once. Billie then flew to Indianapolis on American Airways.

In Indianapolis, Billie first tried to find Hubert Dillinger at his gas station. When he failed to appear, she went to Maywood and gave Audrey $200 and the wooden gun her famous brother used to escape Crown Point. Dillinger was considerate enough to add a letter of authentication:

```
. . . Don't worry about me, honey, for that won't
help any, and besides, I am having a lot of fun. I
am sending Emmett my wooden gun and I want him to
always keep it. I see that deputy Blunk says that I
```

had a real forty-five. That's just a lot of hooey
to cover up because they don't like to admit that I
locked eight deputies and a dozen trustees up with
my wooden gun before I got my hands on the two
machine guns. And you should have seen their faces!
Ha! Ha! Ha! Pulling that off was worth ten years of
my life . . .

  Don't part with my wooden gun for any price for
when you feel blue all you will have to do is look
at the gun and laugh your blues away. Ha! Ha. I will
be around to see all of you when the roads are
better. It is so hot around Indiana . . . So I am
sending my wife Billie . . . I'll give you enough
money for a new car the next time I come around. I
told Bud [Hubert] I would get him one and I want to
get Dad one. Now honey, if any of you need anything
I won't forgive you if you don't let me know. I got
shot a week ago but I'm all right now. Just a little
sore . . . .

                          Lots of love from Johnny

The next day, Billie hooked up with Pierpont's attorney Jessie Levy.
Together, they marched to Matt Leach's office and demanded the personal belongings, mostly clothing, the cops had taken from her in
Tucson. Leach returned it without protest. "Mrs. John Dillinger" then
flew back to Chicago that afternoon. Fellow molls Pat Cherrington and
Bernice Clark were waiting for her when she arrived. An hour later, all
three were on a flight to St. Paul.

    The bad-guys-and-dolls reunion was tempered by more negative
news coming from Lima. After a repetitive, three-day trial, Charles
Makley was found guilty of first-degree murder. The jury recommended no mercy—a ticket to death row. The prosecutors were now
two for two with Russell Clark's trial scheduled for the following
Monday.

    Left with little to go on, Clark's attorneys, Clarence Miller and Levy, tried the same weak defense that had failed with both Pierpont and Makley. They claimed Clark had been at a relative's house at the time of the murder. While Clark's jury was out contemplating that, Pierpont was brought back to court and was sentenced to death. The judge, with a touch of ghoulishness, set the date for Friday, July 13, 1934. Handsome Harry, born on a Friday the 13th, had come full unlucky circle.

A half hour later, Makley was sentenced to die with his friend. Four hours after that, Clark was convicted of murder, but this time the jury recommended mercy, sparing his life. In the cell block, Clark crowed that he'd come out on top. "You poor bastard," Pierpont chided. "You think you got the best of it? You didn't. You've got to serve forty or fifty years in stir. Charlie and I got a sentence of only one hundred eleven days."

Prosecutor Ernest Botkin ended the eventful day by announcing that the show wasn't over. Ed Shouse, who ratted Pierpont and Clark but refused to testify against his pal Makley, was set to face the music next. Harry Copeland would be tried after that.

On March 27, the Lima jail was cleared as Pierpont, Makley, and Clark were escorted under heavy military guard to the Ohio Penitentiary in Columbus. Pierpont was especially anguished over the dismal new surroundings. His tough-guy veneer fading, he collapsed in his cell, nearly suffering an emotional breakdown.

Dillinger fretted over how to liberate his tortured friends before their electrifying date with the chair. He determined once again that overcoming General Bush's forces in Columbus would be too much of a bloodbath. He'd have to wait until things quieted down and the guards grew sloppy. It would be tough on the Shirt Shop Boys, but there were no other options.

The best way to lift their spirits was to keep from being nabbed himself. As long as he remained free, they had hope. With that in mind, he and Billie moved from Minneapolis to the three-story Lincoln Court Apartments at 93–95 South Lexington Avenue, St. Paul. They shared the hideout with Hamilton and Cherrington.

At Dillinger's old haunt in Crown Point, things continued to look bleak for Ernest Blunk and Sam Cahoon. Both were indicted for complicity in the wooden-gun escape. Virtually everyone else involved, including volunteers and hired vigilantes, were severely chastised. Judge Murray, also blasted in the report, turned around and filed contempt charges against his own grand jurors. Mortified, the six citizens apologized and essentially took back their criticisms of him. A victorious Murray dropped the contempt charges and ended their brief terms.

The career casualties left in John Dillinger's wake continued to mount. Prosecutor Robert Estill, unable to escape the photo fiasco, lost his bid for renomination as Lake County prosecutor. The stinging defeat forever crushed his gubernatorial aspirations. Governor McNutt, battered by leaflets reproducing Dillinger's parole order, was eventually left to trade his presidential dreams for the paltry position of high commissioner of the Philippines. The distant, overseas assignment erased him from the public consciousness.

John Dillinger would have been wise to head for the steamy tropical islands himself. Instead, he continued to dance on the edges of the fire. On March 27, he registered for a driver's license in the noted gang stronghold of Minneapolis. Using the name Carl T. Hellman, he gave his age as thirty, height as five feet, eight inches, weight a solid 170 pounds, eyes gray, and hair, oddly enough, red. That may have been in deference to Billie, who was keeping low-key with a mane of carrot-colored hair more befitting a cartoon character than a gangster's moll.

After Pat and Billie spent a day emptying out the local high-end department stores, John took Billie to see the movie *Joe Palooka,* based on the squeaky-clean comic-strip boxer. The news feature before the film was about John Dillinger and included an on-camera interview with John Senior. "John isn't a bad boy. They're trying to make a mountain out of a molehill." John Jr. laughed so hard Billie feared that they would be recognized and arrested.

In touch with his feminine side, the Jackrabbit returned a few nights later to take Billie to see *Fashions of 1933,* which was essentially a filmed clothing report and runway show. Dillinger joked that the twenty-cent movie cost him a bundle because Billie was sure to be hitting the stores again.

On March 30, in the midst of a blizzard, Dillinger spoiled himself with yet another new car, this one a Hudson Deluxe 8 sedan purchased from Pottoff Motors of St. Paul. The car came with cream-colored wire wheels, which the dealer promised to switch to black at a later date to accommodate his customer.

Bernice Clark arrived in St. Paul on April 1 after shaking two G-Men who shadowed her from the Windy City. The Chicago airport was one of fourteen "transportation centers" in the midwest that were being watched around the clock by DI agents. Hoover also had his men lurking around various Terror Gang relatives' houses from Indiana to Ohio. The future FBI boss remained convinced that nabbing the famous fugitive would put his new federal police force on the map. He was sparing no expense to grab the prize before another set of Tucson-like local yokels beat him to it.

He almost accomplished his goal that very week. Two of his special agents were sent to scope out the Lincoln Avenue Apartments after the landlord, Daisy S. Coffey, suspected her new tenants were heavyweight crooks because of their wealth and cautious, nocturnal behavior. In yet another law enforcement slip-up, she was only shown mug shots of the Alvin Karpis and Barker gangs, thugs known to be in the area. Coffey was unable to identify any of them. The agents, their enthusiasm dampened, had no reason to suspect that Coffey's tenants were anything but a band of night owls.

The agents' supervisor, Inspector W. A. Rorer, remained skeptical. Before closing the book, he ordered his men to determine precisely who the mysterious tenants were. Special Agents Rufus Coulter and Rosser L. Nalls teamed with a local police detective, Henry Cummings, to pay them a visit. Nalls waited in the car while Coulter and Cummings entered the building and climbed to the third floor. Knocking on the door around 10:30 A.M., the pair were greeted by Billie, who spoke to them through the narrow crack provided by the chain lock. She gave them the runaround and suggested they come back later in the afternoon to speak with her husband. Refusing to be brushed off, the two said they would wait until she was properly dressed for visitors. Bolting the door, Billie ran to the bedroom and informed John. He sprang from the bed and quickly dressed, throwing the essentials—guns and money—into a suitcase. "Get some clothes on quick! We're getting out of here." After Billie dressed, she found John waiting by the door, a Thompson under each arm. He was stalling for time, expecting Hamilton to return from an errand any moment.

Sensing something terribly wrong, Agent Coulter left Detective Cummings at the door, tracked down Coffey's first-floor apartment, and phoned Inspector Rorer. Alarmed at what he was hearing, he advised Coulter to act with extreme caution and advised him that two additional agents were on their way. After hanging up, Rorer changed his mind and sent the agents to the St. Paul police station to personally round up extra troops. Coulter, expecting more immediate help, returned to the third floor to await Billie's reemergence.

The "U"-shaped, brick Lincoln Court Apartments had a middle stairway near unit 303 that emptied into a narrow rear alley. The new tenants' exclusive use of this secluded route was one of the things that had aroused the landlord's suspicion.

Out front, Agent Nalls waited in his vehicle, unaware of the tension brewing. He watched with moderate interest as a green Ford V8 coupe crossed Lexington and parked on the north side of Lincoln. The driver emerged, crossed the street, and started down a walkway leading to that same rear entrance. The tall, slender figure was wearing a light brown topcoat and a matching felt hat. The dandified Homer VanMeter had come to show off his new threads. Failing to recognize him, Nalls held his ground.

VanMeter climbed the back stairway to the third floor where he encountered Detective Cummings lurking in the hallway outside his friends' room. Instantly sensing a cop, he walked by, intending to proceed to the front stairway and take off. After a few more steps, he ran into Coulter. Homer smiled and asked the agent if he was "Johnson." Informed that he wasn't, Homer continued on his way.

"Who are you?" Coulter called after him.

"I'm a salesman," VanMeter answered. "I sell soap."

"Where are your samples," Coulter asked.

"Down in my car."

"Do you have some identification?" the agent pressed.

"Yes, but it's in the car, too," VanMeter lied. "I'll get it."

Coulter noted that the well-dressed man never questioned his authority to demand such information. It was a tell-tale sign of a crook who knew exactly who he was dealing with. Coulter followed the stranger down the stairs. Reaching the ground-level landing, the agent paused in a six-foot foyer, glanced outside through the glass door, and saw no one. He turned and peered around a doorway to his right, looking down another short stairway. The harmless soap salesman was standing at the bottom, staring up at him with his legs spread and a .45 steadied in both hands.

"You see this, asshole. You wanted this? Here it is!"

Springing back, the hunter was now the hunted. Coulter dashed through the front door and stumbled into the icy courtyard with Van-Meter hot on his heels. The agent clawed at his coat, trying to retrieve his own revolver. Ahead of him, small puffs of snow were kicking up, the only indication he had that he was being fired upon. Aware that he could be hit any second, he prayed to survive the next few seconds. Twenty feet ahead, the building ended. He could hook around the structure, buy himself time, and get the drop on his attacker. Reaching it without being struck, he slid down a sloping yard and finally released his weapon from its holster. He stopped, kneeled, and fired a wild shot just as the felon appeared. Realizing the tables had turned yet again, VanMeter wheeled and ran back inside the building. While Coulter was deciding what to do next, he heard machine-gun fire coming from inside.

Agent Nalls saw the almost comical cat-and-mouse act and went to assist his partner. "Call the police!" Coulter shouted.

"That's the car of the guy who shot at you," Nalls said, pointing to the green V8 at the curb. Coulter angrily approached the vehicle. With a trembling hand, he tried to shoot out a rear tire. It took him three tries to accomplish the point-blank task.

After calming his partner, Nalls sprinted to a corner drug store and phoned the St. Paul police. "We're federal agents in a shoot-out at Lexington and Lincoln. Send all the squad cars you've got!" After delivering that message, Nalls tried to call his own office but the lines were busy.

Upstairs, a similar life-and-death drama was unfolding. After hearing VanMeter's shots, Dillinger indiscriminately fired a blast of .45s through the apartment's wooden door, forcing Cummings to retreat to a twelve-inch offset where the banister joined the wall. The Thompson's earsplitting racket was amplified by the closed quarters, totally unnerving Billie. "For God's sake, don't shoot," she begged as only a hung-over woman would. "I'll stay here. I don't care. You go ahead, but don't shoot."

"Come on, baby, it'll be okay," Dillinger cooed, unwilling to abandon his beloved moll. "Just stay behind me. Grab the suitcases, we're going out." With a noisy Thompson under each arm, Billie's beau worked the doorknob and peered into the hallway. It was empty. "Let's go!"

Struggling to half carry, half drag the heavy suitcases, Billie stumbled down the rear corridor as her man loudly fired warning shots into every hallway and exit. Nine big .45 slugs whistled by the harried Detective Cummings, who was laying flat on the offset. Keeping his head out of sight, he reached out and blindly fired his pistol in the direction of the machine gun that was tormenting Billie.

Dillinger backed his way down the corridor into the rear stairway, covering Billie's agonizingly labored retreat. "Get the car!" John barked, referring to a vehicle in a rented garage 200 feet away. "The keys are in my coat pocket."

George Scroth, a young boy who lived next door, heard the gunfire and naturally came running toward the courtyard to check out the excitement. Daisy Coffey frantically waved him away. He sprinted back into his house and watched with fascination as the frazzled Billie dragged the suitcases into the alley toward the garage while her insensitive boyfriend continued to shatter her senses with his weapon. Scroth's keen young eyes noticed a red stain spreading across the man's left trouser leg, just above the knee.

Billie threw open the garage doors, chucked the hated suitcases into the Hudson, scrambled behind the wheel, jammed the key in the ignition, and pulled the starter switch on the dash, bringing the getaway car to life. She backed out into the alley, cranking the big steering wheel until the vehicle pointed east. "Pull back in," Dillinger ordered.

"Head it out the other way." Exasperated, Billie did as told, busting a fender in the process. The Jackrabbit jumped into the rear seat, leaving a stain of blood on the snow where he had stood. "Head for Eddie's." Billie busted another fender as she backed out and rolled west, the Hudson slipping and sliding in the snow.

VanMeter ducked through the front entrance of the complex, bounded down the same stairway where he tried to ambush the DI agent, and spilled out the back exit. He pondered returning to his car, but saw the two agents guarding it. Taking off west on Lincoln, he hopped on the running board of a slow-moving city sanitation truck. Jerking open the passenger door, he jabbed his gun into garbage man Bernard Kersten's side and ordered the driver, Kersten's brother, to keep driving west on Lincoln. He ripped off his stylish new hat and replaced it with the grubby work cap from Bernard Kersten's head.

As the truck turned into Hemline, VanMeter confessed to the brothers that he'd been ambushed by cops but didn't say why. Crossing the railroad tracks, the big truck lumbered to Snelling and then north on Marshall Avenue. As it approached the Ninth Street viaduct, Homer ordered the driver to stop. He offered the pair ten dollars from a large roll for their troubles, but they declined.

He was just about to jump off and melt into a residential neighborhood when he remembered something of vital importance. He reached back into the cab and swapped headgear, retrieving his spiffy fedora. If all went well, he'd still be able to show it off to his pals.

Chapter 15

The eerie moan of mechanical sirens filled the air around the Lincoln Court Apartments as squads of St. Paul police poured in and fanned out around the building. Special Agent Rufus Coulter, knowing the still unidentified culprits were long gone, supervised a tow truck that carted off VanMeter's green Ford. The nascent federal police force was bolstering their fleet with confiscated vehicles, and this was a prize. They wanted to lay claim before the St. Paul cops got their paws on it.

Inside the fancy Ford was yet another Thompson protected inside an expensive leather case. Its serial number had been filed away. There was also a fully loaded magazine, along with 100-round drum. Opening the trunk, technicians found a .351 Winchester autoloading rifle, serial #46190, and thirteen 20-shell magazines.

John Hamilton, Pat Cherrington, and Bernice Clark arrived from the grocery store to find the complex swarming with cops. Hamilton parked a block away and sent the girls to investigate. He had them carry a sack of food they'd just purchased to help mask their intentions. The two quickly learned about the gun battle and returned to the car. They drove off to find out what had happened to the others.

No one was at the other hideouts, so a concerned Hamilton took the girls to McCormick's Restaurant on Wabasha to huddle with gangster-friendly owner Harry Sawyer. The restaurateur brought them up to speed, and helped Hamilton stash his vehicle. Sawyer then had one of his employees drive the con and the women to his farm at Snail Lake, twenty miles north of St. Paul. A few hours after they left, Homer

VanMeter, still on foot, appeared at the restaurant. Sawyer offered him a similar escape, but Homer chose to stick around town a while.

Billie made it to Eddie Green's place at 3300 Fremont without incident. She went inside and told Green that her boyfriend, waiting in the car, had taken a bullet in his leg and was losing blood by the cupful. Green called Dr. Clayton May, a shady character known to the government as "a known abortionist, dope peddler, and associate of hoodlums," and told him that one of his unidentified friends had been injured. Doctor May rushed right over. When he saw Dillinger's leg, he unknowingly said, "We'd better get you to a hospital."

"To hell with that!" Dillinger responded. "Get me some place private!" The dehydrating outlaw pointed his Thompson at the doctor to stress his point. Doctor May got behind the wheel of the Hudson and drove to a garage in the rear of 1835 Park Avenue. It was the home of Mrs. Augusta Salt, a practical nurse who sheltered women seeking illegal abortions. Dillinger hobbled in and was quickly treated. Once again, he had lucked out. The bullet had passed through and wouldn't require a painful extraction. All he needed were ST37 antiseptic and bandages.

At 2 P.M., the blissful Tommy Carroll remained ignorant of an event that most of St. Paul was already talking about. He parked his gangster special—1934 Hudson 8 Club sedan—a few doors from the Lincoln Court Apartments and went to visit his friends. A pack of square-jawed men in business suits carrying out luggage barely registered. A large, rat pack of neighborhood boys milling about failed to arouse his suspicions, either. He walked another fifty feet until something finally clicked. Filtering in with the youths, he petted a Chow dog and milked them for information. Realizing the bind he was in, he casually circled around, got back in his car, and took off toward Lexington.

The officers were more concerned with taking inventory inside apartment 303 than watching for uninformed criminal associates. They found the usual assortment of weapons, some altered to accommodate compensators that acted as silencers. Two bulletproof vests were discovered, along with five douche bags. Billie, hung over or not, liked to stay fresh for her lover.

The rest of the inventory helped explain her foul mood. There were frilly silk nightgowns, an elastic girdle, a healthy, size-36 "Gordon Uplift" brassier, two bathing suits, a blonde wig, a pair of white pumps, eleven pairs of pink "step-ins," and enough slacks and dresses to stock a boutique.

Dillinger didn't get off easy himself. The cops swept up a closet full of slacks and shirts, a sheepskin-lined leather jacket, two trench coats, a topcoat, a large chinchilla overcoat, and a blue, silk dressing gown.

The gold mine that would rivet everyone from Michigan to Washington, D.C., were some photos Billie carelessly left behind. One showed a small boy perched on a branch. Written in pencil on the back was, "John Dillinger in cherry tree, 10 or 11 years old." Another pictured a sad-looking toddler and contained the inscription, "John after death of his mother, 3 1/2 years." The third was a formal portrait of Dillinger in his navy uniform.

Another major find was a getaway map that designated a bank in Newton, Iowa, as the gang's next target. A scrap of paper next to the map listed Eddie Green's phone number.

The man in the photographs remained at Nurse Salt's house that evening so Doctor May could swing by later, check him out, and collect ninety dollars for his services. Billie stayed into the night, sewing up bullet holes in her beau's pants and coat, and comforting him the best she could. She left to sleep at Green's, unaware that the Feds and cops had her host's phone number.

VanMeter was already at Green's when the temperamental Bessie arrived home. Finding the lanky ex-con hiding inside her apartment popped her cork. "Are you crazy? Next to Dillinger, you're the most wanted man in the whole damned world and here you are under my roof! Why don't you and Carroll just leave a sign on your car that says where you are? You're gonna get us all killed! Don't you ever come here again, ever!"

Heeding her advice, VanMeter and Carroll departed, heading for Mankato, eighty-five miles southwest of St. Paul. If the Feds had been more diligent, Bessie's outburst might have saved the pair's skin. As it was, it took Hoover's paper chasers weeks to follow up on Green's phone number.

In Mankato, the men stopped to have some drinks at the Circle Inn Bar, then continued another twenty-eight miles to New Ulm, before checking into a hotel. On Monday, April 2, they were back in Mankato to meet with some contacts. Carroll had his Hudson serviced, and VanMeter bought a Ford V8 for $748.70 to replace the green one the G-Men had snatched. Tipped that "gangsters were in town," DI agents rushed to Mankato and impounded Carroll's freshly tuned Hudson right at the shop. Carroll escaped with VanMeter and returned to St. Paul to check up on Dillinger.

The news of the Hoosier Hellcat's easy escape from the unsuspecting G-Men resulted in a splash of coast-to-coast headlines that elevated Dillinger's already skyscraping public profile another notch. Hoover fumed in Washington, deflecting intense criticism that his exalted special agents were no more special than all the bumbling Keystone Cops and jailers the bank robber had previously bested. Such criticism was the last thing Hoover wanted for his new elite force. It was sure to hamstring his campaign for expansion funding. Thus, he took it extremely personally.

On the other side, John Dillinger, more than ever, appeared to be infallible.

Nurse Salt, still not sure of her new boarder's identity despite the national headlines, allowed him to stay three more nights. Intrigued by the injured stranger and all his mysterious visitors, Salt's son, Wallace, thirteen, befriended the outlaw and eagerly ran errands for him. Wallace earned his stripes in Dillinger's book when he thought to padlock the garage that hid the Hudson. The teen had figured out who their famous houseguest was from the first day—mainly from the photographs in the newspapers he was fetching—but sensing his mother's denial, kept quiet. Dillinger later paid Mrs. Salt $100 in damp fives from his sweaty pockets for her generosity.

On Dillinger's final night at her home, Mrs. Salt took Doctor May aside and asked if the rumors were true. "Sure, it's him," the doctor responded. "Didn't you know that?"

On April 2, the same day Carroll and VanMeter were escaping the posse in Mankato, Eddie Green asked housekeeper Leonia Goodman to

clean out VanMeter's Marshall Avenue apartment. Hoover's embar-
rassed and angry DI agents were sitting on the place, having traced it
through VanMeter's car. Although Homer had used a false identity to
purchase the vehicle, the janitor of his building, Walter Pommerening,
recognized it from news reports and dropped a nickel. The agents confronted Goodman when she arrived, then told her to complete her
task, return to her nearby home, and wait for Green to pick up the
goods. When he arrived at 5:30 P.M., a nervous Leonia shoved the luggage at his feet and slammed the door in his face. Realizing something
was wrong, Green walked briskly to his car. Two trigger-happy G-Men
claimed that they ordered him to halt before blasting him from behind
with their machine guns. Bessie Green, waiting in the car, jumped out
screaming and cradled her husband's head as he lay bleeding from multiple wounds to his shoulder and head. He was taken to Minneapolis's
Anker Hospital where he hung on for days in critical condition. A
grieving Bessie, her fancy winter coat soaked in her husband's blood,
was gruffly placed under arrest.

While hallucinating and drifting in and out of consciousness, Green
mistook a nurse for Bessie and told her to clear out their apartment and
take everything to "John." A DI agent, listening in, asked where John
could be found. Green mumbled some addresses, including 1835 Park
Avenue, which of course, was Nurse Salt's. Assuming Green was
delirious, the G-Man didn't bother to check it out.

Encouraged by the brutal and questionable shooting, Hoover sent an
army of fifty special agents to the Twin Cities under the command of
two assistant directors, Harold "Pop" Nathan and Hugh H. Clegg.
Assistant Attorney General Joseph Keenan, speaking for Hoover's tight-
lipped G-Men, announced that the mobilization was part of the Feds'
new "War on Crime," instituted a few months earlier. They were in the
Twin Cities not only to get Dillinger, but to bring down the Nelsons,
Floyds, Barrows, and Barkers of the world. By Thursday, April 5, the
G-Men had arrested more than twenty career criminals—none of
which carried the above-mentioned names. Their main target, John
Dillinger, had left the Minneapolis/St. Paul area the night before.

The DI was having better luck adding to their burgeoning motor pool. They hit a bonanza in St. Paul. Aside from VanMeter's Ford and Carroll's Hudson 8, they rather callously grabbed Green's Terraplane 6. In a bit of poetic justice, Lincoln Court Apartments owner Daisy Coffey, the Dragon Lady who ratted the gang, was now battling the Feds over the cars. She filed suit to garnishee the vehicles to pay for the damage to her complex inflicted during the shoot-out.

Bessie Green also filed suit to keep Hoover's G-Men out of her Terraplane. The Feds instead settled with their angry informant, Coffey, for $175.71 and kept the valuable cars. Moll Bessie was shut out.

Dillinger still had his wheels, busted fenders and all. Where they were taking him was anybody's guess. A sighting was filed from La Crosse, Wisconsin, by a sheriff who had some curious details. The petite red-haired woman said to be traveling with Dillinger was wearing an expensive, crème-colored coat, a pink-and-white apron, a garter belt and hose, "and no panties." The sheriff didn't bother to explain how he knew that last detail. A second report had Dillinger traveling around Chicago dressed like a nun. Silly as it was, the sighting was taken seriously and sent right to Hoover. One can imagine how the young DI boss reacted, considering the cross-dressing charges that would haunt the iron-fisted FBI creator after his death.

Johnnie D was in fact at the most obvious place—his boyhood home. On April 6, he and Billie parked the Hudson on a dirt road a quarter mile from his pop's farm and walked through the familiar woods to the house. "I was in bed," John Sr. recalled. "I heard someone knock on the back door . . . soft. A woman was there. I'd never seen her before. She was young and pretty and she looked foreign. Dark, with olive skin and black, flashing eyes. She whispered, 'Johnnie's out by the barn. Is it all right?' 'Yes, it's all right.' I told her.

"She disappeared into the blackness. A moment later, she and John Jr. came into the kitchen. He looked at me a long time, then he laughed out loud. He put a machine gun down on the table and shook my hand. He introduced me to the girl and said they were married, but his eyes laughed when he said it and so did hers. I told John it wasn't safe for them here. 'Probably not, Dad, but I just wanted to see you before . . . well, you know, before anything happens.' We talked all night. Ann

[Billie] just sat there. She was quiet. She didn't say anything all the time they were there."

John retrieved the car before dawn and stashed it in the barn, a risky act considering that Hoover had eyes everywhere.

The next morning, a Saturday, Frances, eleven, and Doris, fifteen, rushed downstairs to embrace their big brother. Hubert walked in unexpectedly a few hours later. John popped around a corner, formed a gun with his thumb and finger, and said, "Stick 'em up!" The brothers went to the barn and painted the Hudson's cream-colored tires black. John Jr. obviously never had the opportunity to switch them at the dealer in St. Paul. While waiting for the Duco lacquer to dry, John carefully painted the cream trim black as well.

"Wanna take a ride with me to Ohio, Bud?" Dillinger asked. Hubert, twenty-one, and recently married, jumped at the opportunity. The pair left that evening at 8 P.M. for another questionable destination, Leipsic. John Jr. wanted to see the Pierponts. Settling in for the three-hour trip, Hubert began to pepper the Jackrabbit with questions. His big brother explained that the limp was due to a police bullet in St. Paul. He downplayed the "brilliance" of the Crown Point escape, casting it off as "one chance out of a hundred when they left the cell block open."

In Leipsic, the siblings discovered that the Pierponts had moved to Goshen, Indiana. Dillinger turned around and headed back to Mooresville, letting Hubert take the wheel so he could sleep. With no one to talk to, Hubert was soon having trouble staying awake himself. At 4 A.M., just over the Hamilton County border near Noblesville, a dosing Hubert slammed the big Hudson into the rear of a slow-moving, spindly Model T Ford driven by Mr. and Mrs. Joseph Manning. The Ford lost a rear wheel and was pushed into a ditch. The Hudson also spit a wheel, this one on the front passenger side, careened across the northbound lane of U.S. 31, tore through a farm fence and plowed 300 feet through a field of tree stumps, narrowly missing them all.

The roller-coaster ride jarred John Jr. awake. He and Hubert ran over to check on the Mannings. The elderly couple had also escaped injury. The outlaw apologized and promised to pay for the damage. As the Mannings went for help, John Jr. retrieved a machine gun from the

Hudson and took off with Hubert. At dawn, they came to a farm three miles from the accident site. John Jr. hid in a hay crib while Hubert hitched a ride with a passing truck, returned to his father's farm, jumped in his own Chevy, and came back to get his brother.

John Jr. tied a handkerchief around a post to alert Hubert where he wanted to be picked up. Spotting it without difficulty, Hubert swung over and the Jackrabbit sprang from the brush and hopped in. They beat it back to John Sr.'s farm.

Hamilton County Sheriff Frank Hattery, inspecting the crash scene, noticed that the Hudson only had 1,400 miles on the odometer, and that the wheels and trim were recently painted over. He phoned Capt. Matt Leach, adding that there were no plates, and a full machine-gun magazine was found in the rear. Within the hour, Leach was in Noblesville inspecting the vehicle in person. Tracing it back to the Pottoff Brothers dealership in St. Paul, Leach quickly got a bead on its suspected owner. "Just look at that," he groused. "There's some more of Dillinger luck! There were trees all over the woods and it didn't touch one of them. Nobody could be that lucky but Dillinger!" Searching for blood, Leach instead found a length of rope and a bullwhip—items he found puzzling as they had never been part of the gang's arsenal. They were, however, part of Dillinger's Jesse James fantasy. According to Hubert, John was planning to use them on Joe Ryan, the one-armed Indianapolis attorney who had run off with his dad's money.

In Mooresville, John Jr. ragged Hubert about his driving skills, and then sent him and Billie to Indianapolis to buy a new set of wheels. The poster boy for auto dealerships was certainly doing his part to pump up the bottomed-out, Depression-era economy. In a time when hardly anybody could afford a bicycle, much less a car, the Jackrabbit was using high-end luxury vehicles like disposable razor blades. The number he'd purchased over the previous six months was nearing double figures—and that didn't include the convoy his various gangs had stolen.

Hubert took Billie to Frank Hatfield Ford at 623 North Capitol Avenue and asked if they had her favorite, a 1933 Essex Terraplane 8. Salesman Ablin Dorsey said they didn't, but convinced her the green Ford V8 on the showroom floor was technologically superior. Billie consented, but said it had to be black, not Homer VanMeter green. Sales manager C. J. Hart promised to have an appropriately colored one that afternoon. Billie killed time shopping, then returned to pick it up at 2:30 P.M., forking over $722. She then drove it off the lot to the farm. Following her as she pulled up was Fred Hancock, twenty-five, his wife Bernita, his mother Audrey, and his sister Alberta, fourteen. Audrey sprang from the vehicle to embrace Johnnie Jr., the beloved little brother that she had raised like her own child. While they enjoyed an emotional reunion, Fred Hancock took the new Ford to Mooresville and stashed it in the garage of another relative.

John Jr., still dangerously sticking around, received a special visitor on Sunday—his dedicated niece Mary. She arrived with Alberta and a gaggle of other relatives. An aspiring beauty school grad, Mary gave her uncle that manicure she'd always promised. Noticing him wince when she bumped his leg, she apologized profusely. "Forget it, kid," he said with a smile. "It was nothing."

The festivities were interrupted when a strange, official-looking man stopped in front of the house and knocked on the door. John Jr. reached for the Thompson as his father answered. It was just a road commissioner come to talk about improvements on Highway 267.

Shortly thereafter, an airplane circled the farm. The others panicked, but John correctly guessed that it was a National Guard training flight out of nearby Stout Field.

The Sunday-night, extended-family dinner featured fried chicken and coconut pie, one of John's favorites. John Sr. noted that his son was "carefree and laughing" and seemed to be the boy he was before all the trouble. "I couldn't figure it out for a while. Then I understood. In those old days, when he was a kid, he didn't have any worries on his mind. When he came out of prison, he had plenty. Bitterness, a desire to get even and restlessness . . . Well, now he'd seen a lot of the country, and he'd got even, and he sensed he was going to die.

"After dinner, he and I walked out over the fields. We just walked, talking, not looking where we were going. Pretty soon we came to the woods on the brow of the hill. I thought a minute . . . I said, 'John, if anything happens to you, what do you want me to do? I've got room for you at Crown Hill right next to your mother.' He looked at me. He was older, quieter. 'That'll be all right, Dad,' "

During a similar walk with Mary, John was moved to clean up his reputation. "No matter what you've heard about the things I've done, I want you to know that I've never killed anyone." The way John Jr. saw it, Sergeant O'Malley fired upon him first and left him no option, so his death didn't count.

John Jr. spent the rest of the evening flying kites, chatting, and posing for pictures. In several historic photos, the suited John Jr. is holding a Thompson under his left arm and the famous wooden pistol in his right hand. They would be the defining snapshots of America's most famous twentieth-century outlaw.

While John Jr. was spending a pleasant Sunday with his family, DI agents were fanned out across Indianapolis looking for him. Astoundingly, they failed to stake out John Sr.'s home. Instead, agents beat a path between Hubert's Shell station in Indianapolis and Hubert's home in Mooresville. They even circled the house of Hubert's father-in-law, Harry E. Baugh, all to no avail. The Feds would weakly argue that because the Dillinger farmhouse was perched on a knoll beside a draw, it had a commanding view of the surrounding area, making undetected surveillance impossible. The agents had to resort to driving back and forth on U.S. 267, trying to catch passing glimpses.

That questionable technique hardly made them less obvious. Mary spotted the shooting-range-duck act, told her mother, then informed her uncle. "I don't like the look of that car," mother Audrey seconded. "John, you and your girl had best leave while there's still time."

Hubert and Fred were dispatched to retrieve the new Ford. Although the Feds spotted them on the way back, they chose to follow Fred in Hubert's familiar Chevy and ignored the trailing Ford, thinking it was unrelated. Fred led them away from the nest, enabling Dillinger to pack without being detected. With Billie driving, Mary Hancock beside her, and Alberta sitting in the back with her fugitive uncle hiding at her feet, the female-filled Ford passed right by the DI agents without raising suspicion.

The loyal family reconvened in Mars Hill at the home of Macy and

Mary Davis, friends of the Pierponts. Gilbert and "Leaping" Lena Pierpont were visiting, and had sent word through the Dillinger family that they wanted to meet with John Jr. They suggested Mars Hill as a safe place to meet. Mary Kinder drove in as well. After saying good-bye to his tearful sister and niece, Dillinger climbed into the Pierponts's Auburn and held a mobile strategy session with Lena and Mary K while Gilbert aimlessly circled the city. Billie followed in the Ford with Audrey's son Norman. An overwrought Lena Pierpont pushed for the funding needed to finance the legal appeals necessary to stall her son's upcoming date with the chair. Dillinger promised to do all he could, dedicating his next bank job to that goal. Satisfied, Gilbert pulled over to the side of U.S. 36 so Dillinger could transfer to the Ford and continue on to Chicago with Billie and Norman.

Warm with family memories, John spoke to Billie at length about settling down somewhere, having kids, and living a normal life. In Chicago, the helpful Norman took a bus back home.

The DI shadows, bolstered by four Indianapolis detectives and ten heavily armed officers, finally decided to act. They raided Mary Kinder's new home on Luet Street, disturbing the evening of Mary's sister, Margaret "Silent Sadie" Behrens, their mother, a family friend named Claude Parker, and Mary herself. "Every flat-footed copper and dick in Indianapolis knew where we lived," Mary squawked to the reporters, explaining the recent move. "They took it as a personal social duty to call on us every day. We moved to get some privacy."

The G-Men in Indianapolis, having once again guessed wrong, retreated and regrouped. Fortunately for Hoover, his Chicago team was having better luck. Tipped that Billie was scheduled to meet a man at the Austin-State Tavern, 416 North State Street, at 8 P.M. on April 9, they placed undercover agents inside and out. Sure enough, Billie arrived on time, kissing John good-bye as he remained in the car a few doors away—an exchange the G-Men somehow missed. Entering, Billie sat with Larry Streng, brother of Harold Streng, the bartender at U Tavern on 639 North State Street. The brothers were supposed to be lining up a place for John and Billie to stay.

The G-Men, enacting Hoover's new "molls-and-all" policy, swept in, some running right by chauffeur Dillinger in their eagerness to arrest small-fry Billie and Streng. Asked how she'd arrived at the bar, Billie shrewdly said she took a cab.

John eased away, then circled the block, clutching his Thompson and waiting for an opportunity to intervene. As more cops poured in, he concluded it was hopeless. He remained close enough to see his beloved Billie shoved into a DI vehicle, a sight that made him unashamedly "cry like a baby."

At the DI field office in the Banker's Building, the agents gave Billie the bare-light treatment, coming at her in waves, denying her sleep, trying to get her to break down and rat her lover. "They kept me up, talking to me until I didn't know what I was saying. Then they'd leave me alone for a long time. I was nearly crazy. They thought John was coming to rescue me."

Despite her fried brain, Billie kept her forked tongue going, misleading the Feds at every turn. She went so far as to claim that the blood on the snow in St. Paul was from her "monthly sickness," and not her boyfriend's leg as the eagle-eyed neighborhood youth insisted.

No matter how much pressure and physical force they applied, Billie stood by her man. Even when G-Man Harold Reinecke smacked her across the face, the tough Native American beauty didn't buckle—in part because there was nothing to sing. Her Johnnie was living out of the Ford and could have been anywhere. Cleverly vengeful, Billie repaid the violent Agent Reinecke by faking a tearful confession that she was to meet John near their old apartment on Addison at a specific time. G-Men and cops flooded into the area, all to no avail. Billie coyly told the fuming agents that they must have been too clumsy and obvious.

Regaining his composure, Dillinger found a phone, called Arthur O'Leary, and relayed the terrible news that "The Whiskers grabbed Billie!" Frantic, John wanted her immediately bailed out. O'Leary explained that Louis Piquett was at the Willard Hotel in Washington, D.C., but would be back the next day to take care of it. Dillinger would have to cool his antsy heels and be patient. He did so by driving forty miles to the Fox River Grove Inn, a popular, gangster-friendly resort and dance hall on the Northwest Highway near Barrington. Neither the big band music nor the thousands of lights in the ornate Crystal Ballroom could shake John out of his lovesick funk. Owner Louis Chernocky's kind-hearted wife Mary led the swollen-eyed Public Enemy to the kitchen and fried him a steak to try to cheer him up.

Returning to Chicago, Piquett discovered that the new federal police were playing fast and loose with Billie's civil rights, refusing to tell him where she was or when she'd be charged and arraigned. The Whiskers were playing hardball with the petite woman, in part, because they continued to be hammered in the newspapers.

Furious over ridicule aimed at his force, Hoover and his minions tightened the vice on Eddie Green's delirious head as well. They posed as doctors in an attempt to get him to reveal more about Dillinger's plans and possible whereabouts. Green rambled incessantly to his "doctors," but was unable to reveal any more than Billie. Nurses, propped up by the Feds, continued to pretend to be his common-law wife Bessie, squeezing reams of mostly outdated information from the badly injured patient. On April 10, Green's fever spiked to 104.6. He fell into a coma at midnight and died an hour later. The information flow, whatever its value, was now over.

Eddie Green's slow death ignited more accusations that he was assassinated in cold blood by the angry Feds. Published reports had him unarmed and shot in the back. Politicians opposed to a federal police force wagged their fingers, screamed "I told you so," lambasted an unchecked "government goon squad," and loudly demanded an investigation. Hoover relented, but was assured by Inspector Clegg that the shooting was legitimate and the uproar would blow over the moment Dillinger and friends hit the next bank. Clegg then secretly whispered that the journalists writing such negative stories had shady pasts themselves and could easily be pressured into zipping up.

Hoover's DI, true to form, clammed up, releasing only bare-bones information that didn't even identify the "nameless and faceless" agents who fired upon Green. An investigation by St. Paul authorities was scuttled when a neighbor in position to witness the event said she instead averted her eyes in disgust because she mistakenly thought a white man was calling on a black woman.

Dillinger, worried about witnesses of a more curious nature, continued to push his grand scheme of surgically altering his appearance. That innovative plan began to take shape on April 12. Piquett decided to throw the lucrative middleman job to an old friend named James Probasco who owned a house at 2509 North Crawford in Chicago. Probasco, a speakeasy operator in dire need of money, agreed, provided that he was given a healthy fee for finding the physician and offering his home as an operating room and recovery hideout. With so many greedy hands extended, Dillinger would have to knock over a few more banks to finance the $5,000 procedure. But first, he needed more armaments.

On Friday, April 13—a date that wasn't lost on the doomed Handsome Harry Pierpont—Dillinger and VanMeter went back to their well of tricks and hit a police station, this one a two-man-per-shift operation in Warsaw, Indiana. The underfunded Warsaw cops didn't produce the bounty that their peers had provided, handing over a single pistol and three steel vests. State police poured into the area afterward, but came away with nothing more than an angry farmer who fired on them because he thought they were coming after him to make him cough up support payments to his hated ex-wife.

Noting the Jackrabbit's less-than-overflowing haul, police departments across three states went on the alert, draining their meager overtime budgets assigning extra officers to guard their gun cabinets.

That same unlucky Friday, Billie Frechette was thawed out and dragged before federal court commissioner Edwin K. Walker on charges of conspiracy to harbor a federal fugitive. U.S. Attorney Dwight Green, claiming that Billie's famous boyfriend had unlimited funds, asked for a bail of no less that $200,000. Walker set it at $65,000—still a staggering sum for the times ($900,000 by today's standards). Billie was then taken under heavy guard to the Chicago House of Corrections.

Unaware of the hearing, Dillinger went to Louisville on Saturday, April 14, in an attempt to have an X ray taken of his aching knee. Recognizing the famous outlaw, Dr. A. David Willmoth claimed that the X-ray office was closed and scheduled the appointment for the following Tuesday at 11 A.M. He then called the police. That Tuesday morning, four special agents and two Louisville police detectives waited in a back room while twenty-two more tried to blend into the scenery outside, pretending to be clerks, office workers, and citizens. Dillinger failed to appear. He was back in Chicago with John Hamilton and Pat Cherrington trying to figure out what was happening with Billie. Piquett was still having trouble getting the Feds to allow him access to his client.

O'Leary then relayed some good news about the plans to alter John's face. Told that it would cost five grand, Dillinger balked, but O'Leary convinced him that it was the going rate for the skills involved. Probasco, eagerly expecting his cut, began looking for bars to invest in, telling various owners that he was coming into a big windfall. So keen was Probasco to collect his cash that he failed to be swayed by the ominous news coming out of St. Paul.

On April 17, G-Men, acting on information from Eddie and Bessie Green, arrested Dr. Clayton May at Nurse Salt's new apartment on 131 East 14 Street. Caught between the law and the gangs, Doctor May had gone into hiding. New at the on-the-lam game, he failed to select a less-obvious location and was easily found. He also failed to cover up his latest illegal activities. The G-Men flushed out a twenty-two-year-old woman recovering from a fifty-dollar abortion. Doctor May was charged with both harboring John Dillinger and performing illegal procedures. His traumatized patient was left stuffed with internal bandages that had to be removed by an authorized physician.

Dillinger, Hamilton, and Cherrington caravanned to Sault Ste. Marie, Michigan, the third oldest city in America, located just across the bay from Canada. Hamilton, fearing that he wasn't long for this earth, wanted to see his sister, Anna Steve, and give her family his Ford V8. Arriving just before dusk on the 17th, they visited until 11 P.M., then returned to Chicago in Dillinger's car. Three days later, the FBI arrested Anna and her seventeen-year-old son, Charles, on charges of harboring fugitives. It was part of Hoover's master plan of making life miserable for anybody—friend or family—who assisted John Dillinger to the slightest degree. (Anna was tried a year later, convicted, and was sentenced to four months in jail and fined $1,000. Charles was acquitted.) Instead of going to his family as intended, Hamilton's Ford was added to the DI's growing fleet.

While Dillinger was in Sault Ste. Marie, Billie was finally being allowed to speak with her attorney, Piquett. They gathered inside the Federal building and took the elevator to Commissioner Walker's eighth-floor courtroom where Billie waived extradition to Minnesota. Tipped about the hearing by Piquett, a mob of reporters were fed embarrassingly exaggerated details of Frechette's arrest. The subsequent coverage incited the police and Feds yet again.

"John Dillinger, the well-known wood carver who has made 'Scarface' Al Capone's career sound like that of a Boy Scout, walked out of a Chicago tavern that was being raided by agents of the United States Bureau of Investigation," *The Chicago American* wrote under banner headlines. The story, quoting Billie, went on to say that both she and her beau had been in the bar that evening, and he had simply strolled off with the crowd when the Feds ordered the legitimate patrons to leave.

Piquett's motive for spinning such damning fiction was no doubt "tit for tat" over the G-Men refusing to allow him to immediately see his client. Chicago DI bosses, scrambling to satiate Hoover's rage, blamed the lies on Piquett's anger over failing to have Frechette's bond lowered. They claimed, correctly, that Billie had never been allowed to even speak to reporters, and referred to Piquett as "a blustering sort of individual."

The DI contemplated revoking Piquett's bond on the Wisconsin securities fraud case, but decided that since he was such a lousy, self-interested attorney, it would best serve the government's interest to allow him to continue to represent Frechette and Dillinger.

Chapter 16

With the heat from the St. Paul escape starting to dissipate, the Twin City Gang decided to reconvene at Louis Chernocky's resort, the Fox River Grove Inn. Baby Face Nelson and Tommy Carroll arrived a few days early and enjoyed the facilities while waiting for the rest of the crew to roll in from various hideouts across the midwest.

The stress and duress of Minnesota had failed to shatter the toddling criminal bond. There was no blame or backbiting, even after Eddie Green walked into a trap while performing a gofer chore for Homer VanMeter. The same couldn't be said for the forever squabbling law enforcement community. Matt Leach didn't share Hoover's "zero tolerance" policy when dealing with Dillinger's relatives. "What good would it do? Dillinger's been and gone, and under the law the old man has the right to protect his son."

Leach's underling, Al Feeney, was then marched out to give the alternative view. "It's unusual for a community to withhold such information for days and then let it reach the newspapers in such a way that it disparages the police. I simply can't understand it."

A Mooresville bank clerk tried to explain it to him. "I wouldn't be afraid if John walked in here right now. He's a town boy, and I don't think he would hurt any of us. We don't even take precautions against him." The clerk had apparently forgotten that the "town boy" had started his career by brutally beating a local grocer.

Others with similarly short memories circulated a petition that again asked the governor to pardon Dillinger, wiping his slate clean in return for a promise to stop being a public enemy. Such a move wasn't without precedent. Frank James, brother of Jesse, was pardoned by Missouri's governor and became a productive, law-abiding citizen. General Lew Wallace, author of *Ben Hur* and governor of the New Mexico Territory, extended a surrender-amnesty agreement to William "Billy the Kid" Bonney in 1879. That one didn't work out so well. The Kid accepted, then was double-crossed when the pardon failed to be granted. He angrily escaped from jail, and was subsequently shot by Sheriff Pat Garrett. (A recent report claims that Garrett, an old friend of Bonney's, may have staged the shooting so the Kid could live under a new identity.)

John Sr. supported the amnesty idea, telling an exasperated Feeney that he thought his wayward son would make a good law enforcement officer. Others suggested that John Jr. run for governor and then pardon himself. Many felt he could actually win such an election on name recognition alone.

The outlaw certainly had that. Dillinger mania continued to rage across the land. A popular lottery based upon his predicted capture date was shut down, without apparent legal authority, by humorless Indianapolis police. In Duluth, Minnesota, an enterprising street vendor offered envelopes purporting to contain "photos of Dillinger." Eager buyers who paid the half-dollar price found that they had purchased nothing but air. "So, he got away from you, too," the vendor chuckled. A billboard was erected in Loretto, Pennsylvania, welcoming the outlaw to drop by and dine at Lee Hoffman's restaurant.

John Sr. was offered a whopping $500 a week in the midst of the Depression to speak on the vaudeville circuit about his famous son. Not being much of a speaker, the seventy-year-old reluctantly declined. A similar offer from a Coney Island sideshow was also passed up. In Hollywood, a gossip columnist reported that an unnamed star had hired a team of private detectives to hunt the bandit down so their vain employer could be in on the capture.

More realistically, the Universal Newsreel Company offered $5,000 to anyone, cop or civilian, who could either arrange Dillinger's capture, or alert them to it. They were obviously eager to record the historic event on film. The nation's most famous criminal defense attorney, Clarence Darrow of the Scopes Monkey Trial fame, sent the outlaw a clear "call me" message through the media when he stated that Dillinger's original jail sentence had been far too harsh. He also chastised the police and government for their tough talk about gunning the robber down at first opportunity.

Holdups in Pana, Illinois, Shreveport, Louisiana, and Flint, Michigan, were all erroneously blamed on Dillinger, with the Michigan job reaching new levels of public hysteria. Four of the six bandits in Flint were identified as John Dillinger. Of the remaining two, one was a woman.

In Brookville, Indiana, Dillinger look-alike Ralph Alsman, twenty-five, was arrested for the seventeenth time at the end of April. Alsman lived in mortal fear that a cop would eventually shoot him on sight as they'd threatened to do with the outlaw he unfortunately resembled.

In Scotland, a ship captain summoned police to his vessel after receiving reports that the American bandit had hopped his boat, the *Duchess of York*, in Halifax. The subsequent uproar led to a search of all ships entering France. Across the channel, Scotland Yard was fanning out looking for the Jackrabbit near Bristol Harbor.

"Dillinger is not just one bad man against the United States," an Indiana newspaper editorialized. "He is, unfortunately, a symbol of crime in its latter day aspects in America. His is crime on rubber tires, crime armed with the finest killing devices known to science. Unlike Billy-the-Kid, Charles Quantrell, the Jameses, Fords, Youngers, and other famous outlaws of the past, this bandit killer is at large over five states. The laws and police of Indiana and neighboring states seem helpless to catch and punish him."

The DI men were desperate to quash such growing sentiments, squeezing Dillinger's family and extracting dubious promises from various members that they would squeal out their infamous relative if he ever returned for another leisurely visit. The DI's hammer was that however unpleasant, a blood betrayal was necessary to protect the rest of the family, including the women, from being imprisoned as accessories. To make sure everyone complied, the DI promised to step up their surveillance of the relatives' homes—even distant second and third cousins spread out across America.

What the Feds didn't reveal was that they had also taken the soon-to-be routine DI/FBI step of renting properties near prospective "hot spots" and having teams of agents reside there until the mission was completed. One such house at 254 1/2 North LaSalle offered a clear view of Hubert Dillinger's Shell station, a place where the heavily interrogated Norman Hancock worked as well.

Hoover's men also put a tap on the phone of Terror Gang defense attorney Jessie Levy, an act that would be considered outrageous today.

Expanding their aiding and abetting threats beyond mere relatives, Hoover instructed his field offices to announce that the G-Men would pounce upon anyone who assisted the outlaws in any manner "regardless of the duress to which they might be submitted by the convicts." It would be a hard law to comply with considering the hardware such desperados carried.

The information-crazy Feds began developing their controversial file system on people's personal habits and peccadilloes that would one day be viewed as civil-rights abuses. A notation in Hubert Dillinger's "jacket" is a prime example: "Associates with various girls of loose character, neglecting his wife to do so." Fred Hancock was given the same damning brand in his "permanent record." The agents wasted no time in turning the snitch tables and threatening to rat little Mary Kinder as well, noting that she "has been living a considerable portion of the time with one Carl Walz at Indianapolis."

If it was any consolation to those being so smeared, Billie continued to expertly play with the agents' heads. Before stepping on an extradition plane to St. Paul under the typical circuslike guard, she turned and addressed the army of lawmen. "Watch out for John. He's the big, bad wolf you know."

Rescuing Billie was at the top of the Big Bad Wolf's agenda as he headed for the Fox River Grove Inn on April 20, to rendezvous with the rest of the gang. He was traveling from Chicago with John Hamilton and Pat Cherrington. Across town, an eager new recruit named Pat Reilly picked up Homer VanMeter, Marie Conforti, and Marie's Boston

Bull puppy at the Velmar Hotel and steered toward the same destination. Baby Face Nelson, his wife Helen, Tommy Carroll, and his moll, Jean Delaney, were already there waiting.

After everyone arrived, Louis Chernocky handed Baby Face a "letter of entry" that was to be presented to his friend, Emil Wanatka, in a place called Little Bohemia, Wisconsin. Wanatka, Chernocky advised, had an out-of-the-way retreat ready for the boys 400 miles to the north.

Wasting no time, the gang pulled out of Fox River Grove early that same morning, driving in four separate cars that left at different intervals. Dillinger, Hamilton, and Cherrington went back to Chicago first to pack for a longer stay, then headed north.

On the way, Nelson sideswiped a Chevrolet coupe at North Leeds Cross Roads Junction, where U.S. 51 intersected with Wisconsin roads 44 and 60 about 130 miles northwest of Chicago. No one was hurt, but there was extensive damage to both vehicles, including the Chevy that was owned by the Midwest Canning Company of Arlington. Carroll and Delaney, trailing Baby Face and Helen from a distance, caught up and followed the Nelsons to the Arlington Motor Company where they arranged to have their car repaired. While waiting, Baby Face went to the Midwest Canning Company and gave a supervisor $83 for the damage to their vehicle.

As usual, the fancy cars and high-fashion molls attracted a lot of attention. Carroll's girlfriend, Jean Delaney, was wearing what the locals called "blue sport pajamas." Mrs. Baby Face was smartly attired in riding breeches and tall leather boots.

Noticing the attention they were receiving, Baby Face decided to continue on in his damaged Ford. They only made it another fifteen miles before the battered car gave out near Portage. Nelson left it at Slinger's Garage, telling A. R. Slinger that someone from the "Oakley Construction Company" would come for it later. Baby Face and Helen then squeezed into Carroll's Buick and headed for Little Bohemia.

Because of the delays, Homer, Marie, and the puppy arrived first, turning off U.S. 51 just after 2 P.M. and easing down a dirt trail lined by tall pines. Homer noted the lodge's ornate welcome sign: DINE, DANCE & SWIM AT LITTLE BOHEMIA, STEAK, DUCK & CHICKEN DINNERS. The secluded camp was thirteen miles south of Mercer, Wisconsin, just north of Manitowish Lake. The main building in the complex was a two-story, log structure 600 feet from the road. The kitchen, dining room, bar, and a large recreation center were on the first floor, while the guest rooms sat above. Some rooms had a view of the gravel parking lot, while the rear units looked out over the eastern shore of Little Star Lake. Several small guest cabins were situated to the right of the parking lot. Although the lodge gave the illusion of being on the same level as the lake, there was actually a ten-foot drop to the beach.

The pleasant, rustic summer resort was still a few weeks away from its busy season and was mostly deserted. The gang found it perfect.

VanMeter, originally scheduled to arrive after Nelson, wasn't carrying the note of introduction from Louis Chernocky. He told Emil Wanatka that it was coming, along with seven more people. Emil was happy for the business with or without the note. His wife, Nan, shuddered a bit, already feeling uneasy about the newcomers. "I hope they don't stay," she whispered to a friend as Homer, Reilly, and Conforti ordered lunch in the dining room and requested a bowl of milk for the puppy.

Much to Nan Wanatka's dismay, Dillinger and crew arrived at 5 P.M., followed fifteen minutes later by Baby Face and his group inside Carroll's Buick. Nelson presented the note, which introduced them as "friends who should be well treated."

Resort employees George Baszo and Frank Traube helped unload the luggage. "There must be lead in this one," twenty-six-year-old Baszo complained as one case nearly took off his arm. "What are these guys, hardware salesmen?"

Not knowing the pecking order, Wanatka gave Dillinger the first room to the left at the top of the stairs. Hamilton and Cherrington shared the quarters next door, with early birds Homer, Marie, and the puppy snagging the unit across the hall with the waterfront view. Nelson decided to take one of the outside cabins with his wife, Carroll and Delaney. Gang wannabe Pat Reilly from St. Paul was told to bunk with Dillinger, a prospect that both excited and scared him. What a story he'd be able to tell, he thought. The first thing he noted was that his roomie slept with the butt of a .45 sticking out from under his pillow. A bottle of expensive, sixteen-year-old bonded whiskey sat on the nightstand, apparently to function as a sleeping aid. Reilly boldly helped himself to a swig.

The Twin Cities Gang kept to themselves the first evening, wary of other visitors. They instructed the girls to remain low-key and socialize only among themselves. Nelson raised eyebrows when he advised Nan Wanatka that his wife would be handling the housekeeping duties for all the rooms they'd rented, including the ones in the main building.

As the group settled in, they became less paranoid. Dillinger played cards with Emil, forty-seven, not bothering to adequately conceal the .45s he carried in twin shoulder holsters. Alarmed, Emil fished through a stack of newspapers in his office until he found one with John Dillinger's photograph. Not knowing what to do about his notorious tenant, Emil rounded up his two collies, Shadow and Prince, and went to bed. Rabbit-eared Nan had other ideas. She kept pestering her sleepy husband about people walking the hallways all night. Nan's hearing was on the mark. Dillinger, Hamilton, and VanMeter were taking three-hour shifts protecting the premises.

Chernocky had figured Emil might be gangster-friendly because the astute businessman from Brumov, Bohemia, was no stranger to the police himself. He was arrested in Chicago in 1922 for the 1920 murder of a business partner in Kenosha. He was also tapped for being part of a large auto-theft ring in Illinois. The slippery Czech beat both charges, and went on to run a bootleg joint called Little Bohemia at 1722 South Loomis Avenue in Chicago. He sold the business to a partner in 1930, then moved to Wisconsin. He and his wife opened The Little Bohemia Lodge on May 27, 1933. Summers bustled with visitors from as far away as Chicago. The long winters were a struggle to book enough loggers, hunters, and Civilian Conservation Corps (CCC) workers to make ends meet.

After a long, chatty breakfast on Saturday, April 21, Emil boldly asked Dillinger to join him in his office. "Emil, what's wrong. What do you want?" Dillinger asked, sensing something was up.

"You're John Dillinger."

"You're not afraid, are you?" the outlaw calmly responded.

"No. But everything I have to my name, including my family, is right here, and every policeman in America is looking for you. If I can help it, there isn't going to be no shooting match."

John smiled and patted the innkeeper on the shoulder. "All we want is to eat and rest for a few days. We'll pay you well and get out. There won't be any trouble."

Tensions eased after all the cards were placed on the table. "He even tried to satisfy me by playing pinochle," Emil recalled. "I cheated him every hand. It was very friendly." So friendly, in fact, that Dillinger borrowed a baseball mitt and played catch with eight-year-old Emil Wanatka Jr., while his mother watched with increasing anxiety. Afterward, the child was sent to a neighbor's.

That same morning, VanMeter sent Pat Reilly on a roadtrip to St. Paul to collect $4,000 that restaurateur Harry Sawyer was holding for him. Pat Cherrington, who wasn't feeling well, went along to see a doctor.

VanMeter, always wary about staying in packs, asked Wanatka if there was another place nearby where he could stay. Emil explained that the surrounding resorts had yet to open for the season. VanMeter may have also been uneasy over the first signs of a fissure in the gang, mostly caused by Mr. Tension himself, Baby Face Nelson. Still smoldering over news reports calling the group "The Dillinger Gang," the temperamental felon with the Napoleonic complex seemed to always be a match away from lighting a fuse. At Little Bohemia, he and Carroll kept their distance from the others.

Dillinger felt an obligation to Nelson for cutting him in on the Sioux Falls and Mason City jobs when he was in desperate need of cash. He tolerated Baby Face's myriad eccentricities, forcing himself to stay cool when the kinetic gangster whined about their accommodations. Because Dillinger had arrived fifteen minutes earlier, Nelson convinced himself that Dillinger's modest dwelling with a parking lot view was better than the expansive, three-room cabin he was assigned. "I'd have let the little bastard have the place if he hadn't been such an asshole about it," Dillinger groused to Cherrington.

Nelson wasn't the only one on edge. Nan Wanatka's anxiety continued to grow. It peaked when she read a story about what happened to Anna Steve, Hamilton's much-hounded sister. Nan's paranoia was just the reaction Hoover and the DI wanted to create. Nan rode her husband about doing something before it was too late, wearing him down. The pair devised a scheme to send a letter to Edward A. Fisher, the U.S. attorney in Chicago, whom they knew. It wasn't the quickest way to alert the law, but Nan was too scared to dial a phone and leave messages.

Nan's brother Lloyd LaPorte lived nearby, so she decided to consult him on what to do. They decided that it would be faster to have their brother-in-law, Henry Voss, drive fifty miles southeast to Rhinelander and contact the Feds. Nan, ever the Nervous Nelly, wanted to run it by her husband first. That evening, Emil reluctantly agreed. Nan scribbled another note, this one to Voss, saying the plan was a go, and adding that the cops should "line up the highways . . . we want to be protected by them the best they can." Nan slipped the missive into a pack of Marvel cigarettes and gave them to Lloyd when he came by the next morning, Sunday, April 22. To allay suspicion, Lloyd brought their mother along for a visit.

After excusing himself, Lloyd went to Voss's home to relay the message. Voss then drove to Rhinelander with his son. LaPorte nervously followed in his car.

Since it was a Sunday, Voss had difficultly finding anybody. He finally connected with a real estate agent who was the son of H. C. W. Laubenheimer, a U.S. marshall in Chicago. Laubenheimer phoned Voss at 1 P.M. and took the message, promising to pass it along to Chicago DI supervisor Melvin Purvis. Extremely interested, Purvis called back, unaware that he was speaking on a busy party line that was the norm in northern Wisconsin. Voss updated the G-Man on the number of people at the lodge, and gave him the license numbers of most of their vehicles. Spilling too much, Voss blabbed that the crooks had been recommended by the owner of the Fox River Grove in Illinois, who was a friend of his brother-in-law, Emil Wanatka. That effectively implicated both men as accessories in the DI's eyes.

Purvis said he'd catch the next plane, and told Voss to wait for him at the Rhinelander airport. Voss was to don a handkerchief around his neck so he'd be identified. Moving fast, Purvis rounded up all available agents and chartered two planes. Notifying Hoover at the boss's home in Washington, D.C., Hoover bolstered the effort by calling in the St. Paul federal troops as well. In a slight to Purvis, Hoover put DI Assistant Director Hugh Clegg in charge. Clegg was still in Minnesota mopping up the mess the DI had made there.

Purvis and eleven agents packed a deadly array of Thompsons, riot guns, and tear gas, then caught their waiting flights. Four additional agents were ordered to drive from Chicago to Rhinelander. The ground crew caught a break because the air posse hit heavy turbulence that bounced the young G-Men around the fuselage, causing many to throw up in misery. It was so bad even a co-pilot became sick.

The agony didn't abate until three hours later when they touched down in Rhinelander. Inspector Clegg and crew were already there, busy trying to obtain cars to drive to Little Bohemia. The Feds were also expecting additional reinforcements from St. Paul, Milwaukee, and Duluth—all within 250 miles.

As the trap was being set, Dillinger was in Little Bohemia making arrangements to check out the next day. Asking how much he owed, Wanatka responded it was four dollars a day per person, or about $120. Dillinger nearly doubled it, giving the man who was about to betray him a generous $110 tip. Emil eagerly accepted the generosity.

A couple of hours later, Dillinger told Emil that that there was a change of plans. They would be leaving that evening around six, as soon as Reilly and Cherrington returned. They wanted one last steak dinner before they departed, to be served at 4 P.M.

The race was on.

Nan Wanatka, filled with some form of bloodlust, now wanted more than just having the criminals flushed from the resort. She asked her sister to rush to Rhinelander and tell the Feds that her customers were preparing to leave. The sister did as told, throwing Clegg, Purvis, and company into high gear. Among the vehicles they commandeered from residents and the local Ford dealership was the prized, 1934 Ford Deluxe coupe, midnight black with cream-colored wire wheels, owned by a very proud Isidor "Izzy" Tuchalsky, twenty-two. The auto had a custom high-compression head to go with an altered rear end, enabling it to top 100 mph. Izzy balked at the request, but eventually was forced to cough his baby up to the grim-faced Feds.

A caravan of five cars, including two appropriated taxis, headed toward Little Bohemia. It was after 8 P.M., extremely dark and bitterly cold. Although the plan was to spread out to divert attention, the Feds found themselves bunching up for safety on the bumpy roads. Halfway there, one car broke down, while a second suffered a flat. Eight displaced agents, some of the same men who had suffered through the queasy flight, now had to bounce in the numbing cold on running boards.

The Feds arrived at Henry Voss's Birchwood Lodge, two miles south of Little Bohemia, just after 9 P.M. Dillinger had wanted to leave three hours earlier, but Reilly and Cherrington still hadn't arrived. Nervous Nan was already hiding out at the Birchwood, leaving her husband behind to experience the fireworks.

Purvis, taking control, waved the posse on, telling his men they'd have to navigate the rest of the way sans lights. The initial plan was that five agents in bulletproof vests would lead a straight-on assault while the others cut off escape routes to the left and right.

Slowing down 100 feet from the main building, Clegg and Purvis nosed their cars together in a V, blocking the building's exit. Agent Arthur McLawhon, driving the third car, stopped behind them. The Feds had successfully arrived undetected. Only Emil's agitated and loudly barking collies—which he failed to warn them about—were aware of their presence.

Dillinger, Hamilton, and VanMeter were upstairs in their rooms. Helen Nelson was also there with Carroll and Delaney, who had moved to the main building the second day. Baby Face was alone in the detached cabin.

Earlier, the lodge's one-dollar Sunday night dinner special had attracted seventy-five locals. By 9:30, the early-to-bed crowd had dwindled down to three, Eugene Boisoneau, thirty-five, from the Mercer

CCC camp, John Hoffman, twenty-eight, an oil station operator, and John Morris, fifty-nine, the CCC camp's cook. The trio had been drinking at the bar and were getting ready to leave just as the agents pulled in. Resort employees George Baszo and Frank Traube joined Emil in walking them out. Emil, sensing a disaster in the making, quickly ducked back inside. Baszo and Traube, slower on the take, remained on the porch as Hoffman cranked his Chevy, clicked on the radio, and wheeled the volume to high. He threw the car into gear and lurched forward, failing to put on the lights. Traube and Baszo, hearing voices and seeing shadows, wised up and joined their boss inside.

DI men Melvin Purvis, Hugh Clegg, Carter Baum, and Jay C. Newman stood in front of their cars armed with machine guns, their hearts pounding under the steel vests as the Chevy approached. "Halt, we're federal officers!" Clegg and Purvis shouted in unison. The three intoxicated revelers heard only the Chevy's powerful radio. "Let 'em have it!" one of the Feds yelled. Purvis squeezed the trigger of his Thompson—but nothing happened. He'd forgotten to release the safety. Dropping it, he fumbled for his .45 as Agent Baum's Thompson began spitting .45 slugs into the Chevy. The others opened fire as well, evaporating the Chevy's side window and blasting holes in the door and cowling. Hoffman took a shotgun blast to the arm and a nearly spent slug to his thigh. Jamming on the brakes, he sprang from car and darted behind Nelson's cabin.

John Morris fell out of the car next and sank to his knees, his body pocked with four hot slugs, all in his right shoulder. "We're federal officers," K. R. McIntire called to him. 'Identify yourself."

"I'm John," a stunned Morris called back, tragically sharing the common first name of the G-Men's main target. Before they could react to that, four shots rang out from the nearby cabin. Seeing the flashes, Purvis fired back with his pistol, engaging in a short battle with Baby Face Nelson before the little bandit hightailed into the inky forest.

Hoffman, still running for his life, approached the garage where the real crooks had stashed their vehicles. There, he ran into Special Agent Harold Reinecke—the man John Dillinger had targeted to die for slapping Billie. Hoffman stopped and threw up his hands.

"Who are you?" Hoffman asked. The gruff agent, mistaking Hoffman for a fellow G-Man, responded, "It's me, Reinecke." Making no sense of that, Hoffman wheeled and sprinted toward the lake. Reinecke ordered him to stop, then fired two shotgun blasts over his head. Hoffman continued to the lake's edge and hit the ground.

Special Agent Sam Hardy took the wheel of one of the V-parked vehicles and drove within thirty-five feet of the riddled Chevy, illuminating it with his headlights. Morris was gone, having climbed to his feet and stumbled over to Nelson's cabin. On the porch, he sat down, took a bottle of whiskey from his hip pocket, and drained what was left—unconcerned with the blood-thinning effect of alcohol. Ignoring orders to halt, he meandered to the main lodge so slowly and painfully that none of the G-Men could bring themselves to shoot him again.

Clegg and Purvis strained their eyes trying to see inside the stricken Chevrolet. A third man remained, moving slowly but making no attempt to escape or fight back. The grating radio continued to blare upbeat Roaring Twenties swing tunes, echoing through the normally dead quiet night.

Behind the main lodge, Inspector Rorer and two agents were looking up at the windows when a figure fell from the eaves of the roof, landed ten feet away, and took off in a sprint. Rorer identified himself, then fired his Thompson into the shadows. Suddenly, from above, a rain of bullets thumped down in front of him. Rorer spun and aimed toward the flashes, shattering glass. As his muzzle lit the scene like a strobe light, he could see two more figures creeping around on the roof. He let them have a few rounds as well, as did agents Melvin and Nichols. Assuming they'd driven the men inside, the G-Men retreated and took cover behind some pine trees.

The jumper who escaped headed north along the lake and nearly tripped over Hoffman. "Is that you, Red?" he asked. Hoffman, still thoroughly confused, didn't answer. The man blew past him.

Inside the lodge, Emil Wanatka was cowering in the basement with Traube and Baszo. Helen Nelson initially ran downstairs, but dashed back up and hid under a bed with Jean Delaney and Marie Conforti. During a break in the action, the three molls skittered to the basement to join Emil and his employees. The girls had just arrived when they all heard John Morris come into the bar upstairs and pick up the phone.

The call was answered by Alvin Koerner, owner of Koerner's Spider Lake Resort a mile and a half away. Koerner's was the designated location of the area's telephone exchange. "I'm at Emil's," Morris coughed. "Somebody's held up the place. Boiseneau's dead and we're shot." Morris then hit the floor with a thump.

Emil asked the girls if they wanted to go up and help him out. They declined. "Damn that Dillinger," Helen Nelson hissed instead. "Ever since we hooked up with him we've been having trouble. The fool never wears his glasses and always walks around in public where everybody can see him." Without Billie there to defend her beau, the statement went unchallenged.

John Hoffman, tired of laying down bleeding into the dirt, lifted himself up and made his way to the Northwood Lodge. Nobody was home. Heading back to Highway 51, he spotted a small man in a brown overcoat and hat walking briskly toward the south. The man, no doubt Baby Face Nelson, stopped, sensed something, and called out, "Who is it?" Hoffman ran back into the woods and hid.

The late-arriving Pat Reilly and Pat Cherrington finally arrived in the midst of the drama, pulling up right behind the jumpy G-Men. "We're federal agents," Baum announced. "Identify yourself." The young gangster wannabe slammed the gears into reverse as the shoot-anything-that-moves Feds fired away with their Thompsons and pistols. Reilly made it back to the highway and slowly drove off, perplexed at what had just happened. Apparently listening to their own loud radio, he and Cherrington never realized they'd been fired upon.

Incredibly, Cherrington convinced Reilly to turn around, pull back in, and let her out so she could snoop around. She had barely left the vehicle when she heard someone yell "Halt!"

"Halt, hell!" she spat over her shoulder as she jumped back into the car without closing the door behind her. "Get the hell out of here!" she ordered. Reilly put the car into reverse, and slammed right into a tree. Shifting again, he spun the vehicle toward the highway, lighting Agent Sam Hardy in his headlamps. Hardy emptied his five-shot riot gun into the fleeing auto as Purvis and John Brennan cut loose with their Thompsons. Someone finally hit a tire, causing it to flop off at the rim.

Shoving two pistols onto Cherrington's lap, Reilly shouted for her to "Shoot! Shoot!" She ignored him and fished for the handle of the suicide door, which opened from a hinge at the rear. The wind caught the wing as she attempted to close it, flinging Cherrington out on her curvy butt. She rolled on her shoulder, splintering it like a chicken bone. Reilly slammed the brakes, reached over, grabbed her good arm, jerked her back inside, and took off on three tires and one screaming metal rim. Glancing over at the distressed damsel, Reilly noticed that she was bleeding from the face where a Fed's bullet had creased her cheek.

After that drama, an eerie silence fell over the grounds. Neither cops nor robbers could see well enough to attack. Purvis and Clegg were certain that they had the bandits trapped inside and surrounded. They ordered agents Hardy, Baum, and Newman to take Izzy's souped-up V8 and return to Rhinelander and bring the expected reinforcements. Purvis, Clegg, and Rorer then huddled and decided to wait until daybreak to make their next move.

During the standoff, Hoffman, his pellet-splattered arm starting to seize up, waited another hour before finding the courage to rise and try the Northwood Lodge again. This time, owner Walter Powell was home and took him in.

Hoffman's drinking buddy, Eugene Boisoneau, remained in the Chevy with the noisy radio. Rorer crawled to the vehicle, checked the blood-covered occupant for a pulse, then switched off the key, silencing the grating music. "I don't know who that young fellow is, but he's dead," Clegg reported to his companions.

Communicating with the local police, the Feds learned that resident Henry Kuhnert of the Northern Lights Resort a mile away phoned to report that his blue-green 1928 Packard sedan was stolen around 10:15 P.M. An all-points-bulletin was sent out for the vehicle across the Midwest.

Agent Hardy, returning from Rhinelander, discovered that a second phone system in the area tapped into all the area resorts. Taking a chance, he rang Little Bohemia. An unidentified man answered, possibly the injured John Morris. Hardy explained the situation and asked that those inside come out with their hands up. The line went dead. After two more tries, Hardy reconnected. This time, Wanatka answered and said he and his two employees would come out if the Feds promised not to shoot them. Hardy agreed. As Emil pondered the true safety of stepping outside, his eyes caught two pairs of headlights approaching. One was a CCC truck bringing in Dr. S. M. Roberts to treat the wounded. The second was his brother-in-law, George LaPorte, carrying the news that a tall, thin man resembling Homer VanMeter tried to flag him down on U.S. 51. VanMeter, suspected of being the first roof jumper, was apparently the thief who hotwired the Packard.

It was close to 11 P.M. when Wanatka, his employees, and John Morris finally emerged. At the same time, John Hoffman reappeared, his arm dangling at his side. He had borrowed a car and returned to find out why he and his friends had been blasted. Morris and Hoffman were reunited aboard the CCC truck and taken to the camp hospital at Mercer. Doctor Roberts then went to the Chevy and confirmed that Eugene Boisoneau wasn't so lucky. He was indeed dead.

Clegg, Purvis, and company were still too focused on the trapped felons to concern themselves with the pending public relations disaster. Wanatka erroneously informed them that the four bandits remained in the building, failing to mention the women in the basement. Hearing that, the Feds reiterated their plan to wait until light and then flush them out with tear gas. Wanatka and the others were allowed to leave with LaPorte, choosing to bed down at Koerner's.

A short time later, Agent John R. Brennan, positioned on the north side of the main lodge, heard four pistol shots in the distance. After a pause, there were nine more. Checking in with central command, the others said they weren't aware of any renewed firing. Instead of investigating, they dug in to wait until dawn.

Aside from VanMeter, one of the men they wouldn't find at first light was the second biggest prize—Baby Face Nelson. After trading shots with Purvis, he had bounded over to the Sylvan Lodge to the south and forced the elderly owners to take him south on U.S. 51. His hostages' Model A Ford only made it a few miles before its ancient electrical system crackled and died—right near Alvin Koerner's place. Nelson herded the couple across the road and headed for the lights. Koerner spotted him coming, grabbed a phone, and notified the agents at the

Birchwood Lodge. Nelson busted in around 11 P.M. and added the Koerners to his quartet of captives.

Wanatka, LaPorte, Baszo, and Traube arrived a few minutes later, with a fifth man, Carl Christenson, a friend of LaPorte's, waiting in the car. The four relieved locals, believing they were finally safe, walked in to find Baby Face and his .45 automatic in charge. Nelson commandeered LaPorte's already warm vehicle, taking Koerner, Wanatka, and Christenson (who was hiding in the backseat) with him. Wanatka, behind the wheel, tried to start the car but it balked. "Turn the damned switch on," Nelson growled, pointing to the ignition toggle. Just as Wanatka did as instructed, Agents Jay Newman, Carter Baum, and the local constable, another man named Carl Christensen (this one spelled with an "e"), pulled up beside them. "We're federal officers. Where is Mr. Koerner?"

Baby Face, seeing them coming, was already out, hiding behind the other side of LaPorte's auto. He sprang from the shadows, thrust his pistol in Newman's face and snarled, "I know who you sons-a-bitches are and I know you're wearing vests. I'll shoot you in the head. Get out of the car!" Newman leaned back to give his companions a clear shot, but they hesitated. Newman then stepped out to the running board, hoping someone would now fire. Someone did—Baby Face Nelson. His first shot glanced off Newman's forehead, knocking him down and nearly out. The dazed agent rolled under a fence and lost consciousness. Nelson continued to fire the erratic weapon inside the car, producing the series of thirteen shots that Agent Brennan heard at Little Bohemia. Christensen spilled out, followed by Agent Baum's machine gun that fell harmlessly on top of him. The constable tried to run, but Nelson cut him down. Baum, twenty-nine, then flopped out, mortally wounded from a bullet fired down through his exposed neck and into his heart, skirting the protection of the steel vest. He staggered to a split-rail fence, fell over it and smacked to the frozen ground gasping for air.

Christensen was lying face up in a small ditch as Nelson continued to pump bullets into him, one deflecting off a coat button right over his heart. The shooting ended only when Baby Face's weapon ran empty. "Nelson gave us a look like he'd like to kill us but didn't have the time," Christensen recalled. "Then he drove off in our car."

"Our car" was Izzy's speedy customized coupe, the one the young man worried about being scratched. As Nelson blasted off, he ran over Baum's Thompson, splintering its stock. Christensen, still conscious, reached out, dragged it over, and tried to shoot it but didn't know how to click off the safety.

Agent Newman came to his senses, saw Nelson escaping, and fired seven times at Izzy's Ford without slowing it down. In the subsequent silence, all Christensen could hear was Agent Baum "drawing one raspy breath after another" as an eerie plume of gun smoke danced in the headlights of LaPorte's car, which was still idling.

Like the slick rat he was, Emil Wanatka used the cover of the shooting to scurry out of the LaPorte car without a scratch and disappear. Carl Christenson remained frozen in fear in the backseat, unscathed, an untouched hunting rifle at his feet. He suspected that Baby Face never knew he was there. Alvin Koerner escaped harm as well, slipping inside the house and bolting the doors. Agent Newman, half conscious, drew his backup .38 on Christenson and ordered him out, not knowing who the man was. Marching to the front door, Newman ordered Koerner to open up. Koerner refused, fearing that the demonic Nelson had returned. Newman, finally realizing Christenson was one of the good guys, asked him to drive them to the Birchwood Resort. After a brief search for the car keys dropped by the deserting Wanatka, the pair sped off. Newman had given up Baum and Constable Christensen for dead.

Wanatka, still running from Nelson, made it back to Little Bohemia. Catching his breath, he tried to relay what had happened. "Jimmy was at Koerner's holding up your men," he screamed, using Nelson's phony name. Purvis, thinking him mad, asked him to spell his name and Manitowish Lake. Wanatka was flabbergasted, arguing that he couldn't spell the Manitowish on his best day. "All your men are dead!" he yelled in the agents' faces. "Did you come here to get Dillinger or me?"

The G-Men rolled their eyes and ignored him.

Chapter 17

Emil Wanatka, still playing both ends against the middle, convinced Inspector Clegg to allow him to pile straw and blankets into the back of his pickup truck so he could rescue the dying men at Koerner's. Agent Brennan, troubled by the thirteen distant shots he'd heard, volunteered to go to provide cover. Inspector Rorer joined him.

Unfortunately, the DI car used to shine its headlights on the civilian Chevy had a dead battery. Moving to the second DI car, they couldn't find anybody who had the keys. Shrugging, Brennan and Rorer tucked their Thompsons under their arms and hopped in with the shifty Wanatka in his truck.

Down the road, Baby Face Nelson, getting a feel for Izzy Tuchalsky's hot rod, encountered a car full of incoming St. Paul agents on U.S. 51. Included in the pack was Werner Hanni, St. Paul's DI field office boss. Nelson blinded them with a custom spotlight, then blew past, leading Hanni to believe that he was a local police officer. The powerful lamp was just another toy Izzy had installed on his cherished Ford.

The St. Paul agents also missed Reilly and Cherrington. The pair bought a new tire at a gas station in Mercer, filled the tank, and went merrily on their way, heading north. Reilly, the young hopeful, had done wonders to prove his colors under fire. Remaining calm and adapting on the fly, he was hardly phased when his headlights went dead and the car became stuck in a mud hole. Cherrington, cold, tired, and hurting, talked her way into a room at a nearby farmhouse while Reilly waited with the vehicle until morning.

Hanni and company, like the single-minded Feds they were, continued forward, arriving at Koerner's just before Wanatka, Brennan, and Rorer. To all the agents' horror, they discovered that Emil had been telling the truth. Agent Baum was dead, leaving behind a wife and two baby daughters. Constable Christensen was critical, and Agent Newman was bleeding but stable. The survivors were taken to Grandview Hospital in Ironwood, Michigan, thirty-five miles to the northeast. There, doctors determined that Christensen had fifteen bullet holes in his sheepskin coat, and had been hit least seven times in the arms, chest, and feet. A nurse commented that "this one's a goner."

The bad news kept coming. While putting out an APB on Nelson, Agent Sam Hardy was told that yet another car was reported stolen, this one a 1930 Model A Ford Coupe, Wisconsin 92652. The suspected culprit? John Dillinger.

The shadowy figures on the roof illuminated by Inspector Rorer's Thompson blasts may not have been driven back inside as the agents thought. Instead, they either leaped from the perch farther down and vanished into the black forest, or they simply slipped out an unguarded back door. Whatever their means of escape, the trio, Dillinger, Hamilton, and VanMeter, crossed U.S. 51 and came upon a modest resort at the southern tip of Rest Lake. VanMeter's presence in this group meant that it was actually Tommy Carroll, an athletic ex-boxer, who had initially jumped from the overhang.

At Rest Lake, the fleeing bandits burst in on the owner, seventy-year-old Edward J. Mitchell, and his bedridden wife. "Now, Mother, I'm John Dillinger, but I'm not so bad as they make me out," the Jackrabbit assured the flu-stricken Mrs. Mitchell, placing a blanket around her. "The police are after us and we need a car. We won't hurt you."

The soothing words put the Mitchells at ease. "For an outlaw, that Dillinger was a gentleman," Edward Mitchell would recall. "He made the others behave. No foul language and cool as a cucumber."

The legendary cool was about to get an acid test. The Mitchells's Model T wouldn't start. The trio tried the hired hand's truck. It wouldn't crank either. Cursing their bad luck, the gangsters were forced to hopscotch to the next cabin where Mr. and Mrs. Robert

Johnson owned a small, V4, 1930 Model A. In no position to be choosy, the escapees woke up Johnson, took his vehicle, sat him up front as a hostage, and plopped Hamilton in the frigid rumble seat. As they puttered away, Johnson saw his wife peering out the window. Figuring he was with friends, she went back to sleep.

Dillinger and company "sped" off at 45 mph, as fast as the Model A could muster. They stopped in Springstead for gas, then gave Johnson seven dollars for his troubles and set him free near the Pixley power substation. That enabled Hamilton to rumble in from the cold. The gangsters then headed south on Wisconsin 13 and west on U.S. 8, heading toward Ladysmith.

At 4 A.M., Inspector Clegg gathered his bolstered forces and prepared to raid the sparsely populated Little Bohemia lodge. Joining in was one angry Izzy Tuchalsky, who'd heard through the grapevine that Baby Face Nelson was now in possession of his rod. An hour later, the veil of inky blackness lifted and Clegg gave the order to fire the tear-gas canisters. The law enforcement battalion watched in shock as the projectiles bounced off the screens and panes and fell to the ground, gassing the officers and agents surrounding the lodge. Angered over the latest bumbling, Agent Ray Suran pulled his .45 and shot out an upper window.

"Stop shooting. We're coming out," a female voice cried. The posse's big catch emerged—Helen Nelson, Jean Delaney, Marie Conforti, and Marie's puppy. The abandoned ladies were arrested under assumed names and taken to Eagle River. Still determined to smoke out the big fish, the agents spent the rest of the morning gassing the Little Bohemia Lodge, then riddling it with bullets, all to no avail. Emil and Nan Wanatka watched in horror, kicking themselves for their decision to bring in the Feds. Had they simply let Dillinger leave and pretended not to know who he was, lives would have been saved and their lodge wouldn't have been nearly destroyed.

Once inside and in control, the G-Men scooped up the usual assortment of guns, clothing, and cars. Purvis took Carroll's Buick coupe, borrowed from Louis Chernocky, to use as his own. Dillinger's black Ford was shipped to St. Paul.

The gang girls were transported from Eagle River to the Dane County jail in Madison where their arrival created a sensation. The news hounds took to calling them the "mollettes" because the sexy, stylishly dressed young ladies appeared to be teenagers. Delaney and Nelson were actually twenty-two and twenty-one respectively, with only Conforti checking in at nineteen.

None of the arrests, of course, made up for the utter fiasco that had occurred at Little Bohemia. Three civilians shot, one killed, one DI agent dead, a local constable in critical condition—and not a single male gang member caught. The DI was blistered like never before. "U.S. Agents in Dillinger Hunt Called Stupid" the *Chicago Herald and Examiner* bluntly blared. *The Chicago Tribune* reported that Hoover's head was about to roll unless he captured Dillinger "real soon." In D.C., various senators and congressmen weighed in with scathing reviews of the federal cops who had once again made Dillinger appear invincible. The usual investigations were launched.

Will Rogers summed it up thusly: "Well, they had Dillinger surrounded and was all ready to shoot him when he come out, but another bunch of folks come out ahead, so they just shot them instead. Dillinger is going to accidentally get with some innocent bystanders some time, then he will get shot!"

The ridicule was such that it even rained down from faraway Germany. Pro-Hitler editors at Berlin's *Zwoelf Uhr Blatt* threw Dillinger in the face of their regime's overseas critics, accusing America of coddling "murderers and the congenitally inferior," and suggested that the infamous felon be sterilized to prevent him from propagating.

Melvin Purvis, taking responsibility even though Assistant Director Clegg was in charge, offered his resignation. It wasn't accepted. In his memoirs, Purvis blamed the failure of the raid on Shadow and Prince, Emil Wanatka's barking collies.

Hoover, in his official report, attributed it to "three drunken . . . members of the Civilian Conservation Corps," and called their shooting "entirely justifiable" because they refused to heed orders they never heard. That wretched excuse didn't endear the Feds with anyone.

The DI was subjected to further scorn when it was revealed that

Washington, D.C., bean counters recommended that the money offered to repair the assaulted Little Bohemia Lodge "not exceed $30." Poetic justice to Nan Wanatka aside, it was yet another public relations disaster that ran counter to the agency's efforts to encourage, or force, the public to cooperate in the capture of Dillinger.

Agent Sam Hardy fueled additional antigovernment sentiment when he brutally assaulted a newspaper photographer in Madison during the arraignment of the mollettes, shattering the 120-pound journalist's costly plate holders. The offended lensman's widely published first-person account painted the faceless DI agents as incompetent goons. The public was further dismayed when Wisconsin's Rhinelander Ford dealership had to resort to a lawsuit to force the DI to compensate them for the vehicles that were taken, abandoned, and damaged.

Ford earned a measure of revenge when a Milwaukee dealer, noting the bandits' recent use of their product, distributed a sales brochure that posed the question "Will they catch John Dillinger?" The answer was inside. "Not until they get him out of a Ford V8!"

Dillinger no doubt agreed. Trouble was, his current wheels fell four critical Vs short. Still saddled with the sputtering Model A, the trio ran into Rusk County Sheriff Carl Nelson at the Flambeau River bridge near Ladysmith, Wisconsin. Relying on skill over speed, VanMeter weaved through a Ladysmith suburb known as Brooklyn, eluding the sheriff and his deputies long enough to hit Wisconsin 46, cross the Mississippi River, and poke into Minnesota at Red Wing. Catching U.S. 61, they headed toward St. Paul.

The tired bandits, thinking more like the outwitted Feds, were leaping back into the fires of the same city that was the scene of their previous escape. Suspecting as much, Dakota County sheriff deputies spotted their Wisconsin tags on a bridge at Hastings, fifteen miles from St. Paul. Close enough to read the tag numbers—B92652—the officers gave chase, only to be blocked by a snail-like cattle truck on the two-lane bridge. Once freed, they made a series of astute guesses and located the blue Model A ten miles farther north at St. Paul Park. Deputy Norman Dieter leaned out the window with a .30-30 rifle and fired at a tire. The slug punched through the thin body of the Model A between the fender and spare, drilled through the rear seat, and ripped square into John Hamilton's back, causing him to scream in agony.

Smashing the window behind Hamilton, Dillinger returned fire with his .45, shattering the offending cruiser's windshield just above Deputy Joe Heinen's head. That set off a whale of a chase right out of Hollywood. The underpowered cops and robbers traded thirty to forty rounds for nearly fifty miles, driving in arches on Highway 3 at Newport, passing by the railway station, barreling up Cemetery Road east and south before circling back west. The bandits finally lost their stubborn pursuers two miles from where they started, then continued their journey, doubling back through St. Paul Park and crossing the Mississippi yet again on the Invergrove toll bridge.

With Hamilton spewing blood from a gaping hole in his back, and the St. Paul police onto them, Dillinger decided to head to Chicago and find a doctor. First, they needed a faster and less recognizable vehicle. VanMeter cut off a 1934 Ford V8 deluxe at City Road 10 and Fifth Avenue. Power company manager Roy Francis, his wife Sybil, and their nineteen-month-old son, Robert, were ordered out as the desperados transferred their meager possessions into one of Henry Ford's finest pieces of machinery. After the injured Hamilton eased in, Dillinger ordered the Francises back inside as well. "Don't worry about the kid," Dillinger assured Sybil, who recognized him instantly. "We like kids."

VanMeter followed in the Model A to Robert Street and Willy Road, where the slow but faithful V4 was dumped. The Francis family was dropped off a short while later a few miles outside of Mendota. The bandits bid them farewell and headed west toward Chicago.

Dillinger and crew weren't the only ones having difficulty finding a place to land after the fireworks at Little Bohemia. The almost comical Reilly and Cherrington continued to have car trouble, eventually being forced to abandon their Ford at a shop in Owen, Wisconsin. Flush with Homer VanMeter's $4,000, which Reilly had been unable to deliver, the pair hired a mechanic to drive them to St. Paul. Concealed in the civilian car, they made the trip without further incident.

The catlike Tommy Carroll only made it fifteen miles north of Little Bohemia before sliding Henry Kuhnert's Packard into a ditch near

Marinesco, Michigan. The vehicle was found the following day, Monday, April 23. Carroll was nowhere in sight.

Despite the advantage of Izzy's souped-up hot rod—license number Wisconsin 166529—Baby Face didn't make it out of the state. Izzy's Ford was found mired in the mud at the mouth of Wisconsin 155 where the road dead-ended, no doubt to Nelson's utter surprise, near Star Lake. He was just twelve miles from where he heartlessly murdered Agent Baum.

The determined Nelson walked eighteen miles to the Lac du Flambeau Indian Reservation. He befriended the Schroeders, a family with Native American relatives who were vacationing in a remote cabin there, a place that conveniently offered no access to telephones, newspapers, or radios. Unaware of Little Bohemia, Mary Schroeder fed the youthful-looking stranger bacon and eggs, gave him some of her husband's clothes, and offered a cot to sleep on. Nelson paid her three dollars and traded his fedora as a souvenir.

The now-famous Ford was returned to Izzy in need of a good wash, but no worse for the wear. After all he'd gone through, Izzy ended up defaulting on the payments and losing it to shrewd collectors.

The ink from the Little Bohemia headlines was barely dry when Dillinger's second St. Paul escape hit the wires. Still pounding on the Feds, The Associated Press took pains to point out that the Dillinger hunt had cost the government nearly $2 million and counting, which they said was four times as much as the bank robber had stolen. The amnesty idea might not have been so crazy after all.

On the Lac du Flambeau Reservation, Nelson was still lingering Monday afternoon when Ollie and Maggie Catfish, Mary Schroeder's uncle and aunt, came by to visit. Ollie and his wife, Chippewa Indians, had heard the news, but kept their lips sealed the moment they saw Nelson's highly recognizable baby face. Nelson, suddenly filled with the rustic spirit, hung around until Thursday evening, chopping wood and helping with the chores. He generously paid Ollie seventy-five dollars for the privilege. Nelson eventually "rented" a blue 1933 Plymouth Deluxe from a rural mail carrier for twenty dollars, a deal negotiated at gunpoint, and took off west toward Wisconsin 70. Ollie Catfish, sixty-seven, served as his hostage/guide to avoid any more unpleasant dead ends. When they reached W-70, Baby Face let Ollie go, circled around a bit to get his bearings, then headed east, searching for a route to Chicago. That reality conflicted with newspaper accounts that had him trapped inside "a foolproof cordon . . . in the dismal swamps of Iron County, Wisconsin, north of Park Falls."

The high-and-dry Nelson switched cars again in Marshfield, this time buying a 1929 Chevrolet coach for $165. He continued 230 miles to Chicago, popping in and out of the Fox River Grove over the next few weeks with various associates, including the resurfaced Tommy Carroll. Obviously more connected to the mollettes than his less-chivalrous mates, he hired a Chicago lawyer to try and spring his wife in Wisconsin. The couple's children, a five-year-old boy and a four-year-old girl, stayed with Nelson's sister at 5516 Marshfield Avenue in Chicago.

Dillinger, VanMeter, and Hamilton were also in Chicago, once again desperately seeking a doctor to treat the festering, untreated, silver-dollar-sized wound in Hamilton's back. They tracked down the unscrupulous Dr. Joseph Moran—the greedy practitioner who had hit them up for $5,000 after the East Chicago job. This time, Moran refused to lend his services at any price, possibly because Hamilton's injury was too severe. Moran suggested they take him to Elmer Farmer's tavern in Bensenville and let him pass away there. Hamilton, his agony increasing by the hour, spent a few days at Elmer's refusing to die. He was subsequently carted to a Barker-Karpis safehouse in Aurora at 415 Fox Street that was being rented by Volney Davis and his irritated moll, Edna "Rabbits" Murray. Ravaged with gangrene and stinking up the place, Hamilton finally gave up the fight on Thursday, April 26.

Dillinger and some of the Barker-Karpis crew buried their digit-challenged friend in a gravel pit near Oswego, Illinois, covering the body with ten cans of watered-down lye to hamper identification. "Sorry, old friend, to have to do this," Dillinger eulogized. "I know you'd do as much for me." Davis placed a nearby roll of rusty wire over the makeshift grave as a marker.

The following day, April 27, Albert W. "Pat" Reilly, Eugene "Eddie" Green, and John "Three Fingers" Hamilton were indicted by a federal grand jury in St. Paul on charges of harboring and conspiracy to harbor. It was a waste of taxpayer's money. Of the trio, only the small-fry Reilly remained alive.

Dillinger stayed in Aurora until the 29th. A former state legislator on the Barker-Karpis payroll, John J. "Boss" McLaughlin, was busted, and Davis feared the man would cave to pressure and start ratting the hide-outs. It was time, once again, to scatter.

While considering where to go next, Dillinger received some unexpected help from an old foe—Melvin Purvis. The Chicago DI chief told The Associated Press that they had received reports that Public Enemy Number One had died from wounds he received at Little Bohemia and/or St. Paul. The DI was in possession of a number of getaway cars, including the Model A, that were drenched in blood, indicating that one or more of the gang members had taken a severe hit. The blood, of course, belonged to Hamilton.

Dillinger was alive, well, and on the road again, traveling in circles to Chicago, Fort Wayne, South Bend/Mishawaka, and back to Chicago. Asked why he didn't leave the areas where he was so hotly pursued, the outlaw told his associates that he felt more comfortable on familiar roads. He also reiterated that Michigan and Pennsylvania police were equipped with radios, making those states particularly inhospitable.

In St. Paul, Eddie Green's common-law widow, Bessie, continued to chirp up a storm, feeding DI Inspector Hugh Clegg a wealth of useful details. The bitter woman exposed the mollettes in Madison, giving away their real names and matching them with the felons whose beds they shared. The Feds used Bessie's information to grill the young ladies further. Unperturbed by the vicious betrayal, they refused to break, holding to their eroding story that they were in Little Bohemia on their own and weren't connected with troublesome gangsters. Finally allowed to speak with an attorney, they promptly clammed up completely.

Oddly enough, John Hamilton's slow, agonizing death did nothing to scare Dillinger and VanMeter straight. On May 3, the pair hit a bank in Fostoria, Ohio. Entering the building through a connected drug-store, they strolled inside, threw open their coats, raised twin

Thompsons, and announced the stickup. While his partner collected the money in the cages, VanMeter didn't hesitate to fire a burst of slugs at employees rubbernecking from an upper mezzanine. He then used the warmed-up weapon to shatter a heavy, plate-glass partition that separated the cages from the vault. Bank president Andrew Emerine and the assistant cashier, William Daub, were marched inside and forced to spin the dial.

Fostoria Police Chief Frank Culp, sixty-seven, happened to be an expert marksman lauded numerous times for his deadly skills. Already in the area, he was alerted to the robbery by an escaping customer. Stepping into the lobby through another side door, he drew his trusty revolver, but couldn't shoot because of the shielding bankers. The less-skilled, yet decidedly better-armed VanMeter had no such qualms, blasting the veteran lawman in the chest, ripping a slug through his lung.

As Chief Culp dropped, a few random shots crashed through the window from the outside. One hit cashier Ralph S. Powley, leaving him bloodied and shaken. VanMeter returned fire, preventing anyone else from being hit.

Leaving through the drugstore, the robbers faced a formidable phalanx of armed citizens stationed all around the building. As usual, the cops and vigilantes couldn't play hero because the bandits had hostages—Daub and a tall, twenty-two-year-old cashier named Ruth Harris. VanMeter held the attractive Harris so tightly as they moved that she could feel the vibration of his machine gun each time he fired—which was often. Keeping the townsfolk at bay, Homer added insult to injury when he put two .45 slugs into the Elk's head over the door of the namesake club across the street to the south. Four vigilantes and witnesses were also shot, none as seriously as the Elk.

The hostages were stationed on the running boards of the duo's latest getaway vehicle, a black Ford V8 with screaming yellow wire wheels that they'd pinched in Toledo. Hightailing it out of town at upwards of 80 miles per hour, VanMeter gripped Harris's wrist with such force she carried his nail prints for weeks.

Daub and Harris were freed after two miles. "Thanks," Dillinger offered, smiling devilishly at the emotionally overwrought lady before he sped off. Once the vehicle was out of sight, Harris promptly fainted.

Despite the excessive shooting, nobody was killed. Chief Culp, hit the hardest, nonetheless recovered. Daub, a large, athletic man who escaped physical injury, never recovered his nerves. Shaken and afraid from that point on, he died within the year.

The amount of cash taken in the holdup was reported to be around $11,000. The value of the bonds was never released, possibly because it was embarrassingly substantial. More likely, the missing accounting was due to the fact that this robbery, until now, was never attributed to John Dillinger. The battered Feds wanted to keep a lid on the superstar outlaw's increasingly successful exploits, and were happy to see this one downplayed.

Media frenzy or not, by all accounts, it was a healthy score, particularly for a "gang" that only had to split the booty two ways.

On May 8, the Jackrabbit was back in Chicago, meeting with Arthur O'Leary and showing off a red, Ford panel-delivery truck with a mattress in the back that was serving as a mobile hideout. Tommy Carroll was now running with Dillinger, as was John Paul Chase. They had purchased the new vehicle at Rimes Motor Company in East Chicago for a thrifty $637. Dillinger queried O'Leary about Billie and the plastic surgeon. O'Leary responded that his boss was working on the first, and reminded the outlaw that they had already arranged the second.

On May 10, Dillinger made a delivery at Hubert's gas station right under the resident DI agent's nose. The unshaven Public Enemy disguised himself in overalls, a blue shirt and tie, brown vest, dark hat, and rimless glasses. Fred Hancock, on duty at the time, initially failed to recognize him. Dillinger gave Hancock a bag with $1,200 in freshly stolen cash, designating $500 each to his father and sister, $100 to Hubert and $100 to Fred. The DI man living across the street, Lish Whitson, viewed the transaction but felt the curious stranger was too tall and heavy to be his prey. Spotting the cleft in the unkempt man's grizzled chin as he was leaving, he decided to follow him. He was only 100 feet behind when Dillinger turned the corner at LaSalle and Washington. When Whitson made the same hook, Dillinger was gone.

The ghostly outlaw left Indianapolis and returned to his latest hideout—in Crown Point! Figuring it was "the last place they'd look for us," he and VanMeter were bunking at a tourist inn there.

In mid-May, fixer James Probasco began steering his friends away from his Chicago home. He offered them a variety of excuses as to why he'd be out of the loop for a while. An unusual theft provided a clue. On May 15, Tommy Carroll stole a medical bag from the car of Dr. W. A. Hornerday outside the Lyndore Hotel in Hammond, Indiana. John Dillinger was getting serious about having his face altered.

That same Saturday, Billie Frechette's trial began in St. Paul. Curiously, her case was bunched with those of Dr. Clayton May, Nurse Salt, and moll-turned-snitch Bessie Green. During the noon recess, Billie filtered in with the spectators and walked out of the courtroom. An alert cop intercepted her in the hallway a few feet from freedom. "I was just going to have lunch with the other folks," she cooed. "I was coming back. Really."

When the trial broke for the weekend, Louis Piquett met with Dillinger in Chicago and delivered a cheerful, optimistic love note from Billie that lifted the outlaw's spirits. In turn, Dillinger gave O'Leary a letter for Billie, and one for Pat Cherrington that confirmed the bad news of her lover's death. Upon receiving the news, Cherrington reacted angrily to the claim that her guy hadn't left her any money. She became hysterical and abusive, arguing that she'd risked her life to bring VanMeter his dough and wanted a cut. Dillinger eventually sent her a stipend from the Fostoria job.

Needing funds for the surgery, Billie's defense, the mollettes' bail and defense, and Pierpont's appeal, among other things, Dillinger and VanMeter decided to go back to work. On May 21, they took down a small bank in Galion, Ohio, that was a dangerous forty miles southeast of Fostoria, and sixty-five miles east of Lima. Dillinger, paying homage to his Jackrabbit days, vaulted over an eight-foot cage to empty the tills of $5,400. When an alarm sounded, the pair decided to abandon the safe and hop out a rear window, possibly spooked by the shoot-out in Fostoria. Shots were fired, but nobody was hit.

The quick exit was also taken because Dillinger read that the government had shipped surplus WWI weapons to Federal Reserve banks nationwide. Many bank presidents had, in turn, distributed the rifles and pistols to hardy area businessmen, forming a defense perimeter around their institutions.

Two days later, on May 23, the verdicts came down in St. Paul. Billie was found guilty of harboring, fined $1,000, and given a hefty two years in a federal women's pen at Milan, Michigan. Doctor May was handed a similar term at Leavenworth. Bessie earned a mere nine-month reduction for her backstabbing cooperation, getting fifteen months behind bars in Alderson, West Virginia. Nurse Salt effectively played dumb and was acquitted.

The convictions were bumped off the front pages of the newspapers by a far more dramatic event that occurred near Gibsland, Louisiana. Grim-faced Texas lawmen set a trap, then gunned down Clyde Barrow, 25, and Bonnie Parker, 23, the star-crossed lovers who would one day ignite the Hollywood careers of Warren Beatty and Faye Dunaway.

The following day, the headlines blared again. Two East Chicago detectives, Martin O'Brien and Lloyd Mulvihill, were found shot to death inside their black Ford on Old Gary Road near the Cudahy Packing Plant. The remote stretch was known as a lover's lane, which doubled as a transfer area for stolen vehicles. The detectives were found just before midnight slumped in their parked, unmarked car. Their weapons remained holstered, indicating an ambush. Powder burns revealed that they'd been shot at point blank with a Thompson and a .38—hit twelve times between them. Neither officer logged their mission that evening, leading to speculation that they were up to no good.

O'Brien left three children. Mulvihill had six. The department, and city, suffice it to say, was outraged. Without evidence to support it, but possibly knowing things he wasn't revealing, East Chicago Police Chief Nick Makar angrily blamed Dillinger. What Chief Makar didn't say was that his department was tearing apart from within, caught between rival factions that despised each other. Detective Mulvihill and the always-deadly Sgt. Martin Zarkovich were mortal enemies who headed up each contingent. Rumors swirled that Zarkovich either performed the hit with his crew, or made a pact to have Dillinger and VanMeter do it. Another theory was that O'Brien and Mulvihill discovered that Zarkovich and his gang had arranged for the cell-block door to be open at Crown Point, enabling Dillinger to make his sensational escape. Armed with the inflammatory information, they were either going to expose their enemies, shake the bandits down, or both.

Dillinger himself would later admit to the shakedown, but refused to comment on the actual shooting. As is usually the case when cops go bad and a department splinters, the situation would grow to be considerably more dangerous than any of the bank robberies.

On a lighter note, the sexism that was the norm in the 1930s paid off for the mollettes. Appearing before Federal Magistrate Patrick T. Stone on May 25, the young ladies feigned ignorance, pleaded guilty to harboring, and were given a probationary slap on the wrist. Judge Stone made it crystal clear why he showed such extraordinary mercy—the girls were to serve as bait. "Undoubtedly, the men . . . will attempt to contact them . . ." he noted, advising Feds to stick to their tails.

The fashionable trio celebrated by shopping for perfume, purses, clothing, and hats. A reporter who tagged along wrote that the two single girls, Conforti and Delaney, were in high spirits. Nelson was less carefree, expressing concern for her heavily hunted husband and their children.

On Sunday, May 27, Billie Frechette's own heavily hunted boyfriend moved into James Probasco's house at 2509 North Crawford (now Pulaski) to prepare for the surgery. Probasco, sixty-six, advised his live-in girlfriend, Margaret "Peggy" Doyle, thirty-three, that the visitor, "Mr. Harris" was from Napierville and would be staying a few weeks. Out of earshot, Probasco brought Dillinger up to speed. The physician he found was Dr. Wilhelm Loeser, another in a long line of fallen healers in need of money. Doctor Loeser was popular among the gangster set for devising a way to alter fingerprint loops using a caustic soda that burned off the skin. He charged $100 a finger. The doc had been his own guinea pig, inventing the procedure while trying to distance himself from his own past. He'd served a stint at Leavenworth for drug violations, among other shady dealings. Assisting Doctor Loeser would be Dr. Harold Bernard Cassidy, thirty-two, a friend of O'Leary's who once practiced with Dr. Charles Eye, the physician who had treated Dillinger's scalp problem. Doctor Cassidy was relatively clean, but was struggling financially because of the Depression. The $600 fee Probasco offered was too big to pass up.

Dillinger opted for the full face and fingertip overhaul at a cost of $5,000, not counting the $35 a day given to Probasco for use of his house. Homer VanMeter would be staying there as well to help with his partner's recovery and monitor the procedure to see if he wanted to go through with it himself. Dillinger gave middleman Probasco $3,000 upfront, with the remainder to be paid afterward. The surgery was scheduled for Monday evening, May 28.

As Dillinger relaxed in preparation, his old friend Pearl Elliott was in town beating the bushes with a furloughed prisoner named Joe Byers. They were trying to locate the outlaw to sell him out for the reward money and a sentence reduction. Among those they attempted to milk was Louis Piquett. The crafty attorney smelled a rat and gave up nothing. Byers, who had weaseled a three-day pass from Michigan City claiming he could find Dillinger, amazingly gave himself up and returned to his dismal cell when his plan failed.

On the evening of the 28th, O'Leary and Doctor Cassidy picked up Doctor Loeser at his home, 536 Wrightwood Avenue. The cautious physician asked to be dropped off two blocks from Probasco's house and walked the rest of the way. Inside, Dillinger was told to strip to his undershirt, go into a small bedroom off the parlor, and lay down. As Doctor Cassidy applied a generous amount of ether, Dillinger swallowed his tongue and started to choke to death. The more experienced Doctor Loeser rushed in, pried the outlaw's tongue forward, and slammed the famous bandit's elbows into his side to jump-start his breathing. The two physicians mopped their brows in relief as their patient gulped for air. Not wasting any more time, Doctor Loeser went to work, removing a mole between the robber's eyebrows, erasing a second mole from his left forehead area, masking a scar on his upper lip, and making an incision under the ear to remove tissue and tighten the face—the standard face-lift procedure. After that, he tackled Dillinger's most distinguishing feature, the dimple in his chin.

Using tissue removed from behind the ears, Doctor Loeser spackled the depression and sutured it with "cat-gut" thread. The final touch was cutting and filling an indentation on the Jackrabbit's nose to give him a more refined look.

Because of the ether fiasco, Doctor Loeser switched to a local anesthetic, meaning Dillinger was semiconscious during the lengthy procedure that lasted until the early hours of Tuesday, May 29. He frequently thrashed and moaned, his warm blood soaking into the white sheets. Still sick from the ether, and having lied about not eating, he vomited repeatedly over the course of the seven-hour operation. Looking on in dismay, O'Leary no doubt was reminded of the movie *Frankenstein* that first shocked viewers a mere three years earlier.

Curious as to what was going on, Peggy Doyle nagged her boyfriend until he confessed that "Johnnie Dillinger" was having his face changed. Peggy was promised a new outfit to "keep my mouth shut."

Doctor Cassidy stayed around for the next few days to monitor the patient's condition. Doctor Loeser returned on Tuesday, June 5, to change the bloody wrappings and administer morphine tablets. From that point, it was just a waiting game—a luxury Dillinger was rarely afforded.

Melvin Purvis, still convinced that Dillinger was dead, announced that his men had undertaken a search for the outlaw's body in southern Indiana. Revealing further details, Purvis claimed that a former Dillinger doctor confessed to interrogators that the outlaw was suffering from three serious wounds, "any one of which could have been fatal." If the exaggerating songbird was Dr. Joseph Moran, it would be the fallen physician's last performance. Hanging with the Barker crew at the Casino Club in Toledo, the intoxicated abortionist started to belittle various gang members, blaming them for his career descent. Fred Barker advised his associates he was going to take the arrogant doc for a "relaxing boat ride" on Lake Erie and escorted him out. Doctor Moran was never seen again.

On Thursday, May 30—Memorial Day—the DI and police were out in force at the famed Indianapolis Motor Speedway, acting on tips that Dillinger and gang would be attending the annual Indianapolis 500. It was one of innumerous false alarms.

At Probasco's, the object of the hunt was doing anything but partying in the pits. Glancing into mirrors during bandage changes, Dillinger growled, "Hell, I don't look any different than I did! It looks like I've been snorting wildcats."

Regaining his considerable strength, Dillinger quizzed O'Leary about Billie. He'd heard that the mollettes had been let off easy and wondered why his gal was hit so much harder. "She's a damned good kid. There won't be any real happiness for me until we're back together. Tell Mr. Piquett to do his very best for Billie."

Texas Ranger Frank Hamer was campaigning to do his very best as well. Flush with blood fever after helping slaughter Bonnie and Clyde, Hamer offered to do the same to the Jackrabbit. "The government men may not give me a chance to kill him," he lamented. "There's a lot of jealousy in this man-hunting game."

That was certainly the case, and it was growing worse by the day. On June 1, Captain Stege and the Chicago police blatantly violated the Feds' policy of letting the gang girls wander free as bait. They barged into room 523 of the Chateau Hotel and arrested Pat Cherrington, Bernice Clark, and Jean Burke, the wife of Arthur "Fish" Johnson. As usual, the veteran molls gave up little of value.

Despite Dillinger's near-death experience and lack of satisfaction with the results, Homer VanMeter decided to go forward with the cosmetic surgery as well. His procedure was scheduled for the following Sunday night. Upon arriving, Doctor Loeser agreed to make further changes on Dillinger's face, and performed the burn job on his fingers. Taking the outlaw into his confidence during the procedure, Loeser revealed that his secret formula consisted of two parts hydrochloric acid and one part nitrohydrochloric acid, used in conjunction with an alkaloid, usually sodium. The fiery liquid was applied to the raw skin after the outer epidermis was cut away.

While Dillinger was still writhing in pain from that nasty combination, Doctor Loeser sliced additional strips from under his ears to "lift" his face. Unwilling to repeat the previous ether experience, Dillinger was said to have endured both operations without any painkillers.

When it was his turn, VanMeter opted to go with the local anesthetic. Doctor Loeser eliminated a scar on Homer's forehead, split his nose to remove a hump, bobbed off some of the end, sliced away a "wedge" on his large lower lip, then attempted, without much success to remove a large tattoo of an anchor and the words "Good Hope" from Homer's right forearm. His face and arm wrapped like a mummy, VanMeter then groggily subjected himself to the finger treatment.

Leaving a healthy supply of morphine tablets, Doctor Loeser noted that Dillinger used them judiciously while VanMeter popped them like gumdrops. Subsequent reports had VanMeter becoming hooked on the powerful narcotic, using both morphine and cocaine from that point on.

Fearing for his life in case his temperamental patients weren't satisfied, Doctor Loeser used part of his $10,000 windfall to secretly rent a house at 1127 South Harvey Avenue to use as his own hideout. It would prove to be a fortuitous precaution.

Chapter 18

The reeling Division of Investigation finally caught a break in early June, when Grandview Hospital officials proudly announced that Constable Carl Christensen was miraculously going to survive. Although the hospital was quick to credit its skillful surgeons and top-flight care, the "miracle" was due more to Baby Face Nelson's erratic shooting. Nelson blasted the lawman twelve times from point-blank range and failed to hit any vital organs. Five of the shots ripped harmlessly through the outer layers of the constable's big winter coat.

The determined Christensen not only refused to succumb, he lived another sixty years, joining Crown Point Sheriff Lillian Holley in bridging the Dillinger 1930s with the 1990s.

Shortly after the Grandview announcement, the DI found itself right back in hot water. An agent trying to flip Marie Conforti caused her, in Marie's exaggerated version, to miss a meeting with her probation officer. Judge Patrick T. Stone made a heated call telling the Feds to stop interfering with the rehabilitation of those under his orders. The DI, in response, gently reminded the judge that he had advised the agents to monitor the girls closely in case they met with a wanted gang member.

That controversy was followed by a report in the *Indianapolis News* that a G-Man had offered Dillinger's father and sister $10,000 if they could persuade John Jr. to turn himself in. "It's up to John as to what he wants to do and I don't think anyone would expect me to turn against him," Mr. Dillinger told The Associated Press. "Life is just as precious to John as to anyone else . . ."

Far too precious to spend it bandaged up in some dank hideout. By June 5, the Jackrabbit was starting to hop all over town again, meeting with associates and hitting taverns with his face still swollen and stitched. Among those he met on these jaunts was Tommy Carroll. It would be the last time Dillinger would see his friend.

On June 7, Carroll, thirty-eight, tracked down mollette Jean Delaney and headed to Minneapolis to visit Delaney's mother. They had some big news to share, and Jean wanted to present it in person. Stopping for gas outside Waterloo, Iowa, a nosey attendant noticed several license plates under a floor mat of Carroll's tan Hudson. Suspecting something wasn't right, he dropped a nickel. Carroll left before the police arrived, but decided to stop in town to shop and have a beer. He parked the Hudson in front of a tavern just south of police headquarters. Confronted by Detectives Emil Steffen and Paul E. Walker as he and Delaney were returning to the vehicle, Carroll instinctively reached for his .380 Colt automatic and was knocked down by a right cross from Walker. Scrambling to his feet, he took off. The detectives, having no clue who he was, shot him four times in the back. As he lingered at St. Francis hospital, he pleaded with the cops to allow him to see Delaney one last time. They refused. He died alone a few hours later.

Among the items confiscated from the Hudson were numerous pairs of silk panties—size small—and Dr. W. A. Hornaday's medical bag that had been stolen in Hammond, Indiana. Despite the shocking events, the smartly dressed Delaney consented to media interviews, explaining that she had dyed her blonde hair black because the other mollettes were calling her Mae West. The faceless G-Men swept in, ended the chats, and relentlessly interrogated her until 4 A.M., mostly to no avail. The pressure, combined with her belated shock over watching her lover shot down on the street, caused her to miscarry the child she was carrying. She told the G-Men she reunited with Carroll because of the baby, conceived at Little Bohemia, and Carroll's promise to marry her. That was the news she was bringing to her mom.

Investigators discovered that the couple had a complicated relationship. Aside from Carroll, whom she initially claimed to be her spouse, Delaney had a legitimate husband in Chicago, along with a boyfriend on the side. Carroll was also married. His wife, Viola, angrily told reporters that Delaney was both a home-wrecker and a rat. "They just turned that woman loose so that she would get Tommy and lead him into a police trap. If I ever see her it will be just too bad for her!"

Viola Carroll's statements exposed the DI to more criticism, especially after the *Madison Capital Times* printed a dark story of how Carroll had been shot right under the noses of special agents that were shadowing the couple, hoping they would lead them to Dillinger. The paper chastised the Feds for using the pregnant young woman as bait in a dangerous cat-and-mouse game.

Unmoved by such reports, Judge Stone revoked Delaney's probation and sent her back to the Dane County jail in Madison, Wisconsin. From there, she was shipped to Alderson, West Virginia, to serve ten months. Within weeks, Stone would yank the probations of fellow mollettes Marie Conforti and Helen Nelsen.

The gas station attendant who fingered Carroll quickly left town. It was a smart move. Baby Face Nelson arrived a few days later to kill him.

On June 8, in keeping with his carefree, out-and-about attitude, Dillinger attended a baseball game between the Chicago Cubs and Cincinnati Reds. Louis Piquett was there, as was Chicago Police Capt. John Stege. Advised of such, Dillinger reluctantly left after a few innings. It was apparent that his "new face" wasn't as new as he had hoped. Having paid good money and suffered greatly, both Dillinger and VanMeter were growing frustrated with Doctor Loeser's alleged skills. "I could see no appreciable difference in their looks than before they were operated upon," Probasco's girlfriend, Peggy Doyle, observed. As a result, Doctor Loeser was becoming increasingly fearful for his life. A heated gripe session at Probasco's was interrupted by the arrival of Baby Face. Doctor Loeser used the diversion to slip away, never to return.

As time passed and the healing set in, Dillinger began to believe the operation hadn't been so bad after all. Dying his hair and mustache black, and donning gold-rimmed glasses, he convinced himself that he was unrecognizable. Frequent outings without incident appeared to confirm his belief. Growing bolder, Dillinger began taking up with a new girlfriend—a woman with a very dangerous girlfriend of her own.

Rita "Polly" Hamilton was a clone of Billie Frechette right down to the troubled youth and Native American blood. She ran away from her frigid home in Fargo, North Dakota, at age thirteen, returned for a while, then left for good at seventeen to join a "show troupe." She ended up in Lake County, Indiana, where she met Anna Chiolak, a local madam who ran a brothel out of a hotel in Gary, Indiana. She worked for Anna off and on as a prostitute until she married a Gary police officer named Roy O. Keele in 1929. They divorced in March 1933. By the summer of 1934, Polly was carting plates and hustling for tips at the S&S Sandwich Shop at 1209 1/2 Wilson Avenue in Chicago. She remained friends with Anna Chiolak, now Anna Sage, who had also moved to Chicago and was living in an apartment at 2858 Clark Street with her son Steve, twenty-four.

One a warm night in early June, Polly was hanging out at the Barrel of Fun nightclub at 4541 Wilson Avenue when she made eye contact with a dapper-looking man who had been staring at her. Intrigued, he approached. "What would happen if I called you up some night?" he asked. It wasn't the best opening line, but it worked—probably because Polly was there at her former madam's behest for the specific reason of attracting this particular gentleman.

"Try and see," she told him with a big smile, eagerly offering the numbers. He called the next day, meeting her after work. The man introduced himself as Jimmy Lawrence and said he worked as a clerk for the Board of Trade. Hitting it off, they hopped a cab to the Stables nightclub for an evening of dinner and dancing. "He was one of the shyest fellows I ever met, but I liked him a lot," Polly recalled.

Since shyness had never been part of the Jackrabbit's persona, her impression was telling. Dillinger had not only changed his appearance, but was affecting a passive, Don Diego de la Vega personality to go along with it, an act he no doubt pinched from *The Legend of Zorro.*

Johnnie and Polly were together from that point on. The first week or so, he always waited outside for her to get off work. He didn't go in because her coworkers, seeing him from a distance in his Don Diego disguise, thought he was indeed a sissy. The glasses, thin mustache, and prim clothing fostered the ironic impression. Up close, he still had the

Zorro scars on his face from the surgery, which he blamed on an auto accident.

Admiring Polly's dark, exotic, Billie-like looks, Dillinger called his new girl "Countess" or "Cleopatra," eventually settling on "honey" as they became more intimate. "She's all right. I like her just the way she is," he told friends. It was obvious he was using Polly as a look-alike bandage to help him get over the loss of his cherished Billie. If she sensed that, however, she didn't care. "He was better to me than any other man I ever knew." She also didn't care when her fellow waitresses began taking a closer look and proclaimed that her not so dainty dandy "looks just like John Dillinger!" Whether Polly knew the identity of the man she was working, or even to what end, is hard to pin down. Her subsequent statements were based upon the knowledge that the Feds were eager to nail her for harboring. The well-practiced 1930s moll credo, after all, was "ignorance is legal bliss."

It's also uncertain as to whether Polly introduced Dillinger to Anna Sage, or whether Anna met the bandit earlier and arranged the meeting at the Barrel of Fun nightclub. Although history until now supported the first proposition, it's more plausible that Anna simply did what she was most skilled at—setting couples up. Whatever the truth, Dillinger began spending a great deal of time at Anna's apartment—a place he seemed to know well from the first visit with Polly—often playing cards with the girls and Anna's son Steve.

If it had just been Polly hooking a new Sugar Daddy, Dillinger may have been in the clear. Anna was an entirely different story. The forty-one-year-old businesswoman was in a world of trouble, and prior setup or not, she immediately targeted her friend's new boyfriend as her ticket out.

A reporter once described Anna as "a woman of the extra sizes, with a metallic jaw and quick adjusted eyes." The references were to the ample figure she carried on her five-foot, three-inch, 167-pound frame, her eight gold teeth, and "snapping black eyes, centered in a not unattractive face." She spoke with a light Rumanian accent and couldn't read or write in English.

Born in Costanza, Rumania, on November 30, 1892, Anna

Cumpanas came to America in February 1909, a month after marrying Mihai "Mike" Chiolak. The newlyweds settled in Chicago, where Chiolak had relatives, renting an apartment at 1452 Fullerton Avenue. The following year, they had their son, Stefan, born on August 16, 1910. Mihai toiled for a cement contractor. Anna labored at Dooring Harvester Works.

Anna separated from Mihai in 1918 and moved to Newcastle, Pennsylvania. She returned to Chicago six months later. In 1921, Anna and Mrs. Leo Bada bought a part interest in the People's Hotel at 1428 Jefferson Avenue in Gary, Indiana. To attract customers, they offered their guests a special treat—themselves. A romp with Anna or one of her girls cost two dollars.

It took the police two years to catch up with her, arresting Anna twice in the summer of 1923. The first case was dismissed, and the second, under the assumed name Katie Brown, cost her a twenty-five-dollar fine. Although an untold number of men had shared her bed, she wasn't officially divorced until February 25, 1924. She smiled coyly at the clerk and signed the divorce papers with an X.

Ducking the heat, the newly single entrepreneur leased the Kostur Hotel at 1249 Washington Street in March 1924, and continued her profitable Gary business. She was arrested again as Katie Brown on May 25, 1924. Charged with operating a house of ill fame, she was found not guilty.

In 1927, she met a Rumanian immigrant named Alexander Sage, the owner of a cigar store on 23 East Ohio Avenue that doubled as a betting parlor. The pair bought an apartment building at 5542 Kenwood Avenue, then celebrated by marrying on May 16, 1929. Despite the marriage, she continued the prostitution business out of the forty-six-room Kostur Hotel, resulting in additional arrests and a few thirty-day jail terms. Her second marriage dissolved in February 1932.

The Federal Immigration Department, noting that she failed to apply for citizenship, issued a warrant for her deportation on June 12, 1933. To stay a step ahead of the Feds and local police, she shifted her operation to the twenty-nine-room Hotel Sheffield at 3504 Sheffield Avenue in Chicago.

Another Sugar Daddy came along, a Scandinavian immigrant named Holger Borglum, and the two quickly became engaged. The bewitched Holger wanted her despite her considerable baggage. After she took him for a chunk of money, they called off the scheduled nuptials. Holger, who barely spoke English, made the rounds of the police and DI complaining about his plight, and telling anyone who'd listen that his duplicitous ex was hanging around with famous gangsters. Nobody paid him any attention.

All considering, there was nothing in Anna's checkered background that alarmed Dillinger. Madams, prostitutes, loose women, and criminals always went hand in hand. What he knew about Anna probably gave him comfort instead of concern. It was what he didn't know that made her so dangerous.

There was one more man in Anna's life that she didn't talk much about. A young Yugoslavian immigrant named Martin Zarkovich began availing himself of her robust charms dating back to his patrolman days in 1920. Married with a baby, Zarkovich's wife Elizabeth cited the affair in divorce papers filed that year. Freed of his family ties, Sergeant Zarkovich rose up the ranks to become East Chicago's deadliest assassin. He was also in charge of lucrative graft payments from Lake County speakeasy owners during Prohibition—the same Lake County underworld figures that later befriended and sheltered John Dillinger.

As Sergeant Zarkovich's fortunes and power rose, so did Anna's protection and political influence—which explains all those "not guilty" verdicts, small fines, and short jail terms. She returned the favor in 1929 when she attempted to dissuade a woman named Julia Barna from testifying against Sergeant Zarkovich and other East Chicago cops and politicians during a wide-reaching corruption probe. Anna was arrested and fined $100 for her efforts. Sergeant Zarkovich was also arrested for taking payoffs, and was jailed in South Bend, Indiana. He was convicted in January 1930, along with his chief, the mayor, and thirteen others. An appeals court tossed out the verdicts on the proverbial technicality and ordered the defendants retried in 1931. When the mayor died of a heart attack, the politically charged case was left to linger and fade away.

Sergeant Zarkovich not only skated, he managed to hang on to his crucial job. He emerged more feared and influential than before.

It's likely that Dillinger met Anna prior to meeting Polly through the double-dealing Sergeant Zarkovich. Rumors swirled that Zarkovich was given a substantial extra payment in his envelop the week of the Crown Point escape, his payoff for helping set it up. The fly in the ointment was the increasingly meddlesome Feds. When Anna came to her longtime lover and protector with her intensifying immigration problems in 1934, it was beyond his reach. There was, however, a way out—John Dillinger.

Unaware of such machinations, the famous outlaw felt safe and comfortable with Anna, so much so that he became a fixture at her apartment. When she tossed the made-to-order Polly into the mix to keep him interested, he couldn't have been more grateful.

In a letter to his father, an upbeat John Jr. mentioned that "I still have some friends who will not sell me out." He added, "I will be leaving soon and you will not need to worry anymore," an indication that he was still dreaming of a Mexico or South American escape. Doctor Loeser, desperate to make up for the oversold surgery, promised to grease such an adventure with an expertly forged birth certificate. The weaseling doctor, playing every angle, later tried to cover himself by writing anonymous letters to Melvin Purvis and J. Edgar Hoover fingering Arthur O'Leary as a link between crooked lawyers and criminals. He also exposed Probasco's house as a haven for bank robbers. The spineless maneuver did little to erase his own culpability, and arrived too late to do anything but bring heat on minor leaguers O'Leary and Probasco.

On the other end of the psychological scale, a tough-minded, adrenaline junkie was once again playfully pushing his luck and nerve to the absolute limit. Secure in his wimpy new "Don Diego" image, the Jackrabbit escorted Polly to the Chicago Police Building at 112 South State Street on Monday, June 11. He was there to help his girl obtain a permit to waitress in a Loop hotel, a process that was mandated after an outbreak of amoebic dysentery the summer before. High on the thrill, he repeated the risky visits three more times, on June 18, 25, and on July 20. At first, he loitered passively in the crowded waiting room, brushing by scores of police officers as Polly filed the paperwork and went through the medical exams. Tiring of that, he began to wander the hallways, ducking in and out of crowded squad rooms, including that of Chief of Detectives William E. Shoemaker. When word of Dillinger's bizarre activities was leaked to *The Chicago Times,* Detective Shoemaker was severely reprimanded and demoted.

Aside from once again embarrassing the police, the sensational appearances flew in the face of Melvin Purvis' statements that Dillinger was dead.

Taking a cue from his infamous buddy, Homer VanMeter began using his new face to court his own girl, which he affectionately referred to as "Mazie." The sultry Mazie turned out to be one Marie Marion Conforti. Learning nothing from what happened to Tommy Carroll, the love-smitten, normally cautious VanMeter was performing a dangerous high-wire act. He was aware that Conforti was being shadowed "everywhere she went," and devised a plan to ferry her away for a long vacation. He swept her up at a designated location, then raced to Calumet City, twenty-five miles south of Chicago. Dillinger went along part of the way for the sheer thrill of it. VanMeter later took his teenaged "bride" to Indian Lake, Ohio, for the promised vacation, renting a cabin at Russell's Point.

Marie, as was the norm, referred to the tall, lanky bandit as her husband, claiming they had married eight months before in St. Paul. VanMeter, always the dandy of the gang, had taken to wearing "pince-nez" glasses void of frames or earpieces. The choice of jewelers and college professors, the spectacles sat precariously on the nose. Homer accented his with a fancy black ribbon that floated from his face to a vest button, the purpose of which was to save them from breaking each time they slid off his reconstructed snout.

The clever disguises were well advised. By the middle of June, the price on Dillinger's head had soared to $15,000. Art McGinnis, among others, was in a frenzy, beating the bushes for information. Even "Leaping" Lena Pierpont turned rat, angry that Dillinger hadn't freed her son or showered them with money. She gave the Feds a map that pinpointed hideouts that were to be used after a spate of late June robberies, including the planned theft of a $100,000 Chrysler Corporation payroll at New Castle, Indiana.

Aubrey Russ of Fort Wayne, a friend of VanMeter's brother Harry, also had designs on the reward, telling DI Division Supervisor Inspector Sam Cowley that VanMeter and Dillinger planned to use his place as a hideout again. Cowley responded by moving agents into Russ's home.

Baby Face Nelson, taking a cue from VanMeter and not his late friend Tommy Carroll, similarly snatched his wife from Chicago and took her to Lake Geneva, Wisconsin, sixty miles from the Windy City just inside the border. A Catholic priest Nelson had befriended in Michigan City, Father Phillip W. Coughlan, was being squeezed by the Feds, who played upon his religious guilt. Agreeing to cooperate, he told the DI that Nelson had gone to some resort, which he remembered as "Lake Zurich." The tip sent a large squad of Hoover's finest on their latest wild goose chase.

Continuing to hammer the uncooperative gang girls, authorities sent Pat Cherrington to the Dane County jail in Wisconsin to await her trial, scheduled for the fall. Bernice Clark was taken to St. Paul and stashed at the Ramsey County jail. She pleaded guilty to harboring and was given a six-month sentence at the Minneapolis Work House.

With his buddy VanMeter on his "honeymoon," Dillinger left Probasco's and accepted Anna Sage's invitation to move into her apartment at 2858 North Clark Street. Once settled, he found a secluded place to meet with his crew, an old frame schoolhouse on Rohlwing Road (SR 53) just south of Palatine. Nelson and VanMeter wheeled in from their hideouts to help plan the next job. The leading candidate was a bank in South Bend, Indiana, home of Notre Dame University. Nelson's California boys, Joseph Raymond "Fatso" Negri and John Paul Chase, were summoned to beef up the dwindling Dillinger Gang, replacing the deceased Carroll and Hamilton. Less recognizable than Dillinger and Nelson, the imports did some scouting and gathered the cars and weapons.

Arthur "Fish" Johnson, always with his ear to the ground, got wind of the plan and appeared at Rohlwing Road on June 22—Dillinger's thirty-first birthday—hawking bulletproof vests he'd acquired from Al Capone's soldiers. Baby Face Nelson bought a pair for a hefty $300 each. Nelson might have been wise to immediately put one on. He and

VanMeter nearly went at it when Baby Face began to rant that Mazie was cooperating with the Feds. "That guinea bitch is no good and you'd better pop a cap on her," Nelson demanded. Chase and Negri moved away, expecting the bullets to fly any second. Instead, Nelson convinced the paranoid VanMeter that he was telling the truth, naming the agent she was seen with. While it was no secret that the Feds were squeezing the girls, the mystery was in determining who, if any, was playing along.

VanMeter jumped in his car to take care of it. Mazie used all her feminine wiles to convince him that she was holding up under the routine interrogations and would never sell him out. His head spun around again, VanMeter blamed Baby Face for nearly causing him to whack his true love. The two killers kept their distance from each other from that point on.

Also darkening Baby Face's mood was the latest bounty tally. The award on Dillinger's head was twice that of Nelson, a slight that made the jumpy bandit seethe with jealousy.

The G-Men were starting to splinter as well. A *Chicago Daily News* story ridiculed the agency for allowing all three mollettes to escape their shadows and reunite with their boyfriends. "A new theory is being discussed," the newspaper deadpanned. "Seize Dillinger and his gang and place them on probation, hoping that the girls will come to see them."

Hoover, who missed nothing, was livid, threatening to roll heads. He launched yet another investigation that produced a flurry of lengthy memos pointing fingers in every direction, including at Judge Stone for setting the mollettes free.

Dillinger was too busy celebrating both his June 22 birthday and Polly's birthday on the 23rd to care about the infighting on either side. He sent his new love two dozen roses, presented her with a beautiful amethyst ring, and took her to the French Casino, a nightclub on Clark Street north of Lawrence Avenue. "The two-day party we had . . . was just about the most important thing that ever happened to me," Polly cooed. "He must have been in love with me. Lots of times he talked about a home and kids of his own."

Polly would have swooned even more if she could be sure that when Dillinger said such things, he was speaking to her, and not the image of Billie she represented.

Audrey Dillinger did her part to remember her brother on his big day, purchasing a classified ad in the *Indianapolis Star*. "Birthday greetings to my darling brother, John Dillinger, on his 31st birthday. Wherever he may be, I hope he reads this." As she expected, other newspapers yanked the notice from the bowels of the tiny want ads and splashed it on their front pages, assuring that John Jr. saw it.

On June 26, Crown Point mail carrier Robert Volk spotted a man he swore was Dillinger in the upper deck of Wrigley Field where the Chicago Cubs played. To his horror, the man moved over from the end of the row and plopped himself two seats away, possibly testing his surgery and disguise. "This is getting to be a habit," Volk choked.

"It certainly is," the stranger replied with a grin.

Volk considered trying to alert a Lake County deputy sheriff who had driven to the game with his group but was sitting lower down. Volk's friend, Kenneth Hanniford, persuaded him to let it slide. Much to Volk's relief, the familiar stranger left after the seventh-inning stretch.

The following day, on June 27, a team of eight G-Men and two local cops swarmed an apartment house at 620 East Franklin in Minneapolis. Pat Reilly's off-and-on girlfriend, Opal Milligan, had sold him out. Unarmed, Reilly was taken without incident. Since he hadn't seen any of the gang since Little Bohemia two months before, he had little information to offer. The $4,000 he picked up for VanMeter was verbally shaved down to $1,000. Of that, he said Pat Cherrington grabbed $400 and Tommy Carroll took $300. The remaining $300 was spent. Agents found only $6.05 in the apartment. What happened to the missing $3,000 was anybody's guess.

Hit with the standard harboring charge, Reilly was carted off to Ramsey County jail to await his trial. He subsequently pleaded guilty, was fined $2,500, and was sent to a Federal Reformatory at El Reno, Oklahoma, for twenty-one months.

In Indiana, Harry Copeland's lady attorney, Bess Robbins, was able to pull a fast one. By pleading him guilty to the Greencastle robbery— which he didn't participate in—he was able to avoid a death sentence in Lima, Ohio. Indiana gave him twenty-five years, enabling him to be paroled in ten to fifteen. Copeland, thirty-eight, was sent back to Michigan City—the place he vowed never to return.

The last day of June 1934, brought clear, warm weather to South Bend, Indiana, a city of 85,000 known for football and making Studebakers. The South Bend police department drove the local product, with its newest vehicle being a 1932 model. The cops did have one-way radios—but no sirens. Michigan Street, which boasted two sets of parallel trolley tracks, was the city's widest boulevard. The point where it intersected with Wayne Street was probably the city's busiest crossroad. Amid the hustle and bustle was Merchant's National Bank, a three-story limestone structure of uncluttered design. Police officers were prevalent in the area, walking various downtown beats.

Just after 11 A.M., a tan Hudson four-door sedan entered South Bend from the west on U.S. 20. The car, a demonstrator, was stolen on May 28 from Butler Motors Inc., 7722 Stony Island Avenue, Chicago. An updated model, it sported steel disk wheels instead of the standard wire versions. The license plate, Ohio C-4018, had been screwed off a car in Toledo. It was the same plate that had adorned a different getaway vehicle in Fostoria on May 3. Five men were packed inside. A sixth waited in a second vehicle outside the city. Only three could be positively identified—John Dillinger, Baby Face Nelson, and Homer VanMeter. The other two inside men were almost certainly John Paul Chase, and another Nelson associate, Jack Perkins. The sixth, according to questionable reports, may have been Fatso Negri, Ed Bentz, or Arthur "Pretty Boy" Floyd.

Whatever the makeup, one thing was certain. It was destined to be John Dillinger's last job.

Chapter 19

South Bend assistant postmaster Robert A. Schnelle carried a densely packed canvass bag into Merchant's Bank and hoisted it on the counter of teller C. L. Shank. It was 11:20 A.M., and Schnelle had arrived right on schedule. As Shank counted and recorded the $7,900 in cash, Schnelle's regular escorts, Police Detectives Edward McCormick and Harry Henderson, gave a half-hearted look around. The post office payroll drop had become so routine that they'd long lost their protective edge. In fact, once Schnelle handed over the dough, the two cops beat it out of the stuffy joint, drove over to nearby Western Avenue, and sat down for what they thought would be a leisurely midday lunch.

Alex Slaby, a local teen with dreams of being a professional boxer, cruised by in his pop's 1928 Ford and nodded to Patrolman Howard Wagner, the area beat cop. Wagner greeted him with a smile. The big cop had attended a few of Slaby's amateur fights and felt that with the right dedication, the kid might have a shot at making a name for himself as a pugilist.

Pleased at being recognized, Slaby turned west on Wayne Street and pulled up to the curb just around the corner from the bank. He snapped off the ignition, opened his door, and started to hop out of the vehicle. Instead, something caught his eye that gave him pause. A large, tan Hudson sedan rolled to a stop and double-parked right next to him. A rat pack of tough-looking men piled out, including a pair who wore overalls. They all carried long, slender objects wrapped in pillowcases, and appeared to be unnaturally bulky, like they were wearing some strange undergarments.

Slaby froze in place as one of the men approached. "You'd better scram, kid," the man growled. The young boxer closed his door and pretended to comply. However, as the men disappeared around the corner, the kid's brawler instincts took over. Fueled by fear and curiosity, he eased out of his car and crept up to the Hudson. The engine was still running! "Mother Mary, " he whispered to himself. "They're gonna pull a job!"

For some inexplicable reason, Slaby found himself reaching inside the Hudson for the keys. Just as he was about to touch them, an angry shout nearly caused him to jump out of his skin.

"What the hell do you think you're doing?" the voice demanded. Slaby, stricken with terror, turned and found himself staring into the famous mug of Baby Face Nelson.

"Na . . . na . . . nothing," the kid stammered as he backed away from the idling car. Figuring this was no time to linger, he didn't stop backpedaling until he was all the way to the other side of the street. Regaining his senses, he ducked inside the first shop he came to and searched for a telephone. The place didn't have one. Slipping back out, he tried the business next door, Colip Brothers Appliance Store.

"I need a phone, please," he gasped. "I think somebody's about to hit the bank!"

A clerk ushered him to the store's phone. Slaby told the operator it was an emergency and was patched through to the police. Catching his breath, he outlined to the desk sergeant what he'd seen.

"You did the right thing, kid" the sergeant praised. "Now stay out of the way. We'll handle it from here."

The jittery young boxer dashed to the store's display window and watched the drama unfold. Baby Face Nelson had already taken position on the corner by the Neumode Shop. The other four men headed toward the bank. Panicking, Slaby glanced at Officer Wagner across the street. The beat flatfoot remained totally oblivious to what was about to go down.

VanMeter fell out of the foursome and positioned himself in front of the Nisley Shoe Store. In the crook of his arm hung a Model 1907 Winchester .351 rifle, modified to fire fully automatic. The barrel had been sawed and the magazine was grossly oversized. The nasty weapon had been further customized to accommodate a Thompson fore grip, along with a Cutts compensator, a device designed to dispel explosive gases and prevent a gun from kicking upward. VanMeter's assignment, Slaby figured, was to shadow the bank's entrance. If anything went wrong, Van-Meter and his lethal weapon were prepared to correct the problem.

John Dillinger, John Paul Chase, and Jack Perkins strolled inside the crowded building without hesitation. The bank was scheduled to close in thirty minutes, and nearly two dozen customers were cued up trying to beat the clock. The civilian mob didn't bother Dillinger a bit. He wasn't planning to wait in line. Besides, the bigger the audience, the better the show.

It was now 11:32 A.M. The Jackrabbit and associates were calm and confident, despite the fact that they'd already made a fatal error—letting Alex Slaby go. Within seconds of their arrival inside the bank, a South Bend police dispatcher sent out an all-points-bulletin alerting area beat officers and radio cars that there was a holdup in process. From every part of town, police officers were jolted from their routines and nervously began to converge on the bank.

"This is a stickup. Everybody stand still!" Dillinger shouted. Only a half dozen people complied. The rest either didn't hear him, or couldn't comprehend what was about to happen. Miffed, Dillinger dropped the pillowcase from his stockless Thompson machine gun, pointed the rapid-firing weapon upward, and squeezed out a burst of shots, just missing an ornate chandelier. The discarded slugs burned through the decorative plastered ceiling and knifed into the hardwood flooring of a second-story conference room. A cloud of white dust wafted down from above, creating a ghostly visual that made the famous felon smile.

It was the jarring sound, not the resulting aesthetics, that gripped everyone else's attention. The crowd instantly knew what was up. Chaos ensued. Several people ran screaming toward the rear lobby, taking refuge in a bank director's private office. Two men dived under a long counter on the opposite side of the lobby. A half dozen others broke for the bathroom, packed themselves inside, and locked the door.

Bruce Bouchard, the manager of an area radio distribution company, felt a sharp pain in his side as he hit the floor. Clutching his waist, he was shocked to discover that he was bleeding. An errant slug from Dillinger's deadly noisemaker had ricocheted off the ceiling and nailed Bouchard in the hip. The outlaw glanced at the fallen executive and shrugged, as if to apologize for the freak accident.

Behind the tellers, Merchant Bank Vice President C. W. Coen disappeared under his desk. He would remain there through the entire incident. His son and coworker, Delos Coen, was standing at his post talking with bank director Perry Stahly when the bullets started flying. Unlike his dad, the younger Coen stood paralyzed in place, mouth agape. He couldn't help but stare directly into the mischievous eyes of the famous bandit. Dillinger, flying on the thrill of it all, lowered his machine gun and gave Coen an unforgettable grin.

While the customers were being distracted by tommy-gun fireworks and their own resulting frenzy, Jack Perkins and John Chase slid into the aisle behind the five teller cages. Perkins, waving an automatic pistol, bullied his way through the hinged door of the first cage, only to discover that it was the paperwork box.

"Where the hell's all the big money?" he growled at Delos Coen and Perry Stahly. It was a rhetorical question. Without waiting for an answer, Perkins and Chase entered the second cage and found that those drawers contained items more to their liking. They began scooping handfuls of cash into the pillowcases, which now doubled as loot bags. They quickly emptied the drawers and repeated the profitable activity at each of the remaining three cages, including the one that held the recently deposited post office windfall.

Outside, Patrolman Howard Wagner was finally jarred from his afternoon bliss by the muffled sounds of gunfire. Pinpointing the shots as coming from the bank, Wagner ran diagonally across Michigan Street toward the building. Local meat market owner Samuel Toth had to swerve and slam on his brakes to avoid flattening the cop. Confused by the sight of a snarling officer pounding his hood, Toth did what most people would at such a moment—he tried to avoid getting a traffic ticket. Almost comically, Toth stuck his hand out of his window and signaled that he wanted to make a left turn. Wagner grimaced at the lame gesture and ordered Toth to stop dead.

To Toth's utter shock, Wagner proceeded to unsnap the flap on his holster. Fortunately for the meat man, the armed officer's deadly attention was focused somewhere else. Wagner danced around Toth's offending vehicle, crossed the trolley tracks, and continued on toward the bank.

Once again, however, the heroic but tragically unaware patrolman failed to notice what the kid boxer had spied from the onset. As Slaby mouthed a silent scream behind the appliance store's plate-glass window, Officer Wagner ran right into a trap. Both Baby Face Nelson and Homer VanMeter spotted Wagner coming and met him with a shower of lead. Wagner was hit so quickly he had yet to pull his weapon. A scorching .351 slug slammed into his abdomen, ripped apart his right kidney, and punched out through his back. Wagner clutched his stomach with both hands, staggered backward a few steps, then collapsed sideways to the street. His head made a sickening thud as it hit the pavement, "like a watermelon falling off a truck," a witness recalled. The officer lay still between two parked cars, drenched in a quickly forming pool of blood.

Toth, to his further dismay, found himself once again linked to Officer Wagner. As Nelson and VanMeter's sprayed the hard charging cop, one of their discharges flew off the mark, shattering Toth's windshield and grazing his forehead. Conscious enough to know he'd tested fate long enough, Toth sprawled across his bench seat and remained there until the incident had long ended.

Officer Neils Hansen was pacing the intersection to the north when he heard the siren sound of Dillinger's Thompson. Hansen arrived on the scene just in time to see the stunned expression on Wagner's face before the bandit's slugs did him in. It took a few long beats before Hansen recovered from the shock of seeing his friend cut down. At first, things were so fuzzy and confusing Hansen couldn't get a bead on who had dropped Wagner. When his eyes finally found the culprits, he was mortified to discover that VanMeter was pointing his souped-up rifle directly at him!

"Duck," Hansen screamed to Officers Sylvester Zell and Emil DeWespelaere, who had taken up the chase and were standing behind him. "That guy's going to shoot us!" Hansen and DeWespelaere dived for cover behind a Pontiac parked on the curb. Zell took off in the opposite direction, crossed the street, and jumped behind a car parked in front of the State Movie Theater directly across from the bank.

Never one to play favorites, VanMeter alternately fired at Hansen, DeWespelaere, and Zell, keeping the trio pinned down behind their respective vehicles. Figuring he needed his own protection, the surgically disguised robber grabbed Arthur Stillson off the sidewalk and was using the terror-stricken car dealer as a human shield. A few minutes later, when VanMeter was momentarily distracted by additional gunfire, Stillson managed to break away, bolting toward the corner. Unfortunately, he ran right into Baby Face Nelson.

"Stop right there and stay put!" Nelson commanded. Stillson did as ordered, watching with fascination as Baby Face calmly removed an empty drum from his Thompson and replaced it with a fresh one as more police began to approach.

Across Michigan Street, a small group of clerks and customers gathered near the display window of Ries Furniture store to catch the action. Aside from the disturbing image of Officer Wagner going down, they watched in horror as VanMeter did a crazed jig as he sprayed the area with slugs to keep the police at bay. The show ended when one of VanMeter's errant bullets crashed into a concrete pillar flanking the entrance of the furniture store. Having had all the excitement they could handle, the clerks and customers ran screaming into the basement.

The furniture store crowd missed VanMeter's definitive display of how to deal with a jammed rifle under intense pressure. Dancing anew, he expertly ejected the magazine, cleared the breach, and popped in a new clip. "It's all right now," he called out to Baby Face, assuring his youthful-looking partner that he was back in action.

Junk dealer Jacob Solomon, somehow failing to notice the commotion and loud shots, chose that moment to amble toward the bank from the south. "Scram, before you get hurt," Baby Face warned. Startled, the daydreaming Solomon turned west on Wayne and headed right for his pal Harry Berg's jewelry store, passing by the still idling Hudson. Before Solomon could reach the store, Berg exploded out the front door, pistol in hand. The jeweler, who fancied himself an expert marksmen, immediately raised his automatic weapon and let one go. At crunch time, Berg managed to back up his boasts. His bullet hit Baby Face square in the back.

Unfortunately, Berg, like Officer Wagner, should have checked with Alex Slaby before trying to play hero. As Slaby noticed from the onset, Dillinger's men were dressed in bulletproof vests.

The jackets were indeed bullet-resistant, but decidedly not pain proof. Baby Face felt like he'd been stung by a giant wasp. Royally peeved, he whirled around and saw a dumbfounded Berg standing on the sidewalk a half block away, pistol still raised. Furious, Baby Face sprayed the area with his Thompson, shooting gangster style from the hip. More than a dozen thundering .45 slugs buzz sawed the front of Berg's store, splintering the wood and shattering the windows. Amazingly, none hit Berg. He emerged from his stupor and dived back into his business.

Jacob Solomon wasn't as lucky. One of the .45s cut into his leg and deflected oddly up to his stomach. Solomon staggered into the jewelry store and crumbled to the floor.

Fifty feet to the north, Homer VanMeter strained his eyes to make out what was happening. He knew Baby Face was frenzied about some-thing, but his view was blocked and he couldn't determine what. Assuming it was a new batch of coppers, he jumped inside the Nisley Shoe Store and began barking orders to manager D. V. Cavendar, employees Kenneth Samper and Helen Chebowski, and two wrong-place, wrong-time customers. "Everybody outside!" he shouted, ges-turing toward the door. Outside was the last place the citizens wanted to be, but Homer waved his rifle and they complied.

VanMeter bunched the shoe store hostages together and took cover, stationing himself directly behind Chebowski. He fired his unique rifle over her shoulder, splitting her eardrums with every retort. Despite the pain, the terrified Chebowski covered her eyes instead of her ringing ears, choosing at that moment to see no evil rather than trying not to hear it.

One of the unlucky customers in VanMeter's fun bunch, R. F. Gibson, seized an opportunity to escape and bolted toward the corner. However, like Arthur Stillson before him, he merely ran into a still-seething Baby Face. Nelson ordered Gibson to freeze, then instructed him to remain close by to further thwart the police.

Joseph Pawlowski, sixteen, was sitting in his family's car outside the Strand Theater, watching as the first act of the wild bank robbery played out. Driven by youth, adrenaline, and raw courage, Pawlowski suddenly sprang from the car and made a beeline for Nelson. Distracted by the police officers, Baby Face never saw him coming. The teen approached from the blind side and without slowing down, leaped upon the famous outlaw's back!

"Shoot him! Grab him!" Pawlowski shouted to no one in particular.

Nelson, still smarting from the jeweler's shot, was in no mood to toy with a boy hero. He reached around and violently smashed the barrel of his machine gun against the right side of Pawlowski's skull, dazing the youth and loosening his grip. Shaking him off, Nelson threw the boy completely through a nearby plate-glass store window. Dizzy and bleeding from various cuts, Pawlowski attempted to rise. Nelson greeted that effort with a burst from the Thompson, ripping a bullet through Pawlowski's palm. The sight of a hole clean through the center of his bloody hand caused the teen to lapse into shock. He fell back and lay motionless, an involuntarily act that saved his life.

Superior Court Bailiff Charles Fisher drove through the intersection and found himself in a hornet's nest. Since his wife and small daughter were in the car with him, he didn't stop to gawk. Flooring it, he drove east to St. Joseph Street where he spied a group of city firefighters who had exited the station house to see the show. The men were smack dab in the center of the street, better to see the action on Wayne and Michigan.

"Hey, you guys," Fisher shouted. "Those bullets can easily travel this far and still kill you! You'd better be careful." With that admonition, the firefighters scattered for cover, leaving the gunplay for their cousins in blue.

Detectives Harold McCormick and Harry Henderson, the post office payroll escorts who had slipped out for lunch, heard the commotion, abandoned their food, and sprinted to their vehicle. McCormick arrived first and grabbed a shotgun. "I'll get there faster on foot," he yelled to Henderson. "You bring the car!"

Dillinger and pals similarly noted the excessive gunplay and knew things weren't going as smoothly as planned. Inside, it was a different story. They had three pillowcases bulging with money, and weren't about to give it up. Dillinger selected three male hostages—injured radio salesman Bruce Bouchard, and bank executives Delos Coen and Perry Stahly—and herded them toward the entrance. The outlaw grabbed Bouchard by the shirt and stationed him front and center as they exited the bank first. John Paul Chase similarly used Coen, while the stout Jack Perkins held firm to Perry Stahly.

Not thirty feet away, Officer Hansen watched the six emerge. He cocked the hammer of his big .32-20 revolver, but couldn't get a clear shot. Instead, he watched Perkins reach into his pocket and slip on a pair of amber-colored glasses to shield his eyes from the midday sun. Frustrated, all Hansen could do was continue observing as the "inside men" and their shields scurried up the street like some bizarre twelve-legged animal, eventually meshing with VanMeter's group in front of the shoe store.

The merger of two separate packs of crooks and citizen shields was jarring. Bandits and hostages separated for a moment, giving Hansen the opportunity he was waiting for. A confident marksman, he took careful aim at Jack Perkins, the biggest target, and fired at Perkin's shoulder, a tactic he felt would result in knocking the dangerous Thompson out of the big man's hand. The shot met its mark, kicking Perkin's shoulder back, but the robber hardly flinched. Miffed, Hansen decided there would be no more mercy. He aimed again, this time for Perkins's massive cranium. Bang! The police bullet slammed into the right side of Perkins' jaw. Only once again, like some horror movie monster, the burly thief hardly flinched. Ignoring his injuries, Perkins continued to make his way toward the getaway car.

The hostages were shuffled back in place around the bandits and the brief opportunity was over—for Hansen anyway. Officers Zell and DeWespelaere weren't as cautious as their coworker. They started firing from their position, seemingly making no concession for the lives of the hostages. Banker Delos Coen took a slug to his left leg just above his ankle.

As they neared the car, Dillinger and Chase let loose of Bouchard and Coen—both bleeding from bullet wounds—in order to climb inside the vehicle. The radio man and banker immediately dove for cover behind the kid boxer's Ford. Perkins, however, already shot twice himself, refused to free Stahly. That proved to be a solid decision. A third police bullet heading directly toward Perkins struck Stahly in the upper thigh instead.

"I've been hit," the banker announced, figuring the injury was his ticket to freedom.

"Keep on going," the unsympathetic Perkins groused. "You're coming with us."

After a few more painful steps, Stahly decided he'd had enough. "The bullets were flying pretty thick because the police were giving the crooks a battle," he recalled. "Suddenly, I just didn't want to play along anymore. I figured my chances of surviving were better if I didn't get in that car. I turned to Perkins and made my point. 'You got your money,' I said. 'Now make your getaway. Let me go now.' Perkins muttered something I couldn't understand, but it was clear he disagreed with my logic. Fortunately, John Dillinger spoke up. 'Come on. Get in. We're going. Now!' With that, Perkins let go of me and ran for the Hudson. I immediately looked for a place to drop out of sight. A car parked near the curb was the quickest solution. However, before I could make it, that SOB Perkins swung around and took a really unnecessary potshot at me. Thankfully, his aim was as rotten as his morals."

Louis Linder and his wife, visitors from Missouri, were parked on the curb just south of the bank. Linder, playing hero like so many citizens that day, ran from his car and canvassed the area stores trying to find someone who had a gun. Failing, he stationed himself at the southwest corner of Michigan and Wayne, pondering what to do next. He was still standing there when Detective McCormick ran by, shotgun in hand.

"Where is he?" McCormick asked. Linder pointed to Baby Face Nelson, still standing watch on the opposite corner. For some reason, McCormick couldn't spot the diminutive bandit. Instead, his eyes were drawn to the action taking place near the getaway car. With trembling fingers, he inserted two 12-gauge, 00 buckshot cartridges into the shotgun's chambers. When he glanced up, he saw Homer VanMeter taking the wheel of the car. Aiming for VanMeter's head, he boomed the first shell. VanMeter slumped forward, then straightened back up. McCormick fired the second shell. VanMeter kicked forward again, but remained conscious enough to thrust the car into gear and get it moving.

"I didn't think he'd get very far," McCormick thought at the time. "I was sure I'd plugged him good both times."

VanMeter's misery wasn't over. McCormick's partner, Harry Henderson, had pulled up through the traffic and stopped thirty feet behind the Hudson, watching as the robbers and hostages made their way to the getaway vehicle. Once the hostages were clear, Henderson had the same thought as McCormick—take out the driver. He lifted his .38 service revolver and fired three times through the Hudson's rear window. As with McCormick, VanMeter slumped over, then popped back up.

"Someone started firing at me, so I had to duck to the floor," Henderson recalled. "As I was down, I heard the bandit car drive away. I couldn't believe it!"

Stahly and Bouchard were also in disbelief, but for different reasons. Despite their attempts to take cover, they both remained in the line of fire. Before he could hit the pavement, two police bullets passed right between Stahly's legs, shredding his trousers. While Bouchard was prone on the pavement, a bullet grazed the heel of his shoe and passed through one side of his pants leg and out the other.

On the road, the Hudson screeched to a stop for an instant to retrieve Baby Face, then roared toward the city limits. Careening a bit, the heavy tan vehicle barely missed colliding with a second car. Inside, South Bend dance teacher Mazine Mollenhour was briefly shaken. Still, she was clear-headed enough to observe that the Hudson's driver was slumped over at the wheel, and the man in the passenger seat seemed to be helping him navigate.

After that close call, the powerful Hudson churned south on Wayne Street and headed into the countryside—with a half dozen police cars in hot pursuit. The chase was on.

Chapter 20

O fficer Sylvester Zell hopped on the running board of a passing police paddy wagon and hung on as they tried to catch the roaring Hudson. Barreling south on Wayne Street, the state-of-the-art getaway car picked up speed and grew smaller as it pulled away. The sluggish truck was no match for the gangster's powerful V8.

Motorcycle cop Bert Olmstead gave it a go on his two-wheeler. "I was doing eighty-miles-per-hour, all the cycle had, and they just walked away from me," he lamented to a reporter. Ten miles outside of South Bend, near Lakeville, Olmstead's outdistanced 1929 Harley fried its engine and gave up the ghost.

Detectives Lucius LaFortune and Fred Miller, in radio car nine, lasted a little longer. Racing after the Hudson, they crossed South Bend and made it to Knox, forty-five miles to the southwest, before hitting a stretch of roofing nails and suffering twin blowouts.

All had better luck than Patrolmen Peter Rudynski and Arden Kline. The duo were on Eddy Street when the bulletin about a robbery in process went out over the air. Although equipped with a radio, they didn't have a siren. They were forced to rely upon their horn to creep through the traffic and make it to the scene. On the way, their 1930 Studebaker cruiser coughed up a gas line, stopping the auto dead. They were out of the game in the first inning.

Even if the pursuing officers had caught Dillinger's heavily armed crew, it's doubtful they would have been able to stop them. The low octane South Bend police were packing handguns and a single shotgun.

The department's only machine gun was still being proudly displayed on a rack at headquarters. Not a single officer was wearing a bulletproof vest. The rash of mechanical breakdowns and power shortages may have resulted from divine intervention.

Despite their decided advantage, the rebuilt Terror Gang was experiencing problems of its own. Shortly after leaving town, the Hudson sideswiped another civilian vehicle, this one driven by a lady who promptly fainted and drove into a ditch. She survived with a few bruises. On a back road eight miles northwest of Plymouth, the nail-tossing robbers suffered their own blowout. They quickly lugged on the spare, leaving the old wheel and tire jack on the road as souvenirs.

Back at the bank, responding police officers arrived to find the scene in chaos. People were slowly emerging from hiding, either hanging around to share stories and rubberneck, or hurriedly taking off in their own vehicles. Ambulances were noisily carting the various victims to area hospitals. Howard Wagner, Delos Coen, and Perry Stahly were taken to Epworth Hospital. Jacob Solomon, the jeweler's friend, was brought to St. Joseph, as were motorist Samuel Toth and the kid, Joe Pawlowski.

Marion Wagner was called and told to get to Epworth ASAP. She was certain it was a mistake because she'd just left her husband fifteen minutes before the shootings started. Curious, she went—only to be informed that she was now a widow. Howard Wagner died in the emergency room shortly after arriving. "It was to be his last day on that beat," she sobbed. "Now it's his last day on any beat."

Outgunned but still determined, neither the police nor the South Bend citizens were about to give up. The cops regrouped in Springfield, borrowed rifles from the local National Guard armory, and set out to find their elusive prey. Radio station WSBT interrupted regular programming to give updates on the route the bandits were traveling. The *South Bend Tribune* paid pilot Homer Stockert to scramble his Stinson Reliant and shadow the crooks by air. Officers Levi Nulf and William Million joined *Tribune* reporter Joe Alvin in the lofty pursuit. Despite the horizontal advantage, they failed to spot the gang.

One reason the superior air power came up empty was that the bank robbers had splintered off into an additional car they'd stashed along the way. Bernice Alcock, playing outside her Grovertown, Indiana, house with her sister Ellen and brother Ralph, saw the famous outlaws as they blew by her home.

"The roar grew louder, and we turned to see a thick cloud of dust coming up behind two cars approaching from the east on Yellowstone Trail," she recalled. "We watched as they neared our corner at breakneck speed. The first car, a black Ford V8 coupe, couldn't make the turn south and shot on past the corner. The second car, a four-door Hudson, took the corner on two wheels and almost turned over. Then the Ford backed up and came around the corner. The Hudson was all over the road, from one side to the other. As they passed our place we knew why. One of the men in the backseat was pulling the driver over the back of the front seat while the man on the passenger side was trying to steer the car. The cars then continued on east and then south into the Red Brush area of Starke County."

Bernice added that she counted two men in the Ford and four in the Hudson.

The robbers' frantic behavior and dangerous speed proved to be unnecessary. An hour passed before the Alcock kids spotted the first police car. It was followed by a long line of law enforcement vehicles, twenty-five or more. The lead cruiser stopped at the corner, looked over the skid marks, then asked the excited children what they had witnessed. Bernice and siblings spilled the details, noting that the bandits had a huge lead.

The Alcocks weren't exaggerating. By 1 P.M., the twin caravan of criminals had blasted sixty miles south and west through Indiana. A farmer named Herb Farrell was working his land three miles northeast of Goodland when he saw a big Hudson stop at the far end of his property. He watched with interest as four men left the fancy vehicle, removed the front and rear license plates, and then climbed in a Ford that followed. Two men sat in the rumble seat near the trunk, while the others squeezed up front. The weighted-down Ford then headed west.

Farrell strolled over to check out the abandoned Hudson. Inside was an empty pillowcase, and the shorn leg from a pair of long underwear, apparently used to conceal the barrel of a Thompson. Empty cartridge casing littered the floor, along with boxes of roofing nails. There was blood on the rear seat. Sixteen small dimples dotted the left side of the vehicle, resulting from shotgun pellets. Both the back and front window had been shattered from a single shot fired by detective Harry Henderson. Two of Henderson's additional slugs hit the car's body, but didn't have the force to penetrate the sturdy metal. The Hudson's gas tank was empty.

Farrell ran back to his house and phoned Goodland Town Marshall Alfred Butler. The marshall called the state police, and then raced out to Farrell's farm. Within hours, the Hudson was being towed back to South Bend to be scrutinized by the DI and local police technicians, including the fingerprint squads.

As with many of Dillinger's scores, there was a furious debate among the citizens, bankers, and witnesses as to whether he had been there at all. Some couldn't pick him out from photos. Others described the men as larger and stouter than the Jackrabbit. Bank Vice President C. W. Coen wasn't vacillating. "If Dillinger looks anything like his pictures, then he was the first man to walk in . . . with a machine gun in his hand."

Complicating things were Dillinger's prior and subsequent attempts to alter his features, including the recent plastic surgery.

The harried state police chief, Matt Leach, in a possible attempt to spin away John Dillinger hysteria and pass the buck, said the violent nature of the South Bend job made him believe it was ruthless "Italian gangsters" from Detroit or Toledo. That raised eyebrows, considering that Dillinger and company, from day one, had long proven they could resort to deadly violence in a flash of a muzzle—sometimes for the sheer hell of it.

Further muddying the waters was the fact that witnesses began spicing their stories with the flair of a tabloid newspaper reporter. One teller insisted that Pretty Boy Floyd was in the midst of the gang. Although they often shared front-page space, Floyd and Dillinger were never known to have met.

Harry Berg, the jeweler who plugged Baby Face Nelson, didn't waste time getting back to business. While the gang was still racing across the countryside, he had already posted a sign in his shop window stating NOT HURT. OPEN FOR BUSINESS.

Joe Pawlowski, the heroic teenager who jumped on Nelson's back and was shot through the hand for the effort, quickly dived back into the swing of things. He grew up to become a noted attorney, concert violinist, and symphony conductor.

The bandits, whatever the final precise lineup, had a considerably dimmer future. They vanished after dumping the empty Hudson on Farrell's farm, and were seemingly home free. However, as usual, the provincial gang didn't go far. By a prearranged agreement, they pulled into a rural schoolhouse yard a few miles northwest of Chicago at 10 P.M. to meet up with Fatso Negri and Clarence Lieder. Negri said both VanMeter and Baby Face Nelson were lying down in agony, with VanMeter bleeding heavily. "I wanted [Lieder] to go out and get a doctor. No, they don't want to get a doctor and get [Lieder] in trouble," Negri later told the Feds. "A bullet grazed VanMeter's head."

Turns out that the bullet, fired by either South Bend Detectives Harry Henderson or Harold McCormick, had not just grazed the Michigan City vet's head, it had tunneled beneath the right side of his scalp for four painful inches. "He's in agony and I think he's dying," Negri reported.

Baby Face Nelson, though not as hurt as VanMeter, was still reeling from the pain of taking Berg's potshot square in the back, his life saved by the bulletproof vest he bought from Fish Johnson. He got up long enough to hand Negri a briefcase with the day's costly take—$28,439. Not bad, but nothing to jump up and down about when considering it had to be split five ways. "Take this with you," Nelson winched. "Lock it in your valise in your room and put it where the maid won't find it. Stay with it 'til we call you tomorrow." With that, the beat-up gang took off again.

At 2 A.M. on July 1, 1934, Dr. Leslie A. Laird was rousted from his bed at his home in North Webster, thirty-five miles southeast of South Bend. One of the two intruders had a bullet wound on his right forearm and required treatment. After being patched up, the unidentified patient demanded some cocaine, ostensibly to kill the pain. The doc professed to have none. His angry patient returned the favor of the house call by slugging him unconscious. It was a solid knockout blow because Doctor Laird didn't regain consciousness for nearly an hour. When he collected his senses, he found his visitors gone and his phone line cut. He jumped in his car, drove to a nearby all-night grill and called the sheriff in Warsaw.

Despite a new set of police now on the lookout, the pair of crooks were in no hurry to leave town. Joined by a third man, they pulled into the busy Lamp Lite Inn four miles south of North Webster on Barbee Lake. They were all wearing short sleeves on the hot night, and sported matching Panama hats with the brim turned down. Since that was the fashion of the day, they didn't stick out. Few of the 150 beer-drinking and partying patrons even noticed that one of the three had a tightly bandaged arm. Days later, when investigators appeared, the trio was identified as Dillinger, VanMeter, and John Hamilton. As usual, others disagreed, putting any number of names to the strangers' faces. Hamilton, for one, was long dead and could have only been there as an apparition.

Both FBI Boss J. Edgar Hoover and Indiana Governor Paul McNutt were incensed by "the latest display of inadequacy in dealing with Dillinger" as one newspaper put it. Hoover and McNutt vowed to implement additional shake-ups in their departments.

As a fascinating aside, a busload of twenty-six Florida newspapermen were returning from a junket to the World's Fair when they stopped for lunch in Kentland, a small town seven miles west of the farm where at that very moment, John Dillinger was saying good-bye to his Hudson. Springing into action, the reporters began knocking out features on how the townsfolk were reacting to the legend of the Jackrabbit.

"The Midwest has come to look on this machine-gun armed modern Jesse James as an incredible wraith who will go on forever," one of the journalists wrote, giving Dillinger equal status to his idol James. "The cream of Florida's reportorial stardom just missed the interview by passing ahead of Dillinger . . . though it seems to be an interview that none desired greatly in the first place. John might not take it the right way."

The roving Sunshine State scribes were long gone when John Paul Chase knocked on the door of Fatso's room at the Fullerton Hotel in Chicago the next day. "You count the money?"

"I don't even know for sure there's money in it," Negri lied. As Chase figured, he'd spent much of the evening counting the cash, which consisted of ones, fives, tens, twenties, and one rare and nifty $1,000 bill. "How is everybody? Is VanMeter dead?"

"He's okay," Chase replied. "They're getting a doc for him. But Nelson damn near got his. Some citizen shot him in the back right there on the street. God saved him with the vest."

Late that evening, Dillinger took the tormented VanMeter back to James Probasco's house. Probasco, eager for another payday, was now claiming to have had veterinarian training and pitched himself as "kind of" a doctor, the "kind of" qualifier causing VanMeter's head to pound even harder. The tipsy middleman began pulling VanMeter's hair out with a pair of tweezers to clear away the wound area, a procedure that sent new waves of excruciating pain through the hood's brain. After Probasco cleaned the wound, VanMeter reported no relief from the pain and demanded to see a real doctor. Probasco relented and summoned Harold Cassidy, the young doctor who had nearly suffocated Dillinger with the ether. Not knowing why he was called, Doctor Cassidy took his time, arriving more than an hour later. By then, VanMeter and his burrowed skull were gone. Brought up to speed, Cassidy returned the next day and found VanMeter waiting. He cleaned the wound with an antiseptic, dabbed it with iodine, and gave VanMeter a tetanus shot.

Feeling better, VanMeter and Dillinger drove to Calumet City to the Finnertys' place. They joined Marie Conforti in a back bedroom, talking privately and plotting their next moves. VanMeter then drove Dillinger through Chicago to Anna Sage's apartment. Returning to Calumet City, William Finnerty finally asked Homer how he'd been injured. Homer blamed it on a car accident.

The gang huddled together the following Monday night at a small lake on Chicago's northwest side. Dillinger, Chase, Nelson, and Negri were in attendance. Dillinger gave Negri $1,000 for "his share," and Chase gave him another $1,500, saying it was from him and Nelson.

Chase explained that he was free to be so generous because they'd soon have more money than they could spend.

"You fellows must have something big lined up," Fatso probed.

"We'll need you again soon," Chase said with a smile.

Things were looking up for some old Terror Gang members as well. On July 3, Pierpont and Makley's lady lawyer, Jessie Levy, managed to postpone their executions. The pair had been scheduled to die on Friday the 13th. Levy called her secretary and instructed the woman to inform the *Indianapolis Star*. The newspaper already knew, their leak system being well oiled. The Feds were also up to speed. They heard the news the same way Levy had—on Levy's phone. Acting on generous wiretapping laws, they continued to listen in on the defense attorney's conversations.

While most in the law enforcement community were grinding their teeth over South Bend, Chicago DI chief Melvin Purvis chose to look on the bright side. The way he saw it, the Feds and cops were slowly but effectively chopping away at Dillinger's second gang. Two of his new associates, Eddie Green and Tommy Carroll, were pushing up daisies. Holdover John Hamilton was no doubt doing so as well. Albert "Pat" Reilly was in jail, and four of the pretty molls—Billie Frechette, Pat Cherrington, Bernice Clark, and Jean Delaney—were busy learning the ropes inside a female prison.

Purvis had already learned of, and had received details about, the Jackrabbit's latest makeover, this one with the help of a scalpel. He figured this gave him an advantage because if Dillinger believed he was just another face in the crowd, he might come out in the open. The new description, which Purvis memorized, was topped with black hair, plucked eyebrows, and was missing a prominent mole. The rat had been Jean Delaney, who blabbed to Eddie Green's widow, Beth, who ran to the G-Men. Delaney also chattered that Hamilton, despite being repeatedly picked out as one of the South Bend crew, was actually six feet under. The remaining members of the once-powerful gang, she continued, liked to hang around the Doll House, a bar four miles from Lake Geneva, Wisconsin. The joint was known to be criminal friendly since it was run by Lucille Moran, ex-wife of noted hoodlum George "Bugs" Moran.

Even more encouraging was the recently announced $25,000 reward the Feds slapped on Dillinger's head. This, Purvis knew, would bring additional people out of the woodwork, loosening the lips of those who had once viewed the bandits as heroes. Instead, they were now being sized up as walking lottery tickets.

Hoover, taking a beating in the press, had opened his purse strings— literally if subsequent cross-dressing accusations are to be believed. The crusty FBI chief tapped into the Federal well and was also authorizing unprecedented manpower on top of the rewards. A field office was established inside the Fletcher Savings and Trust building in Indianapolis—making it both a convenient, on-site headquarters as well as an interesting target.

Hubert Dillinger's gas station was being constantly watched in case big brother paid another unscheduled visit. Mooresville was crawling with suited strangers, while teams of G-Men armed with field glasses hid in a barn across from the Dillinger farm. Agents also crashed the early July funeral of James H. Dillinger, sixty-five, John's uncle. The service was in Knightsville, Indiana, near Brazil, and the elder Dillinger was buried in Indianapolis. The newly made-over nephew, Johnnie Jr., as far as the agents knew, did not show up in either place.

Widespread reports in the media, credited to "police sources," stated that Dillinger was instead holed up trying to heal from an assortment of injuries suffered during his robberies. Some went as far as to say he was once again dying. The FBI traced the source to an Indianapolis police lieutenant who had been misquoted by a local newspaper reporter. Dillinger, in truth, was in fine shape.

On July 5, Probasco called Doctor Cassidy and told him to go to the south end of the Western Avenue streetcar line. "Your patient will meet you there." Doctor Cassidy did as instructed, and was quickly swept inside VanMeter's maroon V8. He was taken to Finnerty's house in Calumet City. The young doctor was escorted to the infamous back bedroom, where he examined VanMeter's wounds and changed the bandage. VanMeter then drove Cassidy back to Chicago.

If Dr. Cassidy was content to play dumb, the same couldn't be said for Bill and Ella Finnerty. When VanMeter returned, they asked him point-blank if he had been part of the South Bend job. He 'fessed up. Finnerty later claimed he asked VanMeter to leave. Instead, VanMeter threatened the couple, monitored their activities, and stopped paying rent. More likely, the Finnertys knew who VanMeter was from the get-go and had to invent such a story to keep from indicting themselves for harboring a fugitive.

Doctor Cassidy, having no such fear, returned to the Finnertys three more times to treat VanMeter, twice bringing Arthur O'Leary along for the ride. O'Leary, however, had the good sense to remain in the car while the doctor did his thing.

On July 8, Baby Face Nelson was feeling well enough to go shopping around Logan Square for some new wheels. He and John Paul Chase took the Ford V8 panel delivery truck they were using as a mobile hideout and started wheeling and dealing with a Hudson-Essex representative at 2501 Milwaukee Avenue in Chicago. Nelson had his eye on a new Hudson four-door sedan, black with black wheels and yellow pinstripping that went for $878. The salesman gave them $560 for their trade because the truck only had 3,000 miles. Nelson paid the difference in crisp bills, registering as "Addie James" a mechanic for Harry Sawyer.

The same day, attorney Louis Piquett was visited again by a relieved but still frantic Gilbert and Lena Pierpont. He didn't have to ask what they wanted. Instead, he asked where they were staying. "At 7923 South Shore Drive," Lena replied. "It's a tourist home."

"Be there at nine o'clock tonight," Piquett advised. "I'll see what I can do."

Although it was exactly what they were seeking, the couple was nonetheless shocked when nine o'clock rolled around and one John Dillinger was standing at their door. "Let's take a walk," he suggested. The couple had no trouble recognizing him despite the surgical makeover. They caught a cab at South Shore Drive and Seventy-ninth Street. Dillinger instructed the driver to circle around without a destination. The notorious bank robber proceeded to ply the desperate couple with a series of comforting lies, assuring them that he was still trying to raise money for their son's appeals. He also claimed that Hamilton was badly wounded but alive, that VanMeter was improving without saying how he'd been injured, and topped it off by denying that he had been in on the South Bend job. Rambling a bit, he told them that he'd used a disguise to trick the G-Men watching Hubert's station. Dressed in overalls and walking with a cane, he met his half-brother right under the Fed's noses in order to prove to the family that despite what they were hearing in the news, he was healthy as a bear.

After pleading poverty, Dillinger reiterated his promise to round up money for Handsome Harry's defense fund. He then gave Lena six bucks for the cab. He motioned for the driver to drop him off a block east of North and Harlem Avenues. Lena watched him vanish down a side street. However, as the cab made a U-turn, she noticed that he had doubled back and was walking toward the corner of Harlem and North where Jimmy Murray's joint, the Rainbow Inn, was perched.

The cab to nowhere ended up costing $7.10, a figure that angered the frayed couple. They felt all along that Dillinger wasn't doing enough to save their son from the electric chair. Despite the risk he took to meet with them, they came away feeling the same. Gilbert Pierpont repeated a threat he'd previously made to turn Dillinger in for the $25,000 reward, which would be used to help their equally criminal son. It was the kind of logic only a parent could understand.

The illogical Pierponts weren't the only vultures circling Dillinger. The reward money had lots of Depression-ravaged folks eyeing the Mooresville legend as their ticket out of whatever misery was inflicting them. Frank Walsh, an associate of Louis Piquett, had plunged into deep financial water promoting questionable securities in the crash-and-burn Lancaster Kilns Corporation. On the day of the South Bend robbery, he paid a visit to DI "Dillinger Squad" supervisor Sam Cowley looking to sell information. He told Cowley he saw Dillinger on June 12 with his face and fingertips bandaged, confirming Dillinger's not-so-secret surgery.

On July 9, Walsh called Cowley to report that he'd overheard Piquett arguing on the phone with someone he suspected was Dillinger. The dispute was naturally over money, and ended with the pair agreeing to meet at 6:30 that evening on the corner of Wrightwood and Clark streets. For whatever reason, Cowley himself didn't follow up on the juicy tip. Instead, Special Agent Gerry Campbell was assigned to see if Dillinger actually appeared. Campbell saw Piquett arrive as promised, then walk into an alley where he proceeded to have a heated argument with an older man. After the verbal combatants parted ways, Campbell tailed the older man to an apartment building at 1127 South Harvey in Oak Park. Pulling rank on the manager, the G-Man learned that the resident, going by the name "R. Robeind" had moved in June 7, and plunked down $240 cash to cover six-months rent.

Sensing a connection, the Feds decided to place special agent Dan Sullivan inside the building. They didn't believe that "R. Robeind" was Dillinger in disguise, but suspected he might have something to do with the crew. They were right. As they would later learn, they'd located the architect of Dillinger's facial overhaul—Dr. Wilhelm Loeser. Since there was no reward for Doctor Loeser, Walsh the rat was out of luck. Still, the DI felt they were one step closer to getting their man.

Pat Cherrington, cut adrift since the death of her sugar daddy Red Hamilton, sent a telegram to the DI in early July 1934 offering to find Dillinger, VanMeter, and Nelson for them in exchange for a full presidential pardon for her husband, who was serving a long sentence at Leavenworth. She also wanted consideration on her own upcoming sentencing for being with the Dillinger gang in St. Paul, Little Bohemia, and assorted other places. Although she promised to betray three big fish, the Feds declined, deeming the cost too high. Cherrington was instead locked away inside the women's prison in Alderson, West Virginia, with Jean Delaney and Bessie Green.

In Ohio, Pierpont and crew were allowed to address the media following their stay of execution. "Newspapers put us here," Pierpont spat. "We didn't do the Lima job. Indiana authorities, from the state house down, know who did that job, but they built up the case against us because we were hot . . . If Johnny Dillinger is raising a $20,000 fund to come to our defense, tell him, if you can, to send us a couple of fins for cigarettes. We owe Dillinger nothing . . . He owes us even less . . . We both hope he's never caught . . . He's one of the grandest fellows that ever lived . . . No, of course, we don't know where he is."

Asked about rumors they were going to kidnap the daughter of Ohio's governor, Makley snapped, "Hell, we didn't even know he had a daughter 'til we read it in the papers."

Pierpont then took the opportunity to complain about the age-old problem of how corrections officers abuse family members. "My wife can't even come in to see me and she's a little girl weighing not more than ninety pounds and couldn't lift a gnat . . . And the way they treated my mother, searching her to the skin, is an outrage."

What Handsome Harry failed to mention was that he'd once been caught with twelve hacksaw blades in his cell, apparently smuggled in by his brother.

When pressed about past statements he'd made regarding his anger toward the police, Pierpont pulled no punches. "When I get out of here . . . if I get out of here and an officer makes one suspicious move in my direction, I will kill him immediately."

It was not the most astute thing for a prisoner on death row to say, especially one desperately trying not be executed.

On Friday, July 13, the day Pierpont and Makley had been scheduled to die, Dillinger and Polly Hamilton met O'Leary on the 1400 block of North Sacramento Boulevard. Dillinger handed O'Leary $500 to cover Doctor Cassidy's treatment of VanMeter. O'Leary had never met Polly before, and Dillinger didn't bother to introduce her. It was the last time O'Leary would lay eyes on the famous outlaw.

The next day, Doctor Cassidy used half of his windfall to put a down payment on a black Ford V8 roadster from Larry Burns Motor Sales on Irving Park Boulevard. Although Cassidy was for all purposes a highly respected citizen, he bought the vehicle gangster style. O'Leary signed the finance note and titled the car in the name of his daughter, Anne Kubat O'Leary. Sensing he was getting in deep, O'Leary left town two days later, July 15, taking his wife and children to northern Wisconsin "to go fishing."

The DI, displaying the no-stone-left-unturned investigative techniques they'd soon be famous for, began interviewing every Dillinger relative and in-law they could track down, trying to get a fix on where Johnnie might be, or might show. More than one weary Dillinger admitted that they'd be glad when John Jr. was either apprehended or killed due to the stress he was causing the family.

The Feds decided to keep a keen eye on Mary Kinder's pad in

Plainfield as well, helped in part by the constant ratting of her ersatz boyfriend, Carl Waltz. A few days before, Mary's sister Mildred's three-year-old bolted from the house and announced to the world that "John Dillinger is inside drinking beer!" Margaret Behrens, a third sister, ran outside, scooped up the precocious youngster and administered a spanking. Nosey neighbors called the police, but by the time they arrived Dillinger was gone.

A couple of days later, a tall man pulled up out front and headed inside. Before he got there, the door opened and Margaret Behrens yelled, "Go get some #$%& whiskey!" The tall man did as ordered, returning with pockets stuffed with booze and his arms full of ginger ale. Before he reached the door, the lanky stranger tripped over the same loud-mouthed child and broke virtually all his bottles. The amused officers staking out the place contemplated sending the kid after Dillinger.

On the night of the 13th, the Kinder residence was the site of a "wild and drunken party with much cursing," as those inside apparently celebrated Pierpont and Makley's stay. However, none of the big star criminals made the noisy bash.

Dillinger officially resurfaced on July 16 at, of all places, a teenage lovers lane. State troopers Filbert Cross and Fred McAllister were routinely patrolling the coincidently named Wolf Road near the intersection of U.S. 41, also known as Higgins Road. Spotting three new, un-teenager-like Ford V8s parked together on a splinter street known as Old Wolf Road, they pulled in to check it out. Approaching the vehicles from the front, they saw a lone woman sitting in the first car. It was Helen Nelson, and she wasn't there to make out with her husband Baby Face. He was, in fact, outside standing behind one of the other cars talking to John Paul Chase, Jack Perkins, and John Dillinger. The officers didn't immediately recognize the famous outlaws in the dark, secluded setting.

"What's the trouble here?" McAllister asked from his car.

"No trouble at all," one of the men called back. Not yet, he meant. Within seconds, a burst of lead shattered the officer's windshield. Cross, twenty-eight, slumped in his seat, hit in the arm, chest, and abdomen.

McAllister was struck in the shoulder. He opened his door, rolled into a ditch and emptied his service revolver at the three cars that were now speeding away.

McAllister didn't have a radio, so he was left to rush his partner to Des Plaines Emergency Hospital and notify headquarters from there. The delay gave the bandits ample time to escape.

Trooper Cross lost a lot of blood and remained in critical condition for days. He eventually beat predictions that he wouldn't survive and pulled through.

Despite the wounding of two police officers, the incident received little attention. Fatso Negri would later explain that the gang was out on Wolf Road going over plans to rob a train. In a story for *True Detective* magazine, Negri explained the gist of the scheme. The target was to be the Chicago/Milwaukee/St. Paul Pacific Railroad mail route, and the take was expected to exceed a million dollars. Gang member Jimmy Murray was said to have a relative who worked for the railroad who would act as their man on the inside, notifying the gang when an especially lucrative shipment was rolling down on the tracks.

The lover's-lane shoot-out delayed the operation. In addition, it was becoming more and more difficult for the gang to meet without someone leading a police or FBI tail to the party. The boys decided to sit tight until things cooled off.

Chapter 21

The world was closing in on John Dillinger. He had few friends, associates, or relatives left that weren't itching to collect the $25,000 reward on his head. Many were diligently at work trying to do so, some on the FBI's payroll. By July, the only people he felt he could trust were fellow gang members who were also wanted, and a pair of prostitutes. An even these longtime associates and bed partners, if captured, might be willing to sell him out to shave years off their sentences.

The once inept chicken thief from Mooresville had become a victim of his own success. He was the biggest fish in the pond, and thus was left without options. He had nothing to trade, nobody to rat that was above him on the Most Wanted evolutionary scale. The police and Feds didn't need any information from him, and therefore had no reason to take him alive.

A smarter felon would have sensed the gig was up and disappeared to parts unknown. The Jackrabbit, however, suffered from the common flaw that eventually brings down most criminals—the hotter things became, the more they prefer to stay in familiar surroundings.

Unable to sit still, he agonized over unfulfilled plans to spring his beloved Billie Frechette, and was similarly wringing his hands over whether he should launch a dangerous scheme to free Pierpont and Makley before they were given a renewed date with the chair. Worn down from a year on the run, he put his trust in the cut-throat Lake County underworld, and the questionable loyalty of a whorehouse madam, Anna Sage. Prostitute-with-the-golden-heart Polly Hamilton was a nice distraction, but he pined for Billie and ached to flee to Mexico with her. Unfortunately, even if the planned train robbery was a roaring success, he'd be going south alone.

On July 17, Dillinger informed den mother Sage that he was going out of town for a few days. She mistook his destination as Stevens Point, Ohio. It was actually Stevens Point, Wisconsin, a city of 13,000 in the central part of the sparsely populated, frigid state. The tracks of the Chicago/St. Paul/Milwaukee Pacific Railroad turned north at Portage and ran through sleepy Stevens Point. That's where he would help stage the ambitious mail train ambush that would enable the Terror Gang II to disappear and retire.

Dillinger and pals weren't the only ones plotting and scheming in Chicago. Anna Sage was eager to put her own plan into motion. She phoned Sgt. Martin Zarkovich and urged her longtime lover to visit the Halstead Street apartment. He agreed, conferring with her on July 19 and setting the stage for their own moment in history.

Anna's underhanded activities were particularly cold-blooded in light of her behavior with Dillinger in the proceeding months. They often dined together at Steven's, a well-known restaurant at 2604 Southport Avenue that had won two World's Fair awards, along with printed praise from respected food critic Duncan Hines. When not ordering takeout, Dillinger and Anna arrived at Steven's just before closing at 10 P.M. to assure themselves a semblance of privacy. The take-out orders generally were steak or pork chop sandwiches. When they dined in, they went fancier, ordering the duck, turkey, or goose accompanied by owner Steve Jankovich's renown apple-and-cheese strudel.

Neither Chef Steve nor his attentive waitress-wife Millie, an immigrant from Yugoslavia, were aware that their "spiffy" dressed, big-tipping late-night diner was the infamous John Dillinger. They knew Anna was a madam, but her escort was just another wealthy "John" from their perspective.

Dillinger even tested their knowledge one evening as Steven was counting the day's take. "That's a big wad of money, Steve," Dillinger said with a devilish grin. "Aren't you afraid John Dillinger might drop in and take it away from you?"

"No, he just robs from the crooked banks," Jankovich replied, going with the popular, Robin Hood–like legends that had been created around the notorious bandit. "If Dillinger knew I needed money he'd probably give it to me."

"Yeah, he probably would," a pleased Dillinger said as he exited.

When Polly came onboard, the socializing was cranked up a notch. Quiet dinners were replaced by whirlwind nights dancing at the French Casino and Chez Paree. Polly noted that her Clark Kent–like boyfriend hardly ever drank or smoked during this period, rarely having more than one beer or a gin fizz. More often than not, he stuck to orange juice. The behavior, not uncommon among high-powered gangsters, spoke of a man who needed to stay in control of his senses and reflexes at all times.

Polly also related to interviewers later that her "Jimmy" rarely resorted to using obscenities, and was a good dancer who was partial to the Carioca, a Brazilian step similar to the samba.

On slower nights, they hung around home with Anna's twenty-four-year-old son Steve Chiolak, and Steve's steady girl, Kay. Steve also saw Jimmy as a dignified businessman who "didn't act tough" or "talk tough," nor did he flash rolls of bills. "He didn't pay much attention out in public to the people around him, but he talked a lot and laughed a lot."

When pressed, Jimmy stuck to his story about working for the Chicago Board of Trade, one of those fancy-sounding jobs that nobody really knew much about and therefore couldn't query him further. It's not known whether Dillinger himself knew the ins and outs of the complicated financial futures and agriculture options exchange beyond the standard "buy low and sell high" cliché.

The friends preferred partaking in their more interesting leisure activities, often double-dating to movies, usually at the nearby Marbro or Granada theaters. One of their favorites was *Viva Villa,* which boasted Fay Wray of *King Kong* fame playing a Latina, and equally Anglo Wallace Beery staring as the mustachioed Mexican revolutionary Pancho Villa. They also caught *You're Telling Me!*, a W. C. Fields/Buster Crabbe comedy. Afterward, they returned to the apartment and played pinochle at a dime a game and a nickel a set.

Dillinger let his newly dyed hair down at area amusement parks. The man who survived dozens of high-speed chases was not surprisingly a roller-coaster junkie. "We never went on one and then stepped off. Three times on each one was the quota, and sometimes we rode more than that," Polly remembered. "You would have thought he had never grown up. Why, he'd yell like an Indian all the way down, and then he'd lean over and kiss me when we went around the curves. Boy, did we have fun."

Another thrill ride wasn't nearly as fun. "Jimmy" started day-dreaming while driving one afternoon and plunged his V8 clear off the road into a ditch. Polly was tossed around, resulting in the standard "cuts and bruises." Her boyfriend was fortunate to get the car back on the road without attracting unwanted law enforcement attention, or requiring nosey mechanical or towing assistance. Either could have been disastrous considering the hefty price on his reconfigured head.

Brushing the accident off, John took the girls to Jackson Park at Sixty-third Street and Stoney Island Avenue to see Steve play in a sandlot baseball league. Dillinger had such a good time cheering for Steve's squad and booing the umpires that he bought beer for both teams afterward, totally unconcerned about being recognized.

At the apartment, Dillinger enjoyed Polly's home-cooked dinners with baking powder biscuits, chicken gravy, and lots of fresh vegetables like tomatoes, green onions, and radishes. The comfort food obviously brought back memories of his days on his father's farm. He also liked ice cream, frog's legs, and yearned for strawberries, which he'd buy a half dozen boxes at a time. Following big meals, he'd let the girls rest while he rolled up his sleeves and did the dishes, an activity he found relaxing.

"There wasn't much pretense about him," Polly continued. "He said he was just an Indiana farm boy and he insisted I was a farm girl, too . . . He never liked to hurt anyone's feeling. He was what you'd call 'on the up-and-up' with me and all his friends every minute."

The man Polly knew as Jimmy Lawrence was also prone to breaking out in song when he was happy, crooning his favorites "All I Do Is Dream Of You," sung by Gene Raymond in the film *Sadie McKee*, which he never failed to dedicate to Polly, and "For All We Know," from band leader Hal Kemp (and later covered by Nat King Cole among others). Polly said he was very loving in private, a prized cuddler, but didn't like to display his affections publicly. He was uncomfortable as well when others around him canoodled. During card games, he would fine any couple that hugged or kissed five cents.

John Dillinger the outlaw returned to Anna's from the train robbery casing mission on the morning of July 20, transforming back into the mild-mannered Jimmy Lawrence. The next day, Sergeant Zarkovich and his captain, Tim O'Neill, were secretly meeting with their Chicago counterpart Capt. John Stege. Zarkovich and O'Neill picked Stege because they thought he might be receptive to their deadly solution to the "Dillinger problem"—the unnerving possibility that the outlaw might connect the corrupt East Chicago cops with the Lake County underworld. Sergeant Zarkovich was particularly vulnerable to such an accusation. If captured, Dillinger might try to link him to the Crown Point escape, the hit on Zarkovich's rival detectives, various payoffs, and possibly even the long-rumored, banker-approved setup behind the robbery of First National Bank of East Chicago that cost Sgt. William O'Malley his life. Zarkovich figured Stege's trigger-happy Black Shirts were the perfect group to handle the sticky situation. "We will deliver John Dillinger to you right here in your own city," Zarkovich pitched to the ambitious Captain Stege. "And we can divvy up the rewards. All you have to do is make sure that he isn't taken alive."

Adhering to standard station house philosophy that cops are always more dangerously corrupt on the other side of the fence, Captain Stege rejected the plan. He had no desire to expand his Special Ops brigade beyond his own trusted men, and wanted nothing to do with the notoriously dirty East Chicago squad.

Captain Stege may have also believed that he didn't need the East Chicago cops and their whorehouse connections. He had his own informant, Art McGinnis, that he was counting on to lead him to Dillinger. McGinnis had been arrested on Wednesday, July 18, then somehow escaped from his unlocked cell at the Marquette precinct station. Stege blasted the slip-up to the press hounds, but many felt he'd actually arranged for McGinnis to slink away so the fink could carry out their plan.

The object of all this law enforcement scheming spent the day playing cards with Polly, then taking her to the beach. With temperatures soaring into the hundreds, Lake Michigan was the place to be. They invited Anna, but she made an excuse and declined. The moment they left, she hit the phone, updating the rebuffed Sergeant Zarkovich. He told Anna that he and Captain O'Neill were working on Plan B and had a sit-down scheduled with Melvin Purvis of the DI later that afternoon. He assured her that there was still a way that she could collect the reward and head off the Feds efforts to deport her.

Martin Zarkovich, as dangerous and cunning as any sullied cop who ever walked a beat, was playing multiple ends against the middle. If everything worked out the way he planned, Dillinger would be silenced, his lover wouldn't be deported, and he and Anna would end up with a healthy pile of reward money.

To set the hook, Zarkovich dangled another carrot, offering to get Anna some face time with Purvis.

"I don't want to be seen going into their building," she responded, the paranoia already eating at her. "We can meet on the street tonight, after dark. Nine o'clock at Fullerton and Orchard, by the Children's Hospital."

Shortly afterward. Captain O'Neill rang Purvis and asked for a meeting. Responding that he had to run it up the ladder, Purvis hung up and conferred with his supervisor, Sam Cowley. Curious, Cowley gave the go-ahead. The meeting was set for 6 P.M. in Cowley's room at the Great Northern Hotel.

Arriving at the beach, Dillinger unveiled a brand-new bathing suit, the skimpier kind "the college boys wear," an approving Polly noted. Her beau was a swimmer, not a sun bather, and went right for the cool water. Before jumping in, he remembered he was carrying a hefty roll of cash. "We had a little council of war," Polly recalled. "The safest thing was to leave someone with our clothes all the time to watch the money. We did this taking turns, and that ended Jimmy's last worry."

When six o'clock rolled around on the blisteringly hot day, the two plotting East Chicago cops, Zarkovich and O'Neill, were laying out a scrubbed-up version of their scheme to the Feds. They had an "insider" who could put the finger on Dillinger. She wanted the reward, and a personal problem taken care of, which the detectives didn't specify. Instead, they said the source would lay it out to the agents in person later that evening. Eager to eyeball the snitch, Purvis and Cowley readily agreed to the clandestine nine o'clock meeting.

Figuring they were on to something, Cowley hit the red line and updated J. Edgar Hoover directly. The legendary DI/FBI chief was pleased with the potential break in the case and asked to be kept apprised night or day.

At nine, all the parties appeared as promised. Purvis and Sergeant Zarkovich waited in one car, while Cowley and Captain O'Neill provided cover in a second vehicle. The area streetlights were shaded by large trees, so the secretive event had an especially dark and eerie feel. Anna left her apartment and walked around the corner, passing the Purvis/Zarkovich vehicle to survey the situation, fearing a trap. Convinced it was on the up and up, she backtracked and ducked inside. The DI brass then caravanned to Lincoln Park, an even more secluded spot on the shore of Lake Michigan—five miles from where Dillinger had earlier spent his fun-filled day. There, the two sides played the usual cop/snitch cat-and-mouse game while Cowley and Captain O'Neill observed from a distance in their car.

Anna outlined what she had to trade and what she wanted in return—the reward and the right to remain in the United States. Purvis shrugged and plead the usual power failure, saying he didn't have the juice to guarantee her anything. Then, after sucking the wind out of her sails, he proceeded to blow some of it back. The way he saw it, if Anna delivered Dillinger, she should be able to pocket a substantial part of the $25,000 reward. He didn't explain why she wouldn't be privy to the entire jackpot, but Anna already expected the cops themselves to slice off a share. The shifty agent danced even harder around the sticky issue of her immigration status. He said he had no authority to grant that, which was true. What he didn't say is he could have easily called in a Federal prosecutor who had such pull. Anna should have demanded as much, but late-night backseat negotiations aren't the same as being represented by a knowledgeable attorney in the comfort of the DI's

Chicago field office. Instead of saying "thanks but no thanks," Anna caved and agreed to rat out her friend the fugitive—a man the government desperately wanted—for nothing more than an undetermined percentage of the reward, and a letter of recommendation from Purvis supporting her immigration case.

For her part, Anna didn't come entirely clean with Purvis, either. Despite her dismal negotiation skills, she was smart enough not to put all her cards on the table. She told the agents that Dillinger visited her apartment on occasion. Actually, he was living there. However, had she spilled that, the G-Men wouldn't have needed her anymore. They could have simply raided the place, scooped up the Jackrabbit, and given her nothing. If she squawked, they had the option of slapping her with harboring a fugitive and further greasing her slide out of America.

Anna, no doubt brought up to speed by Sergeant Zarkovich, was aware that once the FBI contact was made, the Delilah act had to go down fast. The FBI would surely begin to stake out the apartment on their own, and would quickly discover the truth.

In her defense, Anna would later claim that Purvis did in fact trade the stoppage of her deportation for Dillinger. "Your case is nothing compared to getting Dillinger," she recalled him saying. "We'll take care of it." Purvis adamantly denied that version and stuck by his guns that he'd played it by the book.

Either way, the pair were still cat-and-ratting it up to the moment Anna was dropped off. Before they parted, almost as an aside, the desperate madam laid out the soon-to-be world-famous scheme. John and Polly often went to the movies, she advised, usually to the Marbro Theater. If she was around, they'd invite her along. They'd probably go the next evening, a Sunday. If that was the case, she promised to dial the number Purvis gave her and let him know.

Minutes after Zarkovich and Sage left their sight, Cowley was back on the hot line with Hoover in Washington. The bulldoggish FBI general was immediately concerned about the public nature of the takedown site. He feared a repeat of the Little Bohemia fiasco, and didn't want any civilians injured or killed—either by the Feds or by Dillinger. He ordered the agents on the detail to carry only their handguns, and to use every precaution to avoid collateral damage. Before hanging up, he instructed Cowley to take Dillinger alive if at all possible.

Energized with anticipation, Cowley and Special Agent Virgil Peterson drove to 4124 West Madison Street and discreetly began to diagram the exits of the Marbro Theater.

Although he had worked late into the evening, Cowley was up early the next morning preparing for what he sensed was going to be a hell of a day. Starting at 8:30 A.M., he called and began mentally assigning the nineteen handpicked agents he had working under him on the Dillinger Squad. Special Agent Bob Gillespie was one of the first to be contacted that Sunday morning. He was told to stay in his room and stick by the phone until he heard otherwise. The other eighteen agents, plus ten more in the Chicago field office, received similar orders. All vacations and days off were canceled. There would be no splash-happy afternoon at the beach for the G-Men. Instead, they'd be fully dressed and sweltering in the near-record heat.

It was the blistering weather, and not Dillinger, that was the big news in Chicago that weekend. Sunday marked the third day of a deadly heat wave. Seventeen people died on Saturday. Before the sun mercifully set Sunday, another thirty would succumb as the mercury topped 100 in the miserably humid, no-longer-windy city.

The East Chicago cops were determined to add to that number by one. Only the "heat" they planned to apply would come in the form of fiery lead.

The searing temperatures that made the cops and agents miserable was also acting as their alley in one respect. Dillinger was struggling to stay holed up in Anna's third-floor apartment at 2420 North Halstead. He spent most of the morning in front of a metal fan, and the rest of the day would prove to be steamier. Polly had it even worse, working the breakfast-and-lunch shift at the S&S Sandwich Shop at 1209 1/2 Wilson Avenue where she had a part-time job. She returned to the apartment in the midafternoon feint, drained, and colorless. Dillinger put her to bed and went downstairs to the deli to buy her some ice cream. Playing nursemaid, he gave her an extra pillow and aimed a large electric fan her way.

At 5:15 P.M., Anna announced that she was making fried chicken for dinner and needed to go out and get butter. Struggling to stay calm, she exited through the hallway, climbed down the stairs and reached the still-blistering street below. Checking to see if anybody was watching, she grabbed the delicatessen phone and literally and figuratively "dropped a nickel," dialing Andover 2330. "He's just come," she whispered her lie to Purvis. "I'm not sure where we're going—either the Marbro or the Biograph." She hung up, purchased the butter, and skittered back upstairs, perspiring profusely.

Purvis fought off a moment of panic. He and Cowley had a detailed a plan for the Marbro, but nothing for the Biograph. It was a glaring oversight considering that a Shirley Temple movie was playing at the Marbro, and a gangster film starring Clark Gable and William Powell was at the Biograph. It didn't take an FBI profiler to determine which show Dillinger would choose.

The Biograph, one of the Chicago's earliest movie houses, was located at 2433 North Lincoln, nestled among a row of two-story commercial buildings that stood shoulder-to-shoulder along the east side of Lincoln. Anna's apartment was near the south end of this block.

A jittery and sweat-soaked Purvis ordered agents Earle Richmond and Jim Metcalfe to diagram the Biograph and survey the neighborhood. Poring over their notes an hour later, the crew chief frowned as he discovered there were multiple exits in the rear, leading into four separate alleys behind the theater that formed a "K." This was caused by Lincoln running at a forty-five-degree angle to Halstead. The maze of alleys presented the agents with additional headaches.

Purvis and Cowley determined that they needed more manpower. By 7 P.M., an army of thirty armed G-Men gathered in the suffocating heat of the division office in the Banker's Building. Purvis introduced Sgt. Martin Zarkovich, who informed the gathering that John Dillinger would be attending either the Marbro or the Biograph in less than two hours, and would be accompanied by a pair of women. Zarkovich updated the men on the changes in Dillinger's appearance—fuller face, missing mole from his eyebrow, less prominent cleft on his chin, black hair, and pencil-thin mustache. Thanks to Anna, Zarkovich even had the potential clothes down—gray checkered suit, white shoes, and a straw boater hat.

One of the women, Zarkovich continued, would be older and larger than the other, standing five-foot, five-inches, 160 pounds, in her early thirties. The sarge let his ego, or his rose-colored glasses, get away with him there. His lover was forty-two, five-foot, three inches and closer to a chunky 170 pounds. She would be dressed, he continued, in a white blouse over a bright orange skirt—an outfit that would forever erroneously brand her "the lady in red." If they were going to the Biograph, her head would be bare. If they were going to the Marbro or somewhere else, she'd be wearing a white, wide-brimmed hat cocked at an angle.

The second woman, Zarkovich continued with far less embellishment, was twenty-six, smaller, and had dark hair and brown complexion. This woman was, Zarkovich made a point to stress, "Dillinger's lover."

After Zarkovich set the scene, Purvis took the floor. He said he and agent Ralph Brown would stake out the Biograph. Purvis had no doubt finally paid attention to what movies were playing, and was putting his money on Clark Gable. Special Agent Charles Winstead and Sergeant Zarkovich would watch the Marbro while Agent Val Zimmer loitered in the lobby. This pleased Zarkovich because he was still blinded by Anna's light, convinced that the girls would persuade Dillinger to go for mop-top child star Shirley Temple.

The remaining agents were told to cool their heels in the steamy field office until the determination was made as to which movie the trio was catching. Agent Virgil Peterson, weak from a previous illness and drained from the heat, was selected to stay put and coordinate the effort from the base.

The signal to close in would be the lighting of a cigar—either by Purvis at the Biograph or Zarkovich at the Marbro.

With their careers on the line, the rest of Sergeant Zarkovich's equally complicit gang weren't about to let him lead them down the wrong orange-skirted path. Regardless of where Dillinger showed, they insisted that Zarkovich arranged it so they would be major players. "They" were Capt. Tim O'Neill, Sgt. Walter Conroy, and triggermen detectives Glen Stretch and Peter Sopsic. Relenting, Purvis set it up so Stretch and Sopsic would team with Special Agents H. E. Hollis and Clarence Hurt in the critical position near the designated box office. The cop/Fed quartet were given the plum, headline-making assignment of trying to physically subdue Dillinger as he left the theater. More important, the designation would ensure that Sopsic and Stretch were in position to make sure "something went wrong" and Dillinger was silenced.

In the major supporting roles, Special Agents Joe McCarthy and Bob Gillespie were set to roll in behind the arrest team, while fellow G-Men John Welles and Allen Lockerman closed off the front. The rest of the agents would be in the alleys behind the theater or across the street from the box office to cover unforeseen variables.

Before breaking, Purvis felt the need to lay some added pressure on his men, giving a speech that fell on the especially receptive ears of Zarkovich and his henchmen. "Gentlemen, you all know the character of John Dillinger. If he appears at either of the picture shows and we locate him and affects his escape, it will be a disgrace to our bureau. It may be that Dillinger will be at the picture show with his women companions unarmed—yet, he may appear there armed and with other members of his gang . . . It is the desire that he be taken alive, if possible, and without injury of any agent of the bureau. Yet, gentlemen, this is the opportunity that we have all been awaiting and he must be taken. Do not unnecessarily risk your own lives. If Dillinger offers any resistance, each man will be for himself and it will be up to each of you to do whatever you think necessary to protect yourselves."

Zarkovich, O'Neill, and the East Chicago, Indiana, crew traded knowing smiles. Purvis had just given them carte blanche to blow John Dillinger away.

Chapter 22

Unbeknownst to the bloodthirsty East Chicago Five, they had some equally trigger-happy allies among their stiff-necked Federal cousins. Agents Charles G. "Gerry" Campbell, Clarence Hurt, and Charles Winstead were what was unofficially known as "shooters," or "gunslingers." They brought an aggressive, S.W.A.T./military mindset to the party. The trio of marksmen had talked among themselves about the shame and embarrassment Dillinger brought to their beloved Division of Investigation, and swore a pact that it wouldn't happen again.

With Hurt being on the first contact A-Team, that meant the only person in the group remotely harboring the thought of capturing Dillinger alive was Agent H. E. Hollis—and nobody really knew where he stood on the matter.

The one thing the Fed bosses were adamant about was making sure the target was in fact John Dillinger, and nobody else was killed or hurt in the shoot-out. To that end, there were curt memos from higher-ups stressing "extreme precaution" and warning agents about the "hasty opening of fire on any particular car and its occupants, merely from its description."

Hoover feared that in the frenzy of a firefight, some of his pistol-challenged agents might accidentally take out a few cops. In addition, the tragedy at Little Bohemia, and the killing of Tommy Carroll, typified the reckless, ends-justifies-the-means style of law enforcement in the 1930s. The Jackrabbit himself had been shot at two separate times in his younger days before his first prison term.

To lessen the odds of another disaster, Cowley and Purvis decided against informing the Chicago police. They already had enough problems with the meddlesome East Chicago Five, so bringing in the local branch with their own agendas was viewed as counterproductive. Even though the rationale was logical, neither Purvis nor the quick-dialing Cowley bothered to inform Hoover that the Chicago cops weren't being invited to the party.

Around the corner from the Biograph, John, Anna, and Polly finished their fried chicken dinner, washed and dried the dishes, then pulled out the pinochle cards. At 8:30, Anna got up to change into the white blouse and yellowish orange skirt that would make history. Polly, cooled off, fed, and feeling better, selected a tan suit. Dillinger, ever the dandy, pulled out a white Kenilworth broadcloth shirt, a gray necktie flecked in red, and the white buckskins Sergeant Zarkovich had advised everyone about.

The outlaw vacillated over taking his Colt .380 pistol, sliding it in and out of a drawer. It was too hot to wear a jacket and shoulder holster, and his pocket space was limited. This brief, leisurely interlude in his hectic life could vaporize in an instant, so it was necessary to load up with cash at all times. He counted out $3,300 in various bills, banded groups of fives, tens, and twenties together, and spread the one-to-two-inch clumps around his front and back pockets. A smaller stack was stuffed inside his bulging wallet.

Anna tried her best to observe his preparations, making excuses to pass by the door or enter the room. The bank robber wasn't shy about flashing his money around the girls, so that accounting was easy. The more important question this evening—was he packing heat?—proved more difficult to discern. His in-and-out act was making Anna dizzy. By the time they left the apartment, she didn't know what was causing each specific bulge in his pockets.

Dillinger waited until he and girls left the apartment before announcing their destination. *Little Miss Marker*, aka Shirley Temple, would have to wait. They were going to see Clark Gable play the fictional gangster "Blackie Gallagher" in *Manhattan Melodrama*. The selection hardly surprised the ladies.

Despite the still-oppressive heat, the theater was too close to hop a cab. The smartly dressed trio leisurely strolled the short distance.

Around the corner, Purvis and Agent Brown fidgeted in their division car sixty feet south of the Biograph box office. They were doing everything to make themselves obvious. Brown, his pockets jangling with nickels, jumped out every five minutes and hustled to a nearby pay phone to call the field office, asking if Dillinger had appeared at the Marbro. Forty-five minutes of "not yets" made the G-Men increasingly antsy. They began to think it was all going to be for naught. "We were discouraged," Purvis would later write. "We felt that this might be another failure." Their angst is somewhat baffling, since the show times were clearly stated. It was doubtful that John and the girls would arrive early at the single-plex for the nine o'clock show considering how close they lived to the theater, and how steamy it was.

Just as the agents were panicking over the crowd that was gathering out front, filing into the theater, and obscuring their view, the three passed. The sweat-soaked G-Men instantly recognized Dillinger and Anna. They had never seen Polly Hamilton before, but she fit the description. Brown popped out of the car yet again to give headquarters the news and pull the others from the Marbro.

Their prey turned into the entrance without breaking stride and approached the female ticket seller. The ladies waited in front off to the side. Purvis noted that Dillinger was wearing glasses, a *Music Man* straw boater hat, gray trousers, and no coat. The checkered suit that Sergeant Zarkovich mentioned had not materialized, no doubt a victim of the heat.

Purvis's initial reaction to the coatless bank robber was that he probably wasn't armed. The DI file on Dillinger stated that he carried his pistol in his jacket, or used a shoulder holster. Purvis contemplated taking him right then, but concluded that Dillinger's "utter ruthlessness and his entire disregard for human life" made the risk to bystanders on the crowded block too great.

Because of their late arrival, the trio was unable to sit together. Dillinger and Polly found two empty seats up front three rows from the screen. Anna had to sit by herself in the back.

Dillinger enjoyed the movie immensely, laughing, whispering private jokes, and trying to sneak kisses. During one scene, a secretary warned her prosecutor boss, William Powell, against inviting his old-friend-turned-crook, Blackie Gallagher, to his wedding. "Remember what happened to the district attorney in Chicago just for having his picture taken with some gangsters having dinner?" she reminded. It was an obvious reference to Dillinger's Crown Point photo session, and the true-life gangster got a big kick out of it.

By all accounts, the outlaw who had been so cunning, perceptive, and incredibly lucky throughout his reign had no premonition that he had sealed himself inside a deadly trap.

Outside, Brown returned to the car and informed Purvis that Cowley had been advised of the target's arrival. Too nervous to sit still, Purvis approached the box office and checked the running time again. He was told that the movie ran an hour and thirty-four minutes, and was preceded by a half hour of previews and features. That meant they'd have to cool their heels for another 124 minutes.

Unwilling to wait, Purvis bought a ticket, went inside, and tried to spot the bandit and his dates. He was hoping there would be empty seats behind them. His thought was to have two agents join him inside and take the seats. Upon his signal, they would pin Dillinger's arms and grab his head to disable him. That risky plan had to be scuttled when Purvis couldn't locate Dillinger in the jam-packed theater, and didn't want to make himself obvious by walking up and down the aisles for a closer look. On his way out, the jittery agent asked the ticket lady the running time again. It was the same as before, a total of two hours and four minutes.

Despite the long lag time, Purvis became paranoid about his backup. When twenty minutes passed and nobody arrived, he was really starting to worry. The others, in no hurry to wait out a long movie in the stifling heat, finally began trickling in. Agents Joe McCarthy, Bob Gillespie, John Wells, and Allen Lockerman parked two blocks south of the theater. Agents Earle Richmond, Gerry Campbell, and Jim Metcalfe came in the second pack. Clarence Hurt and Ed Hollis followed, bringing East Chicago officers Peter Sopsic and Glen Stretch. Division Supervisor Sam

Cowley swung in from headquarters with East Chicago Capt. Tim O'Neill and Sgt. Walter Conroy. They left their vehicle a block away and walked to the theater.

Checking in from the Marbro, G-Man Val Zimmer was given the news of the unfolding events. He relayed the information to his partner, Charles Winstead, and Sergeant Zarkovich. Winstead took Zarkovich in his vehicle while Zimmer drove a second car and parked it directly across Lincoln Avenue from the Biograph. With everybody onboard, the nineteen federal agents and five East Chicago cops began to take the positions that Purvis had mapped out. G-Men John McLaughlin, Bill Ryan, and Dan Sullivan walked behind the theater to watch the exits and alley at the center and north end. Their associates, Ray Suran, Tom Conner, and Mike Glynn, covered the exits and convergence of alleys at the southeast rear corner.

Agents Richmond and Campbell aligned themselves just north of the box office. Thirty feet to the south, Zimmer and Zarkovich sat in Zimmer's vehicle. Metcalfe slipped into a doorway behind them. Captain O'Neill and Sergeant Conroy hid in an alley fifty feet further south. Sam Cowley, as jittery as Purvis, roamed from station to station, mopping his brow and making sure everybody held their positions.

When he wasn't bothering the ticket lady or chewing on his cigar, the thin, frail-looking Purvis stood in the shadow of a doorway just south of the box office. Across the narrow sidewalk, Hollis loitered beside Brown's car. Hurt and Winstead waited in a dark doorway thirty feet to the south. Lockerman and Wells stationed themselves across the alley behind Hurt and Winstead.

The way Purvis figured it, Dillinger would leave the theater and head south down the narrow sidewalk between the box office and the alley that led back to Anna's apartment. That's why Hurt and Winstead, the shooters and army vets, were there.

Shortly before the movie ended, the ticket lady told her manager, Charles Shapiro, about the sweaty little man that kept asking when the movie was going to end. Looking outside, Shapiro was alarmed to see all the suited figures hiding in every nook and cranny on such a hot night. Fearing a robbery, he called the District 37 police station on Sheffield Avenue.

At 10:25, headlights illuminated the rear alley from three different directions. A plainclothes policeman, armed with a riot gun, jumped out of a car and brandished his weapon at Agent Suran. "Get some identification before you shoot," a voice inside the vehicle suggested.

"Who the hell are you?" the officer demanded.

"We're Federal Agents. Department of Justice," Suran answered.

"Show me your identification. What are you doing here?"

"We're on a Federal stakeout," Suran explained, producing his credentials. "We'd appreciate it if you would back your cars out of the alley but stay close by. We may need you."

At the same time, Chicago detectives approached Gillespie, McCarthy, Sopsic, and Stretch and made them identify themselves. The G-Men took the lead and offered their Federal IDs, figuring the Chicago cops wouldn't be happy to see their East Chicago counterparts working their territory. A third detective confronted Richmond and Zarkovich, now sitting on the front steps of a bakery. Richmond flashed his card. The tense incident, which could have easily gotten ugly, was quietly quelled—with seconds to spare.

As the movie wound down to its final minutes, celluloid gangster Blackie Gallagher made the long, dramatic walk to the electric chair. Stopping at the cell of a fellow prisoner, Blackie offered this advice. "Die the way you lived, all of a sudden. Don't drag it out. Living like that doesn't mean a thing." Passing DA Jim Wade, Blackie sensed that his childhood friend was about to weaken and commute his sentence. "Don't, Jim. You're going to ruin your career? For what? Say, listen, if I can't live the way I want at least let me die the way I want. So long, Jim."

Blackie disappeared into the execution chamber. The prison lights dimmed as the switch was pulled. "There he goes," an inmate called out. "They're givin' it to him!"

A few minutes later, the house lights went up. Dillinger, moved by Blackie's bravado, remained in his seat for a few moments to let it all sink in as the theater cleared.

Seeing the people starting to leave, Purvis felt his knees knocking together. His mouth was dry as cotton. The future of their upstart federal police agency might very well be determined in the next few minutes.

Inside, Anna waited in her seat until she saw "Jimmy" and Polly come up the aisle. She stood and joined them. Polly slipped her arm through her beau's as they proceeded to the lobby. Before exiting, Dillinger adjusted his clear glass spectacles and put on his cheerful hat. There was still a crowd in the lobby, so the going was slow. Polly clung to Dillinger's left arm, and Anna stayed to the right, slightly behind, keeping her distance.

Failing to properly anticipate the jailbreak phenomenon at the end of a movie, Purvis checked the sea of faces so intently his eyes began to burn. The trio emerged, and Dillinger looked Purvis dead in the face as he passed. The doomed outlaw offered no sign that he recognized the thoroughly unintimidating Chicago DI chief. Purvis struck a match to light what remained of the cigar that literally shook in his mouth. That was the signal to the others that the prey was on the way.

Glancing up the street, Purvis noticed in shock that East Chicago assassins, Stretch and Sopsic, didn't catch the signal. They were still being distracted by the frowning Chicago detectives. Purvis fired another match. Still no recognition. His heart pounding, Purvis was relieved to notice that his men, Gillespie and McCarthy, had seen the flame and were quickly approaching.

Sgt. Martin Zarkovich, the man with the most to lose if Dillinger escaped or was captured alive, picked up on what had happened and sprinted across the street toward his cohorts.

Agents Richmond and Campbell were just finishing flashing their credentials to the meddlesome Chicago cops when Campbell spotted the action. "There they go! I'm going to Clarence," he called as he headed into the street to join Hurt just south of the theater. Richmond ran behind him.

DI shooter Clarence Hurt saw the match ignite and swung into his hit-man mode, scrutinizing the theater patrons passing him on the sidewalk. "That's Dillinger with the straw hat and glasses," he whispered to his fellow assassin Charlie Winstead, noting Anna's bright orange skirt. The gangster and his dates passed Brown's vehicle as Hollis watched with feigned detachment.

Suddenly, Dillinger sensed that something was terribly wrong. Polly felt his arm tense. He glanced at Hollis, looked away, scanned the area, then looked hard at Hollis again. He fingered the pistol in his side pocket and created a quick "git map" in his mind. The alley up ahead was his best avenue of escape. It was only a few steps away. He'd have to stay cool.

Hollis, an attorney who was a notoriously bad shot, fell in six feet behind the trio, sliding his hand toward his shoulder holster. Purvis, another attorney with minimal handgun skills, closed in toward the right. Anna had moved up and was now quizzically holding Dillinger's arm as well. They passed the doorway where the military-trained terminators lurked. Hurt casually crossed in front of the trio. Winstead joined the others that trailed.

If Dillinger had any remaining doubts, they were erased when he approached the alley. Agents Lockerman and Welles were standing there with their guns already drawn. Moving forward, Dillinger turned his head and used his peripheral vision to scan the scene behind him. Winstead was practically breathing on his neck. Turning the girls loose, Dillinger crouched and started to run, clawing for the .380 automatic pistol in his right pocket. Checking behind him a second time, he bumped into a woman near the alley and spun partly around. In the instant he took to identify the lady as a civilian, Winstead and Hurt simultaneously fired. Since it was too hot for a steel vest, the famous outlaw was completely vulnerable. One slug burned through his chest at a sideways, downward angle and punched out beneath a left rib. The second, a big .45, slammed into the base of his neck, ripped through the brain stem and spit out beneath his right eye. The impact of the bullets combined with the collision with the lady to spin him around like a top.

Winstead fired twice more as the famous robber began to crumble toward the hot pavement. Hollis also squeezed his trigger. The five reports came so close together that many agents and witnesses would say they only heard a single bang.

Summoning his last ounce of strength, Dillinger caught himself, stumbled into the alley, then fell hard on his elbow and face, shattering an eyeglass lens and snapping the brim of his stiff, straw hat. The Colt .380, its safety still on, remained in his hand. Purvis kneeled down and took the weapon. Winstead leaned in and heard the outlaw attempt to speak. "He mumbled some words that I couldn't understand. That was the end."

Dillinger wasn't the only person prone, nor was he the only one shot. East Chicago cop Walter Conroy hit the ground the moment he heard the noise. He wasn't afraid of the bandit. "I didn't want one of those college boys shooting me in the back," he groused. It was indeed lucky, considering the angles, that none of the agents or officers was hit in the crossfire. The same couldn't be said for the civilians.

There was a long moment of eerie silence as Dillinger's blood spilled out on the cement. Then, as if by some signal, pandemonium reigned. Automobiles and streetcars stopped dead as their passengers poured into the area. Pedestrians swarmed the fallen felon. Within seconds, people were shouting the name "Dillinger!"

Above the din, the anguished voices of two women could be heard. Both were screaming that they'd been hit. The first, Etta Natalsky of 2429 Lincoln, was the woman that Dillinger had bumped into. A bullet passed through her fleshy upper left thigh, spurting blood on her dress. The slug may have been the same one that passed through Dillinger's chest. The second injured lady, Theresa Paulus, twenty-nine, of 2920 Commonwealth Avenue, was leaving the movie with her companion, Fred Kuhn, when a wild volley plunked her in the hip. Neither woman was seriously hurt, but their injuries once again defined the recklessness of the jumpy G-Men.

Agents McCarthy and Gillespie crossed the alley and ducked into a Chinese restaurant to make the victorious call. Dialing the Thirty-seventh Precinct, McCarthy officially informed the local cops that the Department of Justice had made an arrest outside the Biograph. Before hanging up, Agent Brown came in and advised McCarthy to ask for an ambulance.

The six G-Men stationed behind the theater held their ground, resisting all temptation to follow the shots. They stayed in place until they were ordered up front to help with crowd control.

Winstead, still lingering by the body, reported that an unidentified Chicago cop appeared and searched the body. The DI assassin, unaware that Purvis had taken the Colt, asked the officer to look for the weapon he saw the target reach for. Curiously, Winstead was the only person to mention this officer in his report.

Agent Grier Woltz, a bit more observant than his cohorts, noticed that Dillinger was "still kicking and moving around" as he writhed on the pavement. The outlaw's eyebrows were "discolored and seemed to be painted a dark, heavy brown." A gold ruby band on the young criminal's left ring finger glistened in the lights.

Special Agent Gillespie estimated that the Jackrabbit lived about three minutes after the shooting. He was right beside him when the famous Public Enemy gasped and took his last breath.

Agent Tom Conner pulled his vehicle into the alley and illuminated the eerie scene with his headlights. Cowley scooped the shattered spectacles, the crushed hat, and a La Corona cigar that was in John Jr.'s pocket and handed them to Val Zimmer to file at the field office. Cowley then picked up a phone and made the call that J. Edgar Hoover had been waiting for—John Dillinger was dead. Not only dead, but brought down exclusively by G-Men. "Good work, Sam," Hoover said, restraining his jubilation.

Polly and Anna curiously melted into the crowd. "I jumped in fright," Polly recalled. "Then I looked to see what had happened and there was Jimmy lying there shot . . . I ran to the doorway of the grocery next door and bumped right into a gun in the hands of one of the officers, a government man I suppose. He didn't pay any attention to me, so I ran on to the corner. There, in all that crowd, I bumped into a woman who turned out to be Anna, who was running away, too. Then a policeman stopped me. I guess he lost his head or something, for he let me go."

The girls vanished through the alley and went back to Anna's apartment to sort things out. Anna, in on the plot, was acting in character. Polly's instant abandonment of her dying "Board of Trade clerk" lover raises suspicion that she wasn't as innocent and unknowing as she pretended.

As the Lady in Red and Lady in Tan hid, a police van known as "Black Maria" appeared at the mouth of the alley. Agent Woltz led the pack that lifted Dillinger's bleeding body onto a stretcher, carried it to the wagon, and slid it on the floor. Agents Hurt, Glynn, Hollis, Gillespie, and Sullivan hopped in with three Chicago officers. The body was taken to Alexian Brothers Hospital at 1200 Belden Avenue. There, it was decided to save time by having a doctor come outside to the van and declare the outlaw deceased. At 10:55 P.M., Dr. Walter Prusaig appeared, bent over the figure, put his stethoscope to the famous ruffian's chest and announced, "This man is dead." A Chicago homicide detective, "Foley," ordered the body taken to the Cook County morgue on Polk Street. Agents Richmond, Metcalfe, and technician Morris "Max" Chaffetz followed "Black Maria" to the coroner so they could take fingerprints.

At the morgue, the escorts had to wait in line before their prized stiff could be processed. As they lingered, another crowd gathered. Chicago officers asked if they could take a look. The G-Men relented. Deputy coroner Jack Butler finally came out and took control of the circus. The body was placed on a cart, wheeled inside to an elevator, and taken to a basement room designated for washing corpses and preparing them for autopsies. Dr. Charles Parker, a young physician who moonlighted for *The Chicago Tribune*, rushed to the morgue and volunteered to help. Allowed to participate, Parker noted what he saw and heard, paying particular attention to the parade of officers and G-Men who came in to gawk. One, Dillinger's old nemesis Sgt. Frank Reynolds, took the opportunity to ghoulishly shake the dead bandit's hand.

Despite the scarring on Dillinger's fingers, Max Chaffetz was able to take a clear set of prints. He immediately dispatched them to Washington where a match was made. So much for Doctor Loeser's acid tonic.

Agent Dan Sullivan meticulously recorded Dillinger's possessions: one pair of white buckskin Nunn-Bush shoes, size 9D; one pair of black silk socks; one pair of red Paris garters; one pair of Hanes undershorts, white with blue stripes, size 34; one pair of gray pants, laundry mark No. 355 (40); one black belt with a silver buckle; one white broadcloth shirt, Kenilworth brand; one red printed necktie, bearing the tag of Paul Boldt & Sons, 2724 North Clark Street, Chicago; one gold ruby ring, inscribed

"With all my love, Polly:" a yellow gold, seventeen-jewel Hamilton pocket watch, No. 344347, with a photograph of Polly Hamilton inside the hinged lid; a gold chain and tiny knife attached to the watch; a white handkerchief with a thin brown border; two keys tied with a string (one fit the door of Anna's apartment); and a fully loaded, spare magazine for a Colt pistol.

The official record said Dillinger was carrying $7.70 in his pocket. In the ultimate irony, somebody had robbed the dead bandit of $3,000.

Doctors Butler and Parker discovered powder burns on the fatal wound at the base of Dillinger's skull, meaning the muzzle of the G-Man's gun had only been inches away. The jagged exit wound beneath the eye continued to ooze blood and fluid. In addition to the blast through his chest, the doctors noted the old gunshot wound near the knee, and the surgical cuts on his face. Dillinger's eyebrows, as Agent Woltz noticed, were indeed plucked and dyed to match his hair.

Although five shots had been fired at point-blank range, only a pair hit the mark. Two bullets hit civilians, and the fifth went who knows where. The ultimate successful result would act to diffuse this latest example of reckless law enforcement.

A gleeful Purvis allowed the press hounds in at midnight to photograph the body—something that would never be tolerated today. He also ordered that the bandit's watch be taken out of sight to keep anyone from identifying Polly. This was said to have been done in deference to the fact that she had once been married to a cop. The real reason, no doubt, was to conceal her role in the setup.

Later that morning, two separate groups were given permission to make plaster casts of Dillinger's face for future wax museum exhibits. When the Chicago police and coroner objected, some of the masks were seized.

By 2 A.M., throngs of night-owl spectators mobbed Lincoln Avenue outside the Biograph. The "Extra" additions of the newspapers were already on the streets. "John Dillinger died tonight as he lived, in a hail of lead and swelter of blood," one proclaimed. "He died with a smile on his lips and a woman on each arm." Many onlookers dipped their newspapers into the blood that still stained the bricks. Women used the hems of their skirts. A quick-thinking entrepreneur dipped dozens of handkerchiefs, which he sold for a healthy profit.

In Mooresville, Everett and Margaret Moore, publishers of *The Mooresville Times*, drove to the farm to inform John Sr. "So he's really gone," the gentle old man said, tears welling in his eyes. "I just hoped he'd give himself up, but that wouldn't have been John, I guess. It's hard to believe." John Sr. woke up his daughters, Doris, sixteen, and Frances, twelve, and gave them the news. The girls cried hard. Margaret Moore, returning to her home, called a local doctor and asked him to check on the grieving Dillingers.

In Maywood, Audrey and her family were sleeping on blankets in the front yard because of the heat. Two G-Men appeared and told them what had happened. Audrey, Emmett, and Mary quickly dressed and joined John Sr. When they arrived, the yard was filled with reporters. Hubert Dillinger showed up a few moments later and pushed his way through the mob.

"I thought this had to come and I've been expecting it anytime," John Sr. told Bob Butler of the *Indianapolis News* early that morning. "You know, I can't think John was bad all the way through. There are lots of things he did that I don't think he could have done . . . We'll bury him in Crown Hill cemetery alongside his mother. I've got a lot there and I want them to be together."

Francis broke the silence that followed. "Daddy, did he shoot first?"

"No, I guess not," John Sr. accurately answered.

"Maybe they were afraid to try and arrest him?"

They certainly had been—for myriad reasons.

By midmorning, when reporters from distant papers descended upon the farm, Audrey's nerves were fraying. "John wasn't a bad boy," she defended defiantly. "I reared him and I know. They got him. That's what they wanted to do, and there just isn't anything more to say about it."

A weary John Sr. was more patient. "We've had enough pictures spread over the country, but I guess the boys with the cameras have to make their living, too."

Local undertaker Friday Harvey of E. F Harvey's funeral home in

Mooresville was given the task of picking up Dillinger's body. Everett Moore, John Sr., and Hubert Dillinger joined him as they headed toward Chicago in a creaky, 1923 Cadillac hearse. In the back was a dark brown wicker body basket lined with oil cloth.

Homer VanMeter, given the news by Marie Conforti, had no intention of attending the funeral. The pair immediately left Calumet City for Hunter's Log Cabin Camp near Walker, Minnesota, 200 miles northwest of St. Paul.

At the Ohio State Prison, Pierpont, Makley, and Clark naturally took the news hard. Dillinger had been their only hope to escape their fates. "You got a brother?" Pierpont asked a reporter who queried him for a response. "Then you just write about your own brother and you'll have the right dope on Johnnie Dillinger."

"Yeah," Makley agreed. "He was the kind of guy anyone would be glad to have for a brother."

Mary Kinder spoke for many when she offered her feelings: "Well, they got me too in a different way. They took everything away from me that a girl wants in life. I threw it all away for those four months of running around."

At the Federal Detention Home in Milan, Michigan, Billie's reaction was mostly internalized. "That's too bad," she said softly, her eyes filling with tears.

U.S. Attorney General Homer Cummings was more upbeat. "Gratifying as well as reassuring," he responded.

The Chicago PD were neither gratified nor assured. Angry over being shut out of the kill, they boycotted the coroner's inquest held that morning at 11:30, Monday, July 23. During the hearing, deputy coroner John Butler misidentified the photo inside Dillinger's watch as that of Billie, not her clone Polly.

Despite the missing Chicago officers, the jury quickly gave their stamp of approval on the execution, praising the G-Men for their efforts.

When the proceeding ended, Dillinger's body was put on public display at the morgue. The line extended for a quarter mile as thousands of people, mostly women, came to gaze at the Jackrabbit. Clever morgue staffers made multiple copies of his toe tags—"No. 116, July, John Dillinger by District 37, 7-22-34"—put them on the corpse's foot for a few moments, took them off, then gave or sold them as mementos.

A full autopsy was performed by pathologist Dr. J. J. Kearns and his young assistant, Dr. David Fisher. Dillinger's eyes were again curiously noted as being brown, giving rise to a near century of "wrong-body" conspiracy theories. Other than that, however, all the elaborate physical markings were accounted for, including the plastic surgery cuts and finger burns, the leg wound from the St. Paul shooting, the neck and shoulder scars from the Mason City bank robbery, and blemishes left by various childhood injuries. The eye color mystery, as with prior witness reports, was no doubt due to the reflective nature of Dillinger's blue-gray corneas.

The outlaw's brain was removed, ostensibly so doctors, scientists, and physiologists could dissect it in an attempt to determine what made him go wrong. The organ, placed in a jar of formaldehyde, was apparently lost or stolen and has never resurfaced. That, of course, fed "Frankenstein II" tales.

It also no doubt created the popular but unsubstantiated rumor that the bandit's allegedly extra-large penis was removed and saved for posterity. While it's a fanciful tale, there's no official or even moll-relayed confirmation that Dillinger was endowed to the extreme proportions popularized by urban legends.

The brainless, but sexually intact body was put on display again after the autopsy. This time, a throng of 15,000 came to catch a glimpse. Hundreds more were shut out when the doors closed at midnight. Among those who made it inside was Judge William J. Murray of Crown Point.

Another five thousand "morbids," as they were called, swarmed the McCrady Mortuary at 4506 Sheridan Road on Tuesday to watch the body transported to the well-worn Mooresville hearse. Untold thousands lined the route from Chicago all the way back to Mooresville. Five hundred were waiting when the vehicle arrived at the local E. F. Harvey Funeral Home. That number quickly swelled to four thousand. The unruly mob ripped the screen door off the business's entrance, forcing yet another public showing.

The body was then taken to Audrey's in Maywood, where it rested in a $100 coffin draped in lavender cloth under a portrait of John Jr. at age sixteen. People parked as far as a mile away, walking past soda-pop stands and carnival barkers in the 100-degree heat to pay some twisted version of respects. The crowd of rubberneckers and media became so unruly that security guards armed with clubs had to beat them back. Indianapolis police were called in to restore order, ringing the small wooden house. An attempt to provide yet another public viewing was aborted after a drunk nearly stumbled inside the casket.

Ralph Alsman, the Jackrabbit look-alike who was making a career out of being mistakenly arrested, was among the few Audrey allowed inside. He harbored hopes of playing Dillinger in the movies. Little Bohemia's Emil Wanatka had the audacity to send a fancy wreath, which nonetheless was placed by the body.

The burial was announced for Thursday, July 26, at the 560-acre Crown Hill Cemetery in Indianapolis. It was a ruse to fool the public. When more than a hundred police officers began gathering there on Wednesday, word quickly spread. Five thousand "morbids" were on hand by the time Friday Harvey's newer, 1932 "show hearse" arrived just after 3 P.M.

Dillinger would forever share Crown Hill eternity with former president Benjamin Harrison, three vice presidents, two governors, automobile racer "Cannon Ball" Baker, and pharmaceutical giant Eli Lilly. A fierce thunderstorm added to the theatrics, drenching friends, family, and onlookers in the eerie graveyard. Four African-American gravediggers worked the ropes that lowered the casket into Lot 94, Section 44, in the northeast quadrant of the massive Civil War–era cemetery. As John Sr. had promised, John Jr. was laid to rest next to his mother.

While most Americans viewed the assassination as par for the course, the Germans weren't so understanding. "Is a policeman calling a man by his first name before shooting him down a sufficient trial?" asked the *Voelkischer Beobachter* newspaper.

In Chicago, a street artist used chalk to scribble a poem on a brick alley wall near the Biograph:

> *Stranger, stop and wish me well*
> *Just say a prayer for my soul in hell*
> *I was a good fellow, most people said*
> *Betrayed by a woman all dressed in red*

Chicago Coroner Frank Walsh, pausing to reflect, stated that he hoped Dillinger's undignified death served as a warning to young men that he wasn't someone to be idolized. A few hours later, in Los Angeles, an armed twenty-one-year-old man was shot to death by the police. "I'm the new Dillinger!" he screamed before the bullets did him in.

Epilogue

On July 22, 1935, a large sedan stopped at the Crown Hill Cemetery. A veiled, well-bred Lady in Black emerged, glided to John Dillinger's grave, kneeled, and gently placed flowers on the grass. She quickly returned to the vehicle and vanished. The apparition made the same eerie, anniversary appearance for many years afterward. Despite stake-outs, surveillance, and the best efforts of the media, she was never iden-tified. Some speculated that she was Dillinger's long-lost, post-navy, Indianapolis wife.

In the less mythical real world, John Dillinger Sr. declined a $10,000 offer for the corpse of his eldest son. To make sure body snatchers didn't make their own sale, he had the plot sealed inside a tomb of cement and scrap iron.

To combat souvenir hunters, the gravestone wasn't placed until two years after the funeral. That merely delayed the carnage. Ignoring the burial markers of the president and vice presidents nearby, patient mor-bids quickly chipped it away to practically nothing. The marker that stands there today is the fourth replacement.

The Jackrabbit's execution did little to end the madness that sur-rounded his life. James Probasco was arrested by DI agents the week of the shooting and was brought to the Banker's Building for processing and interrogation. He promptly leaped out a nineteenth-story window and splattered on the pavement below. That was the official story. Accusations flew that slippery-fingered G-Men dangled him out of the window by his heels when he refused to talk. A few weeks later, Probasco's girlfriend, Peggy Doyle, similarly "jumped" from a three-story apartment building during a break in her oppressive, all-night interrogation. She survived.

Louis Piquett, Arthur O'Leary, Dr. Wilhelm Loeser, and Dr. Harold Cassidy were hunted down and arrested as well. O'Leary screamed that DI goons, mainly Sam Cowley, broke six of his ribs during an inter-rogation. A battered O'Leary, Loeser, and Cassidy were persuaded to plead guilty. The pugnacious Piquett fought back and won in court, emotionally arguing that he was just doing his job protecting the rights of his client. Crafty prosecutors tried him again for harboring Homer VanMeter, who wasn't his client. This time, Piquett was convicted, disbarred, and sent to Leavenworth for two years. Doctor Loeser was already bunking at the famous Kansas "Big House," serving thirty-six months when Piquett arrived. O'Leary and Doctor Cassidy were given suspended sentences.

To make amends, Doctor Cassidy joined the army during World War II. He was discharged for "nervousness," came home, and shot himself to death.

A month after Dillinger's death, Homer VanMeter was gunned down Bonnie-and-Clyde-style in a St. Paul alley. The local cops who trapped him there fired more than fifty shots. As with Dillinger, it's suspected that the trigger-happy officers pilfered his body of as much as $10,000.

A week later, a desperate Makley and Pierpont constructed prop guns from soap, wire, jigsaw-puzzle pieces, cardboard tubes, and cigarette-pack tin foil, and tried to bluff their way out of the Ohio State Prison. Makley was shot dead on the spot. Pierpont was wounded. Less than a month later, the electric chair finished the job on Handsome Harry.

In late October 1934, Pretty Boy Floyd was killed by DI agents who cornered him on an Ohio farm. He died muttering that his name was "Charles Arthur Floyd." Melvin Purvis led that raid as well, sealing his unlikely status as "America's Number One G-Man."

On November 27, the Feds tracked Baby Face Nelson, Helen Nelson, and John Paul Chase to Lake Geneva, Wisconsin—Chase's girlfriend, Sally Blackman, had ratted them out. After a wild car pursuit, Baby Face, throwing caution to the wind, grabbed a .351 automatic and boldly charged a government-issued Hudson that was providing cover for Inspector Sam Cowley and Special Agent Herman Hollis, the same men who had been Biograph squad leaders. Nelson slaughtered them both. Hit multiple times in return, the crazed bandit still managed to escape with Helen and Chase in the slain G-Men's car. Baby Face's nude body, covered by a blanket, was found the next day in a ditch twenty miles away, his clothing removed by Chase to delay identification.

Cowley and Hollis were the fifth and sixth DI/FBI agents killed in the line of duty—half of whom were taken out by Nelson. To this day, no one has matched Baby Face's inglorious record.

Chase was later captured, convicted of murder, and sent to Alcatraz and Leavenworth for thirty-one years. Paroled over Hoover's objections in 1966, he died in 1973. Helen, fearing a no-nonsense "shoot-to-kill APB," gave herself up and was given the typical twelve-to-eighteen-month mollette wrist slap.

Ed Singleton, the web-fingered "mentor" who ran out on Dillinger during his first robbery, passed out drunk on a railroad track in 1937 and was unceremoniously squashed by a locomotive.

The infamous Lady in Red, Anna Sage, received $5,000 from the DI for her services. She was gypped out of the rest of the $25,000 reward through various underhanded means, and was subsequently deported in 1936. Sympathetic newspapers railed that the Feds sucked her in and then backstabbed her. Pleading with Indiana Governor McNutt for a reprieve, she was denied after Indiana State Police spat that she had done nothing to help them gain the glory and financial windfall of apprehending Dillinger.

A subsequent report stated that Anna opened a nightclub in Timisoara, Rumania, but had to board it up when local gangsters kept trying to shake her down. She escaped to Budapest, then hop-scotched to Italy and Egypt before returning to Timisoara. She passed away there in 1947.

Billie Frechette sowed the carnival circuit for a while, expounding upon her famous beau to rapt audiences. When that waned, she faded into oblivion, dying from oral cancer in Shawano, Wisconsin, on January 13, 1969 at the age of sixty-two.

Polly Hamilton worked at Chicago's Ambassador East Hotel in the room-service department for some time, then drifted out of view as well. Ironically, she died a month after Billie—February 19, 1969—from tongue cancer. Polly was fifty-nine.

Beryl Hovious, Dillinger's only known wife, outlived her replacements by nearly a quarter century. She died of a stroke on November 30, 1993, in Mooresville, just a mile from the Dillinger farm. She was eighty-seven.

Mary Kinder used her notoriety and perky personality to perform in "Scout Younger's Exhibit of Outlawry," a traveling wax museum. Feisty to the end, she made it to 1981, dying at age seventy-two from a combination of pulmonary edema, acute respiratory failure, arteriosclerotic heart disease, and pulmonary emphysema.

Shirt Shop Boy and Lima crew member Russell Clark was imprisoned until 1968. He was let go on a "dying prisoner release" due to lung cancer. He passed away in Madison Heights, Michigan, five months later at the age of seventy.

John Sr. eventually accepted invitations to lecture in stage shows, carnivals, and even at Little Bohemia where the ever-industrious Emil Wanatka divorced his troublesome wife Nan and established a Terror Gang museum. The elder Dillinger was buried beside his son in 1943.

Hubert Dillinger became a mechanic for the once-hated Indiana State Police. A heavy drinker, he died on May 8, 1974. Audrey Dillinger hung on until 1987, reaching the age of ninety-eight. Despite the long passage of time, she, too, was laid to rest in the family's ancient plot at the Crown Hill Cemetery.

Matt Leach, furious at being shut out of the big kill, railed against the DI/FBI, claiming that it was an East Chicago cop, not their agents, who killed Dillinger. He also told reporters that the outlaw was unarmed, and that $7,000 was pinched from his pockets. Under pressure from an annoyed J. Edgar Hoover, Leach was fired in 1937. Returning to the military, he served in the Army Air Corps during World War II, reaching the rank of major. Forever threatening to write an exposé on the Dillinger affair, he finally met with a New York publisher in 1955. Returning home to Gary, Indiana, he and his wife were killed in a traffic accident on the Pennsylvania Turnpike.

Charles Winstead, the agent credited with killing Dillinger, left the FBI in 1943 after a squabble with Hoover over a newspaper interview. He became an intelligence officer in the army, then tried to gain reinstatement to the FBI after the war. Hoover turned him down flat. The grizzled Winstead went on to operate a ranch in Albuquerque, New Mexico, where he succumbed to lung cancer in 1973 at the age of eighty-two.

His "shooter" partner, Clarence O. Hurt, left the FBI to run an

Oklahoma cattle ranch in 1944. Finding the work too demanding, he was reinstated to the bureau in 1945. He retired in 1954, then served two terms as sheriff of Pittsburg County, Oklahoma. He died in 1974.

Melvin Purvis resigned from the FBI a year after Dillinger's death so he could write about his exploits and take advantage of other opportunities that fame showered upon him. His book, *American Agent*, was published in 1936. He hosted a radio "Junior G-Men" show for children; became a newspaper publisher and radio station owner in Florence, South Carolina; was briefly engaged to Janice "Toots" Jarratt, a famous New York model aka "The Lucky Strike girl"; became a JAG colonel during the war (Judge Advocate General); and then went after Nazi war criminals for the War Crimes Office in Europe.

As with his famous prey, the multitalented Purvis died by the gun. Depressed over ill health, he shot himself in 1960. His wife Rosanne claimed he was murdered, but no evidence or motive ever surfaced.

J. Edgar Hoover ruled the DI/FBI with an iron fist until his death from heart failure in 1977. To the day he died, he kept one of the purloined molded masks of John Dillinger's face on the wall outside his office. The mask remains in a vault at FBI headquarters in Washington, D.C.

John Dillinger's thirteen-month reign of terror did more to change law enforcement than any single individual in history. The widespread use of two-way radios in police cars can be credited directly to Dillinger and his gangs. The legendary bank robber steered clear of Michigan and Pennsylvania because those states were already building a radio network. Similarly, police departments upgraded their cruiser fleets to more powerful, eight-cylinder autos, some equipped with bulletproof glass, to keep up with Dillinger's top-of-the-line getaway cars. The creation of reinforced tank cars was another law enforcement innovation that can be credited partially to Dillinger.

It only took a few shootouts for police departments nationwide to realize that a dozen cops armed with six-shot handguns were no match for a single John Dillinger brandishing a .45-caliber Thompson machine gun. To compensate, law enforcement agencies beefed up both their weapons arsenals and their marksmanship skills.

Dillinger's dramatic use of bullet-resistant steel vests, particularly during the East Chicago bank job, motivated police from Florida to Alaska to purchase the body armor for themselves. Frequently, the vests were wrapped around the torsos of a new kind of cop—heavily armed Special Weapons and Tactics (S.W.A.T.) officers sent out to fight Dillinger's gangs on a more even field.

The policemen's bodies weren't the only things getting an extra pound of protection. Thanks to Dillinger's bold attacks on law enforcement gun closets, police departments began building their headquarters with a fort mentality, enclosing them inside walls, many enhanced with barbed wire. Even subsidiary communications buildings were given the bunker treatment.

In the manpower area, the Old West habit of deputizing the public was brought into the twentieth century as rapid-fire citizen mobilization plans were developed to quickly form Dillinger chase posses, erect roadblocks, and protect jails.

Dillinger was also responsible, all or in part, for:

- the arming of firemen and transforming them into special police deputies;
- the use of the National Guard to fight domestic criminal gangs;
- the use of military tanks, troops, vehicles, weapons and aircraft to battle and incarcerate domestic criminal superstars or gangs;
- the government mandated alteration of how people celebrated holidays like Halloween. The intent was to avoid the tragic misidentification of citizens costumed as public enemies, and to temper the excessive glorification of gangsters in the minds of children;
- the use of criminals as advertising endorsement celebrities.

All of the above mentioned law-enforcement advances and counter tactics, extensive as they were, pales in comparison with the creation of the FBI itself. As noted previously, J. Edgar Hoover practically built his agency on John Dillinger's back, using the headline-grabbing, border-crossing bandit to stifle politicians who were vehemently against creating a federal police force. It's no coincidence that the DI/FBI's two most important legislative advances—the ability to carry weapons, and the right to make arrests—occurred during John Dillinger's brief reign.

Using Dillinger as his most effective sledgehammer, Hoover was able to get his boys into the game by pushing for, and obtaining, new laws making various crimes national offenses. Robbing federally insured banks, racing stolen cars across state lines, and felons hopscotching states after escaping prison were all placed under the jurisdiction of the G-Men. These initial Dillinger-attributed laws triggered a legislative avalanche that would roar down the Washington, D.C., mountain and relentlessly expand the FBI's powers over the subsequent decades.

Considering the above, it's not hard to understand Hoover's nostalgia for keeping Dillinger's death mask outside his office.

It's also possible, as Hoover was no doubt keenly aware, that had things played out a little differently, Dillinger may have prevented the creation of the FBI. If the notorious bandit had kept his sensational act going for another year or so, Hoover might have ended up as a footnote in history. Disasters like Little Bohemia, combined with the G-Men's inability to stop Dillinger, would have empowered Hoover's critics and given them the ammunition needed to defeat his design for a massive federal police force.

In a corollary area, Dillinger was responsible for numerous prison reforms. The fear that he would stage additional breakouts led to walls being reinforced with sheet steel, armored cages constructed at exits and entrances, machine-gunners placed in the towers, and in-house S.W.A.T. teams comprised of specially trained corrections officers.

The banking industry was also forced to react to the Jackrabbit, often with higher railings and enclosed teller cages to prevent him from springing over them. Dillinger phobia was also behind the addition of twenty-four-hour security guards, timer vaults, security cages, bullet-proof glass, and the arming of citizen deputies who worked at unrelated jobs in and around banks. These civilian watchdogs were frequently given surplus military weapons.

Even after his death, Dillinger's memory prompted architects to design bank buildings with less windows, stronger walls, and limited numbers of entrances and exits.

John Dillinger, oddly enough, altered the political landscape as well. Aside from turning J. Edgar Hoover into a 500-pound gorilla for the next half century, the outlaw changed the historic timeline on many fronts. Indiana Governor Paul McNutt's presidential aspirations were destroyed over the routine act of signing the parole papers of a faceless con who was, at the time, completely unknown. With each new Dillinger robbery, shoot-out, or escape, McNutt's once-bright career sank lower on the horizon.

A single series of late night photographs plunged a knife into the heart of Prosecutor Robert Estill's public-service ambitions. Estill had his sights set on the Indiana governor's mansion, and John Dillinger was going to be his ticket to electoral glory. The double-whammy of the buddy-buddy photos at Crown Point, combined with Dillinger's subsequent escape, changed Estill from hero to goat and punted him into obscurity.

Sheriff Lillian Holley's status as an inspirational role model for female law enforcement officers was also sucked into the Dillinger abyss. Any thoughts she had of rising up the political ladder were dashed when the famous felon blew out of the Crown Point jail in her own cruiser. Instead of being a trailblazer for equal rights, Holley ended up serving as a poster child for chauvinists who believed that women had no place in law enforcement. Her brief, but highly publicized encounter with John Dillinger may have set back equality for the sexes in police work, and the military, for the next forty years.

In Washington, D.C., Dillinger's presence was felt beyond Hoover's office. The tradition of presidents selecting inexperienced, figure-head attorney generals as a political payback ended, for the most part, in 1933. That's when Franklin Delano Roosevelt put Homer Cummings into the slot and ordered him to do something about the scourge of midwestern bank robbers. Cummings acted by recruiting tough-minded Ohio prosecutor Joseph B. Keenan to be his assistant and enforcer, and by giving Hoover his blessing to go full force after Dillinger. Keenan was instructed to use the power of the attorney general's office to help Hoover concentrate on bagging John Dillinger.

As for Dillinger's legacy among his criminal peers—both past and future—it's hard to find someone that can hold a candle to the Jackrabbit. He was by far the most famous felon of his era, producing more newsprint and newsreel footage than such luminaries as Bonnie and Clyde, Machine Gun Kelly, Pretty Boy Floyd, the Barker-Karpis Gang, and his own wildly jealous partner Baby Face Nelson.

Prior to the Hoosier Hellcat's 1930s era—which author John Toland refers to as "The Dillinger Days"—the most notorious criminals were Old West outlaws like Jesse James and Billy the Kid, and mobsters like Al Capone. The cowboy gunslingers, however, were forced to rely upon horses instead of horsepower, thus rendering them little more than regional nuisances. Mobsters have always been extremely territorial, limiting their impact as well.

Following Dillinger's far-ranging heyday, the balance of power shifted back to law enforcement for the reasons detailed above. This prevented anyone from coming close to matching his accomplishments.

To get an indication of Dillinger's comparative fame today, imagine Charles Manson—after committing his mass murder, Helter Skelter atrocity in California—getting arrested, escaping prison, killing a second batch of Hollywood celebrities, getting arrested again, escaping again, killing a third and fourth gaggle of celebrities, then being gunned down on the streets of Los Angeles by the FBI. And after all that, having Manson's bullet-riddled body put on public display for tens of thousands of people to parade by.

Manson's main "moll," Squeaky Fromme, created some noise when she tried to assassinate President Gerald Ford, but even Squeaky's infamy doesn't come close to matching the enduring image of the Lady in Red, history's ultimate, and most recognizable feminine fatale.

Adding it up, there's never been anyone like John Dillinger before or since. He was indeed America's first, and most enduring, celebrity criminal.

Notes

The Pinkston/Smusyn research from which this book was derived is essentially 2,000 pages of referenced material boiled down from thousands of pages of research documents. A comprehensive listing of the sources would essentially entail reproducing those 2,000 pages, producing a volume four times the size of this work.

The information below contains the most pertinent of the Pinkston/Smusyn citations, much of which was selected by Tom Smusyn and the late Joe Pinkston themselves. A few sources refer to information that wasn't included in the book for space reasons, but are interesting in their own right. There is also tangential material of a footnote nature that future researchers might find helpful.

—Dary Matera

INTRODUCTION

4. In a little more than a year: Financial comparisons—John J. McCusker "Comparing the Purchasing Power of Money in the United States (or Colonies) from 1665 to Any Other Year Including the Present, Economic History Services, 2002, url: http://www.eh.net/ hmit/ppowerusd/

CHAPTER 1

10. The teenage Audrey was thrilled: Much of Audrey Hancock's story comes from an interview she gave to writer Alanna Nash on December 1984 in *The Chicago Reader*. Additional material on Audrey from: *The Dillinger Days*, page 6, John Toland, Random House, 1963.

12. Pop, angry over the defiant: "This Was My Boy, Johnnie," by John W. Dillinger Sr., with H. L. Spade, *Official Detective Magazine*, February, 1941.

13. One of Mrs. O'Mara's students: "The Youthful John Dillinger Recalled," by the late Violet (Lively) Henderson, edited by her daughter, Florence (Henderson) Yeager, Marion County Historical Society Circular, September, 1981.

17. Whatever the motivation, John stuck a revolver: Dillinger's weapon was a single shot, Model 4, and was once on display at the John Dillinger Museum Nashville, Indiana. The museum was sold and moved to Hammock, Indiana.

On Dillinger's early associations: D. C. Stephenson, a gang leader in Martinsville, was Grand Dragon of the Klan in Indiana when, on April 2, 1925, he was jailed for a savage sexual attack on a young Indianapolis secretary who subsequently died. He was convicted of second-degree murder and sent to prison for life. The incident broke the Klan in Indiana.

On Dillinger's early life: Bob Humphreys, *International News Service*, July of 1934 (Humphreys also covered Dillinger's funeral.)

19. The newly uniformed Dillinger completed basic training: The *Utah* was launched December 23, 1909, and saw service in World War I. In 1931, under terms of the 1922 Washington Naval Treaty, she was converted to AG16, a mobile target ship. With her decks reinforced with six-by-twelve timbers to absorb practice bombs, she operated out of San Diego until 1941 when she put in at Pearl Harbor, Hawaii. Just after 8 A.M. on Sunday, December 7, 1941, the *Utah* was struck by three torpedoes dropped by attacking Japanese warplanes. In spite of prior instructions, the pilots had mistaken the *Utah* with her wood deck, for the aircraft carrier *Enterprise* in whose dock (Fox 11) she was moored. The *Utah* capsized and sank in twelve minutes, taking over fifty of her crewmen to a watery grave. Less well known than the *Arizona*, she is, nonetheless, still visible beneath the waters of Pearl Harbor.

20. Whatever the truth, Dillinger surfaced publicly: It is interesting to note that Dillinger would use heart murmur as an excuse for his discharge since he did have rheumatic fever as a child. It would be a point of contention in the autopsy at the time of his death.

20. He proposed within two weeks, and married shorty thereafter: 7ony Stewart, author of *Dillinger—The Hidden Truth,* and great nephew of John Dillinger's wife, Beryl Hovious, provided the information on his great aunt's marriage and divorce, and Dillinger's post-release visit.

   Betty Hovious, Stewart's mom, provided a copy of the Harold C. McGowen and Beryl Hovious' Marriage Certificate. Beryl Hovious' name was misspelled as "Hovis" on the certificate. The Certificate reads:

   HAROLD C. MCGOWEN of Martinsville, Morgan co. Indiana, age 33. BERYL HOVIS of Martinsville, Indiana age 22. June 26, 1929 State of ILLINOIS CO. OF VERMILION. FILED ON JULY 1, 1929, MARRIED AT DANVILLE , IL.

Chapter 2

21. John Sr., weary of his daughter-in-law's nagging: "This Was My Boy, Johnnie," by John W. Dillinger Sr., with H. L. Spade, *Official Detective Magazine*, February 1941.

On Dillinger's preimprisonment years: "Dillinger's Own Story of His Wooden Gun Escape and Other Crimes Now Revealed," by John. W. Dillinger, Sr., *New York Mirror Sunday Magazine*, 25 November, 1934. (This story was most probably "ghost-written" by Basil "Red" Gallagher, an Indianapolis newspaper reporter.)

Chapter 3

42. Faced with the same situation: The teeth-shattering incident came from William Shaw in interviews he gave to Pinkston/Smusyn decades after the robbery. The newspaper accounts of the robbery, and the Indianapolis police department report, failed to mention the assault.

Chapter 4

55. The young couples were coming in: The source for Dillinger fondling the young lady's breast at the Bide-A-Wee Inn was his partner Bill Shaw. Newspapers, in deference to the social mores of that time, probably would not have mentioned the molestation. They certainly would have detailed the pistol-whipping that the young lady's escort was alleged to have taken if he had been cooperative. For whatever reason, possibly embarrassment, there is no such report in the papers.

Shaw, in a written narrative given to the Pinkston/Smusyn researchers in 1958, recounts the assault with the gun but says he doesn't know why John did it. Not until 1976, in an interview with Alanna Nash, would Shaw add the fondling incident. By then, he had also inserted himself into participation in the New Carlisle bank robbery of June 10, 1933, and had Dillinger committing a similar act there, this time on a youthful female bank teller.

Chapter 5

61. Young Crays, the recklessly courageous banker: The true color of John Dillinger's eyes would remain something of mystery over the years, especially once his autopsy report was discovered with a notation that he had "brown" eyes. For more on this see the final chapters.

62. While he showered on night two: The mystery of Dillinger's sudden windfall may be explained by Marion County, Kentucky, indictments that were handed down in early October 1933, naming Maurice Lanham, James Kirkland, and John Dillinger as those responsible for the holdup of the People's Bank of

Gravel Switch on August 8. That was two months after the World's Fair trip, but may indicate that the gang was already active. Two men entered the bank with guns drawn that day at about 11:30 A.M. while a third man remained parked in front of the bank in a car identified as a blue Dodge. The bandits got about $1,300. Three bank employees and the town's postmaster were shoved into the vault as the gunmen sped off. At the time of the indictments, Kirkland and Lanham were in custody but the third man, possibly Clifford Mohler (who may have been misidentified as Dillinger) was never tried in Kentucky. Mohler, arrested in Indiana, was returned to the Indiana penitentiary, confessed to the Gravel Switch job, and confirmed that he, Kirkland, and Lanham had taken $1,220 in cash. Mohler may, however, simply have put himself in Dillinger's role in order to be returned to Kentucky to stand trial for bank robbery rather than remain at Michigan City to serve the balance of a life sentence.

Lanham always denied that he had participated in the Gravel Switch bank holdup and may well have been innocent of the charge. He was given a conditional pardon on December 5, 1935, and lived the rest of his life within the law. James Kirkland died in the Kentucky State Reformatory on July 16, 1935. It is entirely possible that Homer VanMeter or Sam Goldstine may also have been the third man on the job with Kirkland and Mohler.

Another possibility for the money is the May 11, 1933, 2:30 P.M. robbery of The Paragon State Bank, ten miles southwest of Martinsville in Morgan County, Indiana. It was hit by three men, one of whom waited in a car reported to be a Ford roadster. An inside man was described by witnesses as twenty-five, five feet nine inches tall and 155 pounds, while the second gunman was said to be about ten years older, six feet tall and 190 pounds. Both wore dark glasses or "goggles" (the term used by witnesses), and the older man had a large black mustache, believed to be a fake. This same bank had been robbed by Frank Badgley in 1927 with the help of Russell Lee Clark, a future Dillinger gang member.

72. Both Frank and George Whitehouse were later set free: Early on police suspected that Ruby Whitehouse, Frank's sister, was linked romantically with John Dillinger and may have given him shelter. However, it was probably Cliff Mohler to whom she was attracted, not Dillinger. The twenty-five-year-old Ruby worked at the local telephone switchboard in a time when all calls went through an operator. It was later rumored that Ruby had been the operator who delayed a robbery call to the sheriff for some thirty minutes. She was in fact discharged from her job though not prosecuted. In 1995, she admitted to Pinkston/Smusyn that she was working the switchboard but claimed she was on nights, not days. Neither of Ruby's brothers was ever accused in the Gravel Switch robbery.

CHAPTER 6

81. Dillinger, still acting like it was all a minor inconvenience: John Dillinger signed
a bill of sale (#536470) to attorney Jack Egan for the Terraplane at the time of
his arrest. Egan turned the car over to John's half-brother, Hubert, and Hubert
signed it over to "Mrs. John Dillinger," for whom he listed an address of "1052
S. 2nd Street, Hamilton, Ohio," on 6 October 1933, with an Ohio license number
of A63-167. The address was the home of a bootlegger named Wagner that the
gang sometimes used as a hideout. Mrs. John Dillinger, in this instance, was
Billie Frechette.

CHAPTER 7

99. On October 4, Johnnie put pencil to paper: Dillinger's niece, Mary Edna
Hancock, graciously permitted her very personal letters to be quoted by
Pinkston/Smusyn. She would go on to attend Butler University and became a
beloved elementary school teacher. Never excusing what her famous uncle did,
Mary clung to the genuine affection with which she remembers their personal
moments together and refuses to believe he ever killed anyone.

On Dillinger defense attorney Jack Egan: Division of Investigation report by Special
Agent K.R. McIntire, June 16, 1933. Dillinger's attorney, Jack Egan, came under the
scrutiny of the Bureau again in 1936 when the G-Men learned that he had been
retained by Alvin Karpis, a bank robber, kidnapper, and killer. Karpis's wife,
Delores Delaney, was an inmate of the Federal Detention Farm at Milan, Michigan,
when, on May 17, 1935, Egan was suspected of conspiring with Karpis in an attempt
to bribe the federal court judge in her case. After an abrasive confrontation with
Egan, SAC E. J. Connelley reported to Hoover, "This individual is an old, experienced, capable criminal attorney and as indicated previously in the file, is undoubtedly a person who engages in any activity through which he may make money and
is recognized as an underworld attorney and it is difficult and also believed impossible to get any information out of him which would incriminate himself." (FBI
report of June 20, 1936.)

Egan told the agents that he'd had no contact with Karpis but the G-Men
weren't buying it and, on June 12, 1936, Assistant Director Edward A. Tamm noted
in a report to Hoover, "Mr. McKee (Agent S. K. McKee) said that John Egan is
regarded in Ohio as the smartest criminal lawyer around there, and for years he
has represented all of the so-called 'big shots.' I told Mr. McKee that we ought to
make a case of this man if possible, and if we can't convict, we ought to worry the
life out of him."

In his entertaining book, *The Alvin Karpis Story* (Alvin Karpis with Bill Trent,
Coward, McCann & Geoghegan, 1971), Karpis says, "I hired a lawyer in Dayton,
Ohio, to appeal (Delores Delaney's) sentences. The lawyer's name was Jack Egan

and he had a reputation as a first-rate appeals attorney. As soon as he began preparations, the FBI descended on him. They didn't know for sure that I was paying him, but they suspected I was and they wanted to scare him off the case."

Finally, the FBI had a statement from an informant they'd used in the Dillinger case. Thomas B. McAuley, confided to the G-Men that when he was arrested at Dayton with two other men, Egan, through connections with Judge Patterson and Inspector Yendes, had secured his release with a writ so that McAuley "might go to Cincinnati and raise $2,500 as partial 'pay-off' and thus release himself and his two companions." (From FBI report of Special Agent K. R. McIntire, June 16, 1936.)

Similar information found in an article in the *Michigan City News*, by John L. Bach, November 8, 1933.

107. John Dillinger Sr. was asked for his response: "That Was My Boy, Johnnie," by J. W. Dillinger, *Official Detective Magazine*, February 1941. "After John's escape from Lima," Mr. Dillinger wrote, "I thought then, and I still think, that Johnnie was ready to go straight. I don't think he wanted to be taken out of the jail by Pierpont, Makley and Clark."

CHAPTER 8

On Dillinger's October and November 1933 activities: *Chicago Daily News*, November 17, 1933.

122. They toyed with Homer VanMeter's ambitious plan:The Touhy brothers, the most famous of whom was Roger—sent to prison in 1933 for the kidnapping of Jake "The Barber" Factor—were a part of the illicit booze scene in Chicago at the same time as Al Capone. One of Roger's four brothers, Tommy, was convicted of breaking into the L.S. Ayres department store at Indianapolis and was sent to Michigan City. Tommy was paroled from there in June, 1930, almost a year after Dillinger was transferred to that institution. On the first day of 1936, Tommy was again arrested, this time for a mail-truck robbery at Charlotte, and a similar job in Minneapolis in December.

CHAPTER 9

130. Three squads of detectives: In *The Dillinger Days*, author John Toland, apparently basing his allegation on what he'd been told by Lt. John Howe, Sgt. Howard Harder and Art Keller, says that the plan was that an Indiana State Police Lieutenant (presumably Chester Butler, the only lieutenant there) "would simply kill (Dillinger) with a shotgun—as if it were a gang murder."

On the steel vests used by the gang: Some were made by Elliott Weisbrod Company, and some by Dunrite. They were clumsy devices with folding cloth flaps that contained heavy steel plates. Unlike the space-age police vests of the 1990s made from lightweight Kevlar, Spectra or Zylon, the early vests weighed over twenty pounds.

On Dillinger's favorite car: This Terraplane featured a "wet" clutch, functioning in a mixture of oil and kerosene, sold by Hudson as "Hudsonite." Allowing it to dry resulted in clutch failure.

CHAPTER 10

155. The cuddly behavior and generous presents conflict with accounts: Mary Kinder's "My Four Months with the Dillinger Gang," *Chicago Herald and Examiner*, August 2, 1934.

"My Adventures with the Dillinger Gang," by Bernice Clark (Opal Long), *Chicago Herald and Examiner*, September 14, 1934.

Neither moll's stories mentioned anything about Dillinger blackening Billie's eyes or fighting over Ed Shouse. None of Billie's subsequent stories— which included hundreds of speeches at museums and fairs, mentioned such an incident, either.

On Dillinger's far-reaching associations: Frank Zimmerman, 27, also went on trial as a participant in the Streator robbery in December, 1933. Zimmerman denied that he had taken part and called as a witness, a young physician named Harold B. Cassidy. An example of the curious way in which the paths of many of these individuals crossed, Doctor Cassidy was destined six months later to come to grief because of his participation in Dillinger's facial reconstruction.

161. Dillinger was carrying an oblong, black leather valise: The gun valise in the East Chicago robbery, described by some that day as a "trombone case," was actually a rigid, commercial covering made to accommodate the Thompson. Left behind by Dillinger, it was on display at Pinkston's John Dillinger Museum in Nashville, Indiana, through the kindness of Federal Judge Andrew P. Rodovich of Hammond, Indiana, the grandson of East Chicago police chief Nicholas Makar. The museum has since been sold and moved to Hammond.

CHAPTER 11

Rental information on the gangs houses came from the *Territorial Days Dispatch*, the publication of the Tucson Realty & Trust Co., April 1934.

As an aside: On May 4, 1934, J. Edgar Hoover reviewed Special Agent Endres's report mentioning a trip gang members Makley and Clark made to Nogales,

Arizona, and Nogales, Mexico—border towns sharing the same name. He directed the SAC in the Los Angeles field office to have Endres reinterview Madge Ritzer to see if he could learn why Makley and Clark had gone to Nogales and who, if anyone, they'd contacted there. By now, Dillinger had escaped from the Lake County jail and was once again a wanted man. Word of his intention to flee to Mexico or South America may well have reached Hoover's desk by this time, prompting the investigation.

174. John was allowed to hang on to a rabbit's foot charm: John Dillinger's rabbit's foot, along with may other priceless artifacts from the Dillinger case, was on display for years at the John Dillinger Museum in Nashville, Indiana. The museum was sold after Joe Pinkston's death and moved to the city of Hammond in Lake County, Indiana (northwest corner of the state). As of this printing, it was in the process of being reorganized and/or moved again as a result of legal challenges from some of Dillinger's descendents.

178. Lucy Sarber, widow of Sheriff Jess Sarber of Lima: Lucy Sarber, as executrix of her husband's estate, had the Tucson attorneys file a civil suit on January 29, 1934, to lay claim against the gang's money. Submitted were affidavits from Ed Shouse, Dillinger's cellmate Art Miller, and Don Sarber, twenty-four, Mrs. Sarber's son. Now forty-seven years old, Lucy Sarber cited Ohio law in asking that she be compensated for her husband's murder at the hands of the Dillingers, and stating that Jess Sarber was earning $600 a month at the time of his death. By the time the case was heard by Pima County Judge Fred W. Fickett, Pierpont, Makley, and Clark were imprisoned in Ohio, and Dillinger was again a fugitive. On May 28, the court directed the jury to find for Mrs. Sarber and against Pierpont, Makley, and Clark, but to exonerate Dillinger who, the judge said, had no prior knowledge of the jail delivery (breakout). The jury awarded Lucy Sarber $30,000 and Judge Fickett ordered Sheriff Belton to extract the amount from the defendants or seize whatever property they might have. But Belton had to report that, by then, there was no money to be had and he could locate no property to satisfy the judgment. In answer to a subpoena he was ordered to serve on May 22, Belton noted, ". . . made diligent search in Pima County, Arizona, for John Dillinger but was unable to find him."

By June 23, Lucy Sarber appealed to the judge to reverse the ruling exonerating Dillinger in the hope that, if he were caught, some money might be attached. The suit seems finally to have collapsed from fatigue. Lucy Sarber apparently got nothing except a bill from her lawyers for court costs.

179. Addressing an *Indianapolis News* reporter: *Indianapolis News*, January 27, 1934.

CHAPTER 12

Information on Dillinger's Crown Point escape, his connection to the East Chicago underworld, and his connection with a pack of dirty East Chicago cops headed by Sgt. Martin Zarkovich, was pieced together through various sources for this and subsequent chapters. The connection is critical in establishing the truth about Dillinger's death.

"This Was My Boy, Johnnie," by John Dillinger Sr. with H. L. Spade, *Official Detective Magazine*, February 1941.

Chicago Daily News, 31 January, 1934.

Gary Post Tribune, 31 January, 1934.

On the Crown Point Escape: "Crime's Mouthpiece," by J. Edgar Hoover with Courtney Riley Cooper, *American Magazine*, October, 1936, (Hoover rips into Dillinger attorney Louis Piquett, suspected of helping mastermind the Crown Point escape in conjunction with the Indiana Harbor underworld and the East Chicago cops in their pockets. Cooper was a friend of Hoover who wrote numerous books, including *Lions 'N Tigers 'N Everything* in 1924. She was also a film director.)

On the Crown Point escape: In a 1936 syndicated newspaper story, *Dillinger Speaks*, author G. Russell Girardin recounts the story of Piquett and O'Leary meeting Crown Point jail chef Jim Dexter at a Lake County saloon. They bought him a drink and propositioned him to take a business card to Dillinger, which Dexter agreed to do. In *Dillinger, The Untold Story*, (Indiana University Press, 1994, G. Russell Girardin with William J. Helmer) based on Girardin's unpublished 1936 manuscript, this story is changed. Girardin notes that the meeting with Dexter was a fabrication made up to hide the fact that Arthur O'Leary and Meyer Bogue had actually made contact with the East Chicago mob and had thus begun the conspiracy that would soon free Dillinger. O'Leary and Piquett had, Girardin wrote, insisted on the Dexter story to avoid mentioning the involvement of the East Chicagoans, including the cadre of dirty cops, whom they feared. In the new version, Girardin has Sam Cahoon, a jail trustee, delivering the business card to Dillinger. Based on what Piquett and O'Leary told him, Girardin no doubt believed this version but it is so illogical as to suggest that it was actually Dexter who was being protected.

In his 1935 federal trial, Piquett, acting as his own lawyer, questioned a hostile O'Leary on the witness stand:

Piquett: Do you know Jim Dexter?

O'Leary: I do. He was a former chef at the Crown Point jail.

Q: Do you remember introducing him to me?

A: Yes, a few days after Dillinger was brought back from Tucson.

Q: Isn't it a fact that you promised to give Dexter one-third of your fee in the Dillinger case?

A: It is not.

So desperate was Piquett that he then asked O'Leary if it was not true that he, O'Leary, had in fact offered Dexter a generous fee for a copy of the jail floor plan. O'Leary denied the allegation. Dexter himself did little to clarify the issue when he stated later, "Piquett contacted me in Crown Point and asked me to introduce him and O'Leary to Carroll Holley, then Chief Deputy Sheriff, so that he could proceed to consult Dillinger. Piquett represented himself as having been asked by Dillinger's friends in Chicago to act as his defense counsel. I introduced Piquett to Holley. What occurred between Piquett and Holley or anyone else after that, I don't know."

CHAPTER 13

See Chapter 12 notes for continuation of Crown Point escape sources.

209. As they worked. . . . on Dillinger's famous wooden gun: The actual wooden gun used by Dillinger in the Crown Point escape was part of the collection on display at Joe Pinkston's John Dillinger Museum in Nashville, Indiana.

To this day, not everyone buys Dillinger's story that he was the creator and mastermind behind the wooden gun. A popular theory is that it was made by a mysterious German wood craftsman and smuggled into the prison either by Arthur O'Leary, Louis Piquett, or Billie Frechette. That theory, which Tom Smusyn supports, doesn't explain why the pseudo weapon wasn't completed, or why they simply didn't smuggle in a real gun. Smusyn believes they were afraid that a real pistol might have set off an investigation that would have exposed the conspirators. Such an investigation did result, but to no fruition.

Joe Pinkston was never able to pin down the smuggled-in story to his satisfaction, and therefore was not comfortable enough to go with it.

The German craftsman account comes complete with duplicate and prototype carvings that have made their way into the lucrative memorabilia market, further casting doubt on the story. (The actual weapon used is now worth $500,000.)

Author and Dillinger family in-law 7ony Stewart believes the smuggled-in theory. Here are the facts as Stewart sees them:

"The old story was that Dillinger carved the wooden gun from a washboard slat. Not true, but the washboard was found under his jail bed with a piece missing. The washboard was left there to protect all those involved in the escape.

"Those involved included Louis Piquett (name spelled Piquette on his tombstone), Deputy Sheriff (fingerprint expert) Ernest Blunk, and Sam Cahoon, a trustee of the Crown Point jail who did time for being drunk on several occasions. A subsequent claim was made that Judge William Murray was paid $6,000 for his part.

"I later interviewed Jill Blunk, a relative of Ernest Blunk, and she was sure he was in on the escape and collected $5,000 from Dillinger for his valuable help. The wooden gun was indeed made by some German guy in Chicago, but no one knows the gentleman's name. The toy gun was then smuggled into the prison by Piquett as Dillinger would later admit to his girlfriend Evelyn "Billie" Frechette.

". . . There was actually two identical wooden guns made. I have recently located the other one and may have it sent to me for viewing purposes . . . Dillinger gave the real wooden gun used in the escape to his sister Audrey's husband Emmett Hancock.

"The gun was loaned to Piquett by the family, and he gave it to his assistant Arthur O'Leary to return to the family. But O'Leary had the German produce a second wooden gun, an exact copy. He gave the Dillinger family the copy and kept the original hidden away in his house until his death.

"The gentleman who purchased the house found the weapon in a metal box hidden between two rafters in the basement. The box contained several items which included the wooden gun. (I have interviewed the gentleman who found it.) He told me he sold the gun to Joe Pinkston. The gun is worth one half million today."

As for the myriad questions raised by such a series of events, Stewart explains: "Why no grip? And why wasn't it completed? I don't know the answer except to say Dillinger had little choice on the weapon he would receive from O'Leary. He couldn't have pulled it off without wit and courage, knowing that he'd be surely killed if any mistakes were made during this escape.

"According to a statement made by Louis Piquett to G. Russell Girardin (a reporter in the 1930s), Piquett said Ernest Blunk didn't want John Dillinger (who he thought may have underworld connections) pointing a real gun at him even if it was not loaded. Blunk did agree to Dillinger using a fake gun, and O'Leary knew a bearded, bald man with a heavy German accent who lived four miles northwest of Chicago. The man owned a wood shop and once showed O'Leary a toy wooden gun he had made.

"The gun was made of hardwood and had a 3/8 brass rod inserted (press fitted) into the barrel, which clearly proves Dillinger didn't carve the weapon from a washboard. However, if the escape plan failed, Dillinger would say he carved the gun in his cell. The gun also had two small nails that had been filed down to make the gun sights. A lot of work went into this weapon."

A bit more plausible, but the escape plan was a success, and a proud Dillinger still claimed to have made the weapon. In addition, it's hard to imagine a hustler like O'Leary hiding the gun until his death and not trying to profit from it. Similarly, it's hard to imagine the German craftsman not coming forward to take credit for it after the heat wore off.

213. He decided to use the apartment of a former employee: The information on the attempted "love nest" hideout is found in a report of DI agent W. E. Peters of June 4, 1934. A subsequent report, dated October 25, 1934, written by Special Agent R. B. Graham, at the direction of SAC William Larson, does not mention the popular notion of Piquett being drunk and states that Esther Anderson was "fully clothed" when she emerged from the bathroom. Graham's follow-up report was based on interviews with the Lima policemen who had gone to the hotel and is at odds with Botkin's version. The officers did, however, advise Graham that Piquett's guest registration card at the Argonne had been altered to read Louis Piquett and wife. In the first report of Agent Peters, Botkin is quoted as saying that Miss Anderson admitted to him that she had been "intimate" with Piquett on "numerous occasions and numerous places over a period of years." According to Botkin, Piquett and Anderson had taken separate trains to Lima with the intention of sharing a hotel room and "staging a party."

CHAPTER 14

226. Marching toward the bank, Carroll saw: The existence of a movie camera being at the scene of this robbery would be responsible for a legend that the Dillinger gang had brought the equipment in themselves as a ruse while they looted the bank. In truth, it was a bizarre coincidence. H. C. Kunkleman was in town to film another segment of his series: "Things you ought to know about _____ [your town]" Pacific Film Productions (H. C. Kunkleman, 1935). Various towns were featured in the series.

In a related event, in Hollywood, on March 21, Joseph I. Breen of the Motion Picture Producers and Distributors of America, received a telegram from that organization's president, Will H. Hays, ordering a ban on any movie based on Dillinger's exploits. Hays, postmaster general under President Warren G. Harding, had resigned to accept a challenge to clean up the movie industry in 1922 (at a "modest" $100,000 a year!). "This means that if some company outside this organization (MPAA) makes a Dillinger film, they would have no place to show it," the chairman of Hays's advertising advisory council told reporters. Hays's telegram to MPAA members was very specific: "No motion picture on the life or exploits of John Dillinger, will be produced, distributed, or exhibited by any member of the MPAA. This decision is based on the belief that the production of such a picture could be detrimental to the best public interest. Advise all studio heads accordingly, Will H. Hays."

Hays's ban, issued at the urging of J. Edgar Hoover, wasn't challenged until 1945 when an independent studio, Monogram Pictures, produced *Dillinger* starring Lawrence Tierney.

Tom Filben was a half-owner with Jack Pfieffer in the notorious Hollyhocks Club casino.

234. Left with little to go on: Attorney Jessie Levy made reference to the "Scottsboro Boys" during the proceeding, referring to an incident in Alabama in 1931. Nine African American youths, aboard a freight train bound for Memphis, got into a fistfight with several white boys, also riding the rails. When the African Americans threw them off the train, the white boys went to the police. Near Scottsboro, Alabama, police stopped the train, removed the black youths and arrested them. It was then that the officers learned that two white girls, Victoria Price, nineteen, and Ruby Bates, seventeen, were also on the train. Fearing they would be prosecuted as vagrants, the girls claimed that they had been gang-raped by as many as a dozen African-American men, three of whom had detrained earlier.

Less than two weeks later, a jury convicted all nine of the boys in custody, sentencing eight to death and sparing a thirteen-year-old with a life sentence. Northern lawyers took the case to the U.S. Supreme Court. In time, Alabama dropped charges against four of the defendants, after Ruby Bates admitted no rapes had taken place. Four of the others were given early parole. One of the defendants escaped from prison, was caught and convicted of manslaughter in another incident, and died in prison in 1952. The last of the Scottsboro Boys, Clarence Willie Norris, broke parole and moved to New York. In 1977 he applied for, and was granted, a pardon by Alabama Governor George Wallace.

The case was in the early stages of appeal in 1933, when Jessie Levy cited it in her argument for Russell Clark. But much of America, especially the northern states, had come to recognize the injustice of the convictions. (*The Encyclopedia of American Crime*, by Carl Sifakis. Facts on File, 1982.)

On the use of the military to provide security for the Pierpont/Makley trial: The Ohio Highway Patrol was just that in 1934 and not a state police as were Indiana, Illinois and Michigan. Enforcement of criminal laws was the responsibility of county sheriffs and city police. General Bush hinted at this in his report when he noted: "From the very first our relations with the Patrol were most cordial and the detachment at Lima under Sergeant Jonas and his immediate superior, Lieutenant

Mingle at Sidney were most helpful. However, there was some protest over their stepping outside the strict interpretation of the law under which they are constituted and Colonel Black (commander of the Patrol) was compelled to restrict their activities."

Official report of General Harold M. Bush to the Adjutant General of Ohio, April 9, 1934.

236. Governer McNutt, battered by leaflets: "McNutt's Parole Of Dillinger Looked Into," in the *Hammond Times*, 15 March, 1934.

CHAPTER 15
On the aftermath of the St. Paul escape: Letter from O. Baumann to A. J. Pillichody Adjusters, Dayton, Ohio, April 27, 1934.

247. "I was in bed," John Sr. recalled: *Official Detective* magazine, February, 1941, "That Was My Boy, Johnnie," by John W. Dillinger, Sr.

248. The outlaw apologized for and promised to pay for the damage: Despite Dillinger's promise, Mr. and Mrs. Joseph Mannings were obliged to bring legal action against Carl Hellman on April 7, asking for $100 to cover damages. Aware they were unlikely to find Carl Hellman, the Mannings hoped to be compensated when the wrecked Hudson was disposed of. It is unknown whether they ever got their money.

252. Tipped that Billie was scheduled to the meet a man: The informant was probably William E. "Bill" Davis, twenty-nine, a Chicago underworld character and friend of Streng's. Perhaps in an effort to divert suspicion from him, Davis was arrested by Chicago police two weeks after Billie Frechette's apprehension. He was questioned by Lt. John Howe in the presence of Agent Jim Metcalfe and then released.

More on the aftermath of the St. Paul escape: "What I Knew About Dillinger," by Evelyn Frechette, *Chicago Herald and Examiner*, August 1934.

As an aside: In August 1936, J. Edgar Hoover received a letter from Pat Frank of *The Washington Herald* advising that Clark Kinnaird of *King Features Syndicate* had asked him to try to persuade Hoover to write a "prefatory work" for a series they were going to run to be called "Dillinger Speaks." The series would be by Chicagoan G. Russell Girardin and would be based on what he had learned from Louis Piquett and

Arthur O'Leary. (It would also form the basis of the book, *Dillinger, The Untold Story,* by G. Russell Girardin with William J. Helmer, Indiana University Press, 1994.) Hoover chose not to get involved with the articles but did find very interesting an original note the writers had in their possession. It was a small scrap of paper on which was written the name, addresses, and phone numbers of G-Men Harold Reinecke and Melvin Purvis. It had supposedly been written by Dillinger: H H Reinecke 5737 Kenmore; Harold H Rev 6369; Melvin H Purvis 11 Scott Sup 3719.

By November, the FBI laboratory was able to confirm for Hoover that the note was, indeed, in Dillinger's own hand.

The FBI's take on Dillinger's activities during this period: Division of Investigation, "Memorandum for the Director," November 8, 1935 (by this time the organization had become the FBI).

"Memorandum for the Director," Division of Investigation report from Agent R. E. Peterson, April 28, 1934.

Division of Investigation report of Agent E.J. Dowd, April 10, 1934.

"Memorandum for the Director," from Inspector S. P. Cowley, April 19, 1934

246. Encouraged by the brutal and questionable shooting: In the face of charges of corruption in the St. Paul Police Department, Chief Thomas Dahill took Detective Thomas A. Brown off of the Dillinger case on April 4, 1934. Attorney General Homer Cummings had accused "certain segments" of the police department with refusing to cooperate with DI agents. On the day that Brown was removed from the case, Cummings and deputy A. G. Joseph B. Keenan, met in Washington with F. W. Murphy, the president of the Minnesota Bar Association in a discussion on "ways to clean up the crime-ridden Twin Cities."

In a rather curious sidebar, in the summer of 1936, Frank Marron, a reporter for the *Chicago Herald and Examiner,* called on D. M. "Mickey" Ladd, by then the SAC in the Chicago field office of the FBI. Marron had a penciled memorandum from a reporter named Hallberg, a man who had worked for *United Press* at St. Paul. The memorandum questioned details of an alleged $2,500 donation from the Dillinger Gang to Tom Brown's 1934 campaign for sheriff of Ramsey County. The memo suggested it had been the efforts of the G-Men in spreading and perpetuating the bribe story that had cost Tom Brown the fall election. Reporter Marron wanted to know what the FBI's response was.

"(I) refused to comment on this news article," Mickey Ladd reported to Hoover July 23, 1936, "but suggested to Frank Marron that it would be better not to run such an article, but that in the event such an article was run same should deal only with the purported rumor and should make no mention whatsoever of the [FBI] in connection therewith. Mr. Marron promised the writer that in the event this article was used he would eliminate any mention of the [FBI's] purported interest in this matter. It is my desire to call this to your attention inasmuch as it is my recollection Inspector H. H. Clegg did confidentially furnish some similar information to Mr. Hallberg in St. Paul."

255. That same unlucky Friday . . . : Financial comparisons—John J. McCusker "Comparing the Purchasing Power of Money in the United States (or Colonies) from 1665 to Any Other Year Including the Present: Economic History Services, 2002, url : http://www.eh.net/hmit/ppowerusd/

256. On April 17 . . . : It was within a day or two of this St. Paul incident that the gang bought Kentucky license plate 781–779, at Gutherie, Kentucky.

CHAPTER 16

268. A caravan of five cars: Thomas Joseph Dodd was also a member of the raiding party at Little Bohemia. A graduate of the Yale Law School, he became a G-Man in 1933 at the urging of Attorney General Homer Cummings. Dodd left the division in 1934 to join the Justice Department's Civil Rights Chapter, remaining there until 1945 when he played an active role in the trial of Nazi war criminals at Nuremberg. In the years 1953 to 1967, he served first as a congressman and then as a senator, representing the state of Connecticut. It was during this time that Dodd aspired to be the running mate of Lyndon Johnson for the presidency.

Dodd championed the programs of the FBI and enjoyed a warm relationship with J. Edgar Hoover until Hoover learned that he was campaigning to become director of either the FBI or CIA under Johnson. As the sixties drew to a close, Dodd ran afoul of a charge of corruption and, in June 1967, was censured by his colleagues. Denied renomination in 1970, he died in May of 1971. His son, Christopher J. Dodd, is at this writing, a U.S. senator from Connecticut.

Another member of the raiding party at Little Bohemia that night, was Louis B. Nichols. After becoming an FBI assistant director, he left the bureau in 1957 to become public relations director for the Schenley Distilling Company. At least one author claims that J. Edgar Hoover thereafter referred to Nichols as a "Judas" for deserting the FBI.

On the gang's weapons found at Little Bohemia: The DI lab in Washington found the so-called "secret" serial number on the Colt automatic, 14130. The S&W .38 Special was serial number 576426, the S&W Double action was 40399. The Remington .22 was 128096, the .351 Winchester was 41806 and the Winchester

Model 94 was 1046510. The G-Men soon found that the Colt automatic had been sold to a dealer in Fort Worth, Texas, who in turn sold it to Hyman Lebman, Baby Face Nelson's San Antonio gunsmith pal. The lab, using acid, also brought out the number on the abandoned Model 1921 Thompson, serial #6315, and learned it had been shipped to an El Paso, Texas, gun dealer who claimed he had sold it, with fourteen other Thompsons, to the Mexican Consul General. The Mexicans claimed that all of the machine guns had been either "lost or stolen."

On the items found in and on the gang's cars: There were several license plates: Minnesota B419-975, issued to VanMeter as "Art Morton." Minnesota B420-930, issued to Dillinger as "Carl T. Hellman." Minnesota B420-213, issued to Eddie Green as "John Joseph Lavalle." Minnesota B107-811, B38-088, and B47-650, all stolen and with "O"s modified to appear to be "8"s. Tennessee, 127-032, 259-339 and 176-006. Illinois, 642-130. The license plate on Carroll's Buick was California 5-K-1763.

CHAPTER 17

An aside on Emily Wanatka: The genial self-promoter, managed to become something of an irritation to the G-Men. Two days after the battle, he was telling the *Minneapolis Tribune* that he'd written the note asking for help and had then put it in a pack of cigarettes, which he threw out the window of the lodge, not explaining how it then got to the G-Men. The *Rhinelander Daily News*, on that same day, had what it called "the true story," as told by Wanatka. Without naming them, the article told of the part that the LaPortes, George and Lloyd, and Henry Voss had played in the incident and revealed that Wanatka had taken $18 from Dillinger in a poker game.

He'd found two books in Dillinger's room after the shoot-out, Emil told the paper: *The Little Shepherd of Kingdom Come*, and *Murder On The Yacht*. What he did not say was that he had also recovered a .351 semiautomatic rifle which the G-Men had overlooked.

Two months later, Wanatka's name was on an article in the July issue of *Startling Detective Adventures*. The story, captioned, "I Was Held Captive By Dillinger And Saw Him Blast His Way To Freedom," had Wanatka saying, "I know that Dillinger knew the Feds were coming after him . . . for Sunday afternoon a man had driven in from St. Paul to tell Dillinger that Federal Agents were flying and driving for a concentration at Rhinelander, Wisconsin, to swoop down on him." When this statement was brought to the attention of J. Edgar Hoover, agent John L. Madala was sent to pay Wanatka a visit on July 12, 1934. Emil admitted selling the right to use his name to Don Williams of the *Minneapolis Journal* for $12.50, but denied making the statement in the story.

Two years later, on July 26, 1936, D. M. "Mickey" Ladd, by then Purvis's replacement as Chicago SAC, and agent J.W. Coulter (on orders from Assistant Director Ed Tamm) paid another visit to Little Bohemia. Discreetly questioned, in addition to Wanatka, were Frank Traube and George Baszo, the bartenders; Alvin Koerner, at whose home Nelson had killed Carter Baum; and Vilas County Sheriff Tom McGregor. Had anyone, the agents asked, including "newspaper men, magazine writers or government agents," been around asking questions about the 1934 raid on the lodge?" Wanatka and the others were not told so, but what prompted the visit were rumors that had reached Hoover of a potentially embarrassing investigation of the (by then) FBI by the U.S. Secret Service.

Hoover was told, however, that Wanatka was now operating a Dillinger museum, which, in the summer months, was run by John W. Dillinger, John's father. Incensed over a report that Wanatka was displaying a pistol alleged to be slain agent Carter Baum's, Hoover sent Mickey Ladd and agent Kenneth Grace back to Little Bohemia on August 4. Reporting back to the director, Ladd advised that the museum, housed in the small cabin in which Nelson had stayed, displayed clothing left behind by the gang (and returned to Wanatka by Purvis not long after the raid) as well as toiletries, shell-casings, and newspapers which lined the walls.

On display, as well, was "an old .351 caliber rifle" and a glass case inside of which was a .45 Colt automatic pistol, serial # 160461. Admitting that he'd told patrons that the gun was Baum's, Wanatka said he had actually bought it from John Voss and "would immediately discontinue any such statements, inasmuch as they were not correct." Mickey Ladd noted in his report, "[Wanatka] was advised that if he continued informing the public that this property formerly belonged to Agent Carter Baum, or to the government in fact, that the facts would be laid before an appropriate United States Attorney and [Wanatka] assured me that he would not so represent these articles." As Ladd was leaving, Wanatka handed him a faked photograph showing Emil and Dillinger standing together, John with his arms folded before him and Wanatka's arm around his shoulder. He'd created the "novelty," Wanatka explained, by pasting Dillinger's head over that of someone else. Ladd sent the photo on to Washington.

A few months later, on February 26, 1937, Emil Wanatka came to call on the FBI. He was there to complain about Melvin Purvis's new book, *American Agent*, in which Purvis reported that it had been Wanatka who had smuggled out the tip-off note. He was concerned, Emil told Mickey Ladd, that his friends would think him to be a stool pigeon. Nor was Henry Voss happy that his name appeared in print. After being reminded by Ladd that Purvis was no longer with the FBI, Wanatka left, telling Ladd that "he had no ill will against the Bureau."

Then, on May 12, 1938, Inspector W. H. Drane Lester, from the field office at Peoria, Illinois, informed Hoover that Chief Justice John J. Sonsteby of the Chicago Municipal Court, had recently visited at Little Bohemia and had been shocked to find Dillinger's aged father holding forth at the museum there. What the judge found especially shocking was that the substance of the old gentleman's talk, included in the 25-cent admission charge, was "my poor son, John." Noting in his report that "the whole affair had been very nauseating to [Judge Sonsteby]," Lester added that the display should be banned "in the interest of decency and good government." What might scare Wanatka into closing the exhibit, Judge Sonsteby thought, was a stern letter from Hoover.

So far, so good. But then Lester made the mistake of passing along the judge's opinion on one other issue. "Judge Sonsteby also stated," Lester concluded, "that it was his personal opinion that the agents and officials of the [FBI] bungled this raid very badly and that this was the opinion of all citizens in the neighborhood of Little Bohemia and many other citizens throughout the country whom he had met."

Hoover chose to ignore the judge's remarks but did dispatch Special Agent R. H. Klett from the Milwaukee field office to Little Bohemia. Posing as a tourist, Klett reported on his June 21, 1938 visit. "At the lodge there is built a two room (cabin) which has a sign over the door reading 'John Dillinger, Sr.' On the roof of this cabin is painted in large letters MUSEUM, and on the front of same appears the following, PERSONAL BELONGINGS OF JOHN DILLINGER, TOMMY CARROLL, HOMER VAN-METER, JOHN HAMILTON, BABY FACE NELSON."

The elder Dillinger hadn't appeared for the season as yet, Klett advised, but visitors were being shown through by a man named "Pop" Webber. One room in the cabin contained the clothing and other items while a second room with a bed, a table, and two chairs, was fixed up for Mr. Dillinger. Wanatka felt sorry for the old man, according to Pop Webber, and had provided the furniture so that in the summer "he makes enough money to keep him."

He hadn't been able to discover what the museum's income was, Klett concluded, but the sign at the door boasted that "47,651" souls visited Little Bohemia the year before. Locals he had talked to, Klett noted, believed the number to be wildly inflated.

285. Fosteria Police Cheif Frank Culp: Fostoria Police Chief Frank Culp's tip connecting Dillinger to the Fostoria robbery came from the Toledo underworld. The Ohio license plates used on the getaway car were stolen from Toledo as well, leading to the very real possibility that Dillinger and VanMeter had been in that city, trying to recruit another man or two for the planned holdup.

As recounted by Arthur O'Leary, according to G. Russell Girardin in his *Dillinger Speaks*, articles for *King Features* in 1936, the two Fostoria gunmen used their pistols. But, whichever version of this incident is true, it's almost certain that one of the two would have used the Thompson they had, probably firing it in the "single fire" position.

Later information would confirm that the Thompsons used by the robbers had been sold to Dillinger and VanMeter by two Capone Syndicate men, Joey and Bobby O'Brien, later to be the Aiuppas. Operating out of the Hy Ho Club in Cicero, the two were also a supplier of guns to the Barker-Karpis mob.

287. Needing funds for the surgery . . . : "Miss Hazel Nickols Tells of Experience With Bank Robbers," in *The Galion Inquirer*, Galion, Ohio, May 22, 1934.

288. Grim-faced Texas lawmen set a trap: Clyde Barrow, like Dillinger, was impressed with the new Fords. He may have written the company an endorsement letter dated April 10, 1934, mailed from Tulsa, Oklahoma,. It read: "Dear Sir—While I still have got breath in my lungs I will tell you what a dandy car you make. I have drove Fords exclusively when I could get away with one. For sustained speed and freedom from trouble the Ford has got ever' other car skinned and even if my business hasn't been strictly legal it don't hurt anything to tell you what a fine car you got in the V8.—Yours truly, Clyde "Champion" Barrow.
Failing to recognize the name, Ford's public relation staff replied on April 18:

```
Mr. Clyde Barrow, Tulsa, Oklahoma

Dear Sir:
   On behalf of Mr. Ford, we wish to acknowledge your
letter of April 10 and thank you for your comments
regarding the Ford car.

H.R. Waddell, Secretary's Office.
```

Handwriting analysts, as late as 1973, would be inconclusive as to whether the note had been written by Clyde Barrow.

291. If the exaggerating songbird was Dr. Joseph Moran: Dr. Joseph P. Moran, who had a drinking problem, supposedly threatened the Barker boys, Doc and Freddie, in 1935, and they killed him and dumped his body in Lake Erie. A badly decomposed body, with no hands or feet, washed up at Crystal Beach, Ontario, Canada, on September 26, 1935. Dental records confirmed that it was the adventurous Doctor Moran, according to the FBI.

On Bonnie and Clyde: Al Dunlap was the owner of Detective Publishing Company, publishers of pulp detective magazines, and wrote on occasion for

Liberty Magazine. Oddly enough, Detective Publishing also was in the business of supplying equipment to police departments, including so-called bulletproof vests. One of these, carrying a label for the "Dunrite Mfg. Co," was recovered in 1936 from the headliner of the Ford V8 in which Clyde Barrow and Bonnie Parker died. The steel vest had been shot through twice while stored between the headliner and the canvas top of the sedan, probably by .30-06 slugs fired from a Browning Automatic Rifle. The vest was acquired by the John Dillinger Museum of Nashville, Indiana, in 1994.

The guns found in Clyde's car included: 1911 .45 Colt automatic pistols (7), .32 Colt automatic pistols (2), one .380 Colt automatic, one each .20-gauge and 16-gauge shotguns, and three Browning Automatic Rifles (B.A.R.) stolen from a National Guard armory. One hundred loaded magazines, and 3,000 rounds of ammunition were also in the car, along with the steel vest, hidden in the headliner and not discovered until 1936.

Guns used by the six officers in the ambush party were: .12 gauge Model 11 Remington shotgun (00 buckshot) used by Frank Hamer; .351 Winchester Model 1907 auto-loading rifles used by Gault, Oakley, and Alcorn; B.A.R. used by Ted Hinton and a Thompson submachine gun used by Henderson Jordon.

CHAPTER 18

294. The determined Christensen not only refused to succumb: When a day or so later it became obvious that Christensen was going to live, doctors informed him that, because of the broken bones in his hip, he would never walk again. The sturdy lawman fooled them all, however, and soon was walking. In 1935, Congress voted him $7,500 in compensation which President Franklin Roosevelt saw fit to reduce to $3,500. For a while, Christensen operated a tavern not far from Little Bohemia and then went into the construction business at Racine where he later served a term as mayor. Retiring in 1970, he moved to Largo, Florida. In November of 1992, the bullet still in his leg began to cause some pain and surgeons removed it. It was prostate cancer that finally did to Carl Christensen what Baby Face Nelson had been unable to do. He died, at age 92, on April 16, 1994.

294. Shortly after the Grandview announcement . . . : Statements of Special Agent In Charge Werner Hanni, previously at St. Paul, Minnesota, "in connection with possible derelictions in the matter of the attempt to apprehend John Dillinger, et al, at Little Bohemia, Manitowish, Wisconsin, and other statements in connection therewith," by J. Edgar Hoover, June 1934. This memo runs to twelve pages in length.

296. It was apparent that this "new face" wasn't new: Dillinger's dissatisfaction with

his cosmetic surgery is widely reported and accepted. In a statement of August 31 to the G-Men, Arthur O'Leary noted that Dillinger, while still at Probasco's, had told him that "he thought his facial operation was 'bunk,' as in his opinion it had not changed his facial appearance. He said he was going to call up Dr. Loeser and 'give him hell.'"

In a detailed statement of December 7, 1934, O'Leary recounts the episode in an article (probably meant for publication), but does not mention that either Dillinger or VanMeter were unhappy with the surgery. This may be because O'Leary wrote the story while in jail at Waukeegan, Illinois, where he was then held along with Doctor Loeser and Doctor Cassidy. Loeser signed the document as a "witness."

In contrast, G. Russell Girardin, in his 1936 series, "Dillinger Speaks," cites Piquett and O'Leary as confirming that Dillinger was "greatly pleased" with his changed appearance. Arguing that John "always expressed himself as being completely satisfied with the results of the operation," Girardin points out that Dillinger recommended the procedure to VanMeter. The problem, Girardin says, was that Dillinger's face, "chubby cheeks and regular features," was easier to modify than VanMeter's with his "elongated jaw, large nose, thin bony face, low brow and mop of black hair."

298. It's also uncertain as to whether Polly introduced Dillinger to Anna Sage: That Anna Sage knew Dillinger first and set him up with Polly is researcher's Joe Pinkston and Tom Smusyn's conclusion after a half-decade of meticulous research. The evidence is strong based upon how the story unfolded. Dillinger was already connected to Sergeant Zarkovich via Crown Point and the hit on Zarkovich's rival officers. Zarkovich was Anna Sage's longtime boyfriend. It would be an astounding coincidence that Dillinger just happened to meet a Billie Frechette look-alike that was Anna Sage friend—and Dillinger never made the connection between Anna and Zarkovich, and was never told by either that they were longtime lovers.

300. There was one more man in Anna's life: Divorce papers of Elizabeth Zarkovich, 1920, cited Anna Sage as Martin Zarkovich's lover.

On Sgt. Zarkovich: Sergeant Zarkovich's 1930 conviction for taking payoffs, and his jailing in South Bend, Indiana, was covered extensively in the *Chicago Daily News*, *Chicago American*, *Chicago Daily Times*, *Chicago Herald-Examiner*, *Chicago Tribune*, and other newspapers. His subsequent release on an appeals court technicality received heavy coverage as well. Many of the accounts mentioned Anna Sage's attempts to coerce the witness, further establishing the long-term Sage/Zarkovich affair. Legal documents back up the coverage, and clearly establish Zarkovich's connection to the Indiana Harbor underworld.

"A Gangster's Visit," by Judy Gregorich, *Good Old Days* magazine, June 1991.

300. All considering, there was nothing in Anna's checkered background: Among her numerous criminal violations, Anna Sage frequently violated the White Slave Traffic Act of 1910, also known as the Mann Act, after Congressman James R. Mann who introduced the bill. It forbid the transporting of females across state lines for immoral purposes. Designed mostly to protect immigrants and young rural girls from being abducted and forced into prostitution, the law could be a powerful tool for lawmen who sometimes used it even when it was obvious that the female was a willing participant. Responsibility for enforcement of this act had rested with the Division of Investigation since its passage.

On Anna Sage and other aspects of the Dillinger hunt: *Madison Capitol Times*, April 25, 1934.

On Dillinger's whereabouts: According to G. Russell Girardin, Dillinger and VanMeter spent several days in an abandoned cabin in the woods near East Chicago, Indiana, at about this time. VanMeter referred to it as a miserable cottage.

On Dillinger's weapons: The serial number on the .38 Special recovered was 576426. The second, ##40399, was on a .44 frame.

Interesting aside: "BG Woman Once Held Hostage By John Dillinger," interview with Ruth Harris Davidson, by Gene C. Welty, *Sentinel-Tribune* staff writer, March 7, 1981.

303. Aubrey Russ of Fort Wayne: Dillinger and VanMeter apparently did not return to Aubrey Russ's home between May 11 and July 22, when Dillinger was killed. But a humorous epilogue came in April 1936, long after both fugitives were dead. Aubrey's wife wrote J. Edgar Hoover a letter of complaint: "Two years ago this spring I opened my home to your agents in attempt to catch John Dillinger and Homer VanMeter who picked our home to 'hole in' thru no fault of ours. I'm sure you know the details of that terrible visit. We lived at 3702 Abbott at that time. We aided your agents in every way possible giving true information which we heard repeated over last Sunday's broadcast. Some things we told and saw.

"My reason for writing at this time will no doubt surprise you as it's been a long time since your agents were in my home for three months. I was told any damages done in my home would be taken care of after your men left. Mr. Murray, one of your agents called on me and I told him a number of things that had happened to my furniture and rug. He said any claim would be taken care of and he would see what he could do. We have never heard or seen Mr. Murray since or anyone else. When we were in Chicago we called your office there but could never reach anyone we knew. Perhaps if you would see what happened to my furniture you would see I have a just claim. Your men were perfect gentlemen but three men in a house constantly handling guns, etc. will as you no doubt know get restless.

"I had nice things and was proud of my home but since that time I'm ashamed of my things. I have a grand piano that took us years to attain. Mr. White kept his machine gun on that and the bench also. Mr. White knocked over an ash tray hitting the side of the piano. That mar will never come out, another agent burned a hole right thru a rug—also my table. Yes, I feel you should take care of these damages and I've waited long enough to hear from your agents. We are in no position to replace these things as you know our position (I think). Can we expect justice after doing all we could to aid you. Respectfully yours, Mrs. A. G. Russ"

Hoover's response was to order two of the agents to submit reports on the alleged incidents. J. C. "Doc" White, by then stationed in Texas, reported that "during the entire time that this Agent was at the home of Mrs. Russ there never was a machine gun or any other weapon placed on either Mrs. Russ's piano or the piano stool. When Agents did not have the machine guns in their hands they were laid on the floor underneath or behind the Davenport. Mrs. Russ had cautioned Agents to be very careful and not to mar her Grand Piano and during the entire time this Agent was in her residence at no time does this Agent recall of ever having noticed a scar or marred place upon the piano."

As for the mishap with the ash tray, White noted, ". . . this tray was setting on the piano and had some unlighted cigarette butts and ashes in it and someone accidentally knocked this ash tray off the piano and it fell down on the keys and sprinkled a few ashes on the keys of the piano. It did not mar the piano whatsoever, nor was it knocked off the side of the piano."

White had put his best spin on the incident but the image of J. Edgar Hoover, an avid nonsmoker, perusing the travels of the unsavory "cigarette butts" and wondering if they had come from his clean-cut young agents, is irresistible. The next paragraph of Doc White's memo, however, may well have been the undoing for the director who did not take well to learning of "unwanted" incidents two years after the fact.

"The only damage that Agent recalls ever having been done to Mrs. Russ' furnishings or anywhere in the house was when Agent Nichols accidentally let a pistol go off and shot a hole through one of the panes of glass in a side window. This window was fully repaired and paid for by Agent Nichols to the satisfaction of Mrs. Russ."

Hoover's reaction to this belated revelation isn't known to (Pinkston/Smusyn) but can be well imagined. Louis Nichols would, never the less, later rise to the position of assistant director under Hoover.

303. A Catholic priest Nelson had befriended: In April 1935, the Michigan State Police wrote to the FBI indicating they had information to the effect that Father Phillip Coughlan had associated with Baby Face Nelson and others suspected in the robbery of the bank at Grand Haven on August 18, 1933. In a report of April 8, 1936, Special Agent W. M. Bott noted that bank robber Edward Wilhelm Bentz, then an inmate at the Atlanta federal penitentiary, had told police that Father Coughlan "assisted Baby Face Nelson in his preparation for this robbery and that the Buick automobile that was used in the Grand Haven robbery was brought from Chicago to Michigan City and stored in Father Coughlin's garage until it was needed for the robbery."

Whatever the extent of his involvement with Nelson and the others, Father Coughlan was never charged. In the 1950s he was a resident of the Catholic "Providence Home" at Jasper, Indiana, where he had a reputation as an entertaining speaker and capable pianist who had a drinking problem. In 1956, he was a priest in the Diocese of Jefferson City, Missouri, before moving on to Adair, Missouri. Father Coughlan died on April 23, 1970, at the Maria Joseph Living Center at Dayton, Ohio.

CHAPTER 19

On the South Bend robbery: "When The Banks Fought Back," by Ed Sanow, *Guns & Ammo Annual*, 1990.

Article by H.A. Tony Perrin in *Oklahombres* magazine; "A. B. McDonald, Lawman & Author," Fall 1991 issue.

Letter to the Director from S.P. Cowley, June 25, 1934.

Tommy Carroll's Hudson was the one that he abandoned in a garage in Mankato, Minnesota, in early April of 1934. As they frequently did, the G-Men confiscated the car and assigned it to one of their field offices for use by agents.

Report of Special Agent H. E. Hollis, June 27, 1934.

South Bend Tribune, July 1, 1934.

T. D. Bentz was actually the man who "cased" the South Bend bank sometime in 1933 on behalf of Baby Face Nelson. Bentz would be convicted and sent to prison for the August 1933 holdup of the Grand Haven, Michigan, bank—ironically a job in which he had not taken part.

315. A confident marksman: By the time of his identification lineup in February of 1935, Jack Perkins had lost nearly thirty pounds in Federal prison and appeared much trimmer than in June 1934.

CHAPTER 20

328. On July 8, Baby Face Nelson was feeling . . . : Homer VanMeter (and probably Nelson and Tommy Carroll) holed up in a yellow brick warehouse building at 2300 West Division Street in Chicago. The gang, Johnson claimed, simply drove panel truck onto the building's huge freight elevator and then stopped between the first and second floor after first hanging out an OUT OF ORDER sign. Then, in relative safety, they would sleep in the vehicle all night undisturbed. Johnson's revelations appeared in a story by columnist Art Petacque on July 26, 1987, in *The Chicago Sun-Times*. Arthur Johnson, then eighty-one years old, was living at Gary, Indiana.

On the hunt for John Dillinger: According to *The Chicago Times* story, there had been another incident resulting in "Dillinger's capture in Wisconsin some weeks ago being thwarted by a radio message broadcast by Chief Shoemaker, foiling plans of Supervising Captain John Stege to catch the desperado." In this account, Stege had learned from a secret source that Dillinger was in a hideout north of Madison. Delaying because his officers could not make an arrest in the state of Wisconsin, Stege meant to trail Dillinger to the Illinois state line and arrest him. But then, according to the *Times*, a private citizen had given the same tip to Melvin Purvis who in turn contacted Shoemaker to ask that an alert for the outlaw be broadcast on the police low-wave radio system. According to the *Times*, Dillinger's car was equipped with a radio receiver and when he heard the bulletin he fled the area, backtracking into Minnesota in a "brown Hudson with yellow wire wheels." Captain Stege was furious, the *Times* revealed, and criticized Shoemaker for not clearing the broadcast first with superiors. This incident is reported in *The Chicago Times* Sunday, August, 4, 1934.

Madison Capitol Times, June 12, 1934.

327. On July 5 . . . : Statement of William Finnerty to the Division of Investigation, August 29, 1934.

In Ohio, Pierpont . . . : *Columbus Evening Dispatch*, Columbus, Ohio, "John Dillinger Owes Us Nothing . . ." by W. F. McKinnon, July 9, 1934 (Interview with Pierpont).

333. Gang member Jimmy Murray: James Murray would be arrested again in the

holdup of the People's National Bank of Clintonville, Pennsylvania, on October 14, 1938. He was convicted on May 25, 1939.

CHAPTER 21

335. On July 17 . . . : Statement by Anna Sage made on August 1, 1934, to Special Agents S. P. Cowley, J. W. Murphy, and T. J. Connor.

336. Polly also related to interviewers later: "Dillinger's Last Hours With Me, By His Sweetheart," Polly Hamilton, *Chicago Herald and Examiner*, October 1934.

Tangential material: "Mr. Morton" was Special Agent Bliss Morton, assigned to the Indianapolis field office. Morton was one of a handful of agents retained by J. Edgar Hoover when he became the DI's Director in 1924.

References to Dillinger hunt: "Courage Takes Time," by J. Edgar Hoover, *Guideposts* magazine, October 1961.

On Dillinger's last days: *American Detective Cases*, "Dillinger Dies," as told by Samuel P. Cowley to Jack DeWitt, October 1934.

338. John Dillinger the outlaw . . . : The attempted East Chicago/Chicago police plot was confirmed by John Toland in *The Dillinger Days* (Random House, 1962). Toland says that "two out-of-town police officers" paid a visit to Captain Stege on Saturday, July 21, and cites Lt. John Howe and Sgt. Frank Reynolds as his source, stating that both men witnessed the meeting. In October 1935, it would be suggested that the FBI look into this rumor but it was never pursued.

On Dillinger's last days: "Memorandum for the Director," from E. A. Tamm, 10 August, 1934.
"Scarlet Lady Tells All," by Victor Sholis, *The Chicago Daily Times*, 25 July, 1934.

CHAPTER 22

On Dillinger's last hours: Statement by Anna Sage made on August 1, 1934, to Special Agents S. P. Cowley, J. W. Murphy, and T. J. Connor.
"Dillinger's Last Hours With Me, By His Sweetheart," Polly Hamilton, *Chicago Herald and Examiner*, October 27, 1934.
American Detective Cases, "Dillinger Dies," as told by Samuel P. Cowley to Jack DeWitt, October 1934.

347. To lessen the odds: In the late 1950s, East Chicago Sgt. Walter Conroy told

Pinkston/Smusyn that the G-Men insisted the Chicago police not be informed of the trap for Dillinger. According to Conroy, it was a decision that made the East Chicago officers very uncomfortable since they would be obliged to work with the Chicago police even after the G-Men moved on. He and his four fellow officers, Conroy said, were deputized as Federal agents that night to offer them cover. Conroy's allegation seems to have some corroboration from Ed Tamm's July 23 memo to Hoover: "Mr. Cowley stated that last night Captain O'Neal [sic] was all for calling in the Chicago police but he put his foot down and he thinks they feel all right about it now. Before they went [to the Biograph], O'Neal told Cowley if it was a blunder, he could just forget about them; in other words, if they failed it was them and if successful, then O'Neal would get the credit. That was the attitude as O'Neal did not think the Division had enough men to handle it but there were plenty of men."

347. Anna tried her best: At her deportation hearing in September of 1935, Anna Sage contradicted the long-held belief that she told the G-Men that Dillinger was carrying a gun. In her statement, she said she was never able to determine that.

On Dillinger's last pair of pants: The trousers worn by Dillinger the night he died were displayed at Joe Pinkston's John Dillinger Museum, Nashville, Indiana. Experiments by Pinkston confirm that a .380 Colt automatic pistol fits inside the side pocket easily without a revealing bulge. The same was true with the money as reported by Anna Sage and documented in Sam Cowley's "Memorandum for the Director," August 2, 1934.

352. "That's Dillinger with the straw hat and glasses": *American Agent*, by Melvin Purvis, Doubleday-Doran & Co., 1936. The spectacles Dillinger wore, which Purvis remembered as "dark," were actually clear glass and are still in the custody of the FBI in Washington.

On Dillinger's last hours: *The Grapevine*, magazine of the Society of ex-Agents of the FBI, September 1973.
   The Grapevine, an article by Dan Sullivan, October 1978.

357. Later that morning: "John Dillinger's Two Death Masks," by Edward C. and Gail R. Johnson, and Melissa Johnson Williams, *The American Funeral Director*, (p.38), January 1992.

359. Mary Kinder spoke for many . . . : "My Four Months with the Dillinger Gang," by Mary Kinder, *Chicago Herald and Examiner*, August 1934.

359. The Chicago P.D. were . . . : Transcript of the hearing taken by E.F. Wenger, July 23, 1934.

More on Dillinger's last hours: "Dillinger's No Enemy to the Public Anymore," by Patricia Leeds, *The Chicago Sun Times*, 1934
    Inc. column, *The Chicago Tribune*, August 1982.

On Dillinger's corpse being someone else's: Finding of evidence that the corpse had rheumatic fever has been cited, along with the eye color and other physical characteristics, as further evidence the man at the morgue was not Dillinger. This strange theory, first published in book form by Jay Robert Nash and Ron Offen in *Dillinger—Dead Or Alive?* (Henry Regnery Publishing Co., 1971), is dealt with in the concluding chapters of this book.

Interesting aside: In England, in September 1949, Dr. Alexander Kennedy, professor of psychological medicine at Durham University, told a meeting of the British Association for the Advancement of Science that Dillinger might have become a criminal because he once had sleeping sickness. "The great American gangster era of the late Twenties and early Thirties," Kennedy explained, "was linked with an epidemic of encephalitis which lasted from 1918 to 1926. Many young people were affected."
    There is no indication that Dillinger ever had the disease.

Aftermath of Dillinger's death:
    Federal Bureau of Investigation report by Special Agent W. J. Devereux, November 12, 1935.
    Dillinger's father would, perhaps, have been even more distressed had he known that in the future, the brain in the specimen bottle would vanish altogether. It was stored on a shelf in the Cook County morgue according to Kevin Reilly, a retired lab technician, who in 1982 told a reporter that he recalled seeing it as late as the 1960s. A more recent rumor had it located at Northwestern University and then in the hands of a private collector in the western United States.
    "This Was My Boy, Johnnie," by John W. Dillinger, Sr., *Official Detective* magazine, February 1941.

361. Ralph Alsman, The Jackrabbit look-alike: J. Edgar Hoover was able to put a decade-long stop to the making of any Dillinger movies and Ralph Alsman did not get his trip to Hollywood to star in it. It is also worth noting that, despite his claims, the visitor record at the Lake County jail does not show that he was ever there.

On the aftermath of Dillinger's death: *Official Detective* magazine, February, 1941.

The *Associated Press,* (in the *Indianapolis Star*) July 25, 1934.

An affidavit accompanied a snub-nosed .38 Colt Special revolver acquired by the John Dillinger Museum at Nashville, Indiana. The gun was, according to Charles Winstead, the back-up he carried "the night I killed John Dillinger."

EPILOGUE

363. Louis Piquett, Arthur O'Leary, Dr. Wilhelm Loeser: Statement of Dr. Wilhelm Loeser made to Special Agents Virgil Peterson and R. L. Jones at Chicago, August 31, 1934.

   A memorandum to Hoover of March 8, 1935, written by Harold Nathan, refers to an earlier report by SAC Earl Connelley in which Connelley details allegations Doctor Loeser was making against the G-Men. Loeser claimed that after agents searched his home on South Harvey Avenue, a $500 diamond ring and $395 in cash were missing. Loeser also told Albert Woll, special assistant to the attorney general, that "he had been beaten unmercifully in the Chicago [field] office; that as a result of the punishment inflicted upon him he had received a broken rib, and that his nose had been broken in two places. He stated that he had been hit with a chair and after having been forced to the floor he had been trounced upon by various agents."

   Special Agent Virgil Peterson reminded Loeser that he had signed a statement to the effect that no physical force had been used against him during his interrogation, most of which Peterson had taken part in. Loeser replied that this was true, but on one occasion Peterson had left the room and it was then that the remaining agents had worked him over. Loeser believed that Peterson had signaled them to do so.

   "[Loeser] stated that in the event he fails to receive justice in this case," the memorandum went on, "[his] influential friend will immediately contact President Roosevelt and as a result Mr. Woll, as well as Agent Peterson, will have to suffer the consequences."

363. The Jackrabbit't execution: Statement of Margaret Peggy Doyle made to Special Agent In Charge William Larson and Special Agents Dan P. Sullivan and C. R. LaFrance at Detroit, Michigan, August 16, 1934.

   SAC D. M. Ladd in a memo to Hoover of January 10, 1936, advises that an attorney, "named Jacobson, Chicago," wanted to move the Probasco house to an amusement park known as Riverview, and wanted to know if the G-Men had any objection. "He was advised that this office could not give him an expression of opinion concerning this matter," Ladd advised.

364. A month after Dillinger's death: Frank Kirwin, whose real name was Fred Frensdorf, served time for harboring Homer VanMeter, then was in trouble again in the summer of 1939 when, in Chicago, he threatened a motorist with a shotgun. Chased for twelve miles by motorcycle policeman Matthew Boland in what Boland called "a running gun battle," Kirwin was caught when his car rammed a tree.

364: A week later, a desparate Makley and Pierpont: Pierpont and Makley apparently did not have shoe polish available to them as Dillinger had in the jail at Lake County. One possibility offered by Jim Westlake, one-time cell partner with Russell Clark, is that Pierpont may have burned newspapers in his cell and used the residue for coloring. Westlake used this technique when he made a soap gun and tried (unsuccessfully) to escape from prison. The process, Westlake reports, gives a very realistic look to soap.

The John Dillinger Museum at Nashville, Indiana, duplicated these soap guns, working from photographs of the originals and found that Makley's "automatic" was fairly easy to fashion but that Pierpont's "revolver" took considerable skills, even with the proper tools and adequate lighting. What the two condemned men used to carve their soap guns isn't known, but Jim Westlake reports that he sharpened a comb by rubbing it on the floor of his cell and used that to make his gun.

364. On Nov. 27, the Feds . . . : Division of Investigation report #4042, September 26, 1934, Baby Face Nelson.

"Looking For Baby Face" excerpted from *The Vintage Car Murders* by Thomas M. McDade, 1988.

365. Chase was later captured: In his trial for murder in March 1935, John Paul Chase claimed that Cowley and Hollis had fired first. Nelson's V8 did have a bullet hole through the rear window. Chase did not make this claim, however, at the time of his arrest on December 31, 1934.

Evidence that Sam Cowley and Ed Hollis may have worked together outside of the Division hit Hoover's desk on December 21, 1934, in a memo from Melvin Purvis. Attached to the memo was a December 18 article from *The Chicago Daily News* headlined "Work By Slain U.S. Agents Bobs Up In Divorce." The gist of the article was to the effect that a Mrs. Gussie Gundon, described as a friend of Cowley and Hollis, had persuaded the two agents to gather evidence against James C. Clements, owner of the Clements Manufacturing Company, in a divorce action brought by Clements' wife, Daisy. The two G-Men, had they lived, would supposedly have testified that they followed Mr. Clements to a roadhouse where he had a tryst with one Mary Roe. Hoover's reaction to this revelation is undocumented.

"Looking For Baby Face," by Tom McDade, from *The Vintage Car Murders*, 1988.

365. Chase was later captured . . . : "Tom Connor Recalls a Brief But Memorable Career in History Making Period of the FBI," by Miriam Devine, *The Grapevine* magazine, May 1992.

On Nelson : From the personal notes of Special Agent John R. Welles, furnished to Pinkston/Smusyn by his daughter, Mrs. Jacqueline W. Keller.

Chicago Tribune, November 29, 1934.

On Thursday, November 29 . . . Thanksgiving Day . . . G-Man Tom McDade and another agent went to the morgue to view Nelson's body. "It looked like the man who drove the car after us," McDade noted in his diary for that day, "but I would never know him from the (I.0.) photographs."

365. Billie Frechette sowed . . . : 7ony Stewart, author of *Dillinger—The Hidden Truth*, and great-nephew of John Dillinger's wife, Beryl Hovious, provided the information on his great aunt's death, along with the deaths of Billie Frechette and Polly Hamilton.

http://www.johnniedillinger.freeservers.com/index.html

367. Melvin Purvis resigned: On July 30, 1934, J. Edgar Hoover wrote a letter to Melvin Purvis' father, Melvin Purvis Sr. at Timmonsville, South Carolina. Hoover spoke of Melvin's "courageous and fearless act of last Sunday night," remarking that it is an indication of his "sterling qualification of character." Young Purvis had "high personal standards," and "executive capacity far beyond such as is usual at his ages . . ." plus "an unvarying courtesy which has never sacrificed principle for the sake of advantage," all of which made him one of the Division's "most capable executives."

Continuing his praise in this two paragraph letter, Hoover points out that Purvis conducts himself with "that simple modesty which is so characteristic of his makeup," and points out that "During the time when he was subjected to much unfair criticism and attack (after Little Bohemia) he carried on like a true soldier and finally came through to a successful conclusion . . ."

"I am proud of him," the Director concludes, "not only because he is one of our capable executives, but because I can call him a friend, for he has been one of my closest and dearest friends."

Hoover would later seethe at the publicity Purvis reaped from his exploits.

367. Melvin Purvis resigned . . . : By the time *American Agent* came out in 1936, Pretty Boy Floyd had been gunned down near East Liverpool, Ohio as he ran from a group of lawmen led by Purvis.

On the aftermath of Dillinger's death:
Dillinger—Dead Or Alive?, Jay Robert Nash and Ron Offen, 1970.
St. Paul Pioneer Press, August 24, 1934.
Memorandum for the Director, from E. A. Tamm, September 21, 1935.

371. To get an indication . . . : Author Dary Matera previously wrote the Charles Manson book *Training the Beast*, St. Martin's Press, 1998.

MISCELLANEOUS

The Crown Point Thompson machine gun Dillinger took from the warden's office may have been recovered in an Indiana lagoon after the outlaw's death. It was turned over to the G-Men who were able to trace the Thompson through the manufacturer, Auto Ordnance, Inc., of New York City, to Von Langerke and Antoine, a Chicago sporting goods store, which had, in turn, sold the weapon to the Detective Publishing Company. DPC was a multifaceted Chicago company selling police equipment and was run by Al Dunlap, Forrest Huntington's friend. Dunlap also wrote for and published a detective magazine.

There was some confusion over whether this Thompson had been sold by DPC to the police department at Valpraiso, Indiana, or to the Lake County Sheriff's Department at Waukeegan, Illinois. If it was the property of the Valpraiso department, it may well have been one of the weapons Dillinger stole when fleeing the jail at Crown Point, although Dunlap stated that the Waukeegan weapon had also been reported stolen.

J. Edgar Hoover, stung by criticism from Senator Kenneth McKellar that he had never personally made an arrest, accompanied his agents to a rooming house in New Orleans on April 30, 1936, where according to the official FBI version, he personally arrested fugitive bank robber and kidnaper, Alvin Karpis.

John Paul Chase was transferred from Alcatraz to the federal penitentiary at Leavenworth, Kansas, in September of 1954 and a few days later was being considered for parole. Advised of the efforts of several people, including a Jesuit priest, the Reverend Father Joseph M. Clark and James F. Doyle, chief of police at Sausalito, to endorse the parole, J. Edgar Hoover noted to his associates, "Make certain we keep close contact as I want to extend every effort to block Chase's release. We lost two good men due to this rat's actions."

Others disagreed. "Most of the fellows [agents], including myself, feel sorry for [John Paul Chase], as he seems to have been a tool in Nelson's hands," G-Man Tom McDade noted in his diary, December 31, 1934.

McDade visited Alcatraz on October 18, 1950, and while there spoke briefly with Chase. During that conversation, Chase recalled the bizarre incident at Barrington in which he and Nelson had pursued Agents Ryan and McDade. If he'd been driving the V8 and Nelson had been handling the Monitor rifle, Chase told McDade, the two G-Men would be dead now. "With this I had to agree," McDade noted in his diary.

When J. Edgar Hoover learned that McDade had responded to Father Clark's efforts to free Chase, he was furious. McDade's letter to Father Clark, on October 23, 1952, remarks that "the exact part Chase played [in the murders] will always remain a conjecture," and notes that in McDade's opinion and that of several other agents working on the case, Chase was not the same type of individual as [Nelson]. "The risk of releasing [Chase] is one we can well run," McDade advises the priest.

"This is most shameful commentary on an ex-agent interceding in behalf of a man who participated in the murders of two of our agents," Hoover wrote in a January 1, 1955, memo. "See that McDade's file reflects his dastardly action in writing on behalf of Chase."

McDade's diary also produced other valuable information. In a notation made on December 22, 1934, he scribbled: "During the ride, McKee told me of the killing of Pretty Boy Floyd. They fired pistols at [Floyd] but he ran about 200 yards. Sam McKee was behind the others, and yelled for them to get down. Hall, another agent, dropped to the ground, and McKee fired a burst from a Tommy [gun]. It hit the dirt in line with Floyd, who was dodging like a football player. A second burst brought him down. An officer moved to approach, but McKee warned him off when Floyd rolled over with a gun in his hand. Another burst was put into him."

Acknowledgments

Special thanks to Ernie Porter of the FBI, and FBI historian John Fox.

To historian 7ony Stewart, author of *Dillinger—The Hidden Truth*.

johnnieDillinger@aol.com

To Nan Morffi Peterson for her research and editorial assistance, and to Gaylon E. Peterson for taking care of Nan Morffi.

To Mary Dominic Kopitar for her spiritual support.

Special thanks to Fran Matera, Ph.D., of the Walter Cronkite School of Journalism and Telecommunications, Arizona State University, for all her assistance and support. And to Janet Soper and Shana Looney.

To Stedman Mays, Mary Tehan and Fred Hicks for keeping the project alive through the years.

To Dena Nelson, who inherited the phone number of the former John Dillinger Musuem in Nashville, Indiana, and is really nice to people who call her about it.

To Randy Pinkston, Tom Smusyn, and the late Joe Pinkston for making this all happen.

Thanks to my editors at Avalon Publishing, Keith Wallman and Philip Turner, and to my agent, Gene Brissie.

Index

A

advertising, criminals used in, 368
airplane travel, 184, 187, 187-188, 267
aliases. see under individual's real
  name
Alsman, Ralph, 260, 361
American Agent (Purvis), 389
Applegate, Pearl, 157. see also Elliott,
  Pearl
Argus Leader, 218
Arizona Daily Star, 175, 185
Arizona, Dillinger gang visits, 170-
  173
Arthur, Charles (Pretty Boy Floyd).
  see Floyd, Pretty Boy (Charles
  Arthur)
Associated Press, 282
attorneys, for gang. see Levy, Jessie;
  Miller, Clarence; O'Leary, Arthur;
  Piquett, Louis; Robbins, Bess;
  VanBuskirk, John L.
autopsy, of Dillinger, 356, 360

B

Bagley, Frank, ix, 34
Baker, warden, 199-200, 203
bank buildings, fortified, 369-370
bank robberies, 128
  American Bank and Trust,
    Racine, 134-143
  bystanders wounded, 311, 313,
    314, 316, 323
  cancelled, 151
  Central National Bank,
    Greencastle, 112, 113-117
  loot from, 128
  Citizens National Bank, Bluffton,
    Ohio, 69-72, 91
  Daleville, 56-57, 59
  First National Bank, Montpelier,
    65-66
  First National Bank of East
    Chicago, 160-163, 368
  First National Bank of Mason
    City, 226-232
  First National Bank, St. Mary's,
    100
  Fostoria, Ohio, 284-285
  Galion, Ohio, 287
  Gravel Switch, 374-375
  Massachusetts Avenue State
    Bank, 76-77, 152
  People's Savings Bank, 73
  Rockville National Bank, 59-61
  Security National Bank and Trust
    Company, Sioux Falls, 217-222
  South Bend, Indiana, 306, 307-318
bankers, collude with Dillinger, 133,
  136, 167
Barker-Karpis gang, 217
Barns, George (Machine Gun
  Kelly), 82
Barrow, Clyde, 288, 391-392
Behrens, Bill, 57
Behrens, Margaret, 332
Bentz, Eddie, 73, 396
Billy the Kid (William Bonney), 259,
  371

Biograph Theater, 343, 344, 357
Blunk, Ernest, 199-207, 201, 209
  charged with assisting escape, 216,
    235-236
Bogue, Meyer, 233
Bonnie and Clyde. see Barrow,
  Clyde; Parker, Bonnie
bootlegging, 39, 264, 377. see also prohibition
bounty
  on Copeland, 129
  on Dillinger, 129, 225, 302-303, 304,
    326-327, 329, 334
  informants seek. see also Sage,
    Anna Chiolak
  on Nelson, 304
  on Pierpont, 129
  Sage cheated out of, 365
Brenman, Fred, x, 51, 52, 73, 160
Bridgewater, Everett, ix, 33
Brown, Omar, 49, 52, 103
Bucholz, Mary Ann, 61, 62
bullet-proof vests, 162, 163, 167, 303,
  313, 323, 325, 377
  confiscated after arrest, 175
  police, lack of, 320, 368
  stolen, 255
Burns, Joseph, xi, 83-88, 125
Bush, Harold M., 224-225
Butler, Chester, 130-131, 150

C

Cahoon, Sam, 198, 199, 200
  charged with assisting escape, 216,
    235-236
Capone, Al, 39, 40, 122, 149, 371
  and Louis Piquett, 191
car accidents, 152-153, 337
  Billie Frechette, 156-157
  Clarks and Pat Cherrington, 156-
    157
  Hubert and John Dillinger, 248-
    249
  Matthew "Matt" Leach, 366
car chase, 318-322
Carroll, Tommy, xi, xii, xv, 217, 258,
  294-295
  bank robberies, 217-222, 226-232
  gives DI the slip, 243-244
  killed, 294
  on the run, 281-282, 286
cars, 61, 72, 173, 368
  Auburns, 147
  Buicks, 140, 144, 173
  confiscated, 241, 245, 247-248, 256
    at Little Bohemia, 278
  development of, 40
  Essex Terraplane Eight, 40, 41, 62,
    72, 73, 81, 130, 130-131, 132, 145,
    159, 377-378
  Dillinger signs over to Frechette,
    155
  traded in, 170
  wrecked, 156-157
  Ford deluxe coupe, 267-268
  Ford Model A, 280-281
  getaway, 71-72, 134, 140, 144
    disabled, 220-221

  discovered abandoned, 169
  Hudson Deluxe Sedan, 236-237
  Hudson Motor Car Company, 170
  love of, 155-156
  police. see police departments
  purchased, 52, 56, 81, 249-250
  reinforced tank, 367
  stolen, 50, 53-54, 60-61, 66, 68-69,
    72, 73
  Studebaker, 92, 93
  used in Crown Point escape, 205,
    206, 208
cashier stalls bank robbers, 229-230,
  232
Cassidy, Harold Bernard, xx, 289-
  291, 325, 327, 328
  payment for services, 331
  suicide, 364
censorship, 383
Chase, John Paul, xi, xii, 303, 325,
  325-326, 328
  bank robberies, 226-232, 309-318,
    310
  captured, tried and sentenced, 365
  considered for parole, 404-405
  escapes DI raid, 364
  lover's lane shootout, 332-333
  on the run, 286
  trial, 402
Chernocky, Louis, 258-259, 262, 266
Cherrington, Arthur, 102-103
Cherrington, Patricia Long, xv-xvi.
  see also molls
Chicago American, 257, 393
Chicago Daily News, 191, 304, 393
Chicago Daily Times, 393
Chicago, East, police department,
  73-74
Chicago Herald and Examiner, 178-179,
  279, 393
Chicago police department, 149,
  151-152, 215
  and Marbro Theater ambush, 350-
    351, 359
Chicago police "secret squad", 130
Chicago Sun-Times, 397
Chicago Times, 187-188, 302, 397
Chicago Tribune, 143, 148, 159-160, 279,
  356, 393
Chicago World's Fair, 51-52, 59, 61-
  63, 121
chicken stealing, 21-22
children, Dillinger's love of, 63-64
Chiolak, Anna. see Sage, Anna
Chiolak, Steve, 336
Christensen, Carl
  survives, 392
citizens, 189
  identify gang members, 171
  as informants, 255-256
  kill escapee, 95-96
  killed, at Little Bohemia, 268-270
  petition for Dillinger's pardon,
    258-259
  shot at Little Bohemia, 272, 279
  witness bank robberies, 219-222,
    228
Clark, Bernice, 119, 157, 237, xv. see
  also molls

appearance, 145
convicted of harboring, 303
hides money in shoes, 152-153
injured, 152-153
Clark, James, xi, xii, 83-88, 89, 90,
Clark, Russell "Booby", ix, x, xi, xv,
34, 102, 110-111, 119, 126, 375
aliases, 158, 172-173
American Bank and Trust robbery, 134-138
arrested, 171-172
car accident, 152-153
escapes, 83-88
escapes death penalty, 235
extradited to Indiana, 192
later life of, 366
meets Dillinger, 32-33
on the run, 159
springs Dillinger, 104-108
trial, for murder, 234-235
Claudy, H. D., 90, 113, xvi
Claycomb, Noble, x, 41-43, 47, 52, 53,
54
apprehended, 56-57
returns to prison, 57
Clegg, Hugh, 267, 268, 269, 272, 278
Coffee, Daisy, 248
Conforti, Marie Marion, xv, 119, 217,
261-262, 262-263, 325. *see also* molls
and Homer VanMeter, 302
suspected of informing, 304
Constable, Claude, 91
Copeland, Harry, x, xi, xii, 54, 55, 56,
57, 59-60, 65-66, 68, 89
aliases, 78, 103, 144
arrested, 133-134
avoids death sentence, 305-306
expelled from gang, 133
hiding out, 99-100
and Pat Young Cherrington, 103
reward for. see bounty
Coughlan, Fr. Phillip, 395-396
Cowley, Sam, xvii, 329, 402-403
accused of brutality, 363
killed, 364-365
and Marbro Theater ambush, 339-
340, 342, 349-350
mission accomplished, 355
Coy, Wayne, 37, 91, 212
Crays, Roland, 59-61
Crazy Eight, the, 107-108
Crouch, Hilton "Pizzy Wizzy", x, 52,
68, 76-77
APB issued for, 176
arrested, 152
Crown Hill cemetery, 363
Crown Point, Dillinger returns to, 287
Crown Point jail, 189-190
becomes tourist attraction, 215
escape
collusion of law enforcement,
301, 338, 380-381, 381-382
Dillinger on, 233-234
flight, 208-209
Cummings, Homer Stille, 122-123,
370-371

D
Darrow, Clarence, offers services,
260
Daytona Beach News Journal, 155
Death Squad, 188-189, 215
Delaney, Jean, xv, 262, 294-295. *see
also* molls

Dent, Elaine Dekant, 147-148, 148-
149
dental work, on gang members,
121
Depression era, 35, 39, 49
and bounty hunters, 329
and support for Dillinger, 119
DeSoto (car), 72, 76-77
DI. see Division of Investigation
(later FBI)
Dietrich, Walter, x, xi, 158
Dietz, John, 111
Dillinger, Audrey (later Hancock),
10, 14
visits Dillinger in jail, 24
Dillinger Days, The (Toland), 398
Dillinger, Elizabeth "Lizzie" Fields
(Dillinger's stepmother), 11-12,
15, 37-38, xiv
Dillinger family, 247-251, 294, xiv-xv
DI leans on, 260-261, 331
photos taken, 358-359
takes photos, 251
works to parole John, 35-37
Dillinger, Hubert (Dillinger's
brother), 37-38, 62, 251
Dillinger visits, 152
later life of, 366
rats on Dillinger, 82
surveillance of, 261
travels with Dillinger, 248-249
Dillinger, John
aliases, 68-69, 103, 111, 175, 236,
297, 337, 338
Fred Monahan, 68-69, 72, 73
Kirtley, Frank, 154, 155, 158
arraigned in Indiana, 194-195
bank robberies. see bank robberies
captured at Mary Longnacker's,
79-81
childhood, 9, 10-14
death, 354-356, 356
autopsy, 356, 356-357, 360
bloody souvenirs created, 357-
358
body on display, 359-360
funeral, 360-361
gravestone destroyed, 363
money offered for corpse, 363
dental work, 121
discusses burial, 250-251
drinking habits, 191
early criminal career, 17-18, 22-26,
26-27
early "straight" career, 14-16, 20
escapes
Crown Point jail. see Crown
Point jail
Ohio jail, 104-108
Shirt Shop Boys. See Indiana
State Penitentiary
escapes arrest of White Cap gang,
56
escapes stakeout, 130-131
extradited to Indiana, 183-185,
187-190
extradited to Ohio, 91
funeral arrangements, 358-359
girlfriends, 17. *see also* Frechette,
Mary Evelyn "Billie"; Hamilton,
Rita "Polly"
gives policeman his gun, 180
guilt by association, 149
held after capture, 81-83, 97-98
in Arizona, 176-177, 182

heroes of, 16-17
impact on American society, 4-5
indicted for murder, 178
kills policeman, 163, 167, 251
leaps railings, 114
as a legend, 371
letters of, 98-99, 157-158
at Little Bohemia, 264-265
escapes, 277-278
love of cars, 16
marries Beryl Hovious, 20
in the media, 187-188, 190-191, 236
in Minneapolis, 217-218, 236
moves to Anna Sage's, 303
named Number One Criminal,
149
in the Navy, 18-20
photos taken, 251
and Pierpont family, 328-329
plans Pierpont escape, 77-79, 80-
81, 82-83
plastic surgery. see plastic surgery
poem about, 362
quoted in media, 178-179
returns to Chicago, 167-170
returns to Mooresville as public
enemy number 1, 126
reward for. see bounty
robberies. see robberies
on the run, 154, 248-249
after East Chicago, 168-169
scalp condition, 129, 130
serves time at Pendleton State
Prison, 25, 27-31
shot, 229, 232, 239-240, 243
shot by O'Malley, 162-163
sightings of, false, 159-160
in St. Paul, 235-239
talks to informant, 129
visits Audrey, 126, 152, 250, 251
visits detectives' homes, 125
visits father, 169, 247-248
wardrobe, 356-357
taste in women, 131-132. see also
girlfriends
at Wrigley Field, 305
young adulthood, 14-18
Dillinger, John Wilson (Dillinger's
father), 11, 15, 24, xiv
advocates pardon, 259
Dillinger talks about, 179
Dillinger visits, 126, 169, 247-248
discusses Dillinger's burial, 250-
251
lectures about Dillinger, 366, 389-
390
letter from Dillinger, 98-99
makes funeral arrangements, 358-
359
and the media, 107-108, 177, 193,
212, 236
travels to Crown Point jail, 189
Dillinger look-alikes, 159, 260
Dillinger, Mary Brown, 10
Dillinger, Mary Ellen "Mollie"
Lancaster (Dillinger's mother), 10,
11, xiv
Dillinger, Mathias, 9-10, 11, xiv
disguises, 145, 157, 186
of Dillinger, 286, 297-298, 322, 329,
343. *see also* plastic surgery
Division of Investigation (later FBI),
123
accused of brutality, 363-364, 401
accused of theft, 401

and Anna Sage, 339-341
captures Green, 246-247
cars
    comandeered, 267-268, 275
    lawsuit for compensation, 280
and confiscated cars, 241, 247-248, 256, 278
creation of, and Dillinger, 368-369
injured agent survives, 294
interrogations, 252-253, 254
    and suicides, 363
kill Pretty Boy Floyd, 364
kills Baby Face Nelson, 364
leans on Dillinger family, 260-261, 331
at Little Bohemia, 266-267, 267-268, 274-275, 276-277
    agents destroy lodge, 278-279, 280
    agents shot, 274-275, 277, 279
in the media, 254, 257, 296, 304
    embarrassment over, 346
    and Little Bohemia, 279-280, 282
and Marbro Theater ambush, 365
opposition to, 368-369
question witnesses at Little Bohemia, 388-389
raids Mary Kinder's, 252-253
stakeouts
    at citizen's home, 394-395
surveillance, 251-252, 286, 327
    of molls, 294, 331-332
    of Piquett, 329-330
trails gang, 237-239
wiretapping, 326
doctors, for gang, 243, 245, 283, 289-290, 323-324, 325. *see* Cassidy, Harold Bernard; Loeser, Wilhelm
Dodd, Thomas Joseph, 387
Donavan, 72. *see also* Dillinger, John
Doyle, Earl, 73
Dozier, Claude, xvii
drug use, 293
Dyer Act, 123

E
East Chicago police force
    at Marbro Theater ambush, 344-345, 349-350, 352
    officers killed, 288-289
Egan, Jack, 81-82, 98, 376-377
Elliott, Pearl, xv, 89, 103, 112, 134, 157, 290
escape plans, 26-27, 28, 196-197, 378-379
escapes
    from Crown Point jail. see Crown Point jail
    from Indiana State Penitentiary, 83-88
Estill, Robert, xvii, 190, 192-193, 194-195, 195-196
    picture with Dillinger, 212
    political consequences, 236
    referred to, in film, 349
Evans, Albert, 113
extradition, 195-196
extradition, fight over, 180, 182, 183, 183-185
Eye, Charles, 129, 130, 289-290
Eyman, Frank, 178-179

F
FBI (Federal Bureau of Investigation)
    inception of, 123-124
Federal Bureau of Investigation. see Division of Investigation (later FBI)
female sheriff. see Holley, Lillian
fencing, of stolen bonds, 128, 144-145
Fillmore, Charles, 38
fingerprints
    attempt to remove, 292, 293
    failure, 356
    used for ID, 175
Finnerty, Bill, 327-328
firemen, armed and deputized, 368
First National Bank, Montpelier, robbery, 65-66
First National Bank of East Chicago, 160-163
    serial numbers used for ID, 176
First National Bank of Mason City, Iowa, 226-232
First National Bank, St. Mary's, 100
Fisher, Charles, 73
Fisher, Harry, 229-230, 232
Florida, gang visits, 154-156, 157-158
    departure, 156-157
Floyd, Pretty Boy (Charles Arthur), 123, 322
    killed, 364
Ford, Dallas, 171, 172
    receives ring from Makley, 180
Ford, Henry, 62
Ford Motor Company, 40
Ford V8s, 206, 249, 281, 285, 331, 332
    Clyde Barrow endorses, 391
    Dillinger in ads for, 280
    police departments upgrade to, 367
Fort Harrison military base, 124
Fostoria, Ohio Bank, 284-285
Fox, Joseph, 83-88, xi
Fox River Grove Inn, 258-259, 261-262
Frechette, Mary Evelyn "Billie", 119, 124. *see also* molls
    arrested, 176-177, 181
    car accident, 156-157
    charged with harboring fugitive, 255, 257
    and Crown Point escape, 213
    dental work, 121
    and Department of Intelligence, 243
    on Dillinger's death, 359
    does errands, 233-234, 249-250
    domestic skills, 121
    drinking habits, 193-194, 213
    early life, 101-102
    extradited to St. Paul, 261
    files for divorce, 169
    interrogated by DI, 252-253
    later life of, 365
    in the media, 177, 179
    meets Dillinger's father, 247-248
    in Minneapolis, 217-218
    passionate relationship with Dillinger, 108, 177, 213-214
    physical appearance, 111, 145
    in prison, 334-335
    on the run, 154, 159
    and Shouse, 151, 155
    in St. Paul, 235-239
    trial, for harboring, 287, 288

    visits Dillinger in jail, 196-197
Freedom of Information Act, 3
Fromme, Squeaky, 371
funeral arrangements, for Dillinger, 358-359

G
gangs, ix-xi
    extravagant lifestyle, 120-122
    first, 21-23
    Kentucky/Illinois Bunch, 51-52
    major players, xii-xiv
    White Cap, 41-57
Gary Post-Tribune, 168
General Motors, 62
Gilbert, Dan, 158-159
Gillis, Lester (Baby Face Nelson). *see* Nelson, Baby Face (Lester Gillis)
Glegg, Hugh, xvi
glorification, of criminals, 368
    attempts to stop, 383
Goldstein, Sam. *see* Goldstine, Sam
Goldstine, Sam, 51, 52, 65-66, 68, 72, x, xii
    apprehended, 72
Good Old Days magazine, 393
Gordon East Coast Shirt Factory, 32, 34
    and Dillinger's escape plan, 82-83
Green, Bessie, 244, 248, 284, 288, 326, xv
Green, Eugene "Eddie", xi, xv
    bank robberies, 217-222, 226-232
    dies, 254
    and Division of Investigation, 244, 246-247, 254
    indicted for harboring fugitive, 283-284
gun battles, 162-164
    with Division of investigation, 238-241
    at Little Bohemia, 268-275
gun control laws, 40
gun molls. *see* molls
guns, 40
    fake soap, 402
    fake wooden, 201, 209, 233-234, 381-382
        photos taken with, 251
    found, abandoned, 392
    of law enforcement. *see* police departments
    stolen from police station, 109, 112, 255, 404
Guns and Ammo Annual, 396

H
Hamilton, John "Three Fingered Jack", 34, 35, x, xi, xii, xix
    aliases, 153-154, 154
    APB issued for, 176
    bank robberies, 217-222, 226-232
    dies, 283, 284
    escapes, 83-88
    forgets alias, 153
    gang reports death of, 190
    hiding out, 99-100
    indicted for harboring fugitive, 283-284
    indicted for murder, 125
    kills policeman, 147-148
    at Little Bohemia, 277-278

picks up Dillinger after escape, 217
plans Dillinger escape, 103-104
robs First National Bank of East Chicago, 161-163
on the run, 152-153
shot, 163, 230, 232, 280-281
    wounds treated, 168-169
in St. Paul, 241-242
visits sister, 256
Hamilton, Red. *see* Hamilton, John "Three Fingered Jack"
Hamilton, Rita "Polly", 296-298, 304-305, 331, 334-335, 336, 336-337, xv-xvi
later life of, 365
and Marbro Theater ambush, 355
Hancock, Audrey Dillinger, xiv. see also Dillinger, Audrey (later Hancock)
Dillinger visits, 126, 152, 250, 251
later life of, 366
letters, from Dillinger, 233-234
sends birthday greeting, 305
Hancock, Emmett, 11, xiv
Hancock, Fred (Dillinger's nephew), 250, 251, 286
Hancock, Mary (Dillinger's niece), 29, 34-35, 36
Dillinger visits, 126, 152, 250
letters from Dillinger, 99, 157-158
Hancock, Norman, 261
Hanni, Werner, 276, 277, 392
Harris, Jack, 103. see also Dillinger, John
heat wave, 342, 353
Herron, James, xvii
hideouts, rented for historic value, 177
hiding out, 99-100, 120-121 146. see also Florida
Hill, Gladys, 68, xvi
Hite, Ufah Benitta (later Ufah Shaw), 50
Hobson, Delbert, 17
Holley, Carroll, 208
Holley, Lillian, 190, 195-196, 197, xvii
on Crown Point escape, 216
and Crown Point escape
    political consequences, 370
daughters endangered, 193
in the media, 210-211, 216
told of Dillinger's escape, 208
vehicle stolen, 206-207
located, 215-216
Hollis, Ed, 350, 353, 402-403
killed, 364-365
Homer, Leslie, 145-146
Hooten, Naomi, 99-100, 144
Hoover, J. Edgar, 123-124, 124, 192, 245, 324, 367, xvi, xvii
blames civilians for Little Bohemia, 279
and creation of DI, 368-369
cross-dressing, 247, 327
makes arrest, 404
and Marbro Theater ambush, 341-342
and the media, 254, 257, 279, 304, 327
political power, 370
praises Purvis, 403
hostages, 138-139, 140, 141, 142, 162-163, 219, 220-222, 228
in Crown Point escape, 206-207, 207, 209, 209-210

freed, 142-143, 232
as human shields, 230-231, 285-286, 314, 315, 316
at Little Bohemia, 273-274
of Nelson, 282-283
pose for pictures, 143
South Bend bank robbery, 313-314
hot-wiring, of car, 53-54, 205
Hovious, Beryl Ethel, 20, 365, xv
Hovious, Charles E., 34, x
Howe, John, 126-127, 128, xvii
Hudson Motor Car Company, 40-41, 62, 170, 177
Hughes, Howard, 159
Hughes, Shorty George, 48, 50, 68
Huntington, Forrest C., 67-68, 82, 91, 110, 124, 128-129, xvii
and American Bank and Trust robbery, 143-144
confers with Chicago "secret squad", 126-127
informant's cover blown, 132-133
Hurt, Clarence, 346, 349-350, 352-353, xvii
later life of, 366-367

I

Indiana Banker's Association, 67
Indiana Bureau of Criminal Identification and Investigation, 67
Indiana Reformatory at Pendleton, 27-28, 68
Indiana Star, 181
Indiana State Penitentiary
Dillinger gang held, after extradition, 195
Dillinger paroled, 35-37
Dillinger transferred to, 31-37
Dillinger visits, 63
escape from, 83-88
    Dillinger admits role, 191
Michigan City Shirt Shop Boys, ix. *see also* Shirt Shop Boys
political infighting, staff, 90-91
security improved at, 118
Indiana wins extradition battle, 183-185
Indianapolis News, 179, 293, 294, 358
Indianapolis Star, 4, 305
informants, 124. see also McGinnis, Arthur "Art"
children as, 332
citizens as, 255-256, 294, 302-303
    at Little Bohemia, 266-267, 267-268
family members as, 82, 110
gang members as, 57, 68, 72, 150-151, 155, 225, 290, 302, 326
    errand boy, 145-146
jailhouse, 83
molls as, 284, 290, 305, 326, 330. *see also* Hamilton, Rita "Polly"; Sage, Anna Chiolak
and police station holdup, 109
seek bounty money, 334
tip police on Florida trip, 154-155
inquest, on Dillinger's death, 359

J

Jackrabbit, 67, 70, 76, 114, 184. see also Dillinger, John
Jacksonville Union Times, 156

James, Frank, 259
James, Jesse, 16-17, 371
Jenkins, James, 61, 63, 74-75, x, xii
escapes, 83-88
funeral, 96-97
killed by civilian, 95-96
on the run, 92-93, 94-96
John Dillinger Historical Wax Museum, Nashville, Indiana, 3
Johnson, Arthur "Fish", 119-120, 303, xi
Junior G-Men (radio program), 367

K

Kansas City Massacre, 123
Kanter, Benjamin, 95-96, 97
Karpis, Alvin, 376, 404
Keenan, Joseph B., 123, 124, 215, 370-371, xvii-xviii
Keith, Hale, 218-219, 223
Keller, Art, 131, 132
Kentucky/Illinois Bunch, x
kidnapping, 159
Kinder, Mary Northern, 78, 88, 89, 101, 103, 110, 119, 157, 252
in Arizona, 170
arrested, 172, 174, 176-177
disguises, 145
domestic skills, 121, 144-145
extradited to Indiana, 185, 186, 192
as getaway driver, 100
held in Indianapolis, 195
hiding out, 146
later life of, 366
released for lack of evidence, 197
spending, 154
at stakeout, 130
Kirkland, James, 374, 375, x
Ku Klux Klan, 373
Kunkel, Louis E., 90-91, 118, 195, xviii

L

Lac du Flambeau Indian reservation, 282-283
Ladd, D. M. "Mickey", 388
lady in black, 363
lady in red, 371. see also Sage, Anna Chiolak
Laird, Leslie A., 323-324
Lanham, Maurice, 374, 375, x
law enforcement, xvi-xix
equipment, 40
    cars, 367
communications, 306
updated, 117-118, 367
equipment, outdated, 212, 255
federal. see Division of Investigation (later FBI)
local. see police departments
    upgrade to; police officers
law enforcement officers
federal. *see* Department of Intelligence (later FBI)
Huntington, Forrest C., 67-69
Matthew "Matt" Leach, 58-59
and Michigan escape, 86-87
reaction, to Dillinger escape, 211-212
shortage of, in Indiana, 100
shot, 163
trigger-happy, 346-347
Lawrence, Ray, 34, x
lawyers. see attorneys, for gang

Leach, Matthew "Matt", 3, 58-59, 68, 72, 72-73, 117, 124, xviii
  confronts Pierpont, 181-182
  creates "Dillinger squad", 111-112
  and Crown Point escape, 212, 223
  death, 366
  and Dillinger's escape plan, 80-81
  extradites gang to Indiana, 183-185
  fired, after whistle-blowing, 366
  on gang capture, 180-181
  holds witnesses, 100-101
  identifies Youngblood, 233
  in the media, 186, 192-193
  military service, 58-59, 366
  and police station holdup, 109-110
  policy toward Dillinger family, 258
  pursues Dillinger gang, 116-117, 129-131
  rudeness, 81
  and Shirt Shop Boys' escape, 90, 91
  tracks gang to Florida, 154-155
legal defense
  of Dillinger, 195, 196-197
  for Pierpont, 234-235
Legend of Zorro, 296-298
Leslie, Harry C., 31
letters, of Dillinger, 64, 98, 157-158
  to Audrey, 233-234
Levy, Jessie, 234, 234-235, 326, 384
Licanin, Matija. see Leach, Matthew "Matt"
lifestyle, extravagant, of gang members, 120-122
Linton, Ralston "Blackie", 34, ix
Little Bohemia, 262-275, 369, xx
  doctor arrives, 273
  gang escapes, 279, 280-282
  gang stands guard, 264
  gun battle, 268-275
  citizens killed, 268-270
  investigation of raid, 388-390
  weapons found, 387-388
Loeser, Wilhelm, 289-291, 292-293, xx
  accuses DI agents of theft, 401
  arrested, 363-364
  convicted, 364
  found by DI, 329-330
  rats on O'Leary and Probasco, 301
  skips town, 296
Lohraine, Lloyd, 159-160
Long, Opal. see Clark, Bernice
Longnacker, Howard, 65
Longnacker, Mary Jenkins, 61-62, 63-65, 74-75, 79-80, xvi
  marries Claude Constable, 91
loot, from robberies, 117, 128
  confiscated, 243-244
  confiscated during arrest, 174, 175
  serial numbers used for ID, 175
  dividing, 144, 325, 325-326
  spending, 144, 145, 154, 155, 155-156, 249-250
lover's lane shootout, 332-333
Lyle, Victor, 94-95

M

Machine Gun Kelly (George Barns), 82
Madison Capital Times, 295, 394
Makley, Charles, xi, xii, xix, 35
  aliases, 158, 171-172, 172-173

in Arizona, 170
  bank robberies, 134-139
  convicted of murder, 234
  on Dillinger's death, 359
  escapes, 83-88
  extradited to Indiana, 192
  gives ring to policeman, 180
  hiding out, 99-100
  killed, 364
  in the media, 330-331
  meets Dillinger, 32-33
  plans Dillinger escape, 103-104
  and police station holdup, 109
  on the run, 91-92, 152-153, 154, 158
    in Florida, 159
  sentenced to death, 235, 326
  springs Dillinger, 104-108
  talks with governor, 178
Mann Act, 123, 393-394
Manson, Charles, 371
Marion County, 118
Marlbro Theater, 342, 343, 344, 348-353
marriage, of Dillinger, 20
Mason City Globe Gazette, 232
May, Clayton, 243, 245
  arrested, 256
  trial, 287, 288
McGinnis, Arthur "Art", 82, 110, 124, 126-127, 128-129, 302
  arrested and escaped, 338
  cover blown, 132-133
    sought by gang, 146, 160, 190
  payments to, 129
  talks to Dillinger, 129
McNutt, Paul V., xx 37, 82, 111, 125, 212, 324
  and Dillinger parole
    political consequences, 236, 370
  and Terrible Ten escape, 100
media
  and Billie Frechette, 177, 179
  birthday greeting appears in, 305
  coverage of Little Bohemia, 279
  covers Dillinger's death, 357-358
  Dillinger in, 324-325, 371
  Dillinger's father in, 212, 236
  Division of Investigation (later FBI), 304
  exposes Holley daughters' location, 193
  and glorification of criminals, 383
  and J. Edgar Hoover, 327
  and molls, 289, 294
  photograph Dillinger's body, 356-357
  seeks to film Dillinger's capture, 259-260
Meyels, Irving "Happy", 126-127, 128, 133
Michigan City Shirt Shop Boys. ix. see also shirt shop boys
military munitions, Dillinger plans to raid, 124
Miller, Clarence, 234-235
Minneapolis Journal, 388
Minneapolis Tribune, 388
Minnesota, 217
mistaken identity, 159, 260
Mohler, Cliff, 65-66, 74, 375
  rats on Dillinger, 72, 73
Mohler, Whitey, x, xiii, 51, 52
molls, xv-xvi
  acquitted, 289

arrested, 172, 174, 175, 176-177, 278, 279, 292, 303
  released, 185
  bail set, 181
  demand cut of loot, 287
  disguises, 157
  early lives, 101-103
  as getaway drivers, 240-241
  held in Tuscon jail, 184
  as informants, 326
  injured, 152-153
  interrogated, 284, 294
  and jailhouse wedding, 182-183
  at Little Bohemia, 271-272, 276
    escape, 281
  in prison, 330
  spending, 121, 330
  at stakeout, 130-131
  under surveillance, 294, 302, 331-332
Mooresville Times, 212
Moran, Joseph P., 168-169, 283, 291, 391
Morgan, Frank, 38
  signs parole petition, 36
Morton, Art. 154. see also Hamilton, John "Three Fingered Jack"
Motion Picture Producers and Distributors of American (MPAA), 383
mugging, of Frank Morgan, 22-23
museums, Dillinger, 389-390, 392, 398

N

Nathan, Harold "Pop", xviii
National Guard, 118-119, 204, 225, 368
Naval reserve, and police chase, 86-87
Navy, and Dillinger, 18-20, 27-28
Nazi Germany, comments from, 279, 361
Neel, Charles, xviii, 90
Negri, Joseph Raymond "Fatso", xi, 303, 323, 325, 325-326, 333
neice, favorite, of Dillinger. see Hancock, Mary
Nelson, Baby Face (Lester Gillis), xi, xiii, xv, xvi, 73, 74, 117, 119-120, 258, 262, 303, 328
  bank robberies, 307-318
  Dillinger gang refuses to team, 122
  killed, 364
  on Lac du Flambeau reservation, 282-283
  at Little Bohemia, 263, 268, 269
    escapes, 273-274, 274, 275-276
    shootout, 274-275
  lover's lane shootout, 332-333
  record for DI agent killings, 364-365
  shoots policeman, 218-219, 311
  shot, 313, 323
  South Bend bank robbery, 312-313
  in St. Paul, 217
  teams with Dillinger, 217-222, 223-224, 226-232
  violent nature and instability, 228-229, 231, 265, 303-304
Nelson, Helen Wawrzniak, xvi, 270-271, 279, 365. see also molls
Nichols, Louis B., 387, 395
Northern, Earl "The Kid", ix, 33, 78, 83

O

O'Leary, Arthur, xi, xiii, 233, 253, 286, 328
  arrested, 363-364
  skips town, 331
O'Malley, William Patrick, xviii, 161-163, 163-164, 167
  Dillinger as killer, 178, 181, 251
O'Neill, Tim, xviii

P

Palowski, Joseph, 314
pardons, 259
Parker, Bonnie, 288, 391-392
Parker, Paul "Lefty", x, 47, 54
  apprehended, 56-57
  turns informant, 54-55
Patzke, Ursula, 141, 142
  poses for pictures, 143
People's Savings Bank robbery, 73
Perkins, Jack, xi, 119-120, 332-333
  appearance, 396
  bank robberies, 310, 315
Pershing, John J. "Blackjack", 58-59
Pierpont family, 251-252, 331
Pierpont, Fred, 107, 110
Pierpont, Handsome Harry, ix, xi, xiii, xix, 35, 52
  aliases, 155-156, 120, 173 Evans, J. C., 155-156
  American Bank and Trust robbery, 134-138, 138
  in Arizona, 170
  arrested, 172-174, 177
  buys car, 155-156
  chivalry, 144
  confronted by Leach, 181-182
  dental work, 121
  Dillinger assists parole, 49
  on Dillinger's death, 359
  disguises, 145
  early career, 32-34
  escape plan, 83, 187
  escapes, 83-88
  executed, 364
  extradited to Indiana
    held in Michigan City, 192
  as gang leader, 108
  gives policeman his gun, 180
  indicted for murder, 125
  legal defense, 234-235
  and Mary Kinder, 119, 120-121
  in the media, 178-179, 186-187, 330-331
  meets Dillinger, 32
  plans Dillinger escape, 103-104
  police station holdup, 112
  requests jailhouse wedding, 182-183
  reward for. see bounty
  rudeness, 177
  on the run, 88-89
  seeks parole, 77-78
  sentenced to death, 235, 326
  spending, 154
  springs Dillinger, 104-108
  at stakeout, 130
  trial, for murder, 224-225
  violent nature and instability, 112, 113, 182
Pierpont, "Leaping" Lena, xv, 33, 107, 252, 328-329, xv
  rats on Dillinger, 302
Pinkerton Detectives, 3

Pinkston, Joe, 3-5
Piquett, Louis, xi, xiii, 191, 194-195, 195, 196, 214, 253, 328
  arrested, 363-364
  convicted, 364
  criminal record, 257
  defends Frechette, 254, 257, 287
  and Dillinger escape, 212-213
  hired as attorney, 191
  under surveillance, 329-330
  plaster cast, of Dillinger's face, 357
  Hoover retains, 367, 369
plastic surgery, 326, 329-330
  for Dillinger, 255, 256, 286, 287, 289-291, 292
  disatisfaction with results, 392-393
  failure of, as disguise, 296, 297-298
  for Van Meter, 292-293
Plymouth automotive company, 40
poem, about Dillinger's death, 362
police departments
  Chicago
    excluded from Dillinger ambush, 347
    "secret squad", 126-127, 130
  equipment outdated, 167, 284, 319, 333
  equipment updated, 117-118, 143, 367
  guns, 40, 319, 320
    stolen from, 109, 112, 255, 404
    upgraded, 367
  vehicles, 40-41, 92, 93, 130
    upgraded, 367
police officers
  corrupt, 63, 73-74, 195, 217, 288-289, 300-301, 338
  killed, 147-148, 149, 150, 320
  shot, 218-219, 232-233, 285, 286, 288-289, 311, 332-333
police station buildings fortified, 368
police station holdups, 109, 112, 255
political ramifications, of Dillinger crime spree, 370-371
Pretty Boy Floyd. see Floyd, Pretty Boy (Charles Arthur)
priest, associates with gang members, 395-396
prison reforms, 369
Probasco, James, 255, 256, 287, 289, 292, xx
  claims medical training, 325
  jumps to death, 363
prohibition, 35, 39-40, 147, 377
prostitution, 67-68, 296-298, 297-300
public. see also citizens
  views captured gang, 182-183
  views Dillinger extradition procession, 189
  public support, for Dillinger, 119, 128-129, 215, 243, 244, 245, 259, 335-336
    dwindles, 167-168
puppy, 175, 180
Purvis, Melvin, 266-267, 268, 269, 271, 272, 275, 278, xviii
  American Agent, 389
  believes Dillinger dead, 284, 291
  Hoover praises, 403
  kills Pretty Boy Floyd, 364
  later life and career, 367
  and Marbro Theater ambush, 339-341, 343, 344, 344-345, 348, 349, 351-352, 353, 354
  news from informants, 326

offers resignation, 279
  and South Bend bank robbery, 326
  suicide, 5, 367

R

radios, lack of, for police, 284, 333
radios, two-way, become standard equipment, 367
rats. *see* informants
Red Cross posters, 134-138
Reilly, Pat, xi, xiii, 261-262, 263-264, 265, 271-272, 276
  arrested, 305
  indicted for harboring fugitive, 283-284
  on the run, 281
  revenge sought, for James Jenkins, 97
reward. *see* bounty
Reynolds, Frank, xviii-xix, 189
  assigned to Dillinger case, 149
  and Charles Makley, 192
  at Dillinger autopsy, 356
Rhinelander Daily News, 388
robberies. see also bank robberies
  Bide-a-Wee Inn, 55, 57, 59, 81
  City Foods, 41-43
  Eaton's Sandwich Shop, 50
  Haag Drug Store, 47-48, 52-54
  Kroger, 48-49
  Leslie Colvin Construction Company, 57
  open-air market, 49-50
  police stations, 109, 112, 255
Robbins, Bess, 305-306
Rodgers, Will, 279
Roosevelt, Franklin Delano, 39, 122, 370
Rorer, W. A., xix, 270, 272
Russ, Aubrey, 394-395
Ryan, Gene, 130-131, 133, 143-144

S

Saager, Edward, 206-207, 207, 209, 209-210
Saffell, Ralph, 88-89, 100
Sage, Anna Chiolak, xix, xvi, 63, 296-298, 303, 334-336, 344, 393
  biography, 298-300
  criminal record, 393-394
  deported, 365
  plans Dillinger capture
    plan in motion, 338-345
Salt, Augusta, 243, 244, 245
  tried for harboring, 287-288
Sarber, Don, 107, 108
Sarber, Jess, xix, 103-106
  dies, 107
  funeral, 108
  Pierpont indicted and tried for murder, 224-225
  weapon found on Pierpont, 173, 178
  widow files suit, 178
Savage Seven, 132
Scottsboro boys, 384
Security National Bank and Trust Company, Sioux Falls, 217-222
security tower, at Mason City bank, 227-228
Sells, Melvin, 219-222
serial numbers used for ID, 175
Shanley, William J., xix, 147-148

Sharp, Wilber, 104, 105, 106
Shaw, Ufah, 50, 53, 54, xvi
  apprehended, 56-57
  marital problems, 54-55
Shaw, William "The Kid", x, xiii, xvi,
  41-43, 47, 48, 49-50, 52, 53
  apprehended, 56-57
  confesses, 57
  marital problems, 54-55
  rats on Dillinger, 57, 68
Sherman, Chet, xix, 171-172, 180,
  185
Shirt Shop Boys, 52, 58, 217
  escape, 83-88
  hiding out, 99-100, 108, 109
  on the run, 88-89, 91-92
  spring Dillinger, 103-108
Shouse, Edward, xi, xiii
  and Billie Frechette, 155
  captured, 149-150
  escapes, 83-88
  expelled from gang, 133
  indicted for murder, 125
  plans Dillinger escape, 103-104
  on the run, 91-92
  turns informant, 150-151, 155, 225
Singleton, William Edgar "Eddie",
  ix, xiv, 68, ix
  death, 365
  partners with Dillinger, 22-23, 24,
  26
Skeer, Thaddeus, 33, ix
Slaby, Alex, 306, 307
Smusyn, Tom, 3-5
solitary confinement, 192
South Bend Tribune, 396
souvenirs, of Dillinger's death, 357-
  358, 359-360
Spanier, Charles, 86, 87
spending, by gang members, 121-
  122, 154, 155, 155-156
  on cars, 170
  medical care, 168-169
squealers. see informants
St. Paul, Minnesota, 217, 235-236
stakeouts, 129-131, 151-152, 255-256.
  see also surveillance
Stanton, John, 144. *see also* Copeland,
  Harry
Startling Detective Adventures, 388
Stege, John, xix, 151-152, 159, 188, 296
  criminal record, 188-189
  and Crown Point escape, 215, 215-
  216
  hunts for Dillinger, 397
  and Zarkovich, 338
Steve, Anna, 256, 266
suicide
  of Pinkston, 5
  of Purvis, 5
Sumner, Buck, 118
surveillance, 237, 251-252. see also
  stakeouts
  of Dillinger family, 261, 286, 327
  of molls, 294
S.W.A.T teams, invented, 368, 369
syncosis, 129, 130

T
T&T equation, 41
tear gas, at Mason City bank, 227-
  228, 230
Terrible Ten escape, 100, 158
Texas Rangers, 292

Thompson submachine gun, 40, 367
Thornton, Frances Marguerite, 17-
  18
Touhy brothers, 377
train ride, back to Indiana, 186-187
True Detective magazine, 171, 178, 333

U
Universal Newsreel Company, 259-
  260
Utah (ship), 372

V
VanBuskirk, John L., 177, 183
VanMeter, Homer, 49, 51, 54, 217,
  261-262, ix, xi, xiv, xv
  bank robberies, 226-232, 284-285,
  307-318
  and Department of Intelligence,
  241
    escapes from, 242-243
    shootout, 244-245
  and Division of Investigation, 238-
  240
  at the Finnertys, 327-328
  has plastic surgery, 292-293
  hooked on painkillers, 293
  killed, 364
  at Little Bohemia, 262-263
    escapes, 273, 277-278
  and Marie Marion Conforti, 119,
  302
  meets Dillinger, 34
  police station holdup, 255
  shoots policemen, 311, 312
  shot, 317, 321, 323
    wounds treated, 325, 327
vigilantes, 118
Vinson, John, 76-77, x
violence, 135
visitors, denied to Dillinger, 196-197
Voss, Henry, 266-267, 389

W
Waltons, The (TV show), 117
Wanatka, Emil, 272-273, 276, xx
  criminal record, 264
  escapes injury, 275
  IDs Dillinger, 264-265
  implicated as accessory, 266
  later life of, 366, 388-389
  taken hostage, 274
Wanatka, Nan, xx, 266, 267, 366
wardrobes, of gang, 243-244, 262,
  356-357
Wawrzniak, Helen (later Nelson), 74.
  see also Nelson, Helen Wawrzniak
weapons. see guns
wedding, jailhouse, 182-183
Weyland, 139, 140, 141, 142
White Cap Gang, x, 41-57
White Slavery Act, 123, 393-394
Whitehouse, Frank, x, 50-51, 52, 54,
  72
Whitehouse, George, 72
Whitehouse, Ruby, 375
Whiteside, Fred P., 19-20
Williams, Joseph, 36
Winstead, Charles, xix, 346, 350, 352-
  353, 354-355
  later career, 366
  shoots Dillinger, 353-354

wiretapping, 326
Wisconsin Bankers Association, 143
Wisconsin loses extradition battle,
  183-185
witnesses, 115, 132, 322-323. see also
  bystanders
  held by Leach, 100-101
  identify gang members, 144, 157
women
  female sheriff. see Holley, Lillian
  in gangs. *see* molls; prostitution
wooden gun, 201, 209, 210, 233-234,
  381-382
  photos taken with, 251

Y
Youngblood, Herbert, 198-202, 205-
  206, 209
  captured, 232-233

Z
Zarkovich, Martin, xix, 300-301, 335
  and Anna Sage, 393
  and Marbro Theater ambush, 338-
  341, 343, 352
Zimmerman, Frank, 378

About the Author

DARY MATERA's first nonfiction book, *Are You Lonesome Tonight?* was a *New York Times* bestseller in both hardcover and paperback. His other critically acclaimed books include *Get Me Ellis Rubin!*, *Quitting the Mob*, *What's In It For Me?*, *Strike Midnight*, *Angels of Emergency*, *The Pena Files*, *Among Grizzlies*, *Taming the Beast*, *Childlight*, *A Cry for Character*, and *The FBI's Most Wanted*.

Matera's work has been featured on *20/20*, *60 Minutes*, *48 Hours*, *Primetime Live*, *Larry King Live*, *Nightline*, *Expose*, *Donahue*, *Oprah*, *Regis and Kathy Lee*, *Good Morning America*, *A Current Affair*, *Inside Edition*, *The E True Hollywood Story*, *Court TV*, *HBO*, *Hollywood Insider*, *PM Magazine*, and *Personalities* among others.

Formerly a reporter for the *Miami News* and an editor in the book division of Rodale Press, he currently lives in Chandler, Arizona.